Three major waves of anti-Jewish rioting swept southern Russia and Russian Poland in the late nineteenth and early twentieth centuries. In this book, distinguished scholars of Russian Jewish history explore the origins and nature of these pogroms, which were among the most extensive outbreaks of antisemitic violence before the Holocaust.

Using new approaches to the study of Russian history, the contributors examine each wave of violence in turn. They look at the role of violence in Russian society; the prejudices, stereotypes, and psychology of both the educated society and the rural masses; the work of the tsarist regime, especially the police and the army as agents of order and control; and the impact of the pogroms on the sense of Jewish identity and security in the Empire. In his conclusion, Hans Rogger reflects upon pogroms in Russia and then broadens the study by comparing these riots with both pogroms in Western and Central Europe and outbreaks of anti-Negro violence within the United States during the same period.

Pogroms: anti-Jewish violence in modern Russian history is the first comprehensive study of the pogroms in tsarist and revolutionary Russia. It brings together important new research and challenges many of the misconceptions which have continued to characterize the secondary literature on the pogroms. Moreover, this volume appears at a time when inter-ethnic violence and, in particular, anti-Jewish threats have reappeared in the Soviet Union and this recent violence has striking analogies to the events described here. This book will therefore be of interest to students and specialists of Russian, Jewish, and Polish history as well as of the history of mass movements, modern antisemitism, and ethnic group relations.

POGROMS: ANTI-JEWISH VIOLENCE IN MODERN RUSSIAN HISTORY

POGROMS: ANTI-JEWISH VIOLENCE IN MODERN RUSSIAN HISTORY

EDITED BY
JOHN D. KLIER

*Elizabeth and Sidney Corob Lecturer in Modern Jewish History
at University College London*

AND
SHLOMO LAMBROZA

*Associate Professor of History at
St Mary's College, Maryland*

CAMBRIDGE
UNIVERSITY PRESS

Published by the Press Syndicate of the University of Cambridge
The Pitt Building, Trumpington Street, Cambridge CB2 1RP
40 West 20th Street, New York, NY 10011–4211, USA
10 Stamford Road, Oakleigh, Melbourne 3166, Australia

First published 1992
Reprinted 1993, 1995

Transferred to digital printing 1998

Printed in the United Kingdom by Biddles Short Run Books

British Library cataloguing in publication data

Pogroms: anti-Jewish violence in modern Russian history.
I. Klier, John D.   II. Lambroza, Shlomo
305.8924047

Library of Congress cataloguing in publication data

Pogroms: anti-Jewish violence in modern Russian history / edited by John D. Klier and
Shlomo Lambroza.
p.   cm.
Includes bibliographical references and index.
ISBN 0 521 40532 7
1. Jews – Soviet Union – Persecutions.   2. Jews – Soviet Union – History – Pogroms,
1881–1882.   3. Soviet Union – Ethnic relations.
I. Klier, John.   II. Lambroza, Shlomo.
DS135.R9P55   1991
9471.004924 – dc20   90-25617 CIP

ISBN 0 521 40532 7 hardback

UP

Contents

List of plates		*page ix*
List of maps		*x*
Notes on contributors		*xi*
Preface		*xv*
Glossary		*xviii*

PART I GENERAL INTRODUCTION   I

1   Russian Jewry on the eve of the pogroms
    John D. Klier   3
2   The pogrom paradigm in Russian history
    John D. Klier   13

PART II THE POGROMS OF 1881–1884   39

3   The anti-Jewish pogroms in Russia in 1881
    I. Michael Aronson   44
4   "Black Repartition" and the pogroms of 1881–1882
    Moshe Mishkinsky   62
5   Cosmopolitanism, Antisemitism, and Populism: a
    reappraisal of the Russian and Jewish socialist response
    to the pogroms of 1881–1882
    Erich Haberer   98

PART III THE IMPACT OF THE FIRST POGROM WAVE   135

6   The development of the Russian Jewish community,
    1881–1903
    Alexander Orbach   137
7   Tsarist officialdom and anti-Jewish pogroms in Poland
    Michael Ochs   164

PART IV   THE POGROMS OF 1903–1906   191

8   The pogroms of 1903–1906
     Shlomo Lambroza   195
9   The pogrom of 1905 in Odessa: a case study
     Robert Weinberg   248

PART V   THE POGROMS OF 1919–1921   291

10   Pogroms and White ideology in the Russian Civil War
      Peter Kenez   293

Conclusion and overview
Hans Rogger   314

Bibliographical essay
Avraham Greenbaum   373

Index   387

Plates

1   Morgue for victims of the Kishinev pogrom of 1903   *page* 198
2   Wounded victims of the Kishinev pogrom of 1903   199
3   Burial of Torah scrolls desecrated in the Kishinev
    pogrom of 1903 (from the Yiddish publication *Der
    Freynd*)   200
4   A Bund self-defense organization in Pinsk in 1905   220
5   Child victims of the Ekaterinoslav pogrom of 1905
    (postcard published by Poale-Zion, a socialist Zionist
    party)   229
6   Morgue in the city hospital for victims of the
    Ekaterinoslav pogrom of 1905   230
7   Bialystok haymarket, the site of the pogrom of 1906   236
8   Group portrait of the Odessa Bund self-defense group,
    posing with victims of the 1905 pogrom at the
    cemetery. The banner, in Yiddish and Russian, reads:
    "Glory to those who have fallen in the struggle for
    freedom!"   258
9   Members of the Odessa Bund killed in the pogrom of
    1905   258
10 Victims of a pogrom in an unnamed town in the
    Ukraine in 1920   299

Maps

1 European Russia in 1881, showing the provinces of
the Kingdom of Poland and the Pale of Jewish
Settlement   *page xiii*
2 Major pogrom centers in Russia and Poland,
1881–1884   43
3 Major pogrom centers in Russia and Poland,
1903–1906   194
4 Major pogrom centers during the Russian Civil War,
1918–1921   290

Contributors

I. MICHAEL ARONSON was born in Waco, Texas and now lives in Raanana, Israel. He received his doctorate from Northwestern University, and has published numerous articles on Russian Jewish history. He is the author of *Troubled Waters: The Origins of the 1881 Anti-Jewish Pogroms in Russia* (Pittsburgh, 1991).

AVRAHAM GREENBAUM is Senior Lecturer in the Department of Jewish History at the University of Haifa and Research Associate of the Ben-Zion Dinur Institute for Research in Jewish History, Hebrew University of Jerusalem.

ERICH HABERER did his Ph.D. in Russian History at the University of Toronto. He currently serves in the Canadian Ministry of Justice, researching war crimes.

PETER KENEZ is Professor of History at the University of California, Santa Cruz. He is the author of *Civil War in South Russia, 1918* (Berkeley, 1971), *Civil War in South Russia, 1919–1920* (Berkeley, 1976), *The Birth of the Propaganda State: Soviet Methods of Mass Mobilization, 1917–1929* (Cambridge, 1985) and *Cinema and Soviet Society, 1917–1953* (forthcoming). He was co-editor, with Abbott Gleason and Richard Stites, of *Bolshevik Culture* (Bloomington, 1985).

JOHN D. KLIER is Elizabeth and Sidney Corob Lecturer in Modern Jewish History at University College, University of London. He is the author of *Russia Gathers Her Jews: The Origins of the Jewish Question in Russia, 1772–1825* (DeKalb, 1986).

SHLOMO LAMBROZA is Associate Professor of History, St. Mary's College, Maryland. He is the author of numerous articles on Russian pogroms and Jewish self-defense.

MOSHE MISHKINSKY is retired as Professor in the Department of Jewish History, Tel Aviv University. He is the Chairman of the Section on the History of the Jewish Labor Movement in the Chaim Rosenberg School for Jewish Studies. He has published numerous books and articles on Jewish History in Eastern Europe, especially on the history of the Jewish labor movement, and the attitudes of the socialist movement towards the Jewish Question.

MICHAEL OCHS did his Ph.D. in Russian history at Harvard University. He is currently a Professional Staff Assistant at the Commission on Security and Cooperation in Europe, US Congress.

ALEXANDER ORBACH is a member of the Religious Studies Department, University of Pittsburgh. He is the author of *New Voices of Russian Jewry* (Leiden, 1980), and has published extensively on Jewish political activity in pre-revolutionary Russia.

HANS ROGGER is Professor of Russian History at the University of California, Los Angeles. His works include *National Consciousness in 18th Century Russia* (Cambridge, MS, 1960); *Russia in the Age of Modernization and Revolution* (London and New York, 1983); *Jewish Policies and Right-Wing Politics in Imperial Russia* (Berkeley, 1986) and, with Eugen Weber, *The European Right* (London, 1965)

ROBERT WEINBERG is Assistant Professor of History at Swarthmore College. He is currently completing a book on the 1905 Revolution in Odessa.

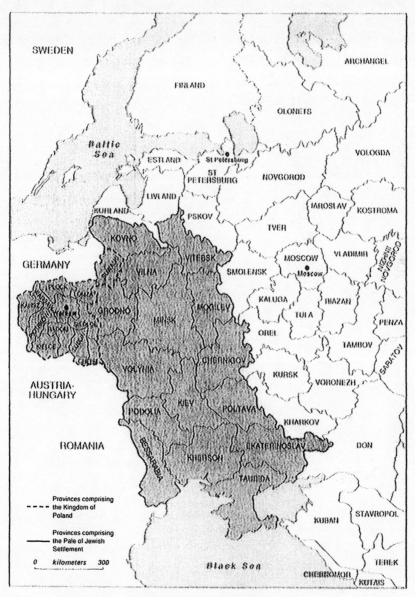

1 European Russia in 1881, showing the provinces of the Kingdom of Poland and the Pale of Jewish Settlement

Preface

In 1984 Professor Shlomo Lambroza conceived the idea of a conference panel and a collaborative publication devoted to anti-Jewish violence in late tsarist and revolutionary Russia. At the time, the project was apparently of academic interest only. The participants were aware that a number of myths and legends surrounded the Russian pogroms of 1881–2, 1903–6 and 1919–21. Almost without exception secondary sources argued that the tsarist authorities actively planned, encouraged or at least welcomed pogroms, in an effort to make the Jews the scapegoats for revolutionary violence, or to channel anti-tsarist protest in a less harmful direction. These claims persist, despite the existence of published scholarship, now over sixty years old, based on primary sources, which effectively refutes these myths.

At the same time, the participants were reluctant to restrict their efforts to the reassertion of old truths. A number of new approaches for the study of modern Russian history lend themselves extremely well to the examination of pogroms. These approaches include the study of violence in Russian society, a better understanding of the prejudices, stereotypes, and psychology of both educated society and the rural masses, and a richer understanding of the tsarist empire as a multi-ethnic entity. Institutional history offers us a more sophisticated understanding of the workings of the tsarist regime, especially the police and the army as agents of order and control. Recent studies offer a better understanding of the workings of the Jewish community in Russia, and the impact of the pogroms on the sense of Jewish identity and security in the Empire. The contributors took as their mandate the incorporation of this research into their work, in the hope of offering a new, integrated view of the pogrom phenomenon.

Ironically, this volume appears at a moment when inter-ethnic violence in general, and anti-Jewish threats in particular, have reappeared in the Soviet Union. This violence has striking analogies to the events described in this volume. In the Caucasus, two terrible pogroms were perpetrated against Armenians, in Sumgait on 29 February 1988 and in Baku on 13 January 1990. These events raised questions which will be familiar to the reader of this volume: what was the complicity of officials, on the local and national level, in the outbreak of these pogroms? Why had a modern state's police and armed forces, some of them stationed in close proximity to the riots, been unable or unwilling to control murder and rapine directed against its own citizens?

The relaxation of official controls has also brought unofficial antisemitic movements into the open. Antisemitic rhetoric which harks back to the period covered by this book has appeared in the ideology of extremist political groups like Pamiat, and in the writings of prominent conservative Russian nationalists. In early 1990, a wave of rumors swept the major cities of the USSR, predicting the outbreak of an antisemitic pogrom on 5 May of that year. In the event, the pogrom did not appear, but the rumors prompted a resurgence of Soviet Jewish emigration, paralleling past responses of the Jewish community in Russia to violence against it. Unwittingly, the essays in this volume have acquired a sharpened contemporary relevance.

All dates in this volume pertaining to the Russian Empire are according to the Julian Calendar (Old Style), in use before the Bolshevik Revolution. Dates relating to the Kingdom of Poland include the date according to the Gregorian Calendar (New Style). The Julian Calendar was twelve days behind the Gregorian Calendar in the nineteenth century, and thirteen days behind in the twentieth century.

Names are given in their most familiar forms (i.e., Alexander and Ignatiev rather than Aleksandr and Ignat'ev). Soft and hard signs are omitted in the text, but included in the bibliographical apparatus. Transliteration follows a modified Library of Congress system, with a few exceptions for personal names, primarily those of German origin.

The maps were designed and executed by Tim Aspden of the Department of Geography at University College London. The assistance of the Faculty of Arts at University College is deeply appreciated.

The photographs illustrating the text are from the collection of YIVO, the Institute for Jewish Research in New York City. Cover illustrations are from YIVO and the American Jewish Historical Society at Brandeis University.

The editing of this volume has been expedited by grants from the Graduate Research Committee and the School of Arts and Sciences at Fort Hays State University, Hays, Kansas, the St. Mary's College Foundation, St. Mary's College, St. Mary's City, Maryland, the Tauber Institute for the Study of European Jewry and the Annenberg Institute. The editors would like to acknowledge the secretarial assistance of Gloria Pfannenstiel of the Department of History at Fort Hays State and Katie Edwards of the Department of Hebrew and Jewish Studies at University College, as well as the editorial assistance of Helen Mingay and Marybeth Burke.

Glossary

The following terms refer to the definitions as used specifically in the text and are not meant to be comprehensive.

artel	a worker or artisan cooperative
ataman	elected Cossack leader; also used to signify leaders of anarchist groups during the Russian Civil War
besporiadki	disorders; official designation for pogroms in tsarist period
boevie otriady	Jewish self-defense squads organized to defend against violence during pogroms
bosiaki	"the barefoot brigade"; vagrants who roamed the countryside in search of work or food especially during times of economic hardship
Bund, the	the General Jewish Workers Party in Russia and Poland (*Der algemeyner yidisher arbeter bund in rusland un poyln*); the Jewish social democratic party founded in 1897
buntartsvo	literally: rebelliousness – term used to express populist faith in the revolutionary potential of the peasantry
Chernyi Peredel	Black Repartition – a revolutionary party founded in 1879 after the breakup of Zemlia i Volia which followed the basic ideas of agrarian Populism
Duma	the legislative body or parliament created after the Revolution of 1905
eruv	a demarcated area of the Jewish quarter of a town or city, set aside for religious reasons
folks-oystand	popular uprising

guberniia	a province of tsarist Russia
halakha	Jewish religious law
Haskalah	the Jewish enlightenment movement of the eighteenth and nineteenth centuries
heder	a private Jewish primary school for the teaching of the Bible and Jewish tradition
hetman	see ataman
Hibbat Zion	literally: Lovers of Zion – first centralized proto-Zionist organization committed to the goal of resettling Jews in Palestine (1884)
intelligent[y]	members of the intelligentsia – usually applied to liberals in opposition to the tsarist regime
Kadets	members of the Constitutional Democrat Party, a liberal political party founded in 1905
kahal	(Heb., *kehillah*) – Jewish community organization responsible for religious, social, fiscal, and at times judicial functions. *Kahals* in Poland had significant authority over Jewish life. Their powers were continually diminished after the Polish partitions and they were abolished under Nicholas I.
kulak	literally: fist. Term used to identify the wealthier segment of the peasant class. They owned large tracts of land and often employed the poorer peasants
maskil(im)	an adherent of the ideas of the Jewish enlightenment (*Haskalah*)
matzoh	unleavened bread eaten by Jews during Passover
meshchantsvo	the judicial estate of townspeople, comprising artisans and petty bourgeoisie; the members of this estate were the *meshchane*
musar	talks by headmasters in *yeshivot* that stressed personal ethics and piety within the structure of *halakha*
muzhik[y]	Russian peasant
nagaika	a Cossack whip
narod	literally: people – specifically used to refer to members of the lower classes, i.e. the workers and peasants

Narodnaia Volia	The People's Will – a terrorist revolutionary party formed in 1879 after the breakup of Zemlia i Volia; its adherents were responsible for the murder of Alexander II in 1881. Members were known as *Narodovoltsy*
narodniki	literally, men of the people; radical Populists
Okhrana	the Russian political police created in 1880
pan[y]	member of Polish nobility, land-owning gentry
Poale-Zion	literally: Workers of Zion – a socialist workers Zionist party (1905)
pogromshchik(i)	one who participates or actively instigates an anti-Jewish riot (pogrom)
shtetl(ekh)	a small town or hamlet in Eastern Europe and Russia
sliianie	literally: merging – the concept of acculturating the Jewish population with the native Christian population
soslovie (ia)	estates or social classes as established by Russian law. Russia had five judicial estates: nobility, clergy, peasants, merchants and towns-people.
szlachta	the middling Polish gentry
Talmud	the comprehensive holy book of Jewish laws and traditions.
ukaz[y]	an official decree of the tsarist government
verst	a measure of distance equalling o·6 miles or 1·06 kilometers
yeshiva (ot)	A school for the advanced study of the Talmud
Zemlia i Volia	Land and Liberty – early Russian Populist revolutionary party, founded in 1876
zemtsvo [a]	elected institutions of local self-government, created in 1864
zhid[y]	in Russian, a Jew: the word had acquired pejorative connotations by the nineteenth century and was replaced in polite conversation by the term *evrei*.

I

General introduction

CHAPTER I

Russian Jewry on the eve of the pogroms

John D. Klier

In the early months of 1881, the Jews of the Russian Empire were poised on the verge of four decades of pogrom violence. Even in the absence of the pogroms, however, this was a significant moment. Russian Jewry had been a target, for just over one hundred years, of a convoluted process of social engineering directed by the Russian state. This process had taken different forms and had been directed towards varying objectives, reflecting the ideology of successive regimes. But by 1881 Russian society displayed a visible disillusionment with past measures, both the apparent successes and the obvious failures. Without the pogroms, dramatic changes in the legal status of Russian Jewry were anticipated. In the face of mass violence, however, the government of Alexander III adopted new policies with uncharacteristic haste. In the end, legal repression was the most visible consequence of the pogroms. The government decided that "Jewish exploitation" was to blame for the "abnormal" relations of Christians and Jews, and moved to deny to the Jews any means to despoil their Gentile neighbors. The pogroms also had a dramatic impact upon the Jewish community itself, calling into question the long-standing commitment of many Jewish intellectuals to forms of integration or assimilation, and providing the impetus for the emergence both of Zionism and distinctly Jewish versions of socialism.[1]

From the perspective of 1881, the initial response of the Russian state to the Jewish communities acquired in the first partition of Poland in 1772 may seem highly ironic, for a number of circumstances made their welcome a warm one. Belorussia, which comprised the territory of the first partition, was poor in population and resources. At first it was utilized as a laboratory for political experimentation by the reform-minded Empress Catherine II. Belorussian Jews were few in number and were scattered throughout

3

the territory.[2] Most of them lived in the countryside, where they engaged in petty trade and leased the feudal prerogatives of the Polish landlords, in particular the right to distil and sell spirits. They served in a variety of middleman roles as buyers of peasant produce for transport to market and as carters and teamsters. As a legacy of the old Polish state, Belorussian Jews were also found in towns, serving as craftsmen and totally dominating trade. Immediately after the first partition, these latter activities caught the eye of Russian officials. Catherine II actively encouraged the growth of urban mercantile centers in the Empire. In a society where most of her subjects were enserfed peasants, bound to the land, urban elements were in short supply. Therefore, Catherine was pleased to accept the Jews as a potential component of urban growth. Russia was a class society composed, at least in theory, of five estates or *soslovie*: the nobility, the clergy, the peasantry, and two urban estates of merchants and townspeople.[3] In 1780, all Jews were ordered to register in one of the two latter estates, with full enjoyment of all corresponding rights, privileges, and responsibilities. Consequently, the status of Russian Jewry was unique for that time anywhere in Europe. This moment did not last, foundering on two obstacles. The first was the resentment of Christian townspeople, accustomed to looking at the Jews as social inferiors, religious pariahs, and commercial rivals who needed no further opportunities. Attempts by Jews to exercise their promised estate rights – chiefly participation in municipal self-government – were greeted with resentment and violence. Russian administrators, faced with the task of maintaining the peace, deferred to the numerically preponderant Christian population. The second obstacle was the growing perception by the same Russian officials that the Jews were not in fact a purely urban mercantile class or the raw material for urban growth. Worse, the Jews were accused of engaging in unproductive, "parasitical," and "exploitative" activity, living at the expense of the peasantry, and "sucking their vital juices," especially through control of the trade in distilled spirits.

No longer would the Russian government accept the Jews as they were. The Jews were seen as badly in need of reform, an objective best attained by moving them into "productive" occupations such as handicrafts, manufacturing, and agriculture. The native population, on the other hand, could be protected from the Jews by "rendering them harmless" through the deprivation of certain rights. Pursuit of these twin objectives mandated special regulations for the Jewish community, which thus became an object for special legislation. Eventually a gigantic corpus of law, supplemented by interpretations of the Senate and administrative rulings by local officials, grew up around the Jews of the Russian Empire. A century-long program of social engineering was now initiated.[4]

The most important restriction on Jewish life in Russia was also one of the first. Under Catherine II the principle evolved that Jews were not permitted to move out of the areas – primarily the lands of partitioned Poland, supplemented by extensive, unsettled frontier areas in the south – where they lived upon first coming under Russian rule. The original intent of this restriction was to protect established mercantile elements in urban centers like Moscow and Smolensk.[5] Even after the second and third partitions of Poland brought hundreds of thousands of Jews under the Russian scepter, these residence restrictions were not immediately a burden. But over time, these first restrictions were joined by efforts to expel the Jews from the countryside and by a number of occupational restrictions which evolved into the notorious "Pale of Jewish Settlement." The Pale was the single most destructive legal burden borne by Russian Jewry, and one of the most enduring.

In 1881 the Pale of Settlement, where most Russian Jews were obliged to live by law, comprised fifteen provinces in the north-western and southwestern regions of European Russia (Belorussia, Lithuania, the Ukraine, Bessarabia and New Russia). The number of Jews in the entire Russian Empire was reckoned at 4,086,650, or 4·2 percent of the population. Of these, 1,010,378 were in the Kingdom of Poland, not covered by the legal regulations of the Pale. Polish Jewry constituted 13·8 percent of the total population. Within the Pale itself, Jews numbered 2,912,165 or 12·5 percent of the population. Of these, 2,331,880, or just over 80 percent, lived in towns or *shtetlekh*, while 580,285 resided in the countryside in peasant villages. Only a minuscule number of Jews, 53,574 or 0·1 percent of the population, lived in the interior provinces of Russia. Most of these were merchants or artisans who resided in St. Petersburg or Moscow. There was always an indeterminate number of Jews living illegally outside the Pale.[6]

Economic conditions in the Pale steadily worsened after the emancipation of the Russian peasantry in 1861 and the construction of a network of railroads throughout the Empire. The Jewish population was increasing at the very moment that employment opportunities were shrinking. Many functions traditionally performed by the Jews, such as teamster services, petty trade, and peddling in the countryside, were becoming obsolete. In urban areas, competition in trade and handicrafts increased. The Pale became choked by a huge, pauperized mass of unskilled or semi-skilled Jewish laborers, whose economic condition steadily worsened.

Contemporaries often debated the impact of the Pale upon the non-Jewish population. Some argued that the conditions of over-competition acted to drive down prices and to provide a buyer's market which was entirely to the advantage of residents who shared the Pale with the Jews. Moreover, those in the Pale were spared the chronic shortage of craftsmen which bedeviled the Russian interior.[7]

Other observers argued that the advantageous features of the Pale were far outnumbered by its negative characteristics. In the ruthless competitive atmosphere of the Pale, they contended, the need of Jews to compete by selling cheap resulted in the production of shoddy, poor-quality goods, or in price-fixing and collusion. The commercial honesty of Jews was the first casualty of the Pale, and willingly or unwillingly Jews were forced to exploit Christians to the fullest possible extent.[8] While commentators differed as to the effect of the Pale on Gentiles, they unanimously agreed that it produced undesirable social and economic abnormalities. Prior to 1881 a broad consensus existed in public opinion that the Pale should be abolished or at least significantly modified. Indeed, one of the first victims of the pogroms was a series of governmental actions relaxing the Pale which had been slowly implemented throughout the reign of Alexander II. Reform proposals were eclipsed by the fear that scattering the Jews around the Empire would spread anti-Jewish violence.

As the Pale of Settlement began to take shape and solidify, it was accompanied by various state initiatives designed to make the Jews more "productive." On the positive side were efforts, exemplified by a special law code for the Jews promulgated in 1804, to direct the Jews into manufacturing and agriculture. The prospect of making the Jews into farmers was especially appealing to the regime, and significant sums of money – albeit collected from the Jews in the form of special taxes – were allocated for the purpose of settling the Jews in agricultural colonies. These efforts proved neither successful nor cost-effective and served as general confirmation to the foes of the Jews that they were incapable of manual labor or of non-exploitative livelihoods. In 1866, the government of Alexander II ended the creation of new state-supported agricultural colonies.[9] Subsequently the government began to transfer the existing colonization fund to other uses, and Jewish efforts to replace state colonization with private initiatives quickly waned after the pogroms.

Official attempts to limit "Jewish exploitation" took the form of periodic attacks on certain areas of Jewish economic activity. These included petty trade and usury, but the most frequent target was Jewish participation in the manufacture and sale of alcohol. There was irony in these initiatives, because the Jews were merely a part of a state-sanctioned system of alcohol production and sale, one which produced significant revenue for the Russian exchequer.

Despite ample evidence to the contrary, Jews were blamed for the impoverishment and intoxication of the peasantry almost from the first moment that Russian officialdom began to study the Jewish Question.[10] A principal motive for recurrent efforts to resettle village Jews into urban centers – thus exacerbating the living conditions of the Pale – was the desire to eliminate them from the liquor trade. In the decade before the pogroms, the government promulgated a new law (14 May 1874) that sought to restrict the regulations under which village Jews traded in alcohol. After the pogroms, the Minister of the Interior, N. P. Ignatiev, struggled long and hard, albeit unsuccessfully, within the Council of Ministers to impose a total ban on Jewish trade in alcohol in the countryside.[11]

In the century before the pogroms, legislation which regulated Jews in the economy was accompanied by statutes motivated by social and political considerations. Russian bureaucrats borrowed from Western Europe the belief that it was not circumstances that directed the Jews into unproductive, parasitical, and exploitative commercial activities, but the teachings of Judaism itself, especially as conveyed by the Talmud. According to Western "experts" and their Eastern epigones, the Talmud preached the undying enmity of Jews towards Gentiles, and encouraged Jews to harm them in any way which would not provoke retribution.[12] In a Christian, agrarian nation like Russia, where Jews were a tiny minority, this goal was best accomplished through trade and commerce, which provided endless opportunities for exploitation.

In the light of these beliefs, would-be reformers were convinced that it was not only necessary to change the occupations of the Jews, as exemplified by the reforms and restrictions noted above, but also to modify the religious ideology which prompted Jewish exploitation in the first place. Judaism itself had to be "purified" through the elimination or modification of the Talmud. If that goal were achieved, Jews would lose their antisocial, separatist characteristics and acquire the virtues of Christians, through a process known as "merging" (*sliianie*) with the native population.

This general objective gave rise to confused and contradictory policies prior to 1881. Virtually all commentators decried, as the foremost cause of Jewish exclusivity and isolation, the system of autonomous local Jewish self-government, the *kahal*, which the Russian state had inherited from Poland. Yet successive Russian governments were reluctant to abolish it. The reason lay in the kahal's utility as an agency to assess and collect taxes and other obligations, and to maintain vital statistics. When the government of Nicholas I abolished the kahal system in 1844, supposedly as an integrationist measure, it promptly replaced kahal officials with other special Jewish bureaucrats, identical in function if not in name with their predecessors. This state of affairs permitted the rise of the pernicious legend that the kahal had not disappeared at all, but continued to exist as an underground institution, reinforcing Jewish social isolation and thwarting the well-intentioned reforms which the Russian government had devised for the Jews.[13]

Another integrationist reform, the imposition of military service upon Jews, had a similarly unfortunate outcome. Implemented in 1827 by Nicholas I, it was designed to make Jewish townsmen – who previously had been able to purchase a collective exemption – serve alongside their Christian counterparts in the army. The rigors of a twenty-five year term of service, the impossibility for observant Jews to practice their faith, and quasi-official efforts to convert Jewish soldiers to Christianity all combined to encourage evasion of military service by Jews. Jewish evasion was met with ever-increasing collective punishment for arrears, including the drafting of communal officials and implementation of the notorious cantonist system, which provided for the draft of under-age children.[14]

One of the first acts of Nicholas' successor, Alexander II, was to revoke these special penalties, thus winning the eternal gratitude of the Jewish community. In 1874, Alexander's reformist advisers implemented a military innovation of their own, a system of universal military service, marked by the elimination of all class exemptions. At first, the Jews were not treated in any special way in the recruitment process. But Alexander, like his father before him, became convinced that the Jews were evading service in disproportionate numbers, and he approved a number of collective punishments for draft evasion. A bitter polemic raged between the friends and the foes of the Jews up to and beyond 1881 on the question of Jewish patriotism and willingness to serve. A state obligation, which had been expected to draw all Russian subjects together, instead became a controversial and divisive element in Jewish–Gentile relations.

The most exotic and variegated attempt at the social reform of the Jews also had its inception in the reign of Nicholas I, and represented another avenue of attack against the isolation of the Jews. It involved the creation of a full-blown educational system, designed to produce teachers and communal religious leaders, as well as to instruct Jewish youth. Young Jews had been offered open admission to all Russian state educational institutions by the Statute of 1804, but few members of the Jewish community displayed any interest in secular education provided by Christian schools. Instead, Jewish youth was educated in a privately run primary school system, the *heder*, before moving on to a more advanced institution, the *yeshiva*. From the government's point of view these schools were breeding-grounds of Jewish isolation and "fanaticism." Instruction was in Yiddish, and study of the Talmud was the central part of the curriculum. After extensive consultation and preparation, Nicholas decreed the creation of an elaborate new state-sponsored Jewish school system, heavily influenced by the German–Jewish model. The system was under the control of the Ministry of Education, and even the principals of individual primary schools were initially Christians. The Jewish community, through a special series of taxes, financed the entire operation.

An idiosyncratic aspect of the reform was the participation of the Russian government in the development of a religious curriculum for the Jewish schools. A confessional element was devised by the reformers who believed that Jews would refuse to educate their children in purely secular institutions. (The government was oblivious to the disquiet which Jews felt towards a religious curriculum developed and overseen by Christians!) In addition to a network of primary and secondary schools, two rabbinical seminaries were also created, at Vilna and Zhitomir, to train teachers for the lower schools, and to educate "enlightened" rabbis, who were to be forced on the community as agents of state oversight and enlightenment.[15] The state further undermined its own reform by permitting the retention of the traditional Jewish heder and yeshiva.

Many historians have emphasized the low enrollment in the state Jewish schools and dismissed the whole project as a quixotic failure. Recent scholarship indicates that, to the contrary, a significant number of young Jews did attend these schools and that an entire generation of Russian Jewish intellectuals had some connection with the schools as either students or faculty. Michael Stanislawski is correct to assert that "these men constituted the literary, intellectual, and political elite of Russian Jewry from the 1840s through the 1870s and the creators of the new Russian–Jewish culture."[16]

Perhaps the most telling testimonial to the success of the Nicholine school system was the decision of the Minister of Education, D. A. Tolstoi, to disband it in 1873. Tolstoi was not just rationalizing failure when he argued that the schools were no longer necessary because so many Jews, male and female, were attending Russian institutions. The stream of students noted by Tolstoi in 1873 became a flood after 1874, when the new military recruitment statute offered generous reductions in the length of service for recruits with secondary and advanced education.

Close to achieving a long-sought goal, the acceptance by at least some young Jews of Russian language, culture, and social values, the Russian government and public opinion began to have second thoughts. School administrators in the Pale reported the alarming phenomenon of the "Judification" of Russian schools, whereby Christian students found themselves either in a minority, or under the unhealthy moral influence of large Jewish minorities in the schools. Jews, it was argued, were too successful in competing for places in secondary schools, and were driving Christians from the school benches. This increased the possibility that the Jews would soon flood into the universities as well. Proposals for restrictions and quotas appeared, highlighted by the famous editorial "The Yid Is Coming," which appeared in the 23 March 1880 issue of the Judeophobe organ *Novoe vremia*. As more Jews did indeed acquire higher education and enter the professions, proposals were advanced to restrict them there as well. The notorious quotas which marked the reign of Alexander III had their spiritual genesis in the reign of his father, Alexander II.[17]

As the above survey suggests, the decade preceding the pogroms of 1881 witnessed a growing atmosphere of crisis surrounding the Jewish Question in Russia. Goaded by an increasingly militant Judeophobe press, Russian statesmen clung to their old prejudiced view of the Jews as a serious economic and social problem, even as the old panaceas of occupational reform, integration, and enlightenment were called into question. The appearance of Jews in the Russian revolutionary movement, and a growing recognition of their economic influence in the western borderlands where Polish and Russian nationalism vied for cultural and political domination, added new elements. Thus, even without the pogroms, new approaches and policies were augured. Some specialists have argued that the government might well have moved towards the complete abolition of the Pale and a general regularization of the abnormal legal status of Russian Jewry.[18] Faced with riot and anarchy in 1881, the regime of Alexander III opted instead for policies of repression and restriction. Subsequent disorders, in the twentieth century, occurred against the background of what had by then become the "politics of despair" concerning the Jewish Question.

NOTES

1 For an excellent discussion of these phenomena, see Jonathan Frankel, *Prophecy and Politics: Socialism, Nationalism, and the Russian Jews, 1862–1917* (Cambridge, 1981).

2 Kh. Korobkhov, "Perepis' evreiskogo naseleniia vitebskoi gubernii v 1772 g.," *Evreiskaia starina*, IV, 4–6 (1912), 164–77.

3 For the reality beyond this abstraction see Gregory L. Freeze, "The soslovie (estate) paradigm and Russian social history," *American Historical Review*, XCI, 1 (1986), 11–36.

4 For a history of the evolution of post-partition treatment of the Jews in the Russian Empire see my work, *Russia Gathers Her Jews: The Origins of the Jewish Question in Russia, 1772–1825* (DeKalb, 1986).

5 Ibid., 75–6.

6 *Obshchaia zapiska vysshei kommisii dlia peresmotra deistvuiushchikh o Evreiakh v imperii zakonov [1883–1888]* (St. Petersburg, 1888), 1–2. Compare these statistics with those from the First All-Russian Census, discussed by Alexander Orbach in chapter 6.

7 Ibid., 281–2.

8 Ibid., 271–3.

9 M. I. Mysh, *Rukovodstvo k russkim zakonom o Evreiakh* (St. Petersburg, 1914), 409.

10 Klier, *Russia*, 62–4.

11 See Iu. I. Gessen, "Graf N. P. Ignat'ev i 'Vremennye pravila' o Evreiakh 3 maia 1882 goda," *Pravo*, xxx (1908), 1631–7; xxxi (1908), 1678–87.

12 See L. A. Chiarini, *Théorie du Judaïsme appliquée à la réforme des Israélites*, 2 vols. (Paris, 1830).

13 See Iakov Brafman, *Kniga kagala* (Vilna, 1869).

14 Michael Stanislawski, *Tsar Nicholas I and the Jews* (Philadelphia, 1983), 13–34.

15 Iu. I. Hessen (Gessen), "Die russische Regierung und die westeuropäische Juden: Zur Schulreform in Russland, 1840–1844," *Monatsschrift für Geschichte und Wissenschaft des Judentums*, LVII (1913), 257–71, 482–500.

16 Stanislawski, *Tsar Nicholas I*, 107.

17 See A. I. Georgievskii, *Po voprosu o merakh otnositel'no obrazovaniia Evreev* (St. Petersburg, 1886).

18 I. M. Aronson, "The prospects for the emancipation of Russian Jewry during the 1880s," *Slavonic and East European Review*, LV, 3 (1977), 348–69. See also Eli Lederhendler, *The Road to Modern Jewish Politics* (Oxford and New York, 1989), 150–3.

CHAPTER 2

The pogrom paradigm in Russian history

John D. Klier

The word "pogrom" is Russian.[1] Its usage became inextricably linked to antisemitic violence after the outbreak of three great waves of anti-Jewish rioting in the Russian Empire in 1881–2, 1903–6, and 1919–21. It was widely charged at the time and since that the Russian government either planned, welcomed, or at least tolerated pogroms for its own devious purposes.[2] Such assumptions were in turn joined to recollections of previous outbreaks of violence against Jews in Eastern European history. These events were invariably tagged as "pogroms" by modern observers, irrespective of the fact that they differed in important respects from Russian pogroms, and in most cases had taken place in territories which were not then part of the Russian Empire. The anachronistic character of using the term "pogrom" to describe earlier events is obvious when they are examined in more detail.

In 1113, for example, upon the death of the Grand Prince of Kiev, Sviatopolk, rioting broke out in Kiev against his agents and the town administration. The disorders were not specifically directed against Jews and are best characterized as a social revolution. This has not prevented historians of medieval Russia from describing them as a pogrom.[3] Another atrocity widely referred to as a pogrom took place in 1563, when Russian armies led by Tsar Ivan IV captured the Polish city of Polotsk. The Tsar ordered drowned in the river Dvina all Jews who refused to convert to Orthodox Christianity. This episode certainly demonstrates the overt religious hostility towards the Jews which was very much a part of Muscovite culture, but its conversionary aspects were entirely absent from modern pogroms. Nor were the Jews the only heterodox religious group singled out for the tender mercies of Muscovite religious fanaticism.

The most dramatic pre-modern pogroms took place in the Ukraine, a region which at that time lay outside the orbit of

Muscovy. In 1648, under the leadership of Hetman Bogdan Chmielnicki, Ukrainian Cossacks rose in revolt. The ultimate target of Cossack resentment was the socioeconomic order of the Polish state, especially the spread of Polish feudalism into the Ukraine. Jews frequently served as the financial agents of the Polish landowning nobility, they lived in the midst of the peasant population and as a consequence were particularly resented and victimized. Nonetheless, the Chmielnicki uprising, complex and confused, was not aimed specifically or primarily against Jews.[4] Similar events occurred in 1768, amidst the social and political turmoil prefacing the first partition of Poland. An anti-Russian noble uprising triggered a peasant and Cossack rebellion, the "Kolivshchyzna," which took a heavy toll of victims from among noblemen, Catholic priests, and Jews. The most notorious atrocity was a massacre of Catholics and Jews at the town of Uman (Human), which claimed 20,000 victims.[5] The Kolivshchyzna was not directed against the Jews alone, although they were a prominent collective victim. Both episodes became firmly established in the heroic lore of the Cossacks. When the pogroms of 1881–2 in the Ukraine reached epidemic proportions, Russian officials were wont to explain them by recalling the "Cossack traditions" of the Ukrainian people. This tradition also was used to account for the absence of pogroms in the northwest (Lithuania and Belorussia), where there were many Jews and economic conditions similar to the Ukraine, but no violence, at least until the twentieth century.

The accompanying essays in this volume provide a collective definition of what comprised modern Russian pogroms, and how the successive waves differed one from another. Certain common features can be identified at this point, however. Among the most striking features of the pogroms were their spontaneous and confused character, devoid of long-term objectives or goals. This was particularly the case in 1881–2, and even the battle cry of the Black Hundreds in 1905 and the White Armies in 1919, "Beat the Yids and Save Russia!" hardly bespoke a sophisticated ideology. Another important feature of the pogroms was their urban nature. To be sure, numerous village taverns, shtetlekh and agricultural colonies were the targets of pogrom violence, but it invariably spread to the countryside from urban areas, as Michael Aronson demonstrates. Peasants were frequently reported to have come to a town or city to participate in the looting that accompanied pogroms, and then carried the idea of an attack upon the Jews back to their village. Before the complete collapse of the political and moral authority of the central government, pogrom violence in the countryside tended to be less brutal and lethal, even though the forces of law and order were weaker and more distant. Finally, the pogroms of the modern period reversed the model of past episodes of violence in Eastern Europe: now it was pogrom violence directed primarily against Jews which spilled over to other groups (such as teachers or zemstvo doctors in 1905–6), rather than the reverse.

The scene of the first Russian pogroms, in the modern sense, was Odessa. These pogroms – which occurred in 1821, 1849, 1859, and 1871 – are worth studying in detail.[6] They were instrumental in creating a matrix of fixed responses and assumptions about pogroms which Russian officials and publicists developed to explain and interpret the Odessa events – a set of preconceptions that can be characterized as the "pogrom paradigm" in Russia. When new pogroms occurred on a massive scale in 1881, interpretations were already at hand to explain the distant and unexpected events raging in the Pale of Settlement.

Odessa was a distinctly non-Russian city with a unique and colorful history. Founded in 1794, it was a free port for the first half of the nineteenth century and the focus of the economic life of newly colonized regions near the Black Sea known as New Russia. It enjoyed explosive growth, becoming the third city of the Empire by the mid-nineteenth century while filling up with many different nationalities. Odessa was famous for its cosmopolitanism, but it was also a hotbed of ethnic, religious, and economic rivalries, as various groups struggled to secure or maintain a favored economic position. The first economic masters of the city were Greeks, whose maritime prowess found a natural outlet in the import-export trade. The Odessa Greeks were famed for their ardent nationalism in the period before the outbreak of the Greek War of Independence in 1821, and the city boasted a branch of the Philike Hetaireia, the secret society which played a major role in the planning and conduct of the Greek revolution. The traditional domination of the Greeks was directly threatened by the Jews, who began to pour into the city in search of economic opportunity. By mid-century, Jews constituted almost one-third of the total population, and were economically diversified. The economic rivalry of Greeks and Jews was accompanied by religious hostility, and further exacerbated by ethnic passions.

The general, and mutual, antipathy of Greeks and Jews in Odessa was made specific by the physical layout of the city and their respective religious customs. The two communities were situated side-by-side in the southeast quarter of the city, above the harbor. The Jewish quarter was a stone's throw, physically and metaphorically, from the principal Greek Orthodox Church, which was the religious and national center for the Odessa Greeks. This unfortunate proximity came into play at least once a year, during Holy Week, the seven-day observance of the passion, death, and resurrection of Christ. The New Testament account of these events emphasizes the role of the Jews in the crucifixion, focused on the accusatory words: "His death be upon us and upon our children!" The solemn Jewish feast of Passover occurred during the same period, and this served to call up the medieval legend that the Jews required the blood of an innocent Christian child in order to make their Passover matzoh. Rumors of ritual murder did surface from time to time in Odessa, as elsewhere in Europe. Finally, the religious ceremonies of Holy Week involved processions outside the church itself. Such public events invariably drew large crowds of curious onlookers, many of whom were Jews. Acts of ridicule or disrespect – devout Christians were supposed to doff their caps to religious processions while equally devout Jews kept their heads covered – could easily lead to scuffles and fights. It was proverbial that squabbles between Jewish and Christian street urchins were an inevitable holiday phenomenon. There was always the danger that holiday ill-feelings, reinforced by the aggressive drunkenness that was an unfortunate side-effect of the Christian celebration of Easter, might escalate into something worse. It was not uncommon throughout the nineteenth century for extra police or army patrols to be added in towns with large Jewish populations. In 1858, for example, the Odessa fire brigade was called out to turn their hoses on a mob that was beating Jews near the Greek quarter.[7] On 30 August 1869, several Jews were badly wounded when they were attacked by Christian apprentices.[8] In 1870, the Jewish newspaper *Den* complained of continuing "demonstrations" by Odessa street urchins against Jews.[9] In an attack on the economic activities of Odessa Jewry in 1870, a writer in the St. Petersburg daily *Golos* took note of past disorders and warned that "this hatred [of the Jews] is so great that sooner or later – I suppose even in the not too distant future – it will force its way into the open." To date, reprisals had only been "payment in kind," bloodless theft, or even destruction of Jewish goods, but such docility could not be guaranteed in future.[10] This theme that pogrom activity was retributive, seeking to destroy property rather than cause bodily injury, became one of the most persistent myths of the pogrom paradigm.

The first Odessa pogrom occurred in 1821 and grew out of events surrounding the Greek War of Independence. At the outbreak of the revolution, in part triggered by the Phanariots, the Istanbul-based Greek servitors of the Ottoman Empire, a Muslim mob attacked the residence of the Greek Orthodox Patriarch in Istanbul, Gregory V, and murdered him. His body was mutilated and cast into the sea, reportedly by twenty members of the city's Jewish rabble. Many Greeks fled from Istanbul to Odessa and on 19 June 1821 the body of the Patriarch was brought to Odessa for a solemn funeral and burial. During the funeral procession, according to one account, a group of Jews were slow to doff their hats and were set upon by armed Greeks. A riot ensued, which was soon joined by a Russian mob, culminating in the death of seventeen people and wounding of sixty more.[11] The streets were finally cleared when Cossacks proceeded to beat anyone found there.

There was only one contemporary account of this pogrom published by the German writer, Heinrich Zschokke, which illustrates the difficulty of assembling an accurate account of such tumultuous events. Zschokke claimed that the attack was planned in advance and even known to the police, who advised the Jews to remain indoors and to close their shops. He reported the charge that the Greeks were instrumental in provoking the attack, but noted that no Greeks were arrested nor were they readily in evidence amidst the largely Russian crowds. The explanation mooted at the time was that the Greeks were wearing Russian clothes, but in the final analysis Zschokke concluded, "the facts remain inexplicable."[12]

Thus in the very first Odessa pogrom questions went unanswered which were to appear again and again in the future: to what extent was the pogrom planned or spontaneous? Who were the instigators? Who were the pogromshchiki and what were their motives?

Little is recorded about the minor pogrom of 22 August 1849, which occurred upon the occasion of a solemn church procession from the Mikhailovskii monastery. Again it is reported that a group of Jews were reluctant to doff their hats when the procession passed and that the Odessa police chief ordered his men to make them do so. The police were joined by civilian volunteers and the ensuing scuffle escalated into a riot. Shops in the Jewish quarter were sacked and looted. On this occasion no special force was required to suppress the disorders and damage was set at the relatively modest sum of 15,000 roubles.[13]

The pogroms of 1821 and 1849 remained local events, attracting no attention elsewhere in the Empire. Lack of rapid communications and the absence of a national press ensured that they would not be widely reported. By 1859 this was no longer the case. Odessa boasted a thrice-weekly newspaper, *Odesskii vestnik*, which was widely monitored in the capitals. In Moscow and St. Petersburg, the monthly journals still ruled the day, but they carried special sections devoted to current events. The censorship was in disarray: the censorship terror of the old Nicholine regime had been relaxed and the state was in the process of devising a more modern and effective system. Moreover, for the first time in Russian journalistic history the Jewish Question had burst into the consciousness of public opinion. The occasion was a hostile description of Russian Jewry by the prestigious periodical, *Illiustratsiia*. When several Jewish journalists responded to the gibes of *Illiustratsiia*, they were ridiculed and insulted. The result was a "literary protest" against the behavior of *Illiustratsiia*, signed by virtually every prominent Russian man of letters, over 100 in all.[14] In this climate the outbreak of physical violence against Jews in Odessa would not pass unremarked.

There are two published contemporary accounts of the Odessa pogrom of 1859 and, as would be the case with subsequent pogroms, they differ sharply. The first appeared in No. 42 of *Odesskii vestnik*, on 21 April 1859. The author noted that the holiday season was especially conducive to orgies and recklessness while the religious aura provided a convenient pretext for the appearance of religious intolerance and fanaticism among the lower classes. To these circumstances was added the large number of foreign sailors in the city. Holy Week had begun, the paper reported, with quarreling between Jewish and Christian children, which escalated into a riot when foreign sailors intervened and began to vandalize the Jewish quarter. One person died and five were wounded in the disorders, although the rapid deployment of Cossacks quickly dispersed the crowd. Later in the week street urchins and drunken Russian workers attempted to revive the violence, but vigorous police measures restricted the damage to some broken glass. In short, the events were nothing serious and a tribute to the timely intervention of the authorities. Regrettably, the disorders also testified to the credulity of the populace, exemplified by the words of one onlooker that "on the first day the telegraph brought permission for a fist-fight."[15]

The prestigious journal, *Russkii vestnik*, published in Moscow by M. N. Katkov, had been in the forefront of the literary protest of the previous year, so it is not surprising that the publication offered its own account of the Odessa pogrom, which differed in important respects from that of the Odessa press. An anonymous author complained that *Odesskii vestnik* had seen the events of the pogrom as no more than a fight (*draka*) and had minimized the violence. As a corrective, the author painted a horrifying picture of the brutal murder of the sole fatality, a hapless orange seller who found himself trapped in the middle of the mob. The lighthearted attribution of the pogrom to the high spirits of Russian holiday-makers drew special condemnation as a slur on the Russian national character. The pogromshchiki, claimed the author, were Greeks.[16]

An account of the pogrom of 1859, published in 1882, offers more detail. The article, appearing in the wake of the Odessa pogrom of 1881, is not overly sympathetic to the Jews and undoubtedly entails some reading back of the events of 1881 to the earlier period. According to the author, the pogrom erupted again after initially being suppressed on the first day of Holy Week, when rumors swept through the city that the Jews had hurled insults at Christians during the rituals of Holy Thursday and that a young Christian had been tortured by Jews. The crowd was described as making an effort to distinguish between "good" and "bad" Jews. (If this detail is not anachronistic, it anticipates similar reports arising from the pogroms of 1881 and given wide circulation in the Judeophobic press of the day.) When the pogromshchiki attacked the Jews they were quoted as shouting "You drink our blood, you rob us," words suspiciously similar to those quoted in newspaper accounts of the 1881 pogroms.[17]

The disturbances of 1859 did not provoke deep analysis. The police response was to round up as many people as could be found on the streets and to give them a birching in one of the city squares.[18] The Governor-General of New Russia, Count A. G. Stroganov, attributed the pogrom entirely to religious fanaticism.[19] *Odesskii vestnik*, as noted above, saw the pogrom as a reflection of the low cultural level of the masses, a judgment with which *Russkii vestnik* implicitly concurred. Paradoxically, such assessments produced a feeling of optimism rather than despair. Russian society was moving confidently into the era of the great reforms. All the shortcomings of the old regime, exemplified by serfdom, were to be swept away and a new society built on its ruins. Unfortunate manifestations of the old days, such as this explosion of medieval religious intolerance, would disappear in the new age. No special alarm need be raised, no special lessons drawn.

This optimistic mood was much changed in the course of the decade that preceded the Odessa pogrom of 1871. The long-awaited abolition of serfdom, like the secondary reforms that followed it, proved prelude only to a new set of intractable social problems. Peasants and left-wing intellectuals alike found the emancipation provisions far from satisfactory. The new institutions of local self-government, the *zemstva*, quickly developed an adversarial relationship with the old bureaucracy. The Polish uprising of 1863 and the appearance of political terrorism encouraged the government to retreat from reform.

As the era of liberal good intentions waned, the benevolent attitude of much of the Russian intelligentsia towards the Jews also changed. Early attempts by Alexander's government to improve the status of the Jews and especially the relaxation of the restrictive Pale of Settlement, failed to attain the objective of the Russianization and integration of the tradition-bound Jewish communities of the Empire's north and southwest borderlands. The vague Judeophilia of liberal Russia in the 1850s constituted the intellectual fashion among men who knew little of the mundane realities of Jewish life. When investigators actually encountered Jewish life *in situ*, they instinctively viewed it as "Jewish exploitation." Dealings with real Jews produced culture shock, disillusionment, and an incipient Judeophobia. Liberals, concerned with the protection of the newly emancipated peasants and committed to the economic theory of the free exchange of goods, saw Jewish involvement in the disintegrating feudal economy as an undesirable brake on peasant prosperity. Intellectuals who had once protested a mild insult delivered to two Jewish authors, now eagerly accepted the exotic theories of a Jewish renegade, Iakov Brafman, who explained the negative features of Jewish life by his claims that the ancient system of Jewish autonomous government in Poland, the *kahal*, still maintained an illegal existence. Allegedly, this secret government joined all Jews together in a "Talmudic municipal republic," which was determined both to preserve the interests of Russian Jewry and to oversee the systematic exploitation of the Christian population.[20]

Brafman's domination of Russian public opinion did not go unchallenged. Jewish publicists, educated in Russian schools, comfortable in Russian society, and frequently employed by Russian periodicals, waged a war of polemics against his accusations, ensuring that the Jewish Question was seldom absent from the columns of the expanding Russian press. Another important phenomenon was the appearance of the first Russian–Jewish newspapers in Russia – appropriately enough, published in Odessa: *Rassvet* (1860–1), *Sion* (1861–2) and *Den, organ russkikh Evreev* (1869–71).[21] The stage on which the nature and causes of pogrom violence could be debated was more extensive and public than ever before. As a consequence, while the pogrom of 1871 took place in Odessa, it became a national event.

The shape of the Odessa pogrom of 1871 emerged in a familiar pattern: disorders broke out during Holy Week, on 28 March and lasted until 1 April. Beyond this barest of outlines, the specific details become more obscure. The official account of 1871 is contained in the reports of the Governor-General of New Russia, P. E. Kotsebu, to the Ministry of the Interior. On 30 March 1871, in the midst of the pogrom, Kotsebu reported that the events were an outgrowth of the traditional fights between Jews and Greeks during Holy Week. The disturbances expanded when the Greeks were joined by Russians motivated by religious antipathy.[22] The following day, Kotsebu noted that the fights were an annual occurrence, but were usually suppressed with ease. The entry of Russians into the fray complicated police procedures. Why had Russians joined in? "The recent events revealed that the [religious] antipathy of the Christians (primarily the lower classes) was joined to bitterness born of the exploitation of their work by Jews and the ability of the latter to enrich themselves and manipulate all manner of trade and commercial activity. In the crowds of Christians there were often heard the words 'the Jews offended our Christ, they grow rich and they suck our blood.'"[23]

The Ministry of the Interior was concerned that the Odessa pogrom might contain a political component and instructed Kotsebu to investigate this point carefully. (The central government displayed an identical concern in 1881.) He replied that while the pogrom arose from brawls, as he had earlier explained, there were indeed instigators who agitated for a riot against the Jews, who led sections of the crowd and who were protected by them. About forty agitators had been arrested. All were common people, often vagrants and, Kotsebu was happy to report, none were under surveillance for political activities.

The methods ascribed to instigators of the crowd by Kotesbu are worth detailing, because several of them regularly reappeared in the reporting of later pogroms. For example, the agitators claimed that an imperial decree had been received by the authorities, permitting three days of violence against the Jews. (This was similar to the rumor floated in 1859.) Others claimed that the Jews had tortured a Christian woman, a charge that also had a precedent in 1859. The most widely disseminated and inflammatory charge in 1871, however, was that the Jews had pulled down and desecrated the cross which stood on the gates of the Greek church. Kotsebu later reported a vague rumor that the body of Patriarch Gregory V, the 1821 victim, was being returned to Constantinople from his burial place in Odessa, recalling one of the presumed motives for the pogrom of 1821.

A final, definitive report on the disorders was sent by Kotsebu to the Ministry of the Interior on 11 April 1871. He emphasized that the economic domination of the Jews in the area produced abnormal relationships between Christians and Jews. In addition, recent violence against the Jews in the Danubian Principalities of Moldavia and Wallachia and in Austrian Galicia had offered an infectious example to the local population. The Greeks, of course, maintained their own religious and economic hatred of the Jews, and this proved sufficient to spark violent unrest. Once the disorders began, the rioters were surrounded by large crowds of curious spectators, who were sympathetic to their activities as long as they were confined to the destruction – rather than appropriation – of Jewish property. Here again was the myth that the rioters were intent on retribution, rather than theft or personal violence. This myth made a powerful impression on Russian commentators – especially Populists who sought to mitigate the guilt of the people – and in 1881 was still being cited by the Populist monthly *Delo* in its explanation of the pogrom of 1871.[24] The presence of the large crowd of onlookers made police measures difficult, Kotsebu reported, and the absence of a political motive made him reluctant to apply too much force, lest the action of troops increase popular resentment against the Jews still more.[25]

In another context Kotsebu complained to Petersburg about the role of the press, complaints that precisely foreshadowed bureaucratic attitudes in 1881–2:

In the Petersburg and Moscow newspapers there continues to appear correspondence about the disorders which took place in Odessa, filled with exaggerated or completely false news. Such correspondence is sent to foreign newspapers. In large part it is written by Jews, with the objective of influencing public opinion everywhere for the assistance of the suffering Jewish community in Odessa.

If our capital newspapers eagerly open their columns to such correspondence, not even knowing the authors, then it meets an even more joyful reception in the foreign press, for this press is found almost everywhere in the hands of Jews or employs their participation as the closest of collaborators.[26]

It is obvious that Kotsebu's reports were designed to do more than describe "exactly what happened" – they were exercises in damage control. First and foremost they sought to justify the actions of Odessa officials, with the governor-general himself at the top of the list. If Greek–Jewish brawls were endemic at holiday time, then the authorities could not have been expected to anticipate that this year they might give rise to a pogrom. Nor could the officials be held responsible for the abnormal socioeconomic relations between Christian and Jew which drew the Russian population into the violence. If the police and army were slow to respond to the escalating violence, it was to protect innocent civilians and, ultimately, for the good of the Jews themselves.

It is surprising that Kotsebu did not emphasize how thin were the police forces at his disposal – perhaps because it was so obvious as to be not worth mentioning. Certainly resort to the army was not the preferred method for maintaining public order. Pre-revolutionary Russia was notoriously under-policed, and the authorities often had little choice or flexibility in dealing with street disorders. At the dawn of the twentieth century, the Department of Police numbered a total complement of 47,866 to police a population of nearly 127,000,000. As late as 1914 there were fewer than 15,000 gendarmes, or uniformed police, in the entire Empire, who were largely responsible for keeping order on the railroads. At the turn of the century, the average Russian province contained only eight to twelve gendarmes. There were a minuscule 8,400 ordinary police sergeants and constables stationed in the countryside. This shortage was made worse by the fact that the political police (the Okhrana) had no responsibility for public order.[27] The implications of these shortages were recognized by the High Commission for the Review of Existing Legislation on the Jews (the Palen Commission) when it observed in its final report that the diminutive numbers of police and troops in Odessa in 1871 gave rise to the popular belief that local officials were reluctant to suppress anti-Jewish rioting, and that the pogrom had been permitted by the higher authorities in St. Petersburg.[28] Despite these suggestive hints, virtually all modern commentators on the pogroms have failed to place them in a wider "law and order" context, although such a perspective would assist the better understanding of the dilemmas and alternatives available to the authorities upon the outbreak of urban or rural riots.

The Kotsebu account became the "official" version, published in *Pravitelstvennyi vestnik*, the official government organ, and widely reprinted, if not always given credence, by most other periodicals. In a summary of the Odessa events on 11 April 1871, the paper reported that troops had been sent to neighboring villages around Odessa, where violence and looting had briefly flared up, a phenomenon repeated in 1881–2. The final tally from the pogrom was two people killed in the disorders, eight fatalities from people who drank themselves to death with plundered liquor, three people wounded by army bayonets, and seventeen victims of contusions. Of the troops involved, three officers and twenty-four men were wounded. In all, 1,159 persons were arrested.[29] A subsequent report by the police chief of Odessa counted 528 houses sustaining broken windows, 335 apartments that had been looted, 151 shops vandalized and 401 shops looted. Damage was set at 10 million roubles.[30]

The first periodical to offer descriptions and interpretations of the pogrom was, appropriately enough, *Odesskii vestnik*. The paper was "official" in the sense that it was under the supervision of the governor-general's office. Doing his duty by publishing official information, the editor did have a certain latitude in the non-official section of the paper. More intimidating than the risk that the governor-general was himself carefully perusing the paper was the authority of the local censorship board, which operated through a system of pre-censorship and which vigilantly oversaw all the contents of *Odesskii vestnik*. This situation was a notorious one. An editorial in *Sanktpeterburgskie vedomosti* later in the year singled out Odessa as an archetypical example of conditions which restrained the satisfactory development of the provincial press.[31] *Odesskii vestnik,* therefore, was faced with the daunting task of justifying the local administration, as well as placing the city of Odessa in the best possible light.

The honor of the administration was preserved by ignoring official actions: *Odesskii vestnik* carried hardly a word, critical or positive, about the actual mechanics of pacification, except to stress that the governor-general was vigilantly at his post. The honor of the city was preserved by minimizing the significance of the disorders. As it had done in 1859, the paper emphasized the high spirits of the holiday crowd and the traditional antipathy of Greeks and Jews. "We think it is safe to say that there was an unthinking sally from one side and a passionate outburst from the other." Once the pogrom was underway, spirits of another kind came into play in the form of large stores of alcohol looted from taverns and warehouses. While not denying the existence of religious intolerance or the activities of "the lovers of other people's property," *Odesskii vestnik* noted the role of drunkenness in provoking the spread and intensity of the pogrom. *Odesskii vestnik*'s first editorial, published when the pogrom was barely over, summarized: "What does this whole story mean? Riots, destruction, religious intolerance? To all this we say no. Of course, there is no doubt that the people are hostile to the Jews. But the affair began with the events at the Greek church – on the strength of a holiday brawl – to which were joined the cheekiness of street urchins and the instigation of criminals."

The problem was explicitly stated: in the short term it was holiday high spirits and irresponsibility, in the long term, the abnormal socioeconomic relationships binding Jews and Gentiles. To resolve the problem, the editor of *Odesskii vestnik* was willing to adhere to the optimistic formulae of the first decade of the great reforms. The intellectual level of the Russian masses must be raised so that they could effectively compete against the resourceful Jews. The Jews, on the other hand, would have to assimilate with the native population. "Assimilation in language, schooling, daily life, customs, historical traditions, assimilation to devotion to one ideal, in recognition of one truth, so that except for religion, nothing might divide the two peoples inhabiting one and the same land, just as nothing separates the French Jew from the native Frenchman in France." Indeed,

there were already educated Jews who fully met these criteria. What
was required was that they assist their own "dark masses" to pursue
this goal.[32]

In a subsequent editorial *Odesskii vestnik* defended this ideal
against those who denied the possibility of Russian–Jewish assimilation, on account of Jewish separatism. The state could assist
this process, it argued, and at the same time benefit Russia by
putting "two million commercial machines to work for her" by
abolishing the Pale of Settlement and permitting the Jews to reside
everywhere within the Russian Empire. Such an act would terminate
the unbalanced economic situation in the Pale, where more Jews
pursued trade and speculation than the region could support.
Odesskii vestnik argued that the Jews were a burden on the local
population, not through any conscious dedication to exploitation of
Gentiles, but as a consequence of forces over which they themselves
had no control. A satisfactory adjustment of the legal system would
culminate in a more acceptable economic life for Russian Jewry.[33]
This view, which dated to the 1850s, still received widespread
support from Russian reformers, but it was also under growing
attack in some circles of the intelligentsia. The pogrom gave them an
opportunity to voice these sentiments.

Outside Odessa, the governor-general lost the protection of the
Odessa censorship and, in the capitals, pre-censorship as well. Well
might Kotsebu complain of the rough handling his administration
received at the hands of the opinion-makers in Moscow and St.
Petersburg. Foremost among these was M. N. Katkov, editor of the
enormously influential *Moskovskie vedomosti*. The year 1871 found
Katkov well along in the intellectual odyssey that moved him from
the liberal camp into the ranks of the most articulate supporters of
the autocracy. But one could be an ardent supporter of the
monarchy and still be a strong critic of its agents, as Katkov proved
throughout his career. He had no use for the inadequacies of the
provincial bureaucracy and made *Moskovskie vedomosti* a rostrum for
attacks upon the malfeasance of the Odessa authorities. The paper
carried its first story, by its own correspondent, on 4 April 1871. This
dramatic account became the version of events most widely reprinted
in the Russian press. It included a number of ingredients which
reappeared in reports of later pogroms but which had not been
mentioned in the accounts of the pogroms of 1821, 1849, and 1859.
Chief among them was the news that Christians had placed icons

and crosses in their windows, to indicate to the crowds that no Jews lived there. Jews who were found in the streets by the pogromshchiki were forced to cross themselves before being freed. Jews were accused of throwing stones at army officers. A later story accused them of engaging in vigilante activity after the pogrom was over.[34] The activities of the administration were described, although not in a favorable light. The presence of the governor-general was noted, but instead of directing overall operations, he was described as engaged in the defense of the home of an influential and wealthy Odessa Jew, David Rafalovich.[35] A description of the pogrom by the Jewish journalist, I. Chatskin, published two days later, also questioned the energy and determination of the authorities.[36]

Moskovskie vedomosti rendered editorial judgment on 8 April, a week after the final suppression of the pogrom. It faulted the role of *Odesskii vestnik*, "the organ of the higher administration," for trying to put everything in the best light and especially for transferring responsibility from the authorities to the general population. The paper was pilloried for suggesting that disorders could have been expeditiously suppressed if the peaceful and law-abiding segment of the town's population had intervened more forcefully to stop the rioters. It wasn't for peaceful citizens to defend taverns, the editorialist noted sarcastically.[37] (In reprinting articles from the Odessa press later in the week, *Moskovskie vedomosti* emphasized those which depicted the assistance of the clergy or the citizenry in putting down the pogrom, or which indicated the indecision and inactivity of the authorities.)[38] In short, every action of the Odessa authorities was tried and found wanting. Cossacks and the fire brigade had used "open force" on the first day of the disorders; the editorialist supposed that minds could have been easily quieted with the simple declaration that those who had vandalized the cross on the Greek church would be arrested and punished. On the other hand, the active measures to which the authorities finally resorted on the fourth day to quell the rioting should have been employed on the second day.[39]

Notably absent from *Moskovskie vedomosti*'s treatment of the pogroms was any consideration of deeper causes. Sufficient explanation was found in the traditional violence between Odessa's Jews and Greeks and the incompetence of the local police and military authorities. No attempt was made to probe more deeply and certainly there was no effort to place any blame on the Jews. This

was compatible with *Moskovskie vedomosti*'s general stance on the
Jewish Question, developed in the aftermath of the Polish uprising.
There was nothing special about the Jews – they were merely
another ethnic minority in need of Russification.

Golos, the St. Petersburg daily, was part of the A. A. Kraevskii
publishing empire and a principal ideological rival of *Moskovskie
vedomosti*. Founded in the midst of the great reforms and faithful to
their spirit, it was one of the best informed and most influential
publications in Russia, earning the ultimate accolade of *The Times* of
London for "approaching the great organs of Western Europe most
nearly."[40] As such, it was a constant critic of the arbitrary exercise
of power which typified Russian provincial administration. The
conduct of the army and police in Odessa was an inviting target.
Golos, its liberal pedigree notwithstanding, was also one of the most
Judeophobe periodicals in the Empire and this fact colored the
paper's interpretation of events in the South.

Golos' own correspondent in Odessa was delayed in getting his
reports to the capital and so the paper had to depend initially for its
news upon reprints from *Pravitelstvennyi vestnik* and *Odesskii vestnik*, the
former emphasizing that order had been restored to the city and the
latter defending the conduct of the authorities. *Golos*' first independent account, published on 10 April, painted quite a different
picture.

The report attacked the account of *Odesskii vestnik* and its
solicitude for its "patron" (i.e., Kotsebu and the Odessa authorities).
Odesskii vestnik had praised "all the diverse and timely measures
taken by the higher authorities." *Golos* offered a critical commentary:

> It's true that these measures were diverse: they whipped, they arrested,
> they stabbed with bayonets, they butted with rifles, they lashed with the
> knout and the *nagaika*... All this is diversity to the extreme; as pertains to
> "timeliness," I beg to differ with the opinion of the author of the article in
> *Odesskii vestnik*... First there was no action taken at all and then suddenly
> troops, Cossacks and artillery. This is one of many examples of how they
> react to street fights. At first they pay them no attention and then suddenly
> they require birch rods, artillery and Cossacks by the hundreds along with
> several army regiments.[41]

Golos was involved in a decade-long explication of the Jewish
Question in Russia and presumably felt no need to use this occasion
to editorialize on the abnormal state of Jewish–Gentile relations, or
to explain its causes. The suspicion with which the paper
characteristically viewed the Jews, however, was to be seen in its

numerous accounts of attempts by Jews to make fraudulent claims as to the amount of damage they had suffered.[42] Jewish vigilante activity was condemned and suspicions raised at the large number of people (allegedly 2,000) arrested as "looters" on the say-so of Jews.[43] (All of these were accusations which reappeared in 1881–2.) The paper waxed indignant at reports of an economic boycott by Jews of Russian taverns. "We live, one would rightly think, not in Russia, but in some Jewish kingdom, where it is necessary for Russians, like a conquered nation, to pay money to Jews."[44]

These charges and concerns were entirely typical of *Golos'* dealings with the Jews. Possessed of the typical liberal love-hate relationship with the "dark masses," *Golos'* editorialists had long feared that the post-emancipation peasantry would be grist for the mills of duplicitous and exploitative Jews, who were firmly lodged in the rural economy. The writings of Brafman, with his emphasis on Jewish monopolies, price-fixing and exploitation, confirmed their worst fears. How predictable then, at this time of crisis, to find the Jews up to their old tricks.

Another paper not adverse to placing the Jews in a darker light was the widely read russifying newspaper of the Ukraine, *Kievlianin*, published by the Kiev academician, V. Shulgin. *Kievlianin*, based in a city with a sizable Jewish population, had long taken an interest in the Jewish Question. By the twentieth century, *Kievlianin* was notorious as one of the most violently Judeophobe publications in the Empire, but under Shulgin's editorship it still made an attempt to provide balanced analysis of the Jewish Question. The paper accepted as a given that the Jews exploited the local population; the only question was whether this was a consequence of impersonal historical phenomena, as most liberals contended, or whether it was a role consciously and freely taken up by the Jews, as claimed in the gospel according to Brafman. *Kievlianin*, since its first appearance in 1864, gradually evolved towards the latter viewpoint.[45]

In 1871, *Kievlianin* did much to articulate the idea of Jewish exploitation as the main cause for the pogrom. In the words of the paper's own correspondent in Odessa:

From everything seen and heard I have reached the opinion…that the chief cause of the disorders is contained in the fact that the Jewish population enjoys great advantages in Odessa: thus, in their hands is a large part of trade, which they abuse; thus, in other fields of endeavor they attain priority and soon all the land in Bessarabia and Kherson provinces will pass under their control; everywhere is the mark of the Jews – doctors, grain-traders, personnel in almost every office, on the railroads and other institutions. Rich Jews, through their means and influence acquire advantageous positions, places, jobs and work for their lesser brothers, at the expense of Russians...To all this is joined the long-standing religious antipathy of the Jews towards the Greeks and the Greeks towards the Jews.[46]

This analysis neatly reversed the explanations offered by Kotsebu: instead of religious-national antipathies reinforced by exploitation, exploitation was the root cause of unrest, to be triggered by chance religious-national tensions. To demonstrate the innocence of the populace and to emphasize that the pogrom was a popular protest against dishonest exploitation, *Kievlianin* drew attention to reports that the crowd discouraged looting by beating looters and shouting "don't you dare loot; we don't want to despoil them to enrich ourselves on their account, let them know that we take nothing for ourselves." In 1881, in an attempt to justify the pogrom violence against the Jews, the conservative publicist Ivan Aksakov quoted accounts that were almost identical as proof of the pureheartedness of the Russian masses and their righteous wrath.[47]

In the main, the reaction of the press to the pogrom of 1871 was entirely predictable, fitting into pre-existing patterns of thought and attitudes about the Jews. For this reason the unexpected analysis of *Sanktpeterburgskie vedomosti* created a minor sensation. *Sanktpeterburgskie vedomosti* under the editorship of V. F. Korsh, was the principal rival of *Golos* for the position of the leading liberal newspaper in Russia. It shared much of the ideology of *Golos*, but was less concerned with the Jewish Question, and was entirely free of *Golos'* Judeophobe proclivities. If anything, *Sanktpeterburgskie vedomosti* was mildly sympathetic to the Jews and was usually counted among the Judeophile press.

Sanktpeterburgskie vedomosti offered the fullest treatment of the pogrom of any newspaper in the Empire. Relying upon official reports at first, it ultimately published a large number of personal accounts, offering a bewildering array of rumors and apocryphal stories. The role of the Greeks was emphasized and the confusion and inactivity of the local authorities generally condemned. There were hints of pre-planning and leadership by mysterious instigators. While over twenty separate articles appeared between 1 April and 24 April, none made a serious attempt to place the disorders into a wider context. If blame was apportioned, the paper was apparently inclined to give the Greeks the lion's share, but editorialists did not go much further.[48] It was a typical "liberal" performance.

Then, unexpectedly, the paper returned to the Odessa events in a series of lengthy editorials, beginning in No. 128 (11 May 1871). The paper warned that the Odessa violence was not a chance, isolated event, and care had to be taken lest the anti-Jewish fury of the population continue to grow. Much had been made of the religious motivation of the pogrom; this was a supposition convenient for the Jews and the local authorities since it negated any need to seek additional causes. Foremost among the neglected causes was the hatred elicited by the Jews' economic domination of the region. The Jews were a "co-operative of kulaks [rural exploiters]," sucking the vital juices from the population. "One can say without much exaggeration that where the Jews have the mass of the population in their hands, they are able to build a many-sided instrument for their exploitation and the people there every minute feel themselves under an unbearable yoke, with which the serfdom of the past cannot even compare." Such an indictment was not incompatible with liberal sensibilities. What was lacking, however, was the essential qualifier usually attached to such attacks, the admission that the situation was not a conscious creation of the Jewish community. Quite to the contrary, by emphasizing the kahal as the agency through which Jewish exploitation took place, the editorialist implied solidarity with the claims of Iakov Brafman, who attributed exploitation to the influence of Jewish religious precepts, and to the conscious direction of the Jewish ruling elite. Within a year *Sanktpeterburgskie vedomosti* had moved away from these extreme anti-Jewish claims, but, from the perspective of the Russian Jewish intelligentsia, the damage had been done. Nowhere was the feeling of disillusionment and betrayal voiced more keenly than in the Russian language Jewish newspaper, *Den*.

Den, edited during the pogrom crisis by S. S. Ornshtein and I. G. Orshanskii, was published in Odessa. Its coverage of the pogroms was incomplete and hesitant, leading many historians to assume that the hand of the censor lay heavily upon the editors. *Den* already had a tradition of difficulties with the censorship as a consequence of its outspoken positions and was under the close supervision of the Chief Board of Press Affairs in St. Petersburg. The paper's treatment of the pogroms, however, was apparently not a serious issue with the Chief Board.[49] Nonetheless, an almost palpable feeling of discouragement and despair pervaded its pages. Historians of Russian Jewry usually emphasize the role played by the pogroms of 1881–2 in arousing dissatisfaction in segments of the Jewish intelligentsia with the old nostrums of integration and in making them more receptive to the lures of Zionism and socialism.[50] The reaction of the editors of *Den* to the pogrom and its aftermath reveals that the process of reassessing the position of the Jew in Russia, and of questioning the existing integrationist consensus, was well under way before 1881.[51]

The most articulate evaluation of the Odessa pogrom from the Jewish side was provided by I. G. Orshanskii in a *Den* editorial forbidden by the censor in 1871 but, due to the vagaries of the censorship system, published in his collected works in 1877. Orshanskii emphasized a theme that he had struck in an earlier history of Russian legislation on the Jews: the law, with its list of exclusive and discriminatory provisions for the Jews, had made them a special category of unequal citizens, the outcasts of society. When Jews succeeded in escaping their unequal position, through economic virtuosity, a society accustomed to perceiving them as a lesser type saw this as impudence, and responded with dissatisfaction and greed.

Every nationality making up the urban population of southern Russia, meeting competition from other nationalities in the exploitation of the area's resources, cannot claim any precedence, since all are equal. Thus, the Russian has no special hostility towards the Greek, seeing him as another citizen with full equality to live and enrich himself. But when facing a Jew, consigned by the law to last place in everything, who has nonetheless gotten rich, he regards him as virtually a thief and as one who can legitimately be plundered.[52]

This argument was repeated, almost word for word, by many Judeophile liberals following the pogroms of 1881–2.

Whatever the press might say, it was the opinion of the government which ultimately was decisive. It is interesting to note that the governor-general of the adjoining southwest region, A. M. Dondukov-Korsakov, fully accepted Kotsebu's analysis of the tensions existing between Jew and Gentile. In his annual report for 1872 to the central government he observed that

the concentration of railroads and other major financial enterprises in Russia in the hands of Jews more and more intensifies the Jewish Question, whose resolution is urgently needed and desired by every inhabitant of Russia... the Governor-General presumes to believe that the regrettable disorders in Odessa lack any political character, and are nothing other than the rude protest of the mass against the failure to resolve this question, together with the preservation of Jewish particularity [problems] which are so much reflected in the life of the trusting but underdeveloped lower classes.[53]

The tendency of the Russian press to assert the causal factor of Jewish exploitation in triggering pogroms, and the willingness of the imperial authorities to accept this explanation, helps to suggest why both press and administration turned so quickly to this interpretation in the midst of the pogroms of 1881.[54]

This brief survey of pogrom violence in Russia before 1881 permits a number of observations that will be helpful in analyzing subsequent pogroms in Russia as well as public and official reaction to them.

1. While not distinctively "Russian" by tradition, nor even an event triggered by or amidst the Great Russian population, the anti-Jewish pogrom was a recurrent phenomenon in Odessa, the third largest city in the Empire. The reappearance of pogroms insured that the pogrom phenomenon became a familiar and unexceptional part of Russian life and one that had already attracted the attention of commentators.

2. The justification for a pogrom became identified in the popular mind with a number of recurrent rumors: the existence of an imperial edict permitting the population to "beat the Jews"; the insult, torture or murder of a Christian by Jews; some offense against the Christian religion by Jews. The Easter season was the traditional time for fights between Christians and Jews, which always had the potential to turn into pogroms.

3. Although pre-pogrom violence was often anticipated by the police or the military authorities, the tsarist forces of law and order proved quite inept at controlling pogroms once they broke out. A major aspect of official failure was due to the inadequacies of the forces at their command, both in numbers and in ability to control urban riots. When a pogrom occurred, the local authorities were inclined to see the disorders as non-political and as directed primarily against (Jewish) property. They thus proved reluctant to take the ultimate measure of shooting into crowds. The reticence and indecision of officials could easily be viewed as tacit approval by the pogromshchiki or as malfeasance of duty by Jewish victims. Whatever the outcome of a pogrom, the authorities were very

reluctant to permit journalists to discuss events or to judge official
conduct during the pogroms. This reluctance gave rise to the
assumption that officials had something to hide. Moreover, by
treating accurate information and wild speculation and rumors in
exactly the same way, officials helped give credence to the latter.

4. By the second half of the nineteenth century, groups of Russian
intellectuals had begun to develop assumptions – which taken
together constituted a paradigm – to explain pogrom violence (i.e.,
Jewish exploitation, religious intolerance, the low cultural level of
the "dark masses," etc.). By the time of the pogrom outbreak of 1881
there also existed criteria, based on past experience, to evaluate the
performance of the forces of law and order, which often stood
accused of negligence or collusion by the very fact that a pogrom had
taken place under their jurisdiction. The contemporary accounts of
Jewish intellectuals are colored by outrage at the events themselves,
a sense of betrayal at the inactivity of local officials to prevent or
repress pogroms, and frustration at their own inability to bring
pogromshchiki before the courts of law or of public opinion. Jewish
perceptions, no less than those of Gentiles, often reflect a hidden
agenda: a desire to influence foreign opinion, to galvanize the
government into more vigorous action, or to discredit local officials.
When subsequent pogroms occurred, observers from the intelligentsia often tried to fit the "facts" of the pogrom into their own
pre-existing paradigm. Many of the most important contemporary
accounts and explanations of pogroms were based on *a priori*
assumptions, engendered by events in 1859 or 1871, rather than
1881. Modern historians of the pogroms must be cognizant of this
pre-existing frame of reference when judging the testimony of
contemporaries.

NOTES

1 Etymologically, "pogrom" is related to the Russian word for thunder
(*grom*), suggesting the destructiveness of national forces. It is more
directly derived from the verb *pogromit'* meaning variously "to break or
smash" and "to conquer." Early uses of the verb in Russian literature
referred to violence attending military operations. A chronicle entry for
1589 notes: "Atamana svoego Stepana...i svoikh tovaryshchen
Cherkas pogromil, a inykh pobil," I. I. Sreznevskii, *Materialy dlia
slovaria drevne-russkogo iazyka po pis'mennym pamiatnikam* (St. Petersburg,
1893, reprint: Akademische Druck U. Verlagsanstalt, Graz, 1955), II,
1022. The Dictionary of the Russian Academy in the early nineteenth
century defined pogrom as "destruction in time of hostile invasion,"

Slovar Akademii Rossiiskoi (St. Petersburg, 1806–22, reprint: Odense University Press, Odense, Denmark, 1970), IV, 1213. The third edition of Dal's famous dictionary, published early in the twentieth century, still associated the word with general destruction by human or natural forces, even though the term was by now widely used in the press for anti-Jewish riots; Vladimir Dal', *Tolkovyi slovar' zhivogo velikorusskogo iazyka*, 3rd revised edn (Moscow, 1903), III, 402–3; I, 981.

2 The first pogroms against the Jews in the Russian Empire were variously described by contemporaries as *demonstratsii* (demonstrations), *gonenie* (persecution), and *draky* (fights). The most common term, however, and the one invariably employed by the government, was *besporiadok* or *besporiadki* (disturbance, disorders, riots). The events in Odessa during Holy Week in 1871 were the first to be widely called a "pogrom," and the events of 1881–2 introduced it into common usage throughout the world. After the Revolution of 1917, the use of the term pogrom evolved in two antithetical directions. In the Soviet Union, the usage grew to include any and all reactionary political disturbances and has been largely stripped of its Jewish connotations. In 1960 the authoritative *Slovar' sovremennogo russkogo literaturnogo iazyka* (Moscow–Leningrad, 1960), X, 201 defined a pogrom as "a reactionary-chauvinistic action, accompanied by mass murders, robbery and destruction of property." Episodes of interethnic violence which erupted in the USSR in 1989 were invariably characterized as "pogroms" in the Soviet press, irrespective of the nationalities of the groups involved. In the West, the Jewish coloration has been retained, along with connotations of official planning or collusion. According to *The Oxford English Dictionary* (Oxford, 1933), X, a pogrom is "an organized massacre in Russia for the destruction or annihilation of any body or class: in the English newspapers...chiefly applied to those directed against the Jews." *Webster's Third New International Dictionary* (Springfield, IL, 1964), offers the definition of "an organized massacre and looting of helpless people, usually with the connivance of officials, specifically, such a massacre of Jews."

3 Fr. Rawita-Gawroński, *Żydzi w historji literaturze ludowej na Rusi* (Warsaw, 1924), XLIV, calls these events a "Jewish pogrom"; Henrik Birnbaum, "On some evidence of Jewish life and anti-Jewish sentiments in medieval Russia," *Viator*, IV (1973), carefully analyzes the events of 1113 and shows that they were not a pogrom, only to use the term in search of synonyms, 244. George Vernadsky, *Kievan Russia* (New Haven, CN, 1959), is careful to specify that the rioting was not a pogrom.

4 For a brief characterization of these events see Salo W. Baron, *A Social and Religious History of the Jews*, 2nd revised edn (New York and Philadelphia, 1976), XVI, 296–308. In a recent survey of the impact of the Cossack revolt upon Ukrainian Jewry, Jonathan I. Israel argues that its destructiveness has been much exaggerated. He contends that

Jews dispersed into the countryside and reassembled later to benefit from the economic dislocation suffered by more established rivals. See *European Jewry in the Age of Mercantilism, 1550–1750* (Oxford, 1985), 121–2.

5 Norman Davies, *God's Playground: A History of Poland* (New York, 1982), 519; Simon Dubnow, *History of the Jews in Russia and Poland* (Philadelphia, 1916), i, 184.

6 It might be noted that beginning in 1849 pogroms in Odessa occurred at approximately ten-year intervals. The pogrom of 1871 was followed exactly a decade later by the great outbreak of 1881. Small fights between Christians and Jews – apparently an urban phenomenon – were common in other towns within the Pale as well.

7 I. Sosis, "Obshchestvennye nastroeniia 'epokhi velikikh reform,'" *Evreiskaia starina*, iv, 1 (1914), 35–6.

8 *Den'*, 17: 7 September 1869.

9 Ibid., 43: 24 October 1870.

10 *Golos*, 160: 7 October 1870.

11 V. A. Ia., "Demonstratsii protiv Evreev v Odesse," *Iug*, 1 (January 1882), 200–3. Hereafter "Demonstratsii."

12 David Kogan, "Pervye desiatiletniia evreiskoi obshchiny v Odesse i pogrom 1821 goda," *Evreiskaia starina*, iii, 2 (1911), 264–5.

13 "Demonstratsii," 203–5.

14 John D. Klier, "The *Illiustratsiia* affair of 1858: polemics on the Jewish question in the Russian press," *Nationalities Papers*, v, 2 (Fall 1977), 117–35.

15 *Odesskii vestnik*, 42: 21 April 1859.

16 M. D., "Goneniia na Evreev v Odesse," *Russkii vestnik*, ix (May 1859), 50–9.

17 "Demonstratsii," 209–10.

18 *Moskovskie vedomosti*, 73: 8 April 1871.

19 "Demonstratsii," 217.

20 See Brafman's work *Kniga kagala* (Vilna, 1869) and Jacob Katz, "A state within a state," in *Emancipation and Assimilation* (Westmead, England, 1972), 47–76.

21 See Alexander Orbach, *New Voices of Russian Jewry* (Leiden, 1980).

22 "Demonstratsii," 217.

23 Ibid., 218.

24 B. Lenskii, "Evrei i kulak," *Delo*, ix (1881), 31–2.

25 "Demonstratsii," 224–5.

26 Ibid., 221. In the aftermath of the pogroms of 1881–2, the censorship began to restrict the reporting of pogroms, ostensibly because such accounts stirred up national antipathies, but more importantly because they discredited Russia abroad. See John D. Klier, "*The Times* of London, the Russian press and the pogroms of 1881–2," *The Carl Beck Papers*, 308 (1984), 1–26.

27 Dominic Lieven, "The security police, civil rights and the fate of the Russian Empire (1855–1917)," in Olga Crisp and Linda Edmondson, eds., *Civil Rights in Imperial Russia* (Oxford, 1989), 235–62; Neil Weissman, "Regular police in tsarist Russia, 1900–1914," *The Russian Review*, XLIV, 1 (1985), 47.

28 *Obshchaia zapiska vysshei komissii dlia peresmotra deistvuiushchikh o Evreiakh v Imperii zakonov [1883–1888]* (St. Petersburg, n.d.), 59.

29 Quoted in *Sanktpeterburgskie vedomosti*, 99: 12 April 1871.

30 "Demonstratsii," 221–2.

31 *Sanktpeterburgskie vedomosti*, 141: 25 May 1871.

32 *Odesskii vestnik*, 69: 3 April 1871.

33 Ibid., 81: 17 April 1871.

34 *Moskovskie vedomosti*, 71: 6 April 1871.

35 Ibid., 70: 4 April 1871.

36 Ibid., 71: 6 April 1871. This was undoubtedly the kind of story against which Kotsebu was complaining in his report to the Ministry of Internal Affairs discussed above. Chatskin's account was virtually the only one which mentioned the incidence of rape. The extent of rape was one of the most controversial elements in accounts of the pogroms of 1881, because of their highly emotional impact and because they contradicted attempts to give a "moral" slant to the pogroms through the claim that they were directed against the property, rather than the person, of the Jews. See Klier, "*The Times*."

37 *Moskovskie vedomosti*, 73: 8 April 1871.

38 Ibid., 74: 9 April 1871.

39 Ibid., 73: 8 April 1871.

40 *The Times*, 29, 867: 28 April 1880.

41 *Golos*, 98: 10 April 1871.

42 Ibid., 107: 19 April 1871.

43 Ibid., 99: 11 April 1871.

44 Ibid., 123: 5 May 1871.

45 See John D. Klier, "*Kievlianin* and the Jews: a decade of disillusionment, 1864–1873," *Harvard Ukrainian Studies*, V, 1 (1981), 83–101.

46 *Kievlianin*, 47: 22 April 1871.

47 *Rus'*, 126: 9 May 1881.

48 See, for example, 111: 24 April 1871.

49 See John D. Klier, "The Jewish *Den'* and the literary mice, 1869–71," *Russian History*, X, 1 (1983), 31–49 and "1855–1894 censorship of the press in Russian and the Jewish Question," *Jewish Social Studies*, XLVIII, 3–4 (1986), 257–68.

50 Jonathan Frankel, *Prophecy and Politics: Socialism, Nationalism, and the Russian Jews, 1862–1917* (Cambridge, 1981), especially 49–132.

51 Steven J. Zipperstein, *The Jews of Odessa: A Cultural History, 1794–1881* (Stanford, 1985), 123–50.

52 I. G. Orshanskii, "K kharakteristike odesskogo pogroma," in *Evrei v Rossii* (St. Petersburg, 1877), 163–4.

53 *Materialy komissi po ustroistvu byta Evreev* (St. Petersburg, 1872), 5–6.

54 See John D. Klier, "The Russian press and the anti-Jewish pogroms of 1881," *Canadian–American Slavic Studies*, XVII, 1 (1983), 199–221; S. M. Berk, *Year of Crisis, Year of Hope. Russian Jewry and the Pogroms of 1881–1882* (Westport, CT and London, 1985), 57–84.

II

The pogroms of 1881–1884

On 1 March 1881 a band of revolutionary terrorists assassinated
Tsar Alexander II. The murder threw the government into
confusion. The first priority was to challenge the revolutionaries.
The strength of the movement was still unknown but the
discovery of mined streets in the capital, St. Petersburg, did
nothing to ease the fears of the new Tsar, Alexander III. He
became a virtual prisoner of the royal palace at Gatchina,
literally looking under the bed in his private apartments for
assassins. Within the councils of the government a struggle was
waged for control of the direction of the state between the
liberal ministers of the late Tsar and a few reactionaries, led by
the Ober-Procurator of the Holy Synod, K. P. Pobedonostsev.
Bizarre rumors, now as ever conscientiously chronicled by the
security police, swept the country, revealing widespread
confusion and discontent.

These rumors reflected local peculiarities. In Odessa, and
elsewhere within the Pale of Settlement, there were predictions
of a pogrom against the Jews. Such rumors connected the
assassination with the Jews, claiming that they had been the
murderers. Yet in this confused atmosphere Jews were not the
only target. The police reported mutterings that the late Tsar's
advisers had murdered him because he wished to give more
land to the peasants.

Despite the assertions of both contemporary Jewish leaders
and modern historians, there is little truth to the claim that the
press conducted a sustained campaign linking the assassination
to the Jews. In the week following the death of Alexander II
accusations that Jews had been the Tsar's murderers were made
directly by *Vilenskii vestnik* and indirectly by *Novoe vremia*, but
both soon dropped the charge. Press accounts of the trial of the
assassins emphasized the leadership of "native Russians,"
Andrei Zheliabov and Sofia Perovskaia. The press denigrated
the role of the sole Jew implicated, Gesia Gelfman, who was
usually portrayed as a stupid and unimportant follower of the
ringleaders. Nonetheless, these accounts were sufficient to
influence the pogromshchiki. Rioters in Kiev, seeking to justify
their actions to the authorities, made Gelfman the symbol of all
the Jews.

A number of contemporaries recalled the period after the

39

assassination as one of a calm before the storm. In this atmosphere of heightened tensions, it is not surprising that social antipathies sought an outlet. In Baku, April brought riots as Christians attacked Muslims. Rumors of anti-Jewish pogroms were prevalent, especially as Easter approached. When a pogrom did finally erupt, however, most of its features were unanticipated. The pogrom did not occur in Odessa, nor did it take place during Easter Week, when special precautions were taken by the police throughout the Pale. Most importantly, the pogrom, when it came, was not an isolated event.

The first anti-Jewish pogrom of 1881 broke out in the town of Elisavetgrad, Kherson province, on 15 April. Throughout the spring and summer others followed, initially in cities such as Kiev and Odessa, from where they spread to peasant villages in the countryside. The authorities were terrified. Was this the long-feared second offensive of the terrorists? The initial impulse, from the Tsar on down, was to seek a political motive and to place the blame squarely on the terrorists. All directives from the Ministry of the Interior to its local agents stressed the need to explore any possible involvement by socialists.

As pogroms continued sporadically through the summer, and then flared up in Warsaw on Christmas Day, a number of important changes in emphasis took place. The reform-minded head of the Council of Ministers, M. T. Loris-Melikov, resigned at the beginning of May 1881 and was replaced as Minister of the Interior by the erratic N. P. Ignatiev. Influenced by the Judeophobe press, provincial bureaucrats, elected officials of local self-government and high state personages alike began to attribute the pogroms, not to revolutionary ferment, but to the conduct of the Jews themselves. The charge that violence was a popular protest against "Jewish exploitation," heard so often in the wake of past Odessa pogroms, now resurfaced. This analysis was formalized by Ignatiev who convoked a number of local commissions throughout the Pale to explore the causes of the pogroms. The agenda given to these "Ignatiev commissions" was a virtual bill of indictment: what harmful practices of the Jews, they were asked, were responsible for the abnormal relations between Christian and Jews within the Pale? The responses of the commissions followed Ignatiev's lead, and heaped blame upon the Jews.

His suppositions confirmed by this analysis from the grass roots, Ignatiev set out to bring order to the countryside by narrowing the scope of Jewish exploitation. His ministry devised a set of measures designed to resettle Jews from the midst of the defenseless peasantry of the countryside into urban areas.

Restrictions were proposed on Jewish trade and commerce, especially for the trade in spirits. Ignatiev's legislative agenda was attacked and weakened by his colleagues in the Council of Ministers, but was finally promulgated in the form of temporary regulations of the Ministry of the Interior. In this form they endured until virtually the end of the tsarist regime. The May Laws, as they were popularly known, prohibited new Jewish settlement outside towns and shtetlekh, prohibited Jews from buying property in the countryside, and banned Jews from trading on Sunday mornings or Christian holidays. The real significance of the May Laws in practice was the scope which they gave to the arbitrariness of local officials, especially the police, who were free to interpret them as they chose. The May Laws accomplished very little in the way of quieting Jewish–Gentile relations. Judeophobes complained that they were easily circumvented, while Jews lamented that they were subject to capricious interpretations. The May Laws, which S. M. Dubnow accurately termed "legislative pogroms," were probably as much responsible as actual physical violence for accelerated Jewish emigration.

Most significantly, the May Laws failed to prevent further pogroms, most notably in Balta, Podolia province, during Easter Week (29 March) of 1882. This outbreak was notorious for the brutality and destructiveness of the pogromshchiki, and the callousness of the provincial administration, who took the occasion to lecture the Jews on their own responsibility for the disorders. As one writer lamented soon afterwards, it was apparent that pogroms had now become an annual tradition in Russia.

A new Minister of the Interior, D. A. Tolstoi, replaced Ignatiev on 30 May 1882. As pogroms reappeared, he resorted to the traditional forms of crowd control. More forcefully than Ignatiev, he made local officials responsible for the prevention and repression of pogroms, and authorized the employment of maximum measures. Deadly force was now used with greater frequency, and the number of Christian pogromshchiki shot down began to exceed the number of Jewish victims. By the late summer of 1882, the central government had regained control of the situation.

But lessons learned were not so easily forgotten. In 1883 there was another episodic outbreak of pogroms, the most violent of which occurred at Ekaterinoslav, Ekaterinoslav province, on 20 July 1883. The final spasm of pogrom violence took place in Nizhnii Novgorod, Nizhnii Novgorod province, on 7 June 1884. Aside from the fact that it was the last in the series which had begun in 1881, it displayed a number of striking features. It took place in the Russian heartland, far distant from the Pale or from a large Jewish community. The victims included the family of a Jewish engineer who was responsible for the construction of temporary bridges for the town's famous annual fair. There could be no possibility of "Jewish exploitation" here, and the pogrom was clearly an example of imitative violence. To complete the grim picture, the pogrom was triggered by a rumor that Jews had kidnapped a Christian child as the victim for a ritual murder, an example of the appearance of an anti-Jewish stereotype which had not heretofore been a popular belief in the Russian interior. The source may well have been the extensive reporting in the Russian press of the infamous Tisza–Eszlar ritual murder trial in Hungary between 1883 and 1884. Finally, the Nizhnii Novgorod pogrom was an especially vicious one, with its victims dispatched with axes and thrown from rooftops. The Nizhnii Novgorod riot proved to be the last in the series which began in 1881. While completing one pogrom era, it anticipated a far more violent future.

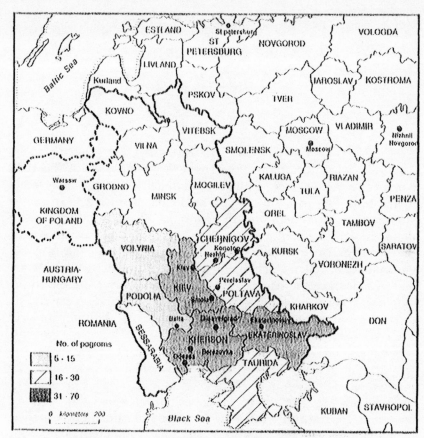

2 Major pogrom centers in Russia and Poland, 1881–1884

CHAPTER 3

The anti-Jewish pogroms in Russia in 1881

I. Michael Aronson

As a rule, when historians have engaged in the study of the 1881 pogroms they have done so under the influence of impressions made by the Jewish tragedies of 1903–6, or the Russian Civil War and its aftermath, or most recently, the European Holocaust. In each of these disasters the hand of the ruling circles was clearly set against the Jews. So it was only natural to assume that the Russian government of 1881, which openly sponsored anti-Jewish legislation and administrative measures, also encouraged or even organized the anti-Jewish violence of that year. But to gain a proper understanding of 1881 we must remove the distorting lenses of hindsight and ask ourselves what the sources really reveal.

To the good fortune of the historian there is at his disposal a wealth of primary evidence which allows him to investigate the pogroms of 1881 from numerous angles and on various planes. The sources include the correspondence of provincial governors, governors-general, the successive Ministers of the Interior, policemen, military officers, and local officials of different ranks, the reports of various individuals, including Count P. I. Kutaisov, the tsarist emissary specially sent in the summer of 1881 to investigate the causes of the riots, and contemporary memoirs and reminiscences.[1] The picture which emerges from these sources is complex, instructive, and fascinating for its divergence from the picture to be found in almost every account written until now. No longer need the events be seen solely from the perspective of the victims; much that was ignored or distorted previously can now be learned about the perpetrators of the pogroms and the governing circles of the time.

First of all, pogroms were almost unknown in the Russian Empire prior to 1881, as contemporaries were well aware. This was a consequence of the late appearance of the Jews in the Russian Empire, and their concentration outside the Russian heartland.

Some of the Empire's new territories, such as the Ukraine, had a tradition of anti-Jewish violence, but not Great Russia proper.[2] Secondly, the pogroms of 1881 caught everyone by surprise. To be sure, the government was apprehensive about unrest *in general* in the uncertain atmosphere prevailing throughout the Empire after the assassination of Alexander II. Judging by the rumors which were widespread at the time, the peasants, under the new tsar, Alexander III, did not know whether they could expect to get their landlords' land or be returned to serfdom, and they seemed ready to riot in either case.[3] The anti-Jewish pogroms were preceded (and accompanied) by persistent rumors to the effect that the Tsar had issued a decree instructing the people to beat and plunder the Jews for having murdered his father and for exploiting the people. Still, before 15 April, the date of the first pogrom, anti-Jewish violence probably seemed a more remote possibility than anti-landlord violence, given the history of the preceding few decades.[4]

And, in fact, the actual outbreak of rioting caught everyone off-guard, as is clearly indicated by the events in Elisavetgrad, the location of the first pogrom of 1881, by the response of the antisemitic press to the riots, and by the successive explanations of them given by the government.

In Elisavetgrad the Chief of Police, I. P. Bogdanovich, enjoyed a reputation for his humane treatment of non-Orthodox Christians and non-Russians. The start of Easter had been greeted with tensions and rumors. The police chief took some precautionary measures against disorders. Then, on the Wednesday of Easter week (15 April 1881), he relaxed some of these measures, because he felt that life had returned almost to normal. He allowed the town's taverns to reopen and he sent the military reinforcements previously called in back to their base camp. During the afternoon a quarrel in a Jewish tavern led to the outbreak of rioting, which it took another day and half to suppress completely, and the anti-Jewish pogrom movement of 1881 was under way.[5]

Meanwhile, some organs of the press had been carrying on an antisemitic campaign since the end of the 1870s. Most often mentioned for their hostility to the Jews were St. Petersburg's *Novoe vremia*, *Kievlianin* in Kiev, *Vilenskii vestnik* in Vilna, and Odessa's *Novorossiiskii telegraf*. After the assassination of Alexander II a number of especially inflammatory articles were published. None called openly for violence and a careful reading indicates that the press initially had no idea that its antisemitic campaign might lead to rioting in the streets. Still, as Easter approached, some newspapers, even vociferously antisemitic ones, began to show concern. Statements condemning physical attacks on Jews appeared. Then, when the first pogrom wave broke, the press manifested great surprise, disarray, and even dismay. The press published all kinds of rumors about what was happening while offering descriptions of events with no attempt at analysis. Soon after the first pogrom, at least one local antisemitic newspaper, *Novorossiiskii telegraf*, felt the necessity to defend itself against charges of having fomented the anti-Jewish rioting and called for forceful measures to end pogroms quickly. An editorial pointed out that the violence had already harmed trade and commerce in general and might turn to direct attacks on Christian property owners.[6]

The editors of antisemitic papers, it seems apparent, never really expected anti-Jewish rioting to take place. They were playing with fire without realizing how ready the fuel was to burst out in flame beyond anyone's control. After all, no major anti-Jewish rioting had occurred in the Ukraine for over 100 years.

During the first few days of rioting it was generally thought that the disorders were simply a manifestation of the usual anti-Jewish feelings which reappeared annually to one degree or another at Easter time. By 18 April however, government officials began to talk about "evil-intentioned instigators," and named the *Narodniki* or socialist revolutionaries, one group of whom was responsible for the assassination of Alexander II. Finally, in the summer of 1881, when it had recovered somewhat from the initial shock of the widespread rioting, the government adopted an explanation of the pogroms more in line with its traditional view of the Jewish Question, namely, that the riots were a spontaneous outburst of popular anger against Jewish exploitation. This was, of course, a gross oversimplification of the circumstances at work in 1881.[7]

We wish to stress a third point. The pogroms of 1881 were initially, and perhaps essentially, an urban phenomenon, the result of Russia's accelerating modernization and industrialization process. The pace of this development and the implications of the changes it was bringing about in the Russian Empire were not always evident to tsarist officials, which helps account for their surprise when the pogrom movement began and their persistence in seeing it as essentially a peasant phenomenon. The changes which occurred in

Russia between 1860 and 1880 created imbalances in the Russian social, economic, cultural, and political systems which made the pogroms possible. The unusual atmosphere prevailing in the spring of 1881, and particular incidents which crystallized out of this atmosphere in various places, provided the added impetus necessary to set the waves of violence into motion.

What we have just said holds true even though, according to one official count, 219 of the 259 recorded pogroms occurred in villages, 4 in Jewish agricultural colonies, and 36 in large towns and townlets, that is, district administrative centers and large settlements having markets and fairs. These latter settlements had an urban character, and numbered populations of not less than 3,000, and in the vast majority of cases more than 12,000 residents.[8]

The pogroms moved in several waves from the large towns and hamlets to nearby villages, and along railroad lines, major highways, and rivers to towns and villages further away. Individuals representing several groups in Russian society were among those who spread and incited the anti-Jewish violence.

After the abolition of serfdom in 1861, the southwest region of the Russian Empire where the pogroms took place entered a period of steady economic growth. Both industrial and agricultural capitalism developed rapidly. Landless peasants and peasants not having enough work in their native villages were attracted to the relatively richer Ukraine from all over Russia. They sought work for the most part as unskilled laborers, especially in the spring, since, as a rule, agricultural and construction work then became readily available.

New arrivals were unusually numerous in the spring of 1881, since an industrial depression which had begun during the preceding winter threw many factory hands – the new urban proletariat – in St. Petersburg and Moscow out of work. These outsiders competed with local peasants who were also seeking employment away from home. The situation was particularly difficult in 1880 and 1881, because of local crop failures which led to near-famine conditions. No one had much hope of finding gainful employment. Outsiders came nevertheless. They tended to wander from place to place as they looked for work. These people were sometimes referred to as *bosiaki*, "the barefoot brigade."[9]

The review of the situation in March–April 1881, reveals the following: the Tsar had just been assassinated. The people were perplexed and uncertain about the future. Rumors about anticipated anti-Jewish rioting were rife. Large numbers of unemployed were to be found in the big towns, often moving from place to place to seek work. Many were strangers far from home.

Both the Great Russian newcomers and the local landless and unemployed peasants undoubtedly felt a strong sense of rootlessness, alienation, and anonymity. Many must have lost all hope of finding employment. They were hungry, homeless, embittered, and given to occasional acts of thievery and assault. Cases are on record of unemployed laborers in this region during this period committing crimes simply in order to be thrown into jail, where they were at least guaranteed something to eat. A pogrom had the advantage of promising, at a minimum, a bellyful of vodka. All of this must be viewed alongside the rowdiness and inclination to rough living characteristic of these men. Any adventure, any outlet, was likely to be eagerly seized upon.[10]

Many urban inhabitants of the southwestern region were also quite embittered, while the Ukrainian peasantry had a long tradition of violent antagonism to the Jews to spur them on. Some resented with special keenness their own dependence on Jews as employers, moneylenders, and suppliers of the necessities of daily life (including liquor). Others felt the growing pressure of Jewish business and professional competition, a consequence of the opportunities offered by the expanding Russian economy during the reign of Alexander II.[11]

The great mass of Jews, however, remained extremely impoverished. Indeed, Russia's economic development, especially the rapid expansion of the railroads, affected some large groups in the Jewish population quite negatively, thereby intensifying the overall pauperization of the Jewish masses. For example, small craftsmen lost business to factory-produced goods, and wagoners, porters, and innkeepers were made superfluous as more and more people and goods travelled by train. The number of Jews who had lately become well-to-do businessmen, industrialists, and professional people was a very small fraction of the Jewish population as a whole. The degree of Jewish success also varied from place to place. Still in recent years, the Jews, especially in the towns, had become more economically visible than ever, since some of them were establishing new stores, shops, offices, warehouses, banks, mills, and factories, wearing fine clothes and jewelry, and buying and building fancy new homes.

Economic and professional rivalry perhaps accounts for the relatively large number of artisans who participated in the urban riots and for the passivity or approval with which the better-off classes looked on.[12] The Jews' well-to-do business competitors – merchants, industrialists, and professional people – while not participating actively in the riots themselves, may have contributed by spreading rumors, reading antisemitic newspaper articles aloud, and even assisting in the impromptu organizing of rioters on the spot, by dividing them up into groups and sending them to different parts of town.[13]

Once pogroms had broken out in towns they were spread to the countryside by itinerant unemployed Great Russians and Ukrainians, railroad workers, contract laborers who traveled in groups by rail, and local peasants returning home after business trips, quests for outside employment, visits to relatives, pilgrimages (especially to Kiev), and so on. By themselves rumors about a tsarist decree to beat the Jews were seldom enough to provoke violence. Eyewitness reports of violence elsewhere often gave just the fillip the village population needed in order to push it over into violence, especially if the witnesses' reports included allegations that officials had failed on purpose to suppress the violence immediately, thus giving weight to rumors of a tsarist decree.[14] Given these factors, in the psychological atmosphere existing in the spring and summer of 1881, any small tavern brawl could escalate into widespread violence.[15]

A few high government officials at the time noted the fact that pogroms were very rare in villages far away from the urban centers. They also observed that because the authorities were so distant, rioting should have been easiest to start and would have had the least chance of being suppressed quickly in these small settlements.[16] The evidence argues against a view of the pogroms as simply a spontaneous outburst of peasant hostility towards the Jews.

The rural population in the Ukraine was clearly quite ambivalent towards the Jews. To some degree relations were good and mutually beneficial. But at the same time they were marked by mutual suspicion and resentment, and occasionally even outright hatred. Village Jews were often on quite friendly terms with their neighbors. They bought their produce, transported it to market, advanced them loans on the security of standing crops or other items, gave them jobs, supplied them with liquor and manufactured products from the towns. On the other hand, loans had to be repaid, and alcohol drunk on credit produced an unwelcome bill for the now-sober drunkard. Moreover, the peasants viewed the Jews as aliens. Their religion, language, food, clothing, and manners were all different, strange, and mysterious. The laws of the Empire marked the Jews as somehow inferior by discriminating against them even more than against the peasants themselves. Yet the peasants found that they were often dependent upon these legal and social inferiors in many ways. They naturally resented this. Some felt a vague sense of guilt and resentment about wasting their money on the Jews' liquor. That such feelings actually became conscious for some peasants is illustrated by cases reported in the Pale at this time of individuals and even whole villages deciding on their own to abstain from liquor altogether.[17] Furthermore, apart from the normal hostility to tradesmen and merchants (as unproductive, non-physical workers) found in every agrarian society, the peasants suspected that the prices the Jews paid for agricultural produce were exceptionally low and that the interest they took on loans, if not the prices they charged for manufactured products, were exceptionally high. The laws of economics which dictated the behavior of the Jews did not interest the peasants. Once aroused to violent action, they may have felt justified that by destroying and plundering the Jews' possessions they were merely appropriating property which did not rightly belong to the Jews.[18]

As a result of this ambivalence, surface relations might be generally calm, while underneath there flowed a current of turbulence. The intrusion of exceptional circumstances could at any time bring this turbulence to the surface in a wave of violence. Such exceptional circumstances existed in 1881. A new, unknown Tsar had taken the throne in the wake of the violent assassination of the "Tsar Liberator." Would the new regime improve or erode the peasants' position? Meanwhile, an economic depression and crop failures had worsened the ordinarily miserable circumstances of the poorer classes. Before Easter a rash of rumors had broken out that the Tsar had given orders to beat the Jews, because they had participated in the assassination of Alexander II. Finally, news arrived of pogroms in the towns. It was hot; everyone was irritable. Tsarist officials were overly placid, and generally incompetent. For decades peace had prevailed. Then, as reverberations from the surge of violence in the towns reached the countryside, the bucolic calm suddenly ended.

After billowing up in one or more places, the rioting moved along, and then died down, only to rise up again at a later date in another area. A relatively small number of towns and townlets were affected; a relatively large number of villages became involved. Nevertheless, the pogroms were more the result of Russia's modernization and industrialization process than of age-old religious and national antagonisms.

A fourth point: Russian governmental policy towards the Jews was shot through with ambivalence and paradoxes. Here are just three examples germane to our topic. On the one hand, as is well known, Russian law severely restricted the rights and opportunities of Jews in the Empire, ostensibly in order to protect the native peasant population; on the other hand, the announced aim of Russian policy was to encourage the Jews to "merge" with the native population. Many responsible Russian officials saw the Jews as a harmful and overly numerous element in the population of the Pale of Jewish Settlement. On the other hand, these same officials supported the government's policies of maintaining the Pale and prohibiting and deterring internal Jewish migration although they were somewhat ambivalent towards the prospects for emigration abroad. Ignatiev, as Minister of the Interior, alternately encouraged and rejected both internal and foreign emigration as a solution to the Jewish Question.[19] Finally, the government and many of its representatives were aware of, and in one degree or another responsive to, the need to protect all the subjects of the Tsar and to foster the rule of law. Nevertheless, officials felt quite comfortable enforcing very damaging discriminatory legislation against the Jews and felt rather uncomfortable protecting these supposedly "harmful" aliens from the "native" Christian population. The Christian population, incidentally, seeing the authorities' maltreatment of the Jews, often drew the conclusion that the latter were not fully under the protection of the law, a point made by almost every Jewish community which submitted a report to the Tsar's special investigator, Count P. I. Kutaisov.[20]

This brings us to our fifth and final point. Contrary to the popularly held view that the Russian government planned, inspired, encouraged, aided, or abetted the anti-Jewish rioting of 1881, the government of Alexander III actually feared all popular violence, including pogroms. It made no difference if such violence was, like the pogroms, ostensibly loyalist in character and directed against persons distrusted and discriminated against by the government itself.

In 1881 the government had no way of knowing where anti-Jewish violence might lead. And there is simply no evidence to confirm that after the assassination of Alexander II the government felt itself cornered and desperate, in need of finding a scapegoat immediately – no matter how hazardous this might be — in order to diffuse a dangerously revolutionary situation.

True, the government's jitteriness immediately after the assassination is evident from the fact that its first response to the outbreak of anti-Jewish violence was to blame the revolutionary socialists. This was only natural under the circumstances, since at the time the government had no way of knowing how weak the socialists really were. But even during the short period when it held this opinion — until about August 1881 – its officials still spoke as if they felt they had overall control of the situation.

Certain objective circumstances indicate why the government would have feared any popular violence. Government officials at all levels expressed genuine anxiety about the dangers of socialist involvement in the pogroms. They thought that the revolutionaries, even if they were not responsible for originating the disorders, would surely try to exploit them for their own anti-governmental purposes. If they had so far remained passive, this was no guarantee that they would not act in the future, perhaps successfully. Such apprehensions could only have been reinforced by the widely held assumption that, even if the revolutionaries had no part in preparing or instigating the pogroms, their propaganda probably contributed to the generally excited state of mind of the population.[21] Alarming also were the reports about politically dangerous rumors spreading among the people. These announced that the violence would begin with the Jews and later turn against the landlords, leading ultimately to a new distribution of land. The situation called for severe repressive measures, perhaps including troops firing on the mobs. But such actions, particularly in defense of Jews, might very well serve only to exacerbate the situation. Consequently, officials feared that given the prevailing circumstances the initial loyalist inclinations of the mobs might easily turn in the opposite direction.[22] Such a possibility was reflected in discussions of the pogroms in the socialist press.[23]

Meanwhile, the local police forces almost everywhere were very short on manpower, poorly paid, poorly trained, and poorly disciplined. Minister of the Interior M. T. Loris-Melikov was well aware of the problem. As early as 12 April 1881 the minister had reported to the Tsar on the need to unify the functions of the police and to reorganize completely the village police forces.[24] Contemporary accounts dramatically illustrate the situation. The governor of Poltava province reported the following: the population

Table 1. *Police resources in Kherson Province,* 1881

Town	Total population	Jews	Christians	Policemen
Aleksandriia	15,980	4,794	11,186	13
Ananev	15,210	7,650	7,560	16
Berislav	6,847	4,525	2,322	7
Elisavetgrad	43,299	13,000	30,299	87
Kherson	49,807	23,000	26,807	138

in the town of Poltava numbered 40,000; 76 policemen served there. In Kremenchug 50 policemen served a population of 35,000. District administrative centers in the province averaged 9 to 16 policemen. Wages were very low, 7 to 12 roubles a month. Only very poorly educated persons would join the force to work for such low wages. The turnover rate of employees was very high. Most had no knowledge at all or else very confused conceptions of the obligations imposed upon officers of the law. Such a police force was unsatisfactory in periods of quiet; it was certainly more so in times of unrest.[25]

The governor of Kherson province reported that the local police force did what it could to keep order, but lacked the means to be entirely successful. It was poorly armed, poorly disciplined, and too small in numbers, as illustrated in table 1. Of the seventeen towns in Kherson province, only Kherson and Elisavetgrad had relatively large police forces. Three towns had 12–16 policemen, 7 towns had 6–10 policemen, and 5 towns had 5 policemen each.[26]

The condition of the army was also a factor which would have deterred the government from promoting popular violence. In the district administrative centers the local garrisons regularly numbered about 70 soldiers. But only about 20 might be available for crowd control, barely enough to guard treasury offices and banks.[27]

Occasionally concern was expressed that there might not be enough military forces to go around in order to protect all the places of Jewish habitation and business that seemed to be threatened. Some officials feared that the whole Russian army would not suffice if troops were sent to every village and townlet requesting them. Given the army's need to engage in summer training exercises and its various other duties in regard to defending the state from foreign attack, peasant uprisings, and revolutionary socialist assaults, this expression of concern may be taken as genuine and not simply a reflection of antisemitic prejudice and unwillingness to protect the Jews. At least one responsible official felt that such large numbers of troops were being pulled back from the borders in order to prevent anti-Jewish riots, that the position there was really significantly weakened, and that this fact should be kept quiet, in order not to make a "disadvantageous impression" within Russia or abroad.[28]

Another objective factor which would have caused the government to fear popular violence was the danger such outbreaks posed to Russia's moral and financial credit throughout the Western world, especially given the influence of the Rothschilds and other Jewish bankers in the European financial community and Russia's dependence on foreign loans at this time.[29]

A more positive indication of the government's opposition to the pogroms is given by the actions it took in defense of the Jews and the punishments it meted out to rioters in numerous instances. In April of 1881 Ministers of the Interior M. T. Loris-Melikov, and in May his successor N. P. Ignatiev, gave orders to take "all measures necessary to prevent possible disorders." Such orders were, admittedly, vague. They prescribed no specific actions. In some cases they may have led to no special steps whatsoever. But this was not the case in the town of Elisavetgrad, home of the first pogrom of 1881, or in the town of Kiev. Careful study of these cases reveals that some genuine efforts to prevent rioting, or to end it quickly, were indeed taken. Sometimes they failed because of errors in judgment, lack of manpower, and outright incompetence.[30]

Not only in Elisavetgrad and Kiev were preventive measures taken before the trouble started. Literally dozens of cases are on record of local officials reporting to their superiors, on up to the Minister of the Interior, measures taken to prevent or suppress pogroms. Many urban and village officials, though not all, of course, were able to report upon the success of their actions in preventing pogroms or in keeping the violence down to clashes between individuals. The contemporary Jewish press contained many expressions of thanks to local officials who had stood firmly against pogroms.[31]

Of what did the measures consist? Most common was the summoning of troops to reinforce the local police, who, as we have seen, were in short supply and poorly trained almost everywhere. The decision to call in troops did not necessarily mean the prevention of, or a quick end to, the rioting. Logistical and administrative problems had to be solved, decisions had to be made about when, where, and how to use the troops available to best advantage, how many to use, and how long to keep them in a particular crisis area. Apart from inexperience, incompetence, inefficiency, and the personal animosity to Jews that local officials may have had, even in the best of circumstances poor decisions were likely, and Jews suffered the consequences.[32]

Other measures were instituted to combat anti-Jewish violence. Night patrols were initiated. Taverns were closed. Jews were warned to refrain from even the least provocative behavior. After the pogrom movement got under way, officials in places where rioting was going on, as well as those in places not yet struck, took other measures. Officials tried to reason with the mobs. Some told the people that the pogrom agitation was seditious. Others explained the ridiculousness of the anti-Jewish rumors, the criminality and culpability of attacking the Jews, and the bad economic consequences which would result. Clergymen, noblemen, zemstvo members, and other local notables, responding to requests by officials, also admonished the people to remain calm. During the late summer of 1881, K. P. Pobedonostsev, as Ober-Procurator of the Holy Synod, sent a circular letter to all the clergy in the Pale, urging them to use their spiritual offices to deter the population from attacks on the Jews.[33] Rumor-mongers and inciters were arrested. Posters calling on the people to beat the Jews were removed by order of the authorities. The passports of residents in hotels, inns, and boarding houses were checked, and anyone who lacked a passport, or who was considered suspicious or a threat to public tranquillity, Jew or non-Jew, was expelled. Large gatherings of people on the streets were forbidden. People were warned not to stand about as spectators if rioting began, because it hindered the police and was dangerous if physical force had to be used against the rioters. Occasionally rioters were killed and wounded when troops resorted to firing their weapons. In a few instances troops immediately flogged arrested rioters and then released them, both as a punishment and a deterrent, although such conduct was proscribed by the legal reforms of 1864.

After 15 April some officials posted public proclamations explaining the falseness of the anti-Jewish tsarist decree rumor, the illegality and punishable consequences of the pogroms, and their harmfulness to the state and the economy. In September 1881 the Tsar signed a law concerning extraordinary measures for the maintenance of state order and public tranquility. This law was motivated by general apprehension regarding the revolutionaries, but was also in part a response to the pogroms.[34]

When discussing the punishments rioters received, the complexity of the legal situation must be emphasized. The available evidence indicates that the pogrom makers of 1881, for the most part, escaped punishment altogether or received exceptionally light sentences. Nineteenth-century Russia was not a state governed by the rule of law. Wide latitude was given to administrative fiat. Consequently, there is some basis for the assumption that if the regime had wanted to ignore the established legal code and court system in order to take a strong stand against the rioters and punish them swiftly and severely it could have done so. However, the unambiguous adoption of such a mode of action was in fact precluded by the framework within which Russian officials acted, quite apart from any sympathy or support they may have given to the pogrom movement.

The points of reference which guided the administration included at least a minimal respect for legal formalism, the underdeveloped character of Russian law, which ill equipped it to deal with attacks by one part of the population upon another (as distinct from insurrection), the complexity of the crimes committed, both in regard to the large number of people and the different types of criminal activities involved, the belief, expressed with apparent sincerity by many local officials throughout the Pale, that strong reprisals would only deepen the hatred of the common people towards the Jews, the fear that the fury of the mob might turn against the regime, and a greater or lesser degree of antipathy toward the Jews as exploiters of the simple people. These concerns alone are sufficient to understand why official behavior was marked by an indecisiveness which left the overall impression of leniency.

The central government by no means approved of clemency toward *pogromshchiki*. Tsar Alexander III noted on a report by his emissary Kutaisov, at the point where the latter complained about the Kiev military courts being too indulgent toward the rioters: "This is unforgivable!"[35] And indeed, there were instances when severe penalties were imposed, including long prison terms and exile to Siberia as well as the extra-judicial infliction of corporal punishment and the billeting of troops in the homes of rioters at the latters' expense.[36] The fact that in many cases such serious punishments were indeed meted out indicates the government's overall opposition to the pogrom movement. Nevertheless, the fact remains that anti-pogrom measures were not always a guarantee against violence. Contrary examples abound throughout the sources – the measures taken were sometimes successful in preventing riots, at other times they failed.

The government was not free to turn the tap of violence on and off at will. It simply was not sufficiently powerful or competent to exercise such control over the population at large or even over its own officials. Some of the latter were more antisemitic than others, some were more competent, imaginative, and energetic than others. The degree to which each official, especially on the local level, fell under the influence of his own antisemitic feelings, together with the degree of his administrative-executive competence, determined his behavior and his success or failure in preventing pogroms.

NOTES

1 Among this material special mention should be made of *Materialy dlia istorii antievreiskikh pogromov v Rossii*, 2 vols. (Petrograd–Moscow, 1923). The first volume, edited by S. M. Dubnow, deals with the pogroms at the beginning of the twentieth century. The second volume, edited by G. Ia. Krasnyi-Admoni and titled *Vos'midesiatye gody, 12 april' 1881–29 fevral' 1882* (herein cited as K-A), is a book of over 500 closely printed pages. These volumes purport to be a full presentation of the relevant documents found in the police archives of the Minister of the Interior. In 1923 the new Soviet regime was interested in publishing historical materials on Russian Jewish history, especially if they reflected badly on the tsarist regime. Dubnow had been arguing for years that the government was implicated in the pogroms. Presumably he would have seen to it that any evidence discovered in support of his claim would be published. Krasnyi-Admoni's volume, however, contains no such evidence.

2 See above, pp. 13–14.

3 Mina Goldberg, "Die Jahre 1881–1882 in der Geschichte der russischen Juden" (doctoral dissertation: Friedrich-Wilhelms-Universität zu Berlin, 1933), 19–21; Hans Heilbronner, "The administration of Loris-Melikov and Ignatiev, 1880–1882" (doctoral dissertation: University of Michigan, 1954), 480–1; K-A, 13, 17–18, 75, 492, 506; S. Valk, ed., "Posle pervogo marta 1881 g.," *Krasnyi arkhiv*, XLV (1931), 153–63; Franco Venturi, *Roots of Revolution* (London, 1960), 713–14; Avram Yarmolinsky, *Road to Revolution* (New York, 1962), 279–80; P. A.

Zaionchkovskii, *Krizis samoderzhaviia na rubezhe 1870–1880-kh godov*
(Moscow, 1964), 391–2.

4 J. G. Bloch [I. S. Bliokh], *Sravnenie material'nogo byta i nravstvennogo
sostoianiia naseleniia v cherte osedlosti Evreev i vne eia*, 1 (St. Petersburg,
1891), 3; "Aleksandr III," *Evreiskaia entsiklopediia*, 1, 826 (hereafter
cited as *EE*); "Pogromy," *EE*, xii, 612, 614; Iu. I Gessen, *Zakon i zhizn'*
(St. Petersburg, 1911) 154; K-Λ, 395–6; *K istorii evreiskikh pogromov i
pogrommnykh protsessov v Rossii. Rechi po pogromnym delam* (Kiev, 1908), 41;
Trudy gubernskikh komissii po evreiskomu voprosu, sect. 5, pt. 1 (St.
Petersburg, 1884), 98 (hereafter cited as *Trudy*); *Obshchaia zapiska vysshei
komissii dlia peresmotra deistvuiushchikh o Evreiakh v imperii zakonov
[1883–1888]* (St. Petersburg, 1888), 81–2, 86 (hereafter cited as *Obshchaia
zapiska*); I. D. Sosis, "K istorii anti-evreiskogo dvizheniia v tsarskoi
Rossii," *Trudy belorusskogo gosudarstvennogo universiteta v gorode Minske*.
(*Pratsy*), vi–vii (1925), 178–9, 181; Λ. P. Subbotin, *Obshchaia zapiska po
evreiskomu voprosu* (St. Petersburg, 1905), 152; Zaionchkovskii, *Krizis*,
391–2.

5 S. M. Dubnow, *History of the Jews in Russia and Poland*, ii (Philadelphia,
1918), 249–51: S. M. Dubnow, "Iz istorii vos'midesiatykh godov,"
Evreiskaia starina, viii (1915) 271–2; *EE*, xii, 612; Goldberg, "Die Jahre
1881–1882," 25; K-Λ, 1–6, 20–6, 226–32, 241–9, 260–86, 471–7; *Trudy*,
sect. 9, pt. 2, 1180–1; *Obshchaia zapiska*, 84–5; P. Sonin, "Vospominaniia
o iuzhnorusskikh pogromakh 1881 goda," *Evreiskaia starina*, ii (1909),
207–10; Sosis, "K istorii," 177, 181–2.

6 See especially *Novorossiiskii telegraf* for 20 March, 25 April, and 8 May
1881, and John D. Klier, "The Russian press and the anti-Jewish
pogroms of 1881," *Canadian–American Slavic Studies*, xvii, 1 (1983),
199–221.

7 B. Ts. Dinur [Dinaburg], "Tokhniyotav shel Ignatiyev l'pitron shailat
hayehudim v'v'idot netsigai hakehilot b'Peterburg b'shnot 1881–1882,"
Heavar, x (1963/5723), 16; Dubnow, *History*, 259–61; Dubnow, "Iz
istorii," 278–9, 270, note 2; *EE*, xii, 614–15; 1, 826; N. Gelber, "Di
rusishe pogromen onhaib di 8oker yoren in shein fun estreichischer diplomatisher korespondents," in Λ. Tsherikover, ed., *Historishe shriften*, ii
(Vilna, 1937), 469–72, 476, 486; Iu. I. Gessen, "Graf N.P. Ignat'ev";
"Vremennye pravila o Evreiakh 3 maia 1882 goda," *Pravo*, xxx–xxxi
(1908), 1632–3; Goldberg, "Die Jahre 1881–1882," 42; K-Λ, 1–6,
46–8, 51–2, 56, 58–9, 128, 202–3, 231, 259–61, 362–4, 384–6, 443–4,
512–14; R. M. Kantor, "Aleksandr III o evreiskikh pogromakh 1881–
1883 gg. (Novye materialy)," *Evreiskaia letopis'*, 1 (1923), 151–3; *Trudy*,
sect. 9, pt. 2, 1204; Λ. Linden [Leo Motzkin], "Prototyp des Pogroms
in den achtziger Jahren," in *Die Judenpogrome in Russland*, 1 (Cologne and
Leipzig, 1910), 29; *Obshchaia zapiska*, 82; *Papers Relating to the Foreign
Relations of the United States*, xi. (Washington, DC, 1881), 1020;
"Proscriptive edicts against Jews in Russia," in *United States Congress,
House of Representatives, Executive Documents*, 38 (1st Session, 51 Congress,

1889–1890), Executive Document No. 47, pp. 52–3; Hans Rogger, "The Jewish policy of late tsarism: a reappraisal," in Rogger, *Jewish Policies and Right-Wing Politics in Imperial Russia* (London, 1986), 29–30; Hans Rogger, "Russian ministers and the Jewish Question, 1881–1917," ibid., 59; Sosis, "K istorii," 93, 180; Zaionchkovskii, *Krizis*, 384–5, 389.

8 T. S. Fedor, *Patterns of Urban Growth in the Russian Empire during the Nineteenth Century*, University of Chicago Department of Geography Research Paper No. 163 (Chicago, 1975), 1–17, 99–102, 183–203; *Obzor postanovlenii vysshei komissii po peresmotru deistvuiushchikh o Evreiakh v imperii zakonov (1883–1888) : Prilozhenie k "obshchei zapiske" vysshei komissii* (St. Petersburg, 1888), 99–100; G. Rozman, *Urban Networks in Russia, 1750–1800 and Pre-modern Periodization* (Princeton, 1976), 50, 58, 212, 285; Y. Slutsky, "Hagiografiia shel praot 1881," *Heavar*, IX (5722), 16–25.

9 Non-resident and unemployed laborers were mentioned in many sources dealing with conditions in 1881. For examples see Ben-Ami, "Odesskii pogrom 1881 goda i pervaia samooborona," *Evreiskii mir*, I, 5 (1990), 39; Bloch, *Sravnenie material'nogo*, 6; P. P. Demidov, *The Jewish Question in Russia* (2nd edn, London, 1884), 98–99; B. Ts. Dinur, "Hamishim shana lapraot," *Ahdut haavoda*, II, 5–6 (1931), 411–12; Dinur, "Tokhniyotav," 28; K-Λ, ix–xvi, 35–6, 39–40, 44, 61, 79–80, 117, 207–9, 439, 452, 456; *K istorii*, 38; *Obshchaia zapiska*, 94–5; Y. Slutsky, "Hapraot b'shnot 1882–1884," *Heavar*, IX (1963 (5723)), 148; Slutsky, "Hagiografiia," 21–2; Sosis, "K istorii," 184; Subbotin, *Obshchaia zapiska*, 152; E. Tsherikover, "Homer hadash l'toldot hapraot b'Rusiya b'raishit shnot hashmonim," *Yehudim b'itot mahapaikha* (Tel Aviv, 1957), 343–4; E. Tsherikover, "Neie materialn di pogromen in Rusland onheib di 8oer yorn," in *Historishe shriften*, II (Vilna, 1937), 446–7; M. I. Tugan-Baranovsky, *The Russian Factory in the Nineteenth Century*, translated by A. Levin, C. S. Levin, and G. Grossman (Homewood, IL, 1970), 265–8.

10 See Demidov, *Jewish Question*, 98–99; K-Λ, xiii–xvi, 44, 117, 452, 456–7; *K istorii*, 38; Slutsky, "Hagiografiia," 21–2; Sosis, "K istorii," 184; Tsherikover, "Homer," 343–4; Tsherikover, "Neie," 446–7.

11 See I. M. Aronson, "Industrialization, pollution, and social conflict in the Ukraine: the case of Pereiaslav in 1881," *Societas*, VIII, 3 (1978), 193–204; Dinur, "Hamishim," 411–13; Dinur, "Tokhniyotav," 28; S. Ettinger, *Toldot Yisrael b'ait hahadasha* (Tel Aviv, 1969), 169; Goldberg, "Die Jahre 1881–1882," 23; N. D. Gradovskii, *Zamechaniia na zapisku kniazei Golitsynykh o cherte osedlosti Evreev* (St. Petersburg, 1886), 135; K-Λ, xxx, 117, 159–60, 299–303, 390, 452, 455, and *passim*; Slutsky, "Hagiografiia," 22–4; Sosis, "K istorii," 181–2.

12 See Dinur, "Tokhniyotav," 28; Dubnow, *History*, 250; Dubnow, "Iz

istorii," 271–2; *Trudy*, sect. 2, pt. 2, 361; K-A, 471, 531–41; *Obshchaia zapiska*, 63–4.

13 H. O. Dahlke, "Race and minority riots: a study in the typology of violence," *Social Forces*, xxx (1952), 425; *Trudy*, sect. 2, pt. 2, 361–2; K-Λ, 21, 23, 77–8, 80, 102, 163, 239, 247, 354, 428–9; Subbotin, *Obshchaia zapiska*, 153.

14 See Bloch, *Sravnenie material'nogo*, 3, 6; Dubnow, *History*, 266; Dubnow, "Iz istorii," 282; K-A, 8–9, 15, 213, 222–4, 249, 402–3, 414, 417–18, 431, 474; *Obshchaia zapiska*, 94–5; *Obzor*, 95–6; *O neobkhodimosti nekotorykh izmenenii i dopolnenii nyne deistvuiushchikh zakonov o prave zhitel'stve Evreev* (St. Petersburg, 1888), 9–10; *Trudy*, sect. 7, pt. 2, 864–5; Slutsky, "Hagiografiiya," 22–3.

15 Ben-Ami, "Odesskii pogrom 1881," 28–9; Bloch, *Sravnenie material'nogo*, 3; I. V. Galant, ed., "Iz proshlogo: Drentel'n i anti-evreiskie pogromy 1881 g.," *Evreiskii vestnik* (1928), 181; Dubnow, *History*, 252; Dubnow, "Iz istorii," 272–3; K-A, 25, 79, 96, 104, 117, 204, 209, 239, 356–7, 442, 489–90; *Trudy*, sect. 9, pt. 2, 1180. The Governor-General of the Odessa Region reported simply that the pogrom began when a Jewish tavernkeeper hit a customer who had smashed a glass, K-Λ, 20, 25, 244.

16 *Obshchaia zapiska*, 94–5; *O neobkhodimosti*, 9–10.

17 I. M. Aronson, "Russian bureaucratic attitudes toward Jews, 1881–1894" (Doctoral dissertation, Northwestern University, 1973), 224; Demidov, *Jewish Question*, 65–7; Gessen, "Graf N. P. Ignat'ev," 1680; N. S. Leskov, *Evrei v Rossii: Neskol'ko zamechanii po evreiskomu voprosu* (Petrograd, 1919; reprint of the private edition of 1884), 31–3, 36–8, 43; *Obshchaia zapiska*, 135, 293–4; Subbotin, *Obshchaia zapiska*, 116, 148–9; *Trudy*, sect. 1, pt. 1, 110–11; T. H. Von Laue, *Sergei Witte and the Industrialization of Russia* (New York, 1969), 103–4.

18 See especially K-Λ, 126; Aronson, "Russian bureaucratic attitudes," 141–273.

19 Hans Rogger, "Government policy on Jewish emigration," in *Jewish Policies*, 176–87.

20 K-Λ, 226–32 for Elisavetgrad, 232–41 for Odessa, 312–21 for Khar'kov, and 425–9 for Kiev.

21 See Dubnow, *History*, 260; Dubnow, "Iz istorii," 278–9; *EE*, xii, 614; Gelber, "Di rusishe," 470–1; Iu. I. Gessen, *Istoriia evreiskogo naroda v Rossii*, ii (Leningrad, 1927), 219; K-A, 44, 79, 272, 362–4, 406; *Trudy*, sect. 5, pt. 1, 97–8.

22 See especially K-Λ, 398–400.

23 See S. M. Berk, *Year of Crisis, Year of Hope: Russian Jewry and the Pogroms of 1881–1882* (Westport, CT and London, 1985), 85–99; J. Frankel, *Prophecy and Politics: Socialism, Nationalism and the Russian Jews, 1862–1917* (Cambridge, 1971), 97–107. See also chapters 4 and 5.

24 N. V. Golitsyn, "Konstitutsiia grafa Loris-Melikova," *Byloe*, x–xi, 4–5 (1918), 180–2; Heilbronner, "Administration," 398.

25 K-Λ, 50–3.

26 K-Λ, 488–9, 494–5.

27 K-Λ, 50–3.

28 See especially Galant, "Iz proshlogo," 181–2; Gessen, "Graf N. P. Ignat'ev," 1681; K-Λ, 19, 35–6, 42, 60, 207, 288, 398, 413, 521; Kantor, "Aleksandr III," 154; Zaionchkovskii, *Krizis*, 391. See also K-Λ, 113–15, 174, 262–3, 285–6, 357, 402.

29 S. Iu. Vitte, *Vospominaniia*, edited by Λ. L. Sidorov, P. Sh. Ganelin and B. V. Anan'ich, I (Moscow, 1960); P. A. Zaionchkovskii, *Rossiiskoe samoderzhavie v kontse XIX stoletiia* (Moscow, 1970).

30 K-Λ, 3–4, 407, 488–9, 494–5.

31 On this last point see Linden, "Prototyp," 31–2.

32 *EE*, XII, 613; K-Λ, 13–14, 19–20, 96, 117, 210–11, 237, 262–3, 282–6, 290, 407, 438; Kantor, "Aleksandr III," 151; E. B. Levin, "Zapiska ob antievreiskikh pogromakh 1881 goda," edited by S. M. Dubnow, *Golos minuvshogo*, IV, 3 (1916), 244.

33 *Odesskii vestnik*, 174: 6 August 1881.

34 Zaionchkovskii, *Krizis*, 402, 407–9.

35 Kantor, "Aleksandr III," 154.

36 Goldberg, 26; K-A, 23, 74, 101, 106, 207, 216–7, 223, 250–2, 263, 288, 290–1, 390–1, 411–12; Kantor, "Aleksandr III," 154, 156; Sosis, "K istorii," 86.

CHAPTER 4

"Black Repartition" and the pogroms of 1881–1882

Moshe Mishkinsky

Zemlia i Volia (Land and Liberty) was the name given to the first Russian revolutionary association with a nation-wide organization. Zemlia i Volia existed from 1876 to 1879. In the summer of 1879 an internal split gave birth to two new organizations, Narodnaia Volia (The People's Will) and Chernyi Peredel (Black Repartition).[1] The differences between the two can be reduced essentially and somewhat schematically to the following. Narodnaia Volia placed the center of gravity for radical change in the absolutist political regime. A central means of change was personal political terror carried out by a revolutionary minority organized along centralist lines against the regime's representatives. In particular, Narodnaia Volia sought to assassinate the Tsar. Chernyi Peredel continued to advance the 1870s idea of Populism (*narodnichestvo*), which spoke of a popular agrarian revolution aimed at land redistribution and envisioned a federal principle upon which the future regime would be based. In this context Chernyi Peredel sought to base its propaganda upon what were thought to be "the people's demands" ("land and liberty") and to introduce the foundations of modern socialism into popular protest. Both organizations saw as the ultimate goal the creation of a socialist society and came to recognize the social revolutionary function as being fulfilled by hired laborers, whether as a class unto themselves or as a special stratum still connected primarily to the peasantry. Actually both, but especially Chernyi Peredel, were conglomerates with respect to their ideas, and in the realm of politics and tactics, their approaches and areas of emphasis underwent constant change. In general, they were affected by the various lessons learned from the results of the activities of the Populists during the 1870s, in which the various methods of "going to the people" had borne but little fruit. Internally, too, changes were noticeable in their basic tendencies. Divergences occurred along personal lines, in the wake of changes in the leadership cadres due to arrests, executions, or emigration, as well as on account of bilateral inter-organizational influences, rapid changes in the Russian political situation, and contacts, mainly on the part of the revolutionary *émigrés*, with Western social democracy and with its Marxist branch, which was steadily growing in strength.

This last phenomenon of internal variegation is of particular importance with regard to the subject at hand – Chernyi Peredel. This organization, whose influence was less than that of its rival, had been destroyed at the beginning of 1881 due to betrayal and arrests. Its leaders, among them figures shortly to be known as the pioneers of Russian Marxism – such as Georgii Plekhanov, Vera Zasulich, the well-known Jewish revolutionary Lev Deich, and his Ukrainian colleague Ia. A. Stefanovich – were forced to flee the country at the beginning of the year. Remaining in Russia was Pavel Akselrod, an active revolutionary since the early 1870s, who had resided abroad, returned, and joined Chernyi Peredel somewhat later than the others. Afterwards he became known as Plekhanov's close colleague and, at the beginning of this century, as the ideologue of Menshevism. While in St. Petersburg, Akselrod laid the foundations for the re-establishment of Chernyi Peredel under the old name of Zemlia i Volia.[2] He himself emigrated shortly thereafter, in June 1880. The renewed organization, not large in size, continued to function independently until the end of 1881 and was regarded as the center of Chernyi Peredel circles. It published the final issues of the periodical *Chernyi Peredel* (Nos. 3, 4, and 5) and of the sheet *Zerno* (*The Seed* – Nos. 3, 4, 5, and 6),[3] a popular publication intended for workers,[4] as well as broadsheets and proclamations. These publications were all printed at a secret press in Minsk that had been founded and operated by a group of Jewish members of the organization – I. Getsov, S. Grinefest, and S. Levkov. These people maintained contact with St. Petersburg and Moscow as well as with other cities in Lithuania and White Russia ("Jewish Lithuania"). The central organization in St. Petersburg was composed of two principal groups – students and naval officers. The chief literary figures in the organization were A. P. Bulanov, a former naval officer; K. Ia. Zagorskii, a Ukrainian law student; and their associate, a Jewish law student, M. I. Sheftel.[5]

The historical literature dealing with the question of the Russian revolutionary movement's relation to the anti-Jewish pogroms of

1881–4 has considered mainly the position of Narodnaia Volia. This
organization stood at the center of the events of the time; its terrorist
activity culminated in the assassination of Tsar Alexander II on
1 (13) March 1881. Afterwards the Romanov throne was occupied
by Alexander III.

In retrospect it can be stated without hesitation that the succession
of the new Tsar ushered in one of the most reactionary periods in the
history of nineteenth-century Russia. At first, though, it seemed that
the successful act of terror provided an opening for undermining the
foundations of autocratic tsarist rule. Both the terrorist revolutionaries and others foresaw and even expected that the assassination
of the Tsar would bring about liberal constitutional concessions on
the part of the new supreme ruler. If not this, it would serve as a
signal to begin a wave of popular insurrection that would sweep
away the existing regime which was considered the principal
impediment to Russia's social progress. A sizeable group within
Narodnaia Volia even looked forward to a "seizure of power" by the
organization. This tense expectation explains the psychological
background – alongside other factors – of the public reaction by
Narodnaia Volia to the first wave of pogroms, which broke out
during April–August 1881 and engulfed the southern part of the
Russian Empire. Concessions were not obtained, and the popular
revolution did not materialize. This was despite sporadic outbreaks
of peasant violence bearing a social character which were directed
against landowners and the rural rich and which at times even
brought about clashes with the authorities.

This reaction found its crudest and most one-sided, extreme
expression – though not its first – in a proclamation published in
Ukrainian following its approval by a majority of the Narodnaia
Volia executive committee (*ispolnitelnyi komitet*), the heart of the
organization, which had been reconstituted following the arrests and
executions that had been carried out after the Tsar's assassination.
The proclamation, which appeared on 1 (13) September 1881,
looked with favor upon the pogroms as the beginning of a popular
revolution. In general this position was maintained by Narodnaia
Volia until 1883.[6]

In contrast to Narodnaia Volia, the reaction of Chernyi Peredel to
the pogroms has been neglected in the historical literature. It has
often been ignored altogether and, when mentioned, it has been only
in a fragmentary fashion on the basis of partial documentation and

with one-sided – not to mention distorted – judgments.[7] Even if there can be various opinions about the weight carried by Chernyi Peredel in the Russian revolutionary socialist movement during this period, it cannot be denied that the organization served directly as a bridge to a new stage in the movement's history – the appearance of Marxist social democracy as expressed organizationally in the establishment of Gruppa "Osvobozhdenie Truda" (Group for the Emancipation of Labor) in 1883. As we shall see, an examination of Chernyi Peredel's stance on the pogroms will contribute to a more correct reconstruction of the manner in which the fathers of Russian Marxism initially related to them.

However, there is an objective difficulty in studying this affair. The difficulty stems from the very nature of Chernyi Peredel, the vicissitudes of its history, and the condition of the historical sources. In the first place, unlike Narodnaia Volia, whose executive committee served as its spinal cord internally and as its sole authorized representative externally, Chernyi Peredel did not maintain any degree of real organizational continuity. Even the use of the collective name Chernyi Peredel is conditional since it possessed general validity only for an extremely short time, and stood for a conglomeration of related organizations and groups. It is advisable to distinguish four broad groupings that overlap both chronologically and in terms of personal composition:

1. the initial activity of Chernyi Peredel to the time when its founders went abroad;
2. the Southern Russian Workers Union of Kiev, whose founders, Elisaveta Kovalskaia and Nikolai Schchedrin, had been members of Chernyi Peredel in Petersburg;
3. the association Zemlia i Volia, founded by Akselrod in St. Petersburg, sometimes known as the Second Shift of Chernyi Peredel. Most of the issues of the newspaper *Chernyi Peredel* and of *Zerno* were edited by members of this group on their own responsibility;
4. *the émigrés*, led by Plekhanov and Akselrod.[8]

Another distinction worth noting is that in contrast to the centralism of Narodnaia Volia, Chernyi Peredel was characterized from the start by decentralized, federalistic tendencies. The articles written in the periodical *Chernyi Peredel* were often signed with the authors' full names, with recognizable initials, or with pseudonyms;

this was an outward indication of varied if not contradictory opinions. This fact was epitomized in the response to the pogroms.

Finally, the various documentary materials relating to Chernyi Peredel – newspapers, letters, and even testimonies of participants – were published only gradually during the Soviet period, so that the study of the organization's history began relatively late.[9]

The Kiev Union should be separated from this general framework, as its influence was quite marked relative to the conditions of the time. Its founders had formerly been associated with Chernyi Peredel in St. Petersburg, but they had taken issue with the direction in which Akselrod had wished to lead the organization before he went abroad. They continued to emphasize semi-anarchistic principles, to cling to their faith in the elementality (*stikhiinost'*) of popular movements, and to sanction economic terror in both the agrarian and manufacturing sectors. Following the founders' arrest, those who carried on the organization operated independently of St. Petersburg and Moscow. The association was greatly influenced by the special conditions and traditions that prevailed in Kiev and the Ukraine as a whole. In the present context it should be pointed out that the Union had dealt with Jewish matters even before the pogroms and that the proclamation published at the time of the pogrom in Kiev at the end of April 1881 essentially marked the end of its activity. For all of these reasons, this group merits a separate discussion.[10]

The first two issues of the newspaper *Chernyi Peredel*, published by the organization's founders, made virtually no mention of Jewish issues. The same was true of the two initial issues of *Zerno*. The first two responses to the pogroms came during the month of June 1881; one took the form of a special proclamation in the name of Zemlia i Volia in St. Petersburg, and the second was contained in an article published in the third issue of *Zerno*.[11]

The uniqueness of the proclamation lies in the fact that it clearly rejected the pogroms and linked its rejection both to the fundamental socialist tenets of the revolutionary movement and to its political interests. Even two years later the proclamation was mentioned in a revolutionary periodical; it was also noted in police sources and distributed outside St. Petersburg. Nevertheless, there are no tangible indicators of the specific influence the proclamation exerted on the public, which is true of the overwhelming majority of underground publications. Still, the proclamation is of particular importance in expanding our familiarity with the range of opinions that had made inroads into the central circles of the various branches of the revolutionary movement during this time. The specific position expressed in it justifies and even mandates its detailed examination.

The publication is, according to its tone and style, a sort of explanatory declaration, a statement of opinion rather than a call to action. Yet despite its brevity it clearly expresses an opinion on the nature of the pogroms and their causes as well as the regime's relation to them and aspects of the overall Jewish situation. The date of its appearance, 15 June 1881 – exactly two months following the outbreak of the pogrom in Elisavetgrad, the first pogrom of the 1880s – is indicated in the body of the text. Before that time a few small handbills and proclamations against the pogroms had been circulated, perhaps by revolutionary circles; but these had been extremely short and anonymous, and were not preserved.[12] Immeasurably more significant is the proclamation published by the underground Southern Russian Workers' Union in Kiev, for it aroused a relatively strong response throughout Russia and beyond. Nonetheless, this proclamation, which was mainly anti-pogrom, did not lack a certain tone of ambivalence. In contrast, the proclamation under discussion, which appeared in the capital, St. Petersburg, was unequivocal in its principled stance and was directly connected to one of the principal streams of the revolutionary movement. Moreover, the Kiev proclamation, which was written in anger and under pressure, bears the marks of haste, and a sense of panic apparent both in its language and in its formulation. This was not the case with the St. Petersburg proclamation, which leaves the impression that it was clearly thought out and faithfully expressed the views of those responsible for its publication.

The reason for the appearance of the declaration of Zemlia i Volia was the statement of the Tsar, Alexander III, to the Jewish delegation that met with him in the aftermath of the pogroms. The idea of sending a delegation to the Tsar appealed greatly to the circle of Jewish notables of St. Petersburg. They assumed that the Tsar possessed full power to order that drastic measures be taken to stop the further spread of pogroms and to suppress them quickly if they continued, and they hoped that he would do so. Evidently there was an additional special reason for their action: the agitators and instigators of the pogroms took care to spread the rumor that the

Tsar himself had ordered that the Jews be punished.[13] This rumor
was joined by another that the Jews had had a hand in the murder
of the Tsar's father, who was still remembered by many as the
"Tsar-Liberator." An appropriate statement by Alexander could
provide an effective weapon against the instigators of the pogroms,
their active accomplices, and those within the administration who
took a passive attitude towards the pogrom agitation and the riots
themselves or even, it was charged, actively encouraged them.

Participating in the delegation were the leaders of the capital's
Jewish community: Baron Horace Gintsburg (Guenzburg), the
banker A. I. Zack (Zak), the attorney A. Passover, and others well
known for their connections with the imperial court. The interview
with the Tsar took place on 11 May 1881 and was widely reported
in the press.[14] The apparently favorable response given by the Tsar
to the delegation, however, soon was revealed as a two-edged sword.

Alexander III's personal attitude toward the pogroms became
known following the revolution, when government archives were
opened and reports that had been sent to the Tsar by his ministers
during 1881–2, together with the Tsar's handwritten comments in
the margins, were discovered.[15] These comments reveal that while
Alexander may have been a definite Jew-hater, he was not
comfortable with the pogroms. The Tsar's feelings were confused
and ambivalent: he wondered about the pogroms' causes and the
identity of both instigators and active participants, displayed
bitterness over the disturbance of public order, and expressed fear
that the pogroms might spread to the point of endangering the
regime. On the other hand, he was also affected by a deep desire not
to serve as protector of the Jews.[16]

Alexander's response to the members of the Jewish delegation was
in two parts. The first, widely publicized, was his statement, noted
by the Zemlia i Volia proclamation, that the pogroms were "the
work of anarchists," that is, revolutionaries whose actions were
directed against the existing regime and for whom the Jews were but
a pretext.[17] The inspiration for this statement is generally attributed
to N. P. Ignatiev, the recently appointed Minister of the Interior.[18]
He had already advanced the same explanation for the pogroms –
placing the blame upon the revolutionaries – in a memorandum
dispatched to the provincial governors on 6 May 1881, the day after
he had taken over his post from M. T. Loris-Melikov.[19] Ignatiev's
assumptions, however, had been anticipated. On 4 May the Tsar's

brother, the Grand Duke Vladimir Aleksandrovich, told Baron
Gintsburg that the government had discovered that the source of
the pogroms lay not merely in anti-Jewish feeling but in a desire to
"arouse a general insurrectionary chaos."[20] Jewish circles advanced
this explanation as well, for their own reasons. They thought that in
this way they could encourage the administration to suppress the
pogroms. They also apparently hoped to relieve somewhat the
feeling of desperation and panic among the Jews by spreading the
word that the regime wished to put an end to the disturbances.

It is reasonable to assume that Ignatiev in particular influenced
the second part of Alexander's answer, in which he attributed the
pogroms to hatred toward the Jews resulting from their economic
domination and their exploitation of most of the country's
inhabitants.[21] Only a few days earlier the Tsar had found this
argument surprising.[22] The claim of "Jewish exploitation" is
especially significant, for it shaped both the positive and negative
attitudes of revolutionary circles towards the pogroms. From the
government's point of view, there was past precedent for dual
explanations of pogrom activity.[23]

It is doubtful whether the first explanation, which placed
responsibility for the pogroms upon the revolutionaries, was ever
really believed by those in the government who advanced it. Even if
it did reflect a certain bewilderment over the source of the pogroms
or an intention to besmirch the revolutionaries in the eyes of the
Jewish public and especially public opinion abroad, it was most of all
a fear for the future. The fear was that the anti-Jewish movement
would spread and evolve into a campaign directed against the regime
and the upper classes as a whole, for there was no doubt that this
movement joined with a deep social ferment among the peasantry
and even among certain classes of the urban population. Moreover,
police reports indicated that the accession of the new Tsar had
somewhat weakened the popular affection – so-called "naive monarchism" – for the "Little Father" (although to a lesser extent than
imagined by revolutionary circles). Attribution of the pogroms to the
revolutionary movement was not consistent with official claims
before 1881 that the revolutionary movement was essentially a
Jewish one – but then, the anti-Jewish movement has never been
noted for excessive consistency in its arguments.[24] In the case of a
hypocritical opportunist like Ignatiev, consistency was hardly to be
expected. In any case, the opinion that held the revolutionaries

responsible for the pogroms was quickly rejected in favor of the
second of "Jewish exploitation." This was a very old accusation
which now was sharpened anew in accordance with the needs of the
hour. It placed the blame for the pogroms upon the Jews themselves,
turning them into a scapegoat for the evils caused by the regime, and
it proved an efficient political distraction. Further, the exploitation
argument was used to justify the continuing stages of an anti-Jewish
policy formulated under Ignatiev's leadership, which remained in
force, with variations, even after his dismissal at the end of May
1882.[25] The changing emphasis of the government did not go
unnoticed among alert Jewish circles.[26] Not so alert were those who
were supposed to be the most active opponents of the regime within
the revolutionary camp – the spokesmen for Narodnaia Volia. They
were themselves trapped by the same distorted stereotype concerning
Jewish exploitation.

Consequently, the appearance of the delegation of Jewish notables
before the Tsar, the nature of his response to them, and press
reactions to the event represented a focal point of public and
political attention during the pogrom wave of spring and early
summer 1881. The event underlined the dilemmas faced by both the
regime and the revolutionaries in dealing with pogrom violence. The
proclamation of Zemlia i Volia referred only to the linking of the
pogroms and the revolutionaries, although the Tsar's words were
quoted neither fully nor accurately. The proclamation totally
rejected the Tsar's contention from two perspectives: the connection
itself, and his motives for raising it.

The Zemlia i Volia pronouncement on the ties of the revolutionaries to the pogroms took a principled approach in contrast to
the evaluations offered by Narodnaia Volia spokesmen, and others.
The lead article in the first number of *Listok Narodnoi Voli* (The
Narodnaia Volia Sheet) published in August 1881, observed that
"The anti-Jewish movement was neither aroused nor formed by us,
yet nevertheless it is an echo of our activity in both its essence and
its timing." Alongside the statement (correct as far as it goes) that
Narodnaia Volia had not actively initiated or directed pogroms, the
proclamation spoke explicitly about a fundamental interconnection
rather than an accidental congruity between the pogrom movement
and revolutionary propaganda.[27] Similarly, the sixth number of
Narodnaia Volia, for October 1881, published an article entitled
"Internal Outlook," which declared, while speaking of the Tsar's

linking of the revolutionaries to the pogroms, that "to a certain extent there is truth in this statement."[28] Such agreement, no matter how tentative, between the organization from whose ranks came the Tsar's assassin and his legitimate successor, is deeply significant. This is true also with regard to the opposite conclusion in the statement of Zemlia i Volia, which reviewed the Tsar's statement as a trick designed to further his reactionary policies.

Neither of these positions was new, but reflected assumptions developed in the revolutionary movement since the first half of the 1870s.[29] The first position placed the Jewish population as a whole in the category of exploiters of "the people" (that is, the peasantry and those social strata close to it). The Jews were seen purely as a distinct social category. The attitude drew on the stereotypical image of the exploiting *zhid*, an image that carried with it a heavy burden of negative associations and hatreds. In reality, this conception either ignored the social differentiation among the Jewish population and the bitter poverty of its overwhelming majority or refused to attribute to this reality any importance in evaluating the essence of the Jews' group character, their historical relations with non-Jewish society, and their status in the configuration of political and social forces in the Empire as a whole. This background helps to explain why the majority of the Narodnaia Volia executive committee saw no contradiction between its general recognition of the principle of solidarity among peoples and rejection of national hatred and oppression on the one hand and an attitude toward the pogroms as a fundamentally progressive popular social outburst or at least an outburst that fostered the revolutionary struggle against the existing regime. In consequence Narodnaia Volia ignored the fact, obvious to others, that the pogroms, although directed against the Jews in general, injured mainly the poor and laboring classes.

The proclamation of Zemlia i Volia offered an opposite view. It did not separate the pogroms from the overall political and social setting in Russia but without the specific rubric of "Jewish exploitation." The pogroms were seen first of all as a product of the people's situation, for which the regime and not the Jews as a whole was to blame. If pogroms contained a measure of social protest, this protest still could not be viewed positively. The Jews would not be viewed as a single, reactionary, social stratum to be rejected in *a priori* fashion following the basic tenets of socialism. The pogroms

took place within the context of "fostering national antagonism,"
and "inflaming national passions" – activities totally opposed to
revolutionary socialism's fundamental principles. Such activities
were to be rejected practically as well, for they posed an obstacle to
revolution, which mandated fellowship among peoples. The proclamation thus found no basis for the view that the pogroms were
likely to serve as a preparatory stage for the revolution. On the
contrary, the pogroms served the reactionary policy of the Tsar, who
sought, as all autocrats do, to divide and conquer.

The proclamation offered other reasons for the pogroms. One of
them was the crowding of the Jews in the Pale of Settlement, a
cornerstone of tsarist policy. An obvious corollary was that the Jews
were also victims of the existing regime, a view not in the forefront
of Russian radical social thought about the Jews. The proclamation
of Narodnaia Volia, after all, placed the Tsar, *pans* (lords), imperial
officials, and all Jews in a single category. The organization's other
publications likewise failed to appreciate the significance of the
special discrimination meted out to the Jews. Zemlia i Volia, on the
other hand, recognized that antagonism among Jews, fostered by
official treatment of them, was of potential utility for the forces of
change. This point could be reached from another direction as well
– from the principle, clearly expressed in the proclamation, that the
Jews were included as an integral element in the solidarity among
people that, together with other factors, made the victory of the
revolution possible. This idea, too, was a controversial one during
the 1870s. If the approach that rejected socialist activity among the
Jews took its cue to a certain extent from M. A. Bakunin, it is not
accidental that the pioneer Jewish socialist A. S. Lieberman (Liberman) was tied to P. L. Lavrov and his colleagues, who supported his
activities.

Therefore, the diversionary tactic of divide and conquer attributed
to Alexander III in the proclamation took on a dual significance, to
the extent that it was directed against both the "Russian people,"
from whose ranks the perpetrators of the pogroms came, and their
victims.[30] It followed that the Tsar's remarks attributing pogroms to
the "anarchists" was an attempt to besmirch the revolutionaries in
the eyes of the Jewish population, itself a target for socialist
activity.[31] Concern at these tactics is apparent in a proclamation
issued by a revolutionary circle in Vilna at the end of July 1881. This
proclamation, according to an eyewitness, pointed to the intent of

"government agents" to distract the public's attention and asked the Jews not to believe that the "nihilists" (another common name for the revolutionaries) had incited the masses to riot.[32] At the root of this response – and perhaps even more in St. Petersburg, which was beyond the Pale of Settlement, than in Jewish Vilna – lay a principled approach to the possibilities existing within the Jewish environment for socialist action.

Regarding the source and causes of the pogroms, this declaration did not mention the alleged organizing hand of the government or of reactionary political circles close to it.[33] Rather it saw in them an inevitable outburst of popular violence in protest over the people's "desperate situation" and "unimaginable oppression." This was also the version presented in Narodnaia Volia sources, but in this case no attempt was made to place the blame upon the Jews themselves. Zemlia i Volia fixed responsibility for the condition of the people and the form of its protest (pogroms) upon the government and "all exploiters." But the government's causal responsibility was not confined to the results of its general policy toward "the Russian people" but also of its "medieval policy of crowding the Jews into a relatively small territory." This can be interpreted to mean that the crowding in the Pale of Settlement had exacerbated tensions between Jews and the surrounding society until they had reached the flash point. However, the reference might also pertain to the Jews' lack of rights and the discrimination to which state law subjected them, residence restrictions being the most unique and burdensome. Because of their distinct legal position, Jews were perceived as both different and unprotected. Representing the path of least resistance, they inevitably drew violence toward themselves. This explanation of the pogroms was quite common among the Jews as well as among Russian liberals and even to an extent in the revolutionary press.[34]

What does this proclamation reveal about the evolution of attitudes towards the pogroms by adherents of Chernyi Peredel, especially the leadership of the central organization, Zemlia i Volia, in St. Petersburg? This question can be answered first by explaining the origins of the anti-pogrom stance of the June 1881 proclamation, and then by relating this stance to subsequent publications of the group.

As has been mentioned, Pavel Akselrod re-established Chernyi Peredel in St. Petersburg. Akselrod was not satisfied with adherence to the narodnik tradition of worshiping "the people" and "popular ideals" that appeared in the first issues of the periodical *Chernyi Peredel*. He explained the return to the name Zemlia i Volia as an indication of reservations about the notion of an ineluctable popular insurrection conjured up by the ambiguous name Chernyi Peredel.[35] In his discussions and arguments with the members of the St. Petersburg association Akselrod maintained that only the progressive aspirations of the people should be supported, not their reactionary desires. As an example of the latter he raised the hypothetical possibility that the people might want to riot against the Jews or forcibly prevent the separation of Poland from Russia. Indeed, there were some revolutionaries who believed that in order to foster revolutionary outbursts it was fitting to take advantage of popular hatred of Jews and Poles.[36] It is possible, therefore, that Akselrod's opinion left its mark upon the association's activists given his stature as a long-standing revolutionary and his seminal role in building the St. Petersburg organization. It logically came to the fore a short time later, after his departure, when the matter of "beating Jews" became timely and demanded just the sort of concrete response as was embodied in the association's proclamation.[37]

However, at the same time, dissident voices were heard. In the same month of June 1881 a special propaganda article about the pogroms appeared in the third issue of *Zerno*.[38] What was the background of the pogroms? According to *Zerno* the answer was obvious: "Jewish plunder, which has become unbearable for the working people." The Jew-kulak was almost everywhere: "The Jew operates taverns and inns, rents real estate from the estate holders and leases land to the peasants at triple the price, buys up the peasants' crops before they have been harvested, and carries on usury." In addition the author portrayed all of the institutions of the regime and its representatives as defenders of the Jews during the pogroms, coming to their aid with whips and rifle butts. They were joined by landowners and priests, who feared that the riots might encompass more far-reaching targets than the Jews alone. This helps to explain the article's satisfaction that the people did not fall for speeches and blandishments and took to chasing the Jews and destroying their property, "which in any case they stole from the people." The article made no attempt to account for the fact that the major pogroms occurred in the cities rather than in the countryside. Moreover, the entire discussion centered on damage to property, failing even to mention the atrocities against persons.

If, to this point, the article was consistent, the author then deviated to an idea different both in content and in form. For the first time, the issue of class divisions was raised. But first there were practical considerations: whatever the people have done has not helped them in the least; they have merely fallen prey to reprisals by soldiers and Cossacks. This led to a number of wider questions, of a transparently emotional tone. Are the people well off in places where there are no Jews? Are Jews the only exploiters? What about the Russian kulaks and usurers? On the other hand, not all Jews are rich. Many of them work by the sweat of their brow and are exploited; the Jewish kulaks trample upon them no less than upon others. "Why, then, we ask, have the miserable huts of Jewish craftsmen been destroyed; why have their meagre possessions, acquired with the pennies they have earned by their labor, been plundered and vandalized?" Hence the call: "Desist from hatred toward those of other peoples and religions.[39] Remember that all those who labor, no matter what their religion or nation, must unite in order together to fight the common enemy... Do not waste your strength in vain; do not hate workers of another people, even Jews."[40] Here the article approached the position taken by the Zemlia i Volia organization, while also viewing the relations between workers of different ethnic groups from a revolutionary perspective. This position envisioned a number of goals: the transfer of land for use by the peasants, and of factories and workshops to the control of workers' *artels* (cooperatives); and at the start of the insurrection, replacement of the previous authorities by "elected and reliable" people, who will begin to manage and to "implement the new."

Several months later, the final edition of *Zerno* once again made reference to the pogroms, this time in a lengthy portion of its lead article.[41] The context was a discussion of insurrections as a positive phenomenon, which was contingent on the rebels "knowing why they are rebelling and what to insist upon." This means that revolutionaries from the start must inject a conscious awareness into an elemental movement. Such a position was again anti-pogrom, and its rationale identical to that of the latter part of the article in the third issue of *Zerno*.

Thus far, we have observed in the publications of the St. Petersburg Zemlia i Volia three components which comprise the organization's attitude to the Jews and the pogroms: (1) rejection of

the stereotype of the Jews as an exploitative minority, both in their
relations with non-Jewish society and in their internal structure; (2)
condemnation of the pogroms as a part of the retreat from unreserved
affirmation of all popular outbursts, no matter what their motives or
manner of expression, because of their damage to the revolutionary
cause; and (3) the trumpeting of solidarity among all workers
including the Jews, without regard to religion or ethnicity.
Nevertheless, one ought not to ignore evidence of inconsistency and
deviation from these positions, which indicates hesitation and self-
doubt among the organization's spokesmen. The available sources
do not permit us to draw exact conclusions as to the meaning of this
phenomenon. There is one episode, however, which casts some light
on the problem.

I. Getsov, a member of the Minsk group of Chernyi Peredel and
foreman of its printshop there told, over forty years later, of an
article about the pogroms that Zagorskii had sent to be printed in
Zerno.[42] According to Getsov, this article, agitationist in spirit,
viewed the pogroms as the beginning of the revolution and
encouraged the people to continue them while at the same time
moving on to estate owners and the police. The Minsk group,
revolted by these ideas, decided not to set the article in type and sent
Getsov to St. Petersburg. Getsov argued with Zagorskii, claiming
that the pogroms were not a class movement but an ethnic (*plemenny*)
one, based upon prejudice and superstition, in which the victims
were mainly impoverished proletarians just like the pogromshchiki.
He maintained further that police agents, capitalist exploiters, and
others had instigated the pogroms as part of the struggle against the
revolution. Getsov described Zagorskii's reaction in graphic detail:
he made no objection to Getsov's argument, tore up the manuscript
copy, and on the spot wrote a new article in an entirely different
spirit. This article was printed in *Zerno*.

Getsov's dramatic story has generally not been contradicted; in
fact, some commentators have presented it together with moralizing
comments about how a few young Jews managed to save the honor
of Chernyi Peredel. To be sure, Getsov did not invent this story,
which is built around a kernel of truth. Nevertheless, certain
questions persist about the details of Getsov's own story and the
wide-ranging conclusions scholars have drawn from them. A special
article about the pogroms appeared only in the third issue of *Zerno*
in June 1881, and, as has been noted, its two parts stood in

contradiction to one another. There is evidence from testimony that this article was indeed written by Zagorskii, who evidently wavered between two positions, was influenced by the arguments of the Minsk group, and significantly altered one part of the article.[43] This would be consistent in part with Getsov's story. However, Getsov states emphatically that the incident followed the publication of the pro-pogrom proclamation of *Narodnaia Volia*, which came later, towards September. It is possible that Getsov erred in the sequence of events, but it may also be that he is referring to a piece that appeared in the sixth issue of *Zerno*, published in November. While not a special article on the pogroms, an unequivocal anti-pogrom statement was incorporated into it. The inescapable conclusion is that the honor of Chernyi Peredel (to the extent that this is at issue) was saved first of all by the Zemlia i Volia proclamation of June 1881, not mentioned by Getsov. There is no other plausible explanation for the fluctuations in Zagorskii's attitude, but neither is everything clear with regard to the Minsk group. Even if the latter were beset by conflicting emotions and showed restraint when they printed the bifurcated article in the third issue of *Zerno*, this does not explain why they did not respond to related items published in the organization's other, older, and more theoretical and propagandistic periodical, *Chernyi Peredel*, the principal organ of the St. Petersburg group.*

The first mention of the pogroms in *Chernyi Peredel* is found in its fourth issue (September 1881). It consisted mainly of two reports from pogrom-infected areas in the Ukraine as well as a short paragraph in an editorial. The reports dealt with the attitudes prevailing among the peasants and agricultural laborers as revealed in conversations with them.[44] The articles also reveal the attitudes of the reporters, themselves declared revolutionaries, to what was happening. This subject seems worthy of more extended discussion, in order to explore the dilemmas facing socialist activists in the field, as they came into actual contact with "the people."

The reports all offer a description of the emotional fervor that gripped the populace, the uncertainties and expectations which followed the assassination of the Tsar and the flood of diverse and strange rumors that circulated and shaped its opinions. The atmosphere surrounding the pogroms assumed a primary role in this process. "A Letter from the South" reported that the peasants

* Compare the treatment of this episode in chapter 5 in this volume by Erich Haberer, pp. 113–14.

themselves made no accusations against the Jews which revealed a religious or ethnic basis. Everything was centered about the issue of the economic exploitation of the masses. The reporter accepted this general claim, adding the caveat that one could easily discern "a second motive as well... the traditional hatred of the *muzhik* toward the yid." This hatred was even stronger than the anger felt for the pan. The argument raised by the correspondent, that most of the land was owned by one or another pan and that therefore the pan was the greatest enemy of the people, was completely ineffective.[45] The peasants responded that the rule of the pan was not as insulting as the rule of the yid. Individual anger toward the Jews was thus greater than that toward the estate owners. Among the people there existed a hierarchy of enemies: first, the kulak of another religion, next, the Orthodox kulak who was foreign to the local environment, followed by "our own" kulak who had emerged from the peasants themselves. It seemed, then, that there really was a firmly rooted ethnic and religious hatred which played a formative role. Certainly there were understandable reasons for caution on the part of revolutionary intellectuals in their contacts with the peasants. However, this ought not to have prevented them taking a principled look at assertions intended for an underground publication. In the end, the reporter concluded that the anti-Jewish pogroms were merely a prelude "to a more serious and purposeful movement" and optimistically added that under present conditions they were an essential stage on the road to an uprising against the regime. He told of how he had awaited a possible pogrom that did not ultimately materialize and drew the lesson that what was lacking was organization among the people. The reporter did not sense the contradiction in which he had become entrapped, for the peasant conception of the stages leading up to insurrection was quite different from his. "Popular thinking" in the countryside associated the pogroms with a redistribution of the land. Once the Jews were expelled (or, worse), the Tsar would order all land divided among the peasants.[46] The reporter himself did not claim that this belief was consistent with the revolutionary perspective of "a more serious and purposeful movement." The hope that the people placed in "the socialists," and which the reporter regarded as important, would likewise not lead to a serious movement, even though this hope was significantly tied to the belief that "the socialists" had somehow initiated the pogroms.[47]

In another article entitled "From the Village," the tendency is similar and even more unequivocal. In the author's opinion the pogroms, especially severe in his region, strengthened a mental (*umstvenny*) process among the people which might promote a peasant revolt aimed at land redistribution. This article too sought to offer a qualified picture of a decline in the popular belief in the Tsar. It stressed peasant complaints against the Tsar and the soldiers who in his name beat the Christians who took action against the "bloodsucking" Jews. They sought a sign of approval from the Tsar for the expulsion of the Jews, and this reporter too registered no objection to this expectation.

There were no editor's notes in this issue of the newspaper specially devoted to the testimony found in the articles or to the interpretations provided by the reporters. However, one of the two editorials in the issue did contain something relevant.[48] This editorial revealed more emphatically the change in the position of Chernyi Peredel towards the possible value of a constitutional regime as well as a more positive evaluation of political terror as a whole and of the regicide of 1 March in particular. This approach was again connected to the popular experience, which continued to stand at the center of the organization's world view and its conception of the revolution. The greatest utilitarian importance of terrorist activity lay not only in defending the legitimate rights of man and the citizen but in strengthening and arousing the positive qualities of the people — "the sense of strength, energy, and right, the belief in the foremost rights and the willingness to defend them to the utmost with weapons in hand."[49] The pogroms against the Jews served as proof of this positive excitement. Indeed, aside from the role of 1 March in bringing about these outbursts, decisive importance should be attributed to "the whole complex of historical and current conditions in which the local populace lives." This formula paid no attention to the argument raised in other publications of the organization regarding the role of religious-ethnic hatreds in the pogroms. As in regard to terror, the only justification for the pogroms lay in the utilitarian value of the action, a concept which, incidentally, was also denied by other publications.

The question of the pogroms was raised again in the fifth issue of *Chernyi Peredel* (December 1881), this time in a report from the Elisavetgrad area, which had been hard hit by pogroms, and also in a significant editorial.[50] The twisted line was evident once again, although this time in the direction of a more sober appraisal of the events and a more complex view of the relations between the Jews and the surrounding society. The reporter connected the anti-Jewish movement with dissatisfaction among the large oppressed majority of the population, a dissatisfaction inexpressible except through physical force. Why did the movement assume "such a narrow character and a rather ugly form," since alongside the Jewish exploiter there were non-Jewish exploiters as well? The former, however, is especially visible. He is faster, more mobile and noisier, and thus becomes the scapegoat. But this conspicuousness applies to all Jews, for all were denied even the few minimal rights that the state had granted its subjects. Their presence caught the eye and they were easier to hurt. Added to this was "the *national-religious* antipathy held by the Russians toward the Jews" [emphasis in original], a hatred with historical roots.

The author believed that the anti-Jewish movement also fanned the embers of revolt after the fact and he recounted several instances of violent outbursts against estate owners and government authorities that offered a portent of the future. This view, however, did not prevent him from analyzing the causes of the pogroms realistically and especially from pointing out who, in his opinion, had instigated them. On this latter point he went further than the proclamation. Describing agitation conducted by the widely distributed *Novoros-siiskii telegraf* in the South and the spread of rumors long before Easter about the forthcoming "yid beating," he concluded that the initiative for the pogroms did not come from the masses themselves but from "those that suck their blood" and "elements foreign to the people" (i.e., from among the merchants and petty officialdom).[51] He concluded with the observation that both Jewish artisans and the Jewish poor were injured.[52] The desire to hurt the Jewish competitors was decisive, with no thought given to the interests of the people.

The accompanying editorial, which evidently was written by Bulanov, dealt mainly with the role of the organized revolutionary intelligentsia in the face of sporadic outbursts of popular violence.[53] The pogroms revealed that the newly awakened populace had not yet learned to identify its real enemies and the reasons for its distress and thus attacked "the most conspicuous object it sees." Their ethnic-religious differences and their juridical rightlessness made the Jews stand out with special sharpness from the masses. The editorialist too regarded it as probable that the pogroms were but a prelude to a broader and more general movement, but still regarded their role as negative.[54] The pogroms were indeed born against the background of unbearable distress, but rather than helping to focus popular consciousness upon this fact they "preserved the senseless idea of tsarism and made concrete the tradition of national hatred." Thus in no way did they represent an attempt to inject new foundations into the governmental and social regime. To the extent that it is possible to speak of guilt in this context, that guilt falls, in the editor's opinion, upon the revolutionary intelligentsia and not upon the populace, "which has remained faithful to itself"; – a phrase that should not necessarily be read as praise of or idealization of the populace, as was the fashion among many narodniki.[55] Everything depended upon the ability of the organized revolutionary intelligentsia to create a conscious and united nucleus among the populace that could lead the people from partial rebellions with vague demands to a real nationwide revolutionary popular insurrection. The question of the revolutionary intelligentsia's responsibility stood at the center of the article, and there can be no doubt that in the author's opinion the struggle with pogromist tendencies should be an inseparable part of the efforts of the revolutionary intelligentsia to deepen the social and political consciousness of the masses. He did not approve of looking passively at the pogroms as a "prelude." Clear common lines proceeded from this point to the sixth issue of *Zerno*, which had appeared a month earlier. The main editor of the fifth issue of *Chernyi Peredel* was A. Bulanov, who was Akselrod's outstanding student.

To summarize, the stand taken by the so-called Second Shift of Chernyi Peredel on the pogroms was not quite as sporadic or one-sided as it has often been described. It is apparent that a uniform characterization, whether positive or negative, of the revolutionary movement's attitude in the 1880s toward the pogroms – the forebears of things to come during the 1905–6 revolution and after the revolution of 1917 – is impossible. Insofar as individual and unique approaches can be discerned, Chernyi Peredel should be regarded as the principal contemporary representative of the anti-pogromist trend. It is not surprising to find that interest in the pogroms brought about discussion of the overall Jewish situation. Typically, the theoretical baggage and the actual knowledge of Jewish affairs in the revolutionary movement was quite limited. The historic failure of Narodnaia Volia's response to the pogroms at the time of its greatest success and subsequent decline were in part a result of this. But this circumstance was also a source of puzzlement and a certain zigzagging in Chernyi Peredel. This ambivalence in turn reflected another aspect of the problem.

The two major branches of the revolutionary movement underwent periods of substantial change throughout this period, although it is impossible to establish a direct deterministic relationship between these permutations and the attitudes of the revolutionary groups towards the Jewish Question. An organization like Narodnaia Volia, which strayed far from the style of 1870s Populism towards political radicalism, reassumed many of its previous attitudes at the time of the pogroms. One can discover in the movement influences of Slavophile, Populist, and pseudo-Populist Judeophobia. On the other hand, in Chernyi Peredel, usually viewed as the true spiritual heir of 1870s Populism, clear voices were raised against popular Judeophobia. The Chernoperedeltsy instead emphasized the need to introduce a conscious awareness of means and ends into the areas of popular psychology and action as well.[56]

From the above discussion, it should be apparent that the significance of the Jewish Question in Russia was preserved in the revolutionary movement as well. It should not be viewed as a marginal matter, to be dismissed in a few random sentences (as has often been done), but as an integral feature of that history. The interest shown in the Petersburg proclamation, and the treatment of pogroms in the pages of *Chernyi Peredel* and *Zerno* testify to this fact. There is another aspect of the matter as well – the participation of Jews in the revolutionary movement and their impact upon contemporary socialist attitudes towards the Jewish Question. In this connection, one should consider the episode of the workers in the secret Minsk print shop, the exact role of Sheftel, whose work has not been satisfactorily explored, especially in regard to the subject at hand, although he was one of the three principal activists of Chernyi Peredel and, finally, the peregrinations of Akselrod.[57]

With the publication of the fifth issue of *Chernyi Peredel* the activity of the central St. Petersburg group ceased. A month earlier the editor, Bulanov, together with Stefanovich and others, had moved over to Narodnaia Volia. A short time later the Minsk print shop was seized, arrests were made, and the group ceased to exist. What remained, apart from various local groups, was the *émigré* group abroad: Plekhanov, Akselrod, Zasulich, Deich, and a few others, who comprised the so-called First Shift of Chernyi Peredel. This group cannot be considered a real organization, and it had no journal of its own. Nevertheless its members, especially the first two, found ways and opportunities to make their views known. They enjoyed the authority of veterans of the revolutionary movement within the European socialist arena as well. After a while they began to style themselves "former members of Chernyi Peredel." Collectively and individually they now went through a process of accelerated evolution, not without contradictions, which led to the founding of the Marxist "Group for the Emancipation of Labor" in 1883, a pioneer of Russian social democracy. Their attitude towards the pogroms and to the Jewish Question overall found expression in internal discussions, in correspondence among themselves and with other well-known revolutionaries, and in various publications. *Émigré* connections with Russia were at the time tenuous. Full and reliable reports about their reactions to the discussion about the pogroms in *Zerno* and *Chernyi Peredel* are therefore lacking. Nevertheless, in a very real sense a line led from the First Shift of Chernyi Peredel to the Second to the Third and onward. Continuity was embodied in Pavel Akselrod more than in anyone else. The special transformation undergone by that group during the years 1881–3 from *narodnichestvo* to Marxism occurred, not by accident, during a time of crisis in Russia overall, for Russian Jewry and its intelligentsia, and for Russian revolutionary socialism. This crisis, as well as the fate of the foremost participants in it, justifies a special discussion.

NOTES

1 A full-scale monographic study of Chernyi Peredel has not yet been published either in the USSR or in the West. A brief description, containing various details that must be treated with caution, is contained in A. Yarmolinsky, *Road to Revolution* (Toronto, 1962), 223–6. See also chapter 21 of F. Venturi, *Roots of Revolution* (London, 1964), which deals with Narodnaia Volia until the time of the assassination of Tsar Alexander II in March 1881. See also E. R. Ol'khovskii, "K istorii 'Chernogo Peredela' (1879–1888)," in *Obshchestvennoe dvizhenie v poreformennoi Rossii* (Moscow, 1965), 124–78; and the same author's "K istoriografii 'Chernogo Peredela'," *Istoriia SSSR*, II (1967), 63–81.

2 Akselrod tells of this in his memoirs: *Perezhitoe i peredumannoe* (Berlin, 1923), 349–55.

3 *Chernyi Peredel, organ sotsialistov-federalistov, Zemlia i Volia* (cited according

to the reprint edition: *Chernyi Peredel, organ sotsialistov-federalistov, 1880–1881g.*, Moscow–Petrograd, 1923). This book opens with a preface by V. Nevskii and an introductory article by the veteran revolutionary and Chernyi Peredel member O. Aptekman. At the time of publication there was in the entire Soviet Union only a single copy of the fifth issue, and it was damaged in several places.

4 *Zerno, rabochii listok* (cited according to the reprint edition: V. I. Nevskii, *Ot "Zemli i Voli" k gruppe "Osvobozhdeniiu Truda,"* Moscow 1930). *Zerno* also served members of Narodnaia Volia in their agitation among the workers. As late as 1887 copies of this newspaper were found in possession of an underground figure from Białystok, see P. Korzec, *Pół wieku dziejów ruchu rewolucyjnego Białostoczyzny (1864–1914)* (Warsaw, 1965), 93.

5 The discovery of the foundation and operation of the print shop in Minsk came only during the 1920s, first noted in a letter sent by I. Getsov to L. Deich in January 1923. The letter was first published in Deich's book, *Rol' Evreev v russkom revoliutsionnom dvizhenii* (Berlin, 1923), 316–35. R. M. Kantor, a bitter critic of the book because of the selectivity of the author's memory, found the letter "the only thing of value" in it, *Katorga i Ssylka* (henceforth *KiS*) vii–viii (1926), 373. Cf. note 42 below. Zagorskii soon disappeared from the public arena. His memoirs are not enlightening regarding our topic. Sheftel became known later as a lawyer, a Jewish public figure, a delegate to the Duma, and a member of the Cadet party. On Bulanov, see O. Bulanova, "A. P. Bulanov," *KiS*, xii (1924), 291–6. Entries on Bulanov and Zagorskii are included in the Russian bio-bibliographical dictionary of participants in the revolutionary movements of the 1870s; see note 42 below.

6 The proclamation is included in the article by S. N. Valk, "G. G. Romanenko," *KiS*, xlviii (1928), 35–59.

7 See Appendix I, pp. 91–2.

8 On the continuation of narodnik influence on the tradition of Chernyi Peredel during the 1880s, see N. Sergeevskii, "'Chernyi Peredel' i narodniki, 1880 g.," *KiS*, lxxiv (1931), 7–58; Ol'khovskii, "K istorii 'Chernogo Peredela,'"; D. Offord, *The Russian Revolutionary Movement in the 1880s* (Cambridge, 1986), chapter 3. Except for a mention by Sergeevsky (50), of a proclamation issued by a narodnik circle in Kharkov containing expressions of support for the pogroms I have not found that this phenomenon has any bearing on our subject.

9 Here we shall mention only the examination of the history of the *Chernyi Peredel* print shop, the history of the periodical's appearance, the number of issues, and the identity of their editors, all of which have been treated in a large literature of historical detection that has often been characterized, even down to our own time, by inaccuracies, contradictions, and uncertainties. It is not clear to me why the existence of the Minsk printing house escaped the attention of – or perhaps was ignored

by – the authors of the study: I. G. Levitas, M. A. Moskalev, E. M. Fingerit, *Revoliutsionnye podpolnye tipografii v Rossii* (Moscow 1962), 42.

10 See my article, "The attitude of the Southern Russian Workers' Union toward the Jews (1880–1881)," *Harvard Ukrainian Studies*, VI, 2 (1982), 191–216. The agitational writings of this organization, too, insofar as they were directed towards the peasants, used the popular name Zemlia i Volia.

11 For the wording of the proclamation, see Appendix II, p. 93. In the first issue of *Chernyi Peredel* (15 January 1880) there is an article about "The Rostov Rebellion of 2 April [1879]" that describes the mass riots in that city, including episodes connected with two Jews: a moneylender who averted calls from the crowd to rob him, and a distiller ("a crafty yid") who rolled a barrel of liquor into the street for the rioters, "and alcohol put out the fire." The third edition of the newspaper (dated March 1881) was actually completed on 21 May. It contains a reaction to the assassination of the Tsar but no mention of the pogroms.

12 Government officials attributed such proclamations to the Jews themselves. This is reflected clearly in the report of Count Kutaisov, who was appointed to investigate the pogroms. The report was published in the early 1920s in the collection by G. L. Krasnyi, ed., *Materialy dlia istorii antievreiskikh pogromov v Rossii* (Moscow 1923), II.

13 On such a rumor in Elisavetgrad, see, for example, the Russian Jewish weekly *Rassvet*, 21 (23 May 1881), 802; 22 (30 May 1881), 843.

14 *Rassvet*, 20 (16 May 1881), 762–4; *HaMelits*, 18 (12 May 1881), 379. A week later *HaMelits* published an expansion of the story based upon foreign periodicals without mentioning the names of the sources (395).

15 See R. M. Kantor, "Aleksandr III o evreiskikh pogromakh," *Evreiskaia Letopis'*, 1 (1923), 149–58.

16 There is later evidence (from 1882) for the latter tendency.

17 *HaMelits*, 395; Kantor, "Aleksandr III," 153. The Russian revolutionaries generally referred to themselves as "Revolutionary Socialists"; this explains the quotation marks around the word "anarchists" in the proclamation of Zemlia i Volia.

18 S. M. Dubnow, *History of the Jews in Russia and Poland*, II (Philadelphia, 1918), 261.

19 The full text of the circular was printed in *Rassvet*, 19 (9 May 1881), 724–5. See *HaMelits*, 18, 373–4; *Evreiskaia Entsiklopedia*, XII, 15. According to information presented in August 1881 by the Austrian ambassador in St. Petersburg, Ignatiev stated that the Jews and the Poles formed the basis of the "secret nihilist organization"; P. A. Zaionchkovskii, *Krizis samoderzhaviia na rubezhe 1870–1880 godov* (Moscow 1964), 380.

20 *HaMelits*, 17 (5 May 1881), 354–5; *Rassvet*, 19 (9 May 1881), 754. The interview with the Tsar was evidently arranged through Vladimir. *HaMelits* reports that the antisemitic newspaper *Novoe vremia* also stated

that "the hand of the rebels is [recognizable] in the affair." The Hebrew-language weekly supported this opinion and elaborated on it in its own article, *HaMelits*, 364.

21 Dubnow distinguishes between the first, comforting part of the Tsar's response to the delegation, which was published in the newspapers, and the second part, which became known "through rumor." In fact, *HaMelits*, 29, 395, specifically published the second part citing an anonymous foreign periodical. On the other hand, the weekly saw fit to soften the impression and even claimed that the Tsar had agreed to refute the charge of exploitation in response to delegation member A. Zak. In contrast, *Rassvet*, 20 (16 May 1881), 762, entirely ignored what had been said about exploitation in its report of the meeting. Perhaps, because it was published in the Russian language, it had wanted to avoid giving even greater currency to this charge. *Russkii Evrei* and *HaTsefirah* behaved in the same way. Moreover, *Rassvet* was also quite cautious and restrained regarding the Tsar's accusation about the role of the "anarchists" in the pogroms. This charge was used by the weekly mainly to prove that Jewish actions or inactions had not caused the pogroms. Unlike other Jewish organs, which reacted with real or forced enthusiasm to the episode of the delegation to the Tsar, *Rassvet* maintained a certain reservation. Evidently this practice was not accidental but consistent with the stand taken on many issues by the radical, secular, educated elite among the Jews that coalesced around the newspaper at that time. *Rassvet* both raised the idea of "Jewish patriotism," and drew a distinction between the wealthy class of Jewish society and the impoverished majority. Cf. *Jewish Chronicle*, XII, 635 (27 August 1881).

22 On 1 May, ten days before he met the Jewish delegation, the Tsar received a report on the pogroms in Kiev province. This report spoke of "deep hatred" on the part of the local population for "the Jews who enslave them." Alexander underscored the words "deep hatred," adding in the margin, "surprising," Kantor, "Aleksandr III," 152.

23 An early example of this phenomenon can be found at the time of the pogrom in Odessa in 1871. See chapter 2 by John Klier in this volume, pp. 20–1.

24 This contradiction did not escape the notice of bystanders, such as the Austrian ambassador in St. Petersburg, Kalnoky; see N. M. Gelber, "Di rusishe pogromen onheyb di 80-er yorn in shayn fun estraykhisher diplomatisher korespondents," *YIVO Historishe Shriftn*, II (Vilna, 1937), 1470–1. Kalnoky, by the way, passed on a minute devoted to the Jewish delegation's discussion with the Tsar (which he characterized as "noted for its accuracy"), without mentioning the Tsar's comments about the anarchists. Ibid., 469.

25 The Tsar's appointment of Count Kutaisov during the first half of May underscored the belief in a connection between the pogroms and the activities of the revolutionaries; Krasnyi, ed., *Materialy*, II, 47. However,

Kutaisov's detailed report from the end of July negated this version of events and transferred the blame to Jewish "exploitation." This is the controlling line in Ignatiev's report to the Tsar, which was drafted around the same time, as well as in the establishment of the "provincial committees" (August 1881) and in the "Temporary Regulations" of May 1882 (the so-called May Laws). As early as March 1881, before he had been appointed to his position, Ignatiev noted that "a powerful group of Poles and Yids exists in St. Petersburg, and it directly controls the banks, the stock exchange, the legal profession, most of the press, and other social functions. By numerous legal and illegal ways and means it wields enormous influence over the bureaucracy and over the course of events in general." Zaionchkovskii, *Krizis*, 338.

26 The diversionary tendencies of the pogroms, as well as the changing explanations for them, were already dealt with in a memorandum prepared in 1882 by Emmanuel Levin, who was associated with the Jewish notables in the capital. The memorandum was anonymously published in part only in 1909 in *Evreiskaia starina*: "Evreiskii vopros i antievreiskoe dvizhenie v Rossii v 1881 i 1882," 1 (1909), 88–109, 265–76. Compare "Mitokh tazkir al hapra'ot b'shnot 1881–1882," *Heavar*, IX (1962), 78–81.

27 On the weakness of the version claiming active participation of the revolutionary organizations in the pogroms, as well as on the small degree of participation in them even by individual revolutionaries, see A. Linden [L. Motzkin], ed., *Die Judenpogrome in Russland*, I, 1909, 46–47, 57–58, 63. Motzkin's own solid and comprehensive article has somehow, unjustly, been pushed out of the historiographical memory.

28 Evidently the words "to a certain extent" were intended to limit the force of "the truth of the matter" to "an echo of our work," to use the newspaper's expression. The two publications appeared in two editions before the First World War as *Literatura sotsial'no-revoliutsiannoi partii "Narodnoi Voli"* (n.p., 1905), and *Literatura Partii "Narodnoi Voli"* (Moscow, 1907).

29 M. Mishkinsky, "Al Emdatah shel haTenu'ah haMahapchanit haRusit legabei haYehudim biShnot ha-70 shel haMe'ah ha-19," *Heavar*, IX (1962), 38–67, X (1963), 212–13.

30 The term "Russian people" was used, even though quite a few Ukrainians took part in the pogroms, especially in the rural areas and in the small towns. This distinction does not appear to have been intentional, for the terms were often interchanged. On the tendency to arouse dissatisfaction with the revolutionary movement among the Jews, see, in a broader context, Linden, *Judenpogrome*, I, 66.

31 Mishkinsky, "Attitude," 206–11. Cf. 52 below.

32 J. Ruelf, *Drei Tage in Juedisch-Russland* (Frankfurt-on-Main, 1882), 73–5. Ruelf, the rabbi of Memel, saw the Russian-language proclamation (or as he called it, the "Plakat") pasted on the doors of the

synagogue. The contents, as were translated for him, ran approximately thus: "We are not your enemies. Government agents are the ones who did this, in order to divert the furor of the enraged people from the government and to turn you over to the force of the people's wrath. Be sure you know who your enemies really are." Ibid., 74. Ruelf indicates that the proclamation was signed by "The famous revolutionary committee"[?]. The Minsk group of Chernyi Peredel had connections with Vilna, but this does not tell us anything about the identity of the writers of the proclamation under discussion. Ruelf mentioned the proclamation once again in a later work, in which he added several details and explanatory notes: *Die Russischen Juden* (Memel, 1892), 31.

33 In 1882 the aforementioned memorandum (see note 26 above) made the clear assumption that the pogroms had been organized "down to the minutest detail" by an "anti-Jewish league" participating in which were "numerous representatives of both the provincial and central government." There was even a hint about the role of the Slavophiles in preparing the pogroms. This matter has been discussed widely in the historical literature, but it is still not possible to draw final conclusions as to the identity of the organizing body and the actual extent of its influence. But see John D. Klier, "German antisemitism and Russian Judeophobia in the 1880s: brothers and strangers," *Jahrbücher für Geschichte Osteuropas*, XXXVII, 4 (1989), 524–40.

34 *Rassvet*, 20 (16 May 1881), 763; Levin, "Evreiskii vopros"; *Voskhod*, IV (1881), 50–6; *Evreiskaia Entsiklopediia*, XII, 614. See also below regarding the editorial in the fifth issue of *Chernyi Peredel*.

35 See Mishkinsky, "Attitude," 196, note 17.

36 For a fuller discussion, see ibid., 199–202. (Please note that in note 33 of "Attitude," Akselrod's memoirs are incorrectly cited; see note 2 above.)

37 Measured doubt about the accuracy of Akselrod's memory is raised in A. Ascher, *Pavel Axelrod and the Development of Menshevism* (Cambridge, MS, 1972), 72, 78. However, there are various proofs of Akselrod's unusual sensitivity during this period to oppression, discrimination, and prejudice directed against religious and ethnic minorities, as well as to his demands for a federal, autonomist solution to the problem of the status of the various national groups in the Empire.

38 "Russkaia Zhizn'," *Zerno*, III (June 1881) 413–16. The entire issue contains twelve pages, of which the lead article, dated 1 June, takes up six. This article is almost entirely identical to that which opened the second issue (395–403). The piece in question here is based upon the pogroms of "the last month," meaning from mid-April (the first pogrom at Elisavetgrad). Thus in the final analysis it relates to the first two stages of the riots of 1881. See Y. Slutsky, "HaGe'ografiyah shel Pera'ot 5641," *Heavar*, IX (1963), 16–18.

39 As an example of the damage done by hatred between peoples the author mentions the exploitation of hatred towards the Poles during the

Polish uprising of 1863. The Russian peasants aided the authorities, but the beneficiaries of this cooperation were the Russian landowners who received the lands confiscated from the Polish pans. But with regard to the pogroms the author clings to his formula, expressed in the first part of the article, that the authorities at all levels together with the propertied classes repudiate pogroms entirely, for fear that they will spread against the regime as a whole. This contrasts with the statement of Zemlia i Volia, which characterizes the authorities' position as one of "divide and conquer."

40 To be sure, the word "even" sounds like a bit of a concession to popular prejudices, but in the present context it is insignificant.

41 *Zerno*, VI (November 1881) (the date 10 November appears at the top of the article). See Appendix III (pp. 96–7).

42 See note 5 above; also the entry "Getsov, Iosif," *Deiateli revoliutsionnogo dvizheniia v Rossii*, III, 2 (Moscow 1934), 791–2.

43 Thus according to the testimony of A. Bulanova, Bulanov's wife, who was herself active in Chernyi Peredel in St. Petersburg. See Ol'khovskii, "K istorii 'Chernogo Peredela,'" 143.

44 "Letter from the South," 303–7; "From the Countryside," 308–15. The first article is signed by Prokopenko, the second by Niedolia. I have been unable to determine who these are. The first article deals with a wider region, and it appears that the author spent several years in the area. The second, on the other hand, deals with a single village and its environs, and the length of the author's stay there ("in the guise of a St. Petersburg *intelligent*") came to half a year. Most of the inhabitants were Ukrainians, but there was an admixture of people from Great Russia that is indicated, *inter alia*, in the language.

45 This is the only reservation to the anti-Jewish arguments that the author raised indirectly in his discussions with the peasants.

46 "There are those who propose to transfer them across the Amur, others to an area in Egypt; the more radical [say] simply to drown them in the Dniepr," "Letter from the South," 306. The strong attachment to historical associations characteristic of the Dnieper area comes through strongly.

47 The author contends that the hopes placed by the people in the "socialists" are merely the fruit of Jewish propaganda to the effect that the pogroms are the work of the socialists. The concluding sentence states that this hope is already too important a matter "for purely practical purposes in the countryside" (307) but there is no elaboration upon what these purposes are.

48 1 March 1881, *Chernyi Peredel*, 4, 295–303. According to Sergeevsky, "Chernyi Peredel," 25, the author was Zagorskii. On disagreements between Zagorskii and Bulanov, see B. P. Verevkin, *Russkaia nelegalnaia pechat' 70-kh i 80-kh godov XIX veka* (Moscow, 1960), 120.

49 *Chernyi Peredel*, 298. At this point the author takes hold of an almost

poetic analogy when he compares the influence of the terrorist act to that of metabolism on an organism or to a breeze that fans a flame.

50 Ibid., 319–20, 345–9.

51 Incidentally, the author is usually quite strict about placing the pejorative expression "yid" ("zhid") in quotation marks. For a different opinion concerning the attitude of the possessing classes toward the pogroms, see note 39 above.

52 This contrasted with what was written in the fourth issue of Chernyi Peredel and accorded with the actual situation. The pogrom movement originated in the cities; in the countryside there were few Jews, most of whom were innkeepers, who were themselves generally poor and did not own land. These people could not, therefore, serve by themselves to provoke a movement.

53 Chernyi Peredel, 307–26. This time, too, as in the brief reaction in the editorial of the fourth issue, the sentiments of descriptive reports were reflected in editorials. On the identity of the author, see Aptekman, Chernyi Peredel, and Bulanova, "A. P. Bulanov."

54 For some reason the author believes that this prospect "may serve to comfort the Jews." He supports the likelihood of this prospect with an analogy from the histories of France and Germany; in these countries the Jews were only the first scapegoats for the masses, and in the wake of outbursts against them came the revolutionary events. This example also appeared in the press of Narodnaia Volia (supported by a statement of Marx), but in a pro-pogrom rather than an anti-pogrom context. The author mentions together with this a certain rebellion against the landowners of Tver province, of which he gives no details.

55 "As everywhere and at all times the masses behaved according to their immediate instincts, to emotions that reached the boiling point, and to interests that were immediately – if superficially and falsely – apprehended," Chernyi Peredel 320. When speaking of the rural environment in particular he indicates that "unresolvable contradictions reside in it; enlightened ideals often take on the monstrous form of dark prejudice," 322.

56 See also my article "Did the Russian Jacobins (Blanquists) have a special attitude toward the Jews?" in A. Rapoport-Albert and S. Zipperstein, eds., Jewish History: Essays in Honour of Chimen Abramsky (London, 1988), 319–41.

57 Should access to Soviet archives and the publication of sources be broadened, our knowledge of these points as well is likely, of course, to be enriched.

Appendix I
Bibliographical note

The subject of the attitude of Chernyi Peredel to the pogroms was raised to some extent in the historical literature before the First World War, for instance, in Plekhanov's polemic against the book of the historian V. Bogucharskii. My intention is to point out the way in which the subject has been reflected in recent historical literature. I shall not deal here with the proclamation of June 1881 (see Appendix II), for even after it was published a second time in 1978 it escaped the notice of almost all writers.

The subject is treated on the basis of a wider range of sources than is usually encountered in Claudio Sergio Ingerflom, "Idéologie révolutionnaire et mentalité antisémite: les socialistes russes face aux pogroms de 1881–1883," *Annales: Économies, sociétés, civilisations,* XXXVII, 3 (1982), 434–53. However, Ingerflom's analysis and certain other features of his article do not justify the generalized title.

David Vital, *The Origins of Zionism* (Oxford, 1975), 56–7, deals briefly with the attitude of Narodnaia Volia, basing his discussion upon the Ukrainian proclamation of summer 1881 and placing special emphasis, as is quite common, upon the use of the term *zhid,* notwithstanding the fact that at the time this was the only designation for a Jew in the Ukrainian language. He makes no mention of Chernyi Peredel. The "other currents" which he discusses are confined to Kropotkin and Lavrov, thus creating certain problems of incompleteness and, as regards Lavrov, of inaccuracy as well.

Jonathan Frankel, in his remarkable monograph *Prophecy and Politics: Socialism, Nationalism, and the Russian Jews, 1862–1917* (Cambridge, 1981), cites several statements from the organs of Chernyi Peredel, but had he made use of the later issues of both newspapers it is doubtful that he would have written that

"Narodnaia Volia and Chernyi Peredel had welcomed, were even inciting, the pogroms...," 102.

Offord (see note 8), ignores Chernyi Peredel altogether in his discussion of the pogroms. Stephen M. Berk, *Year of Crisis, Year of Hope: Russian Jewry and the Pogroms of 1881–1882* (London, 1985), 90, defines the position of Chernyi Peredel as one of "ambivalence" and "inconsistency," although he bases this conclusion upon two quotations from a single issue of *Zerno* and *Chernyi Peredel* taken from a secondary source; he does not prove that his characterizations are applicable.

From the literature in Hebrew, an essay by a non-professional historian is worth special mention: Y. Erez, "Yahas haMahapchanim laPera'ot beRusiyah biShenot haShemonim" [The Revolutionaries' Relation to the Pogroms in Russia of the 1880s], *Shenaton Davar* (Tel Aviv, 1952), 232–74. He is more careful in distinguishing between the positions of Narodnaia Volia and Chernyi Peredel; but since he used only some of the sources, his conclusions are tenuous (cf. 264, 267, 274). Y. Maor, who had earlier dealt with the attitude of the revolutionary movement toward the Jews, states in his book *HaTenu'ah haTsiyonit beRusiyah* [The Zionist Movement in Russia] (Jerusalem, 1973), 37, that certain circles of revolutionaries "from the Narodnaia Volia party joined their voices and encouraged antisemitic agitation." He then rushes to the generalization that "the anti-Jewish pogroms were for the Russian revolutionaries a means of achieving their revolutionary goal." The case of Chernyi Peredel, which the author ignores, does not confirm this hasty generalization. B. Pinkus, *Yehudei Rusiyah uVrit haMo'atsot* [Russian and Soviet Jews] (Ben Gurion University, Be'er-Sheva, 1986), 119, confuses the various "shifts" of Chernyi Peredel and states sweepingly and summarily that "they did not differ much in their outlook from Narodnaia Volia," a statement that is not adequate.

Appendix II
From the ZEMLIA I VOLIA Society

Alexander III informed a delegation from the Jews that the beating of their fellow Jews in the South was caused by "anarchists'" agitation; this announcement by the Tsar clearly reveals that he has decided to take advantage of the disturbances in the South for the benefit of his reactionary policy.

The ZEMLIA I VOLIA Society finds it necessary for its part to declare that fanning national antagonism stands in complete contradiction to the fundamental principles of the revolutionary socialists, who regard international solidarity as one of the primary conditions for the revolution's success.

Stirring up national passions is almost certainly liable to serve Alexander III, who, like all despots, knows quite well the meaning of the Roman saying, "Divide and Conquer."

The beating of the Jews is the result of the desperate situation of the people and of the medieval policy of squeezing the Jews into the confines of a relatively small territory.

Let then the governmental responsibility for the violence that has been caused to the Jewish population in the South fall upon the government and upon the exploiters in general, who through immeasurable oppression have brought the Russian people to express its protest in such fashion.

THE ZEMLIA I VOLIA SOCIETY
Petersburg 15 June 1881

The signature ZEMLIA I VOLIA SOCIETY was generally attached to the publications of the so-called Second Shift of Chernyi Peredel, whose central circle was in St. Petersburg. The proclamation in question was not mentioned in society's periodicals, *Chernyi Peredel* and *Zerno*. The fact of its publication as noted in *Kalendar Narodnoi Volii na 1883*, published in Geneva. Years later the proclamation was cited in a publication that originated in a secret police report (*Khronika sotsialisticheskogo dvizheniia v Rossii, 1878–1887: ofitsialnyi otchet* (Moscow, 1906). The original French version of this report was distributed among official agencies in a small number of copies in 1890. The portion dealing with the content of the proclamation (205) reflects its spirit faithfully.

The proclamation was not included in any collection of documents on the revolutionary movement and was not reprinted. Similarly, as far as I know, it was never included in discussions of the revolutionary movement and the Jews in the historical literature. It was first republished by this author in the late 1970s (*Mehkarim beToldot Am Yisra'el veErets Yisra'el* [Studies on the History of the Land and People of Israel], iv, edited by U. Rappaport (Haifa, 1978), 266–7.

The copy of the proclamation was at first preserved in the archive of Vladimir Burtsev; a copy of it was made by Boris Nikolaievsky, who was good enough to make a copy available to me (as attested in his letters to me of 17 June 1962 and 30 June 1963).

According to information I received from Plekhanov House in Leningrad in 1963, a limited number of copies of the proclamation have been preserved in various archives in the Soviet Union, but it was not indicated whether these were printed or stencil copies. Nor did Nikolaievsky know about the manner in which the proclamation had been published. Sergeevski, "Chernyi Peredel," and Ol'khovskii, "K istorii 'Chernogo Peredela,'" 142, stated briefly that the proclamation had been printed in the clandestine print shop in Minsk, but they offered no evidence for this statement. I. Getsov, in Deich, *Rol' Evreev*, however, does not include it in the list of Minsk imprints. It is reasonable to assume that if the episode of Zagorskii's article about the pogroms in *Zerno* was preserved so well in his memory, he would recall this publication, which bore such an unequivocal anti-pogrom character. This is not merely a technical detail, and perhaps the matter will be finally clarified in the future.

Finally, a divergence should be noted between the published version of Tsar Alexander's remarks, which spoke of the "handiwork of the anarchists," and the version in this proclamation, which refers to the *agitation* of the anarchists. The former version appears to be more farreaching than that used by the Zemlia i Volia Society.

ОТЪ ОБЩЕСТВА «ЗЕМЛЯ И ВОЛЯ»

Александръ III заявилъ депутаціи отъ евреевъ , что избіеніе ихъ соплеменниковъ на Югѣ вызвано агитаціей «анархистовъ»; это заявленіе царя ясно показываетъ, что онъ рѣшилъ воспользоваться безпорядками на Югѣ для своей реакціонной политики.

Общество «ЗЕМЛЯ И ВОЛЯ» считаетъ съ своей стороны необходимымъ заявить, что возбужденіе національной вражды находится в полномъ противорѣчіи съ основными принципами революціонныхъ социалистовъ, которые международную солидарность признаютъ однимъ изъ главныхъ условій успѣха революціи.

Разжиганіе національныхъ страстей можетъ оказать скорѣе всего услугу Александру III, который, как всякій деспотъ отлично знаетъ значеніе римскаго изреченія «раздѣляй и властвуй».

Избіеніе евреевъ есть результатъ отчаяннаго положенія народа и средневѣковой политики скученія евреевъ в предѣлахъ сравнительно небольшой территоріи.

Такъ пусть-же правительственная отвѣтсвенность за причиненное еврейскому населенію на Югѣ насиліе падетъ на правительство и эксплуататоровъ вообще, доведщихъ русскій народъ безмѣрнымъ гнетомъ до появленія протеста в подобной формѣ.

ОБЩЕСТВО «ЗЕМЛЯ И ВОЛЯ»

Appendix III

Not long ago, this summer,[1] so-called riots against the Jews occurred in many cities and towns, and to an extent in the countryside, in the South. The crowd stormed Jewish houses and destroyed the property in them; the authorities arrested many from among the crowd and carved the manifesto of the new Tsar on their backs with whips. The people gained nothing from this rebellion; but could anything possibly have been gained by working without purpose and without any preparation. Instead of striving to change unbearable conditions to better ones, the people merely poured out its wrath upon the Jews. But are Jews the only ones who oppress them and exploit their labor for nothing? Are the kulaks among the peasants or the landowners any better?[2] Are not they the ones who took the land from the peasants and who force them to work as before at serf labor? Will a Russian factory owner flinch before extracting from the worker the last penny of his wages? Ethnic origin and faith are of no concern here: every person belongs to the people into which he was born and clings to his faith according to the dictates of his conscience. For this no one is subject to praise or blame. At the same time, robbery and oppression do not distinguish among different peoples or faiths. Even among the Jews there are many who must live by their labor and who are oppressed by their wealthy fellow Jews no less than the Russian manufacturer oppresses his Russian workers. Jewish workers, too, need better conditions, just like Russian workers. Thus their cause is the cause of all: to institute a better governmental arrangement in the country and to guarantee full wages to anyone who wishes to work by himself, no matter whether he be a Russian, a Jew, a Tatar, or a Pole. This is what we must aim for and strive to achieve (*Zerno*, VI: November 1881, 451–2).[3]

NOTES

1 *Zerno*, VI (November 1881).
2 Evidently the reference is to the third stage of the pogroms of 1881, which began at the end of June.
3 The comparison between kulaks and Jews served as the subject of a controversial but thoughtful article that appeared at approximately the same time in the radical monthly *Delo* as B. Lenskii, "Evrei i Kulak," IX, 2 (1881), 27–60.

CHAPTER 5

Cosmopolitanism, antisemitism and Populism: a reappraisal of the Russian and Jewish response to the pogroms of 1881–1882

Erich Haberer

The Jewish response to the pogroms of the early 1880s has been of great interest to historians concerned with the rise of modern Jewish national consciousness and its politico-cultural expression, Zionism. To some this response was akin to a "revolution," to a sharp break with previous assimilationist tendencies, which "necessarily undermined the authority of groups most clearly identified with Jewish adaptation to Russian life": the *maskilim* grouping around Baron Gintsburg's Society for the Promotion of Culture among Jews; and the socialist Jews, who themselves underwent a deep spiritual crisis that affected their commitment to the revolutionary cause of Russian Populism.[1] Others, while recognizing the momentous impact of the pogroms on Russian Jewry, have cautioned us not to overemphasize the political and psychological effects of the crisis since for many Jews this did not result in "a complete rejection of assimilation and cosmopolitan radicalism and a wholehearted return to the Jewish masses and Jewish nationalism."[2] Historians of either viewpoint agree, however, that the loss of retention of "faith in socialist cosmopolitanism" was a crucial factor in deciding whether or not a Jewish Populist remained loyal to the Russian revolutionary movement. This faith, the argument goes, had been seriously challenged by the massive anti-Jewish riots of the *narod* and even more so by "the fact that two major revolutionary parties showed clear signs of sympathy with the pogroms..."[3] In other words, popular antisemitism and corresponding sentiments in the principal revolutionary groupings of Russian Populism – the People's Will (Narodnaia Volia) and the Black Repartition (Chernyi Peredel) – compelled Jewish socialists to reconsider their allegiance to revolutionary Populism. For these parties had dismally failed to live up to their "professed internationalism" in the face of brutal anti-Jewish persecution. Thus, according to conventional interpretations, antisemitism – particularly among Gentile revolutionaries – undermined a Jewish socialist's cosmopolitan *Weltanschauung* and forced him either to renounce his Russian-centered revolutionary convictions or, paradoxically, confirm them anew in time-honored "cosmopolitan-assimilationist" fashion. That renunciation rather than reconfirmation of the "faith" was the prevalent reaction of Jewish radicals is the predominant opinion and was most succinctly expressed by Louis Greenberg when he wrote:

Most of the Jewish narodniki were stunned by the open antisemitism revealed in the ranks of their Russian comrades, a sentiment directed even against the Jewish socialists. Because of this hostility Jewish revolutionaries left the ranks of the narodniki, some even joining the newly formed Zionist groups.[4]

Clearly, for Greenberg and others like him, "revolutionary antisemitism" was the decisive variable in the set of circumstances which drove many, if not most, Jews to abandon the revolutionary movement. Like its antidote, "socialist cosmopolitanism," it has been accepted as an axiomatic truth in analyzing the Jewish response to the pogrom crises.

While the above seems to be a neat interpretation – particularly within the context of Jewish national awakening in the form of early Zionism – it does not always square with the facts, nor does it always make sense conceptually. Factually, there is no proof that the majority of Jewish socialists "deserted" the revolution and that they reacted in a uniformly negative way to the pogroms. As will be shown, the assertion of a negative attitude was in many cases a gradual process that did not exclude indifference to, or even approval of, the riots; nor did the eventual opposition to the pogroms result in a large-scale withdrawal from the Russian revolutionary movement. Although it is impossible to verify precisely how many Jews left the movement, we do know for certain that the vast majority of Jewish Narodovoltsy and Chernoperedeltsy, as the followers of Narodnaia Volia and Chernyi Peredel were called, remained "loyal" to their respective parties – a loyalty that was augmented by hundreds of other Jews who embraced the revolutionary cause in the years following the pogroms. Conceptually, this fact – as well as the fact that some Jews did "desert" the movement – cannot be explained satisfactorily in terms of "revolutionary antisemitism" and "socialist cosmopolitanism." For this would mean that sometimes the latter sustained a Jew's loyalty in his hour of doubt and soul-searching, and sometimes the former destroyed his belief in the revolutionary movement's "professed internationalism."

The question here is, can we have it both ways? Are we to assume that the "loyalists" were assimilated "non-Jewish Jews" who themselves shared the antisemitic sentiments of their gentile comrades, and that the "deserters" were unassimilated "Jewish Jews" whose cosmopolitan affliction was cured with the advent of "revolutionary antisemitism"? If so, how are we to explain that most Jews, including the "loyalist" majority, reacted in the course of time negatively to the pogroms and to pro-pogrom manifestations in the ranks of their Gentile comrades? Obviously, something is amiss with the cosmopolitan-antisemitic paradigm. Since "faith in socialist cosmopolitanism" was indeed a principal motif among Jewish radicals, it would seem that the other variable of the equation – revolutionary antisemitism – is both insufficient and problematic for analyzing Jewish, as well as Gentile, behavior during the pogrom crises: insufficient because it does not, except through tautological argument (once a cosmopolitan, always a cosmopolitan), explain the continuous revolutionary dedication of most Jews; problematic because it applies the antisemitic brush to the revolutionary movement as a whole, including its unrepentant Jewish participants. Hence, in the first place, is it correct to characterize the revolutionary response to the pogroms in terms of antisemitism and, secondly, is it convincing to consider the "cosmopolitan tautology" a satisfactory explanation for the persistent "revolutionary loyalty" of Jewish socialists? These are the questions that will be addressed in the following pages in an attempt to arrive at a proper assessment of the true nature of the Russian–Jewish socialist reaction to the violent anti-Jewish riots in 1881–2.[5]

The outbreak of massive anti-Jewish riots in southern Russia came as a surprise to Jewish and Gentile revolutionaries alike. Bewilderment and disorientation marked their initial reaction. At the most they sensed some kind of an "inner connection" to the Tsar's assassination on 1 March 1881.[6] However, they soon convinced themselves that this was in fact a *positive connection* linked directly to their own revolutionary expectations. The dust had hardly settled over the first pogroms in Elisavetgrad, Kiev, and other places in the spring of 1881 when many began to herald the pogromshchiki as the vanguard of revolution, as the *enfants terribles* of a spontaneous, popular fury against the oppressive order of autocratic Russia. For them this appeared as the beginning of that revolutionary upheaval which they had dreamt of for years, and had especially expected since the murder of Alexander II. Finally, "the people" had awoken! No longer clamoring for a tsarist "golden charter," they had taken things into their own hands: this was *buntarstvo*, the great rebellion; this was the making of a cataclysmic revolution. True, so far the narod had attacked only the Jews, that stratum of "oppressors" least capable of defending itself – the "weakest link," as it were, in the overall system of oppression. But, as far as they were concerned, there were already numerous signs – pogrom-related attacks on landlords, police, and other officials – to show that in time the riots would lose their anti-Jewish focus and reach out to those who stood behind the Jews, the gentry, and the government. Thus, the task of the revolutionaries was to speed up this process towards a general conflagration by directing the enraged masses away from the Jews against the established order and its true representatives: the Tsar and his officials, the indigenous bourgeoisie, and landed aristocracy.[7] *Summa summarum*, this was the so-called "antisemitic" pro-pogrom attitude of revolutionary Populists.

The "place of honor" in proving the supposedly antisemitic character of revolutionary sympathy with the pogromshchiki has been reserved for Gerasim Grigorevich Romanenko who, in August 1881, issued an extremely pro-pogrom proclamation: "To the Ukrainian People," which is said to have represented the "official position" of Narodnaia Volia.[8] For, as will be elaborated later on, this document bore not only the official imprint of the Executive Committee, but its blatantly anti-Jewish statements were justified by Romanenko in the October issue of the party's official journal, *Narodnaia Volia*.[9] His views, the argument runs, must have been shared by the party since it had apparently sanctioned the printing of the infamous proclamation – and since the document was filled with antisemitic clichés, "the most influential factor shaping the attitude of the narodniki toward the pogroms was outright traditional antisemitism..."[10] According to serious scholarly opinion, there was nothing exceptional or surprising about this antisemitic motif. It had existed in revolutionary circles throughout the 1870s. The pogroms merely brought to the surface such dormant sentiments. The Romanenko proclamation and other less explicitly pro-pogrom statements were seen as "wholly consistent" with this underlying, long-established antisemitic current in the Populist movement. For Elias Tscherikower this is also demonstrated by "the well-known fact" that in contrast to their gentile counterparts, Jewish socialists reacted wholly negatively to the pogroms: since their ideology and revolutionary conviction were similar, antisemitism evidently accounts for their difference in attitude.[11]

Contrary to the "official opinion" of respected historians, a close friend and personal assistant of Pavel Akselrod, V. S. Voitinskii, wrote in 1924 that the positive pro-pogrom response

had nothing in common with antisemitism however: to the majority of revolutionaries the pogroms appeared not as a manifestation of national hostility, not as an attack against people of a certain nationality, but as a broad popular social movement, as a revolt of the impoverished masses against oppressive exploiters that must be followed by other outbursts culminating in a social revolution.[12]

If one accepts this proposition, as I do, one is nonetheless forced to ask: how valid was this perception and expectation of the average revolutionary? Was it not, after all, rooted in antisemitic sentiments which, as many have argued, enabled them to persist in their wishful thinking, shameless Machiavellianism, and apocalyptic Bakuninism?[13]

Leaving aside the question of morality and insensitivity to human suffering (likely to be ignored by the people thinking abstractly of achieving the salvation of mankind), it is only fair and prudent for historians to recognize that the Populists were children of their time and, like anyone else, subject to contemporary prejudices in assessing the pogroms. Thus, it comes as no surprise that, while cognizant of "honest" and "poor" Jews, they usually fell in with the popular stereotyping of Jews as exploiters, swindlers, and usurers – in short, the Jew as the *zhid* who was the curse of the peasantry, their idealized revolutionary clientele.[14] Like any prejudice, this belief had some substance in fact, as was particularly visible in this case. One did not have to be an antisemite to lament the socioeconomic profile and status of nineteenth-century Russian Jewry. Even the *maskilim*, and later on the Zionists, were not immune to the negative images Jews had assumed in the public mind as a consequence of the lopsided Jewish occupational structure. That this fact was generalized and amplified to the point where it lost all resemblance to truth did not, unfortunately, occur to most Russian socialists. Instead of coming to terms with popular misconceptions of Jewish exploitation, they uncritically accepted the negative public image of Jewry and conveniently convinced themselves that the pogroms were directed against Jews as a parasitic class rather than as an ethno-religious entity. But, with the possible exception of Romanenko, there is no evidence that this rationalization and the prejudicial conceptions which fed into it were antisemitically motivated. This was also recognized by Leo Motzkin, an outspoken Zionist critic of revolutionary complicity in the pogroms, who stated in his well-researched report, *Die Judenpogrome in Russland*, that "regardless of how one may describe the revolutionaries' role in the pogroms, it certainly did not emanate organically from antisemitic principles or sentiments."[15]

This exonerating statement still begs for an answer to the question: what prevented the Russian Populists from seeing the pogroms for what they really were – Judeophobic mob violence which harmed the Jewish poor and whose "cheer-leaders" were reactionary monarchist elements? Anti-Jewish prejudices undoubtedly contributed to this blindness. But the full answer must be sought elsewhere: namely, in their emotional and ideological make-up which was rooted in idealization of the narod and the expectation of a revolutionary upheaval.

The assassination of Alexander II had not yielded any political dividends. Instead of gaining a constitution or igniting a revolution, this act of terrorism destroyed Narodnaia Volia organizationally and isolated it more than ever from "the people." A bleak and hopeless future indeed. Short of a miracle, the Narodovoltsy faced a dead-end avenue – in short, political bankruptcy. It must have appeared to many like a miracle when the pogromshchiki "rescued" them from their predicament. In their desperation it was easy enough for them "to read an apocalyptic meaning into the pogroms."[16] Imbued with the Bakuninist romanticism of the peasants' volatile communistic instincts, they did not have to be antisemites to perceive the riots as an authentic expression of popular revolutionary will – of *buntarstvo*. Add to this the old, quintessential Populist notion that the revolutionary activist ought to identify himself with the aspirations of the narod, that he must merge with the peasantry – and a fairly complete picture emerges of what motivated Populists to sympathize with the pogroms. In short, the positive response is best understood as a product of frustrated expectations, Bakuninist *buntarstvo*, and romantic "muzhikophilism." It allowed them to view the pogroms as a revolutionary phenomenon. In this perspective the pogroms could be, and were indeed, seen as signaling the beginning of social revolution; and, by the same token, it made good political sense to utilize the riots as *tactical means* of mobilizing the masses towards desired revolutionary ends.

But how realistic was the belief that the pogroms had the potential of sparking a genuine revolutionary bonfire? Was it, as has been generally argued, merely the *fata morgana* of Populist imagination, a self-serving deception to justify a politically and morally inept Machiavellianism?[17] If we examine these questions in the context of autocratic Russian political culture, we find a sound basis to suggest that, contrary to conventional wisdom, the revolutionaries' apocalyptic hopes were not as irrational as may appear at first glance. For different reasons, the same view was prevalent among officials who were terribly afraid that the riots might get out of hand. This premonition was clearly articulated by the State Comptroller, D. M. Solskii, when he said of the pogromshchiki: "Today they are harassing the Jews... Tomorrow it will be the turn of the so-called kulaks..., then of merchants and landowners. In a word, if the authorities stand by passively, we can expect the development of the most devastating socialism."[18] As can be seen, this view coincided with the revolutionaries' own assessment of the pogroms. Although they exaggerated isolated incidents of pogrom-related attacks against non-Jews, they were essentially right in recognizing that disorders of any kind, originating spontaneously, threatened the social and political fabric of the autocratic state.[19] In this they were definitely less naive than some of their comrades – and latter-day historians – who thought that the pogroms were engineered by the tsarist officials themselves "to divert the Russian people's anger at oppression" to the Jews.[20] As Hans Rogger has demonstrated convincingly, the authorities were more frightened than gratified by the pogroms, which they tried to suppress for precisely the same reasons as the revolutionaries tried to utilize them.[21] The shared expectation that the anti-Jewish disorders might unleash a terrible *buntarstvo* in the countryside was probably unwarranted. Yet, while this may have been an unfounded fear in government circles and an illusionary hope in revolutionary circles, the pogroms nonetheless confirmed rather than contradicted "political reality" as perceived by both the tsarist officials and Populist activists in the wake of Alexander II's assassination: neither questioned the "inner connection" between the pogroms and tsaricide, and the latter had at least as much reason to be "gratified" as the former to be "frightened." Hence, whether or not the revolutionaries resorted shamelessly to a "Machiavellian calculation" in their pro-pogrom behavior is a moot question.[22] For them this was an act of political expediency in a desperate situation; far from being an irrational response nourished by antisemitic sentiment, it was a rational act easily explainable in terms of Populist ideology and contemporary political reality.

The Populists' "gratification" was not unqualified, however, nor was it translated into action. Among the Narodovoltsy this was clearly expressed in their unwillingness to promote the exclusivist anti-Jewish nature of the pogromshchiki's "rebellion," and, above all else, in their opposition to precisely such an attempt by G. G. Romanenko, who resorted to antisemitic agitation to incite "the people" to further pogroms in order to speed up the revolutionary process. At issue was his proclamation, "To the Ukrainian People," in which he wrote:

The people of the Ukraine suffer most of all from the Jews. Who takes the land, the woods, the tavern from out of their hands? The Jews!... Wherever you look, wherever you go – the Jews are everywhere. The Jew curses you, cheats you, drinks your blood... But now as soon as the muzhiki rise up to free themselves from their enemies as they did in Elisavetgrad, Kiev, Smela, the Tsar at once comes to the rescue of the Jews: the soldiers from Russia are called in and the blood of the muzhik, Christian blood, flows... You have begun to rebel against the Jews. You have done well. Soon the revolt will be taken across all of Russia against the Tsar, the *pany* [landowning gentry], the Jews.[23]

The antisemitic rhetoric of this agitational tract went far beyond the accepted ethical and political norms of revolutionary behavior and expediency. With the possible exception of Lev Tikhomirov, all leading Narodovoltsy found Romanenko's unscrupulous demagogy morally and politically reprehensible regardless of his subsequent claim that he was motivated solely by revolutionary considerations.[24] Those socialists who responded positively to the pogroms, always understood that these events made sense only if their perpetrators could be induced to shift their wrath away from the Jewish people to the rich and privileged classes. Instead of fueling the antisemitic violence of the mobs, they meant to redirect this violence into revolutionary non-Jewish channels. Romanenko's agitation invalidated this principle and, as such, was considered a self-defeating exercise.

Utterly appalled by Romanenko's unscrupulous and inexpedient utilization of popular prejudice, members of the almost defunct Executive Committee scurried to destroy all remaining copies of the proclamation.[25] But, alas, too many were already in circulation to undo the damage. They irrevocably tarnished Narodnaia Volia's reputation, not only antagonizing its Jewish membership but also furnishing ample ammunition for historians to "prove" the party's – if not the revolutionary movement's – antisemitism and concomitant "official position."[26] That neither the Narodovoltsy nor the Chernoperedeltsy could bring themselves to disavow publicly the Romanenko proclamation merely compromised them even further in the eyes of their critics. Was this not just another manifestation of the revolutionaries' "antisemitic mood"? Again, the truth lies elsewhere: namely, in their proverbial desire "to have their cake and eat it too" – to have the pogroms *qua* revolution minus antisemitism.

That this was not possible would soon have become obvious to most, had they actually participated in the "pogrom-rebellion", to give it its proper revolutionary twist. To be sure, some did and were "out in the streets, 'on picket duty,'" watching the mob, studying its mood and "doing everything possible to lend the disturbances a revolutionary character'."[27] Predictably, they quickly realized their quixotic role of trying to play the holy "nihilist guard" of revolutionary purity in an unholy mob of antisemitic impurity. But these were isolated incidences of participation and recognition.[28]

For the most part the revolutionaries limited themselves to ambiguous declarations disapproving indiscriminate "beating of Jews" while tacitly approving the "pogrom-rebellion." This duplicity is exemplified in two publications by the Chernoperedeltsy. The first one was issued as a proclamation by the South Russian Union of Workers in Kiev, April 1881, and addressed the pogromshchiki in this pogrom-ridden city in the following words:

Brother workers... You should not beat a Jew [*zhid*] because he is a Jew and prays to his own God – there is, after all, one God for everybody – but because he plunders the people [and] sucks the blood of working men... But the other Jew, who, perhaps, earns his slice of bread through hard work no easier than we do, by some trade or labor, should we plunder him also?... If we are to hit out, then let's hit out at every plundering kulak... at every authority that defends our exploiters, that shoots at the people on behalf of some miserable millionaire [like] Brodskii...[29]

The second publication, an article, appeared in *Zerno*, the workers' paper of the St. Petersburg Chernoperedeltsy, and put forth a similar argument:

Why did they [the pogromshchiki] beat only Jews? Yes, you, brothers, look closely at the Jews themselves and you will see that not all by far are rich, not all are kulaks. There are many poor among them who earn their bread by the sweat of their brow, who are squeezed by kulaks and masters no less than you... Understand that all workers of whatever religion and nation must unite, must work against the common enemy.[30]

But lest the call for universal brotherhood stifle the rebellious instinct of "the people," this passage was followed up with the all too familiar theme of Jewish exploitation: "The Jew owns the bars and taverns, rents the land from the landowners and leases it out to the peasants at two or three times the rate, he buys wheat from the field, goes in for money-lending and charges percentages so high that the people call them simply 'Yiddish' rates."[31] The ambiguity expressed in these two documents speaks for itself and reveals, as J. Frankel notes, "clear signs of inner confusion."[32]

Perhaps representative of a generally more sensitive attitude toward the specifically antisemitic nature of the pogroms on the part of the Chernoperedeltsy, the views expressed in these pronouncements are nonetheless similar in motivation to the positive response of the mainstream Narodovoltsy: namely, to utilize the pogroms for political ends by transforming the energy generated antisemitically into revolutionary power. Thus, instead of condemning the anti-Jewish riots *in toto*, of chastising their perpetrators without qualification, the revolutionaries took care not to insult popular sentiment lest this might endanger their reputation among "the people" or, even worse, create a rift between themselves and the volatile masses – the sole *raison d'être* of their political existence. This sort of inner conflict, between political expediency and higher socialist principles, was also at the source of the failure of prominent Populists like Georgii Plekhanov and Petr Lavrov, neither of whom can be suspected of antisemitism, to take a firm public stand against the pogroms and their most outspoken advocate, G. G. Romanenko.

As the acknowledged leader of the Chernoperedeltsy, both inside and outside Russia, Plekhanov was particularly anxious to clear his party of pogrom complicity. Defending himself years later against the accusation that in 1881–2 neither he nor his comrades openly voiced their opposition to the Romanenko proclamation, Plekhanov insists that, "except for only a few," the Chernoperedeltsy did not share the pro-pogrom attitude of the Narodovoltsy and that, in fact, they were opposed to it.[33] Although this contrasting of respective attitudes is exaggerated, there is much truth in this claim. He rightly notes that in Russia a former Chernoperedelets, Iakov Stefanovich, was instrumental in suppressing the Romanenko "antisemitic declaration of the Executive Committee," and that abroad his own party, as well as other *emigrés*, refused to cooperate with the Narodovoltsy in the publication of a new journal (*Vestnik narodnoi voli*) as long as their leader, Lev Tikhomirov, tolerated the views expressed by Romanenko. Apparently, Tikhomirov yielded to this pressure and even promised to write an article "denouncing the pogroms in the name of the revolutionary movement." For his part, Plekhanov intended to publish a detailed refutation of the pogroms entitled "Socialism and the antisemitic movement."[34] So far so good. There was no lack of good intentions and, as a matter of fact, we do know for certain that Plekhanov and his group of Chernoperedeltsy were deeply distressed when the news of the pogroms reached them in Switzerland.[35]

In defence of Chernyi Peredel, Plekhanov could have cited the protracted attempts of his party to mobilize the revolutionary community abroad to issue a brochure to denounce the pogroms. He preferred not to mention it, for the project never materialized because political expediency prevented its sponsors, including Plekhanov, from renouncing publicly what they repudiated privately. Strictly speaking, they were at a loss how to square their own revolutionary aspirations with the popular antisemitism of their supposed revolutionary clientele, the narod. This dilemma was clearly articulated in Lavrov's response to Pavel Akselrod's request to collaborate in writing the said brochure. Refusing to apply himself to this task, Lavrov justified his decision thus:

I must admit that I consider the [pogrom-Jewish] question extremely complicated, and, practically speaking, highly difficult for a party which seeks to draw near to the people and arouse it against the government. To solve it theoretically, on paper, is very easy. But in view of current popular passions and the necessity of Russian socialists to have the people wherever possible on their side it is quite another matter.[36]

Few disagreed with this assessment of the "practical difficulties" of opposing "popular passions." Thus to remain silent appeared to be most realistic under the circumstances. In other words, they simply dropped the issue of an anti-pogrom declaration because they did

not know how to deal with the so-called "antisemitic movement" in
the context of revolutionary politics. Rather than taking a definite
position one way or another, they were hoping that the whole
pogrom affair would pass into oblivion. That this was on Plekhanov's
mind at the time is clearly shown in his pathetic apologia why he did
not release his own article on the pogroms:

I withdrew [it], since I became unbearably ashamed to demonstrate
truisms [*azbuchnye istiny*]. I admit, in those days I did not think that the
pogroms would continue to erupt periodically. Had I known differently
then, I of course would not have been ashamed of truisms and would have
published my brochure.[37]

The ambiguity which characterized Plekhanov's and Lavrov's
hesitation to state in print their stand on the pogroms was common
to almost all revolutionaries, regardless of whether they responded
positively or, like them, *negatively* to this unsightly spectacle. In either
case, political expediency and ideological abstractions governed
their reaction: it motivated the former to adopt a pro-pogrom
attitude while condemning its extremist manifestation in the form of
Romanenko's proclamation; it inhibited the latter from adopting an
explicitly anti-pogrom attitude in the form of a public criticism of the
document. But neither of the respective responses and failures to
repudiate Romanenko "officially" was conditioned by "the existence of *bona fide* antisemitic sentiments above and beyond the
demands of political expediency" and nourished by "a definitely
antisemitic current in the ranks of the early Russian socialists..."[38]
Surely, antisemitism does not explain why the Romanenko proclamation "called forth an outburst of indignation among the
revolutionaries," nor does it account for their reluctance – as
exemplified by Plekhanov and Lavrov – to vent this indignation
publicly.[39]

Antisemitism aside, are we to conclude that the reluctance of
leading Narodovoltsy and Chernoperedeltsy to take a definite stand
on the pogrom issue "left statements such as Romanenko's as the
official position of the Russian revolutionary movement"?[40] By default,
in a formal sense, the answer is yes. In practice, however, this was
clearly not the case. Although most Populists shared many of
Romanenko's anti-Jewish prejudices and fallacious rationalizations,
they were not prepared to equate their own hazy views of seeing the
pogroms as a touchstone of revolution with his vulgar extremism in

actively encouraging the pogromshchiki's orgy of destruction as a positive act in itself.[41] No revolutionary of any standing, inside or outside Narodnaia Volia, endorsed Romanenko's antisemitic transgression. Evidently, Romanenko had managed to usurp the authority of the Executive Committee which, in the person of Tikhomirov, failed to prevent his proclamation from being printed on its party press. While this blunder does not absolve the Executive Committee from its responsibility, it is wrong to equate the Romanenko proclamation with Narodnaia Volia's or even the revolutionary movement's "official position."[42] Such an interpretation, like its antisemitic correlate, contributes little to our understanding of the Populist response to the pogroms, which, if anything, exhibited many *ambiguous positions*. It obscures the fact that this response was highly differentiated and hardly antisemitic even in its pro-pogrom expression. It simply distorts the complex picture of Populist emotions and motives. Finally, by speciously projecting Romanenko's views on to the movement as a whole, we are ill-equipped to comprehend the reaction of Jewish Populists both to the pogroms in general and the pro-pogrom response of their gentile comrades in particular.

In his skilful analysis of the Russian Populists' apparent pro-pogrom attitude, Leo Motzkin finds it rather intriguing that the presence of many Jews in the revolutionary movement should not have had a corrective influence on their comrades' distorted perception of the pogroms. "Yes," he asks rhetorically, "where were the *Jewish* social revolutionaries, what was their stand?" As he implies, in their ranks there was nothing but silence or, even worse, conformity with the general pro-pogrom sentiment.[43] This, of course, conflicts with Tscherikower's thesis that "the pogroms called forth a completely contrary reaction in all Jewish circles than was the case in [antisemitically inclined] Russian Populist circles."[44] What accounts for these contradictory statements? One reason is undoubtedly that Motzkin, in contrast to Tscherikower, quite rightly does not link antisemitism with revolutionary behavior. The other reason is that both fail to appreciate the complexity of the Jewish response. Just as historians have been overly simplistic in their generalizations of the Gentile response, they have labelled the pogrom reaction of Jewish socialists as either positive or negative – neither of which is entirely true. Moreover, this response varied in time and location.

The initial response of radicalized Jewish youth to the pogroms is perhaps best characterized by Isaak Gurvich who, with reference to his home town, Minsk, writes:

The pogroms made a deep impression on the Jewish public. A Palestinian movement arose among the [local] youth. But we, in our revolutionary circles, remained indifferent to the whole thing. [Like our gentile comrades] we were also under the influence of the theory that the pogroms are a popular uprising [*a folks-oyfstand*], and any *folks-oyfstand* is good. It revolutionizes the masses. Certainly, the Jews suffered as a consequence – but all the same, the gentile revolutionaries of the nobility also called on the peasants to rise up against their fathers and brothers![45]

A similar account emerges from the pages of Abraham Cahan's autobiography. Describing the mood of his Jewish comrades who, like him, were associated with Narodnaia Volia circles in Vilna, Vitebsk, and other places in the northeastern regions of the Pale of Settlement, he states that, while the pogroms caused some Jewish youngsters to rediscover their own people and to work on their behalf for emigration to America or Palestine:

I must admit that these new nationalists comprised only a small group. And Jewish revolutionaries who fell in with the nationalist movement also comprised a small group. Among the Jewish revolutionaries were some who considered the antisemitic massacres to be a good omen. They theorized that the pogroms were an instinctive outpouring of the revolutionary anger of the people, driving the Russian masses against their oppressors. The uneducated Russian people knew that the Czar, the officials and the Jews sucked their blood, they argued. So the Ukrainian peasants attacked the Jews, the "percentniks." The revolutionary torch had been lit and would next be applied to the officials and the Czar himself.[46]

As Cahan admits, he himself was not beyond this sort of reasoning. The same can be said of Gurvich who, just prior to the pogroms, wrote a pamphlet in which he resorted to popular antisemitic sentiments in order to incite the Belorussian peasantry to rebel against the landowners and tavern-owners.[47]

Neither Gurvich nor Cahan, nor the majority of their Jewish comrades experienced the pogroms at first hand. This may well explain their indifference to Jewish suffering, which in many ways was merely an extension of their general indifference, if not hostility, towards traditional Jewish life. For the average Jewish socialist this life, like the tsarist order which sustained its parasitic and backward existence, was doomed to disappear. Unattached to the moorings of Judaism, which for him was "a repulsive religion" and "a form of social parasitism," he could master no affection for his own people.[48] Viewing reality through Populist spectacles, he saw things as did his Gentile peers: Jews were essentially an "unproductive petit-bourgeois, shopkeeping merchant class," the incarnation of social evil; in contrast, peasants were a genuine productive class, "the repository of virtue and the potential architect of a Good Society."[49] To be sure, many Jewish Populists did not wholly subscribe to this distorted black and white dichotomy; and, emotionally, they were never quite at ease with their idealization of the authentic narod at the expense of completely negating the Jewish people. But this uneasiness usually gave way to a higher sense of dedication to a cause that would also benefit the Jews, even though some of them – especially the rich – might suffer as a result of socialistically inspired pogroms. As one historian put it rather felicitously, "just as Abraham felt he had to break a personal tie in order to display devotion to a higher being, so Jewish revolutionaries, too, compulsively disavowed their Jewish ties and ignored immediate injustices for the sake of a higher cause."[50] Like their comrades of the gentry, they would have to sacrifice their own kind on the altar of revolutionary progress. Thus, already alienated and often physically remote from the Jewish world, the response of committed Jewish socialists to the pogrom was conditioned by a misplaced sense of loyalty that was rooted in their identification with the revolutionary movement and its lofty ideals. Consequently, they at best remained indifferent to the victims of the pogromshchiki or at worst promoted their action. Indeed, notes Abraham Cahan, who himself had been under this spell of indifference:

in their blind theorizing according to preconceived formulas, most of the active Jewish Nihilists shut their eyes to the actual state of things and joined their gentile comrades in applauding the riots as an encouraging sign of the times as "a popular revolutionary protest."[51]

This indifference did not last for long, however. Neither their ideological blinkers nor their emotional attachment to the revolutionary movement could prevent them from seeing and sensing the exclusively antisemitic nature of the so-called *folks-oyfstand*. How this "awakening" occurred has been graphically illustrated by M. B. Ratner, a Populist and latter-day Socialist Revolutionary, who related the story of one Jewish Narodovolets for whom the Kiev pogrom of April 1881 was a real eye-opener. In anticipation of witnessing the revolutionary transformation of the riot, this individual -- wearing a red blouse in peasant fashion -- mingled with the pogromshchiki to observe and possibly encourage their primeval rebellious instincts. But when the mobs had completed their destructive work in the poorest quarters of the Jewish community, he witnessed with horror that they had no desire whatsoever to carry on the "rebellion" against the bourgeoisie and the authorities. So devastating was his disillusionment that he almost went mad in his recognition of the "actual state of things."[52]

For most Jewish revolutionaries such an "enlightening experience" was not readily available, nor indeed necessary, to raise grave doubts about the wisdom of supporting the pogroms. Less drastic, but in the long run equally effective, in changing their attitude was their growing awareness that the pogroms were directed against the impoverished Jewish masses as an ethno-religious group, rather than as a social class of exploiters. A good example of this process of recognition relates to the already mentioned pro-pogrom proclamation which Isaak Gurvich had prepared on behalf of the Jewish Chernoperedeltsy and Narodovoltsy in Minsk. Commenting on this affair, Gurvich reminisced:

Well, I wrote this proclamation in which...I called on the peasants of the Vilna, Minsk, and Mogilev provinces to rise up against landowners and innkeepers. I gave the proclamation to Grinfest [printer of the *Chernyi Peredel* press in Minsk]. Several days later I met him again and asked what he thought of my proclamation. He told me rather nicely that it had been decided not to print the proclamation because of its appeal [to the peasants] to beat land-and-tavern owners alike. "Who are those innkeepers in the villages? Aren't they all Jewish paupers?" – he asked me. I agreed with him...Perhaps, you might say that it was class instinct which spoke in him: his father owned a tavern...He knew from experience that the poor Jewish innkeeper of that time had nothing in common with the rich gentile innkeeper of central Russia who was the owner of the whole village.[53]

Once the pogroms were in full swing, Grinfest's objections became ever more relevant and quickly gained support among his friends who, at first, had been rather ecstatic about the "pogrom-rebellion." This sense of growing disillusionment is well documented by their reaction to the original manuscript of the already cited pogrom article of the St. Petersburg section of Chernyi Peredel, which they were supposed to print for *Zerno*, the party's paper for workers. I. Getsov, one of the printers of the Minsk press, noted years later:

The article was written in an agitational tone, viewing the pogroms as the beginning of revolution. [It] encouraged the people to continue, and to move on against the police and landowners. On us, the typesetters, this article had a repulsive effect. Unanimously, we decided not to print it. However, it was necessary to bring its author to reason... This mission was entrusted to me. With the article in my pocket I hurried to St. Petersburg. To Zagorskii's [the author's] credit it must be said that I had no difficulty convincing him that these pogroms were not a class movement, but were based on superstition, prejudices, misunderstandings, etc., that its victims were in general as impoverished and proletarian as the *pogromshchiki* themselves; that this was the doing of the government agents to fight the revolution and also of capitalist exploiters [resenting Jewish competition]. Zagorskii listened to me without objections, destroyed the article and immediately wrote another, completely different in spirit. Triumphantly, I returned [to Minsk] by the next train... I was happy and my comrades were delighted.[54]

As Getsov points out, the Chernoperedeltsy abroad were equally delighted with the revised article when it appeared a month later in *Zerno*.[55] Clearly, the disillusioned Minsk Chernoperedeltsy had taken the initiative in disassociating their party from prevailing pro-pogrom sentiments. Yet, their negative reaction to the pogroms did not translate into a complete rejection of the whole phenomenon.

As shown in the previous discussion of the *Zerno* article, this document was still ambiguous, even after it had been rewritten in a "completely different spirit." That the Jewish Chernoperedeltsy were nevertheless "happy" with the final version shows that they themselves shared an ambivalence which, as in the case of their Gentile comrades, merely showed that they were still very much under the influence of Populist abstractions and political thinking. But, all the same, elated they were! Perhaps rightly so, since it must have given them great emotional satisfaction that they had been able to convince others of the immorality and inexpediency of supporting the pogroms *in toto*. Their joy was considerably dampened, however, with the release of the Romanenko proclamation.[56] It might have been a consolation to them had they known that this tract called forth a similar response among the Jewish Narodovoltsy as their own to the original *Zerno* article.

For a long time it has been assumed "that the text of the proclamation had been approved by a member of the Executive Committee who was Jewish by nationality..."[57] Calling the culprit by name, Lev Deich accused Savelii Zlatopolskii – the only Jewish member of the Committee in 1881 – for having sanctioned "the cowardly proclamation" (*di nidertrekhtige proklamatsie*).[58] In an attempt to clear the "good name" of Zlatopolskii once and for all, A. N. Pribyleva brought up the issue in her memoirs:

In January 1882…I was in St. Petersburg together with Zlatopolskii, and often happened to witness how he, time and again, objected to the [anti-Jewish] theme of the proclamation. He was not able to talk quietly about it. Each time he was in a state of strong emotional distress. He said that the proclamation left an indelible stain on the reputation of the Executive Committee, and that under no circumstances could he forgive the Committee for such an action. When the proclamation was published in Moscow, Zlatopolskii was preoccupied with current affairs in St. Petersburg. However, knowing about its appearance, he dropped everything and went to Moscow. There, he immediately forced the decision to destroy the proclamation.[59]

Thus, instead of sanctioning the proclamation, Zlatopolskii was responsible for its removal. Like his fellow-Jews in Chernyi Peredel, he vigorously opposed extremist pro-pogrom statements and, like them, he was fully supported by his comrades in Narodnaia Volia (except that, unlike Zagorskii, Romanenko did not rescind his views).

Unfortunately, the ill-functioning Committee was in no position to destroy the proclamation completely despite energetic efforts by leading Narodovoltsy.[60] In the absence of effective controls over local circles and a clear policy statement denouncing the proclamation, it was inevitable that some copies should remain in circulation.[61] That nonetheless only a few were distributed in the provinces was also due to the fact that Jewish Narodovoltsy in Odessa and other places had refused to distribute the proclamation.[62] Like their "star" in the Executive Committee, these "lower-rank" activists were unwilling to cooperate in Romanenko's illicit enterprise.

Ironically, several weeks prior to the Romanenko leaflet, Jewish Narodovoltsy in Vilna had issued a proclamation in Yiddish in which they announced:

Jews! – they try to tell you that we, the Nihilists, have been inciting the mobs against you. Do not believe it, we are not your enemies. This has been done by government agents in order to direct the wrath of the agitated people away from the government against you. Now you know who your enemies are.[63]

This document clearly marked a reversal of previous pro-pogrom attitudes. Accounting for this change, it has been rightly noted that

the revolutionary circles in Vilna consisted of Jewish intellectuals who, in such centres of Jewish population like Vilna, could not overlook the large number of Jewish proletarians. Therefore, it was easier for them to find the right standpoint toward the pogroms... [64]

This evidently was also the case with Jewish revolutionaries elsewhere. For instance, despite their Populist disposition and alienation from Jewish life, the Minsk Chernoperedeltsy were still sufficiently embedded in Jewish reality to recognize more quickly than many of their Gentile comrades that they had been mistaken in their positive perception of the pogroms. Because of this, but also because of a lingering sense of Jewish identity (clearly visible in Grinfest and Zlatopolskii), the Jewish radicals in Vilna, Minsk, Odessa, and other locales woke up to the foolishness of equating anti-Jewish violence with revolutionary virtue. Hence, from an initial sense of indifference to, and/or approval of, the pogroms, Jewish socialists had undergone a process of disillusionment which, quite soon after the inception of the riots, caused them to oppose pro-pogrom manifestations – so much so that they played a crucial role in fostering anti-pogrom sentiments in both parties. Yet, what was still lacking was an all-party resolution in the spirit of the Vilna declaration.

The attempts and eventual failure to come up with such a declaration went right to the heart of the dilemma facing Jewish socialists, especially those who insisted that the revolutionaries must publicly repudiate the antisemitic dimension of the pogroms and its approbation by people like Romanenko. This concern was particularly pronounced among Jewish *émigrés*. Unlike their compatriots in Russia, they had no illusions about the pogroms and were deeply disturbed by the bad news. Expressing this mood, Rozaliia Plekhanova wrote:

Deep down in the soul of each of us, revolutionaries of Jewish birth, there was a sense of hurt pride and infinite pity for our own, and many of us were strongly tempted to devote ourselves to serving our injured, humiliated and persecuted people. [65]

Since, however, they could not envisage "a return to the Jewish people" at the expense of leaving the revolutionary movement, the least they felt compelled to do was to let the Jews know that the revolution had not forsaken them. Tragically, this desire to fulfil their moral obligation as Jews yielded no concrete results, even though one of their comrades, Pavel Akselrod, had already drawn up a brochure to this effect. The brochure in question was none other than the one for which Akselrod had unsuccessfully sought Lavrov's assistance.[66]

The genesis and demise of the Akselrod brochure testify to what one historian has termed "a conflict between Jewish loyalty and revolutionary dedication."[67] As far as "Jewish loyalty" was concerned, the pogroms caused almost all Jewish revolutionaries, sooner or later, and to varying degrees, to rediscover their Jewishness and to identify more closely with the predicament of their own people. This change of attitude, and the vocal anti-pogrom manifestations on the part of outspoken Jewish Chernoperedeltsy and Narodovoltsy elicited, as we have seen, a sympathetic and accommodating response from their Gentile comrades. But when faced with the reality of revolutionary politics, the failure of their respective parties to renounce publicly pro-pogrom statements, Jewish revolutionaries were caught in the dilemma of how to reconcile their Jewish sensibilities with "revolutionary dedication" — sentiments that appeared irreconcilable at a time when nationalism and socialism were considered mutually exclusive by Russian socialists. Although it occurred to some – even prior to the pogroms – that there was not necessarily a conflict between the two, for most the *Zeitgeist* dictated that a choice had to be made between "Jewish national" or "Russian revolutionary" loyalty.[68] The process of taking sides was extremely tortuous and many wavered before deciding whether their loyalty belonged to the Jewish people or, ultimately, to the Russian revolutionary movement.

What made this process so tortuous? What were the ingredients which tipped the scale this way or that in what has been considered an unprecedented "crisis of consciousness" among Russian–Jewish socialists? Was it merely a question of "faith in socialist cosmopolitanism" that was more prevalent in some than others, or were there additional factors which perhaps proved more decisive in making the tragic choice to "go national" or to remain a Russian socialist? To answer these questions let us turn to three Jewish revolutionaries: Grigorii Gurevich, Pavel Akselrod, and Lev Deich, all intimately involved with the unsuccessful venture of an anti-pogrom brochure.

The Narodovolets Gurevich personified those Jews for whom it was seemingly least difficult to break ties with the Russian revolutionary movement. Having been most persistent in demanding an anti-pogrom declaration, he was utterly disappointed when his efforts brought forth nothing but the stillborn Akselrod brochure.[69] Consequently, he felt there was no longer any future for Jews in a movement which was prepared to sacrifice a whole people for the sake of humanity's salvation. He broke his long-standing ties with the revolutionary movement and, after a short spell of passionate advocacy of Palestinian emigration, dedicated himself solely to Jewish affairs, both as a writer for Russian–Jewish journals and as a secretary of the Jewish community in Kiev, where he was also active as a member of the local chapter of Zionist–Socialist territorialists.[70]

But Gurevich was not representative of the choice made by most Jewish revolutionaries. More characteristic for resolving – or perhaps repressing – the conflict between "Jewish loyalty" and "revolutionary dedication" was the capitulation to *political expediency* in the name of *revolutionary solidarity* of Pavel Akselrod and Lev Deich. They both abhorred the pogroms and were in agreement that their party, Chernyi Peredel, should issue an appropriate statement in cooperation with Narodnaia Volia. But when Akselrod applied himself to this task, in the form of a brochure addressed to "the Jewish socialist youth," Deich strongly disagreed with its format and ideas. While the actual content of this document need not detain us here, the Deich–Akselrod correspondence relating to it is of considerable interest. It offers a rare insight into what motivated Jewish socialists to remain loyal to the revolutionary movement not only in spite of, but also because of the pogroms.[71]

Akselrod felt that the pogroms demanded a fresh look at the Jewish Question and the role of Jewish revolutionaries in the movement. Under the influence of Gurevich, he seriously considered including in his brochure the idea of emigration to Palestine for Jews persecuted in Russia.[72] This reasoning was not well received by Deich who, speaking on behalf of the Geneva Chernoperedeltsy, declared:

We, as socialist-internationalists, should not at all recognize special obligations toward "co-nationals" [*soplemenniki*] ... Of course, we do not say that one ought to remain indifferent ... But our approach to the [Jewish] problem must be based on a universal-socialist standpoint that seeks to fuse nationalities instead of isolating one nationality [the Jews] still more than is already the case. Therefore ... do not advise them to move to Palestine where they will only become still further frozen in their prejudices ... If they are to emigrate – then [let them go] to America where they will merge with the local population.[73]

In his argument Deich derived much strength from the fact that his "universal-socialist standpoint" had been reinforced by an international authority, the French geographer and anarchist Elisee Reclus, who, wrote Gurevich, "categorically dissuaded us [Jewish socialists] from devoting ourselves to the colonization of Palestine" because it is "a country unsuited for settlement – there Jews could live only by trade and exploitation of the native population."[74] The message was clear: instead of helping Jews, conditions in Palestine would reproduce the age-old pattern of "unproductive" Jewish existence and, consequently, generate conflicts between Jews and Arabs – the local "productive" population. Even for a fervent *Palestinets* like Gurevich, this uninviting prospect was sufficient for him to discard "completely the question of Palestinian colonization."[75] Needless to say, Akselrod followed suit. Though for him there was another "major motive" that militated more than anything else against the idea "to transform Palestine into a Jewish fatherland": namely Elisee Reclus' "comment that [Jews] would clash ... with the Arabs for whom Palestine is their fatherland not only according to tradition, but also [by virtue of] actual [residence]."[76]

For Deich the Palestinian solution, like any other issue concerned with Jewish rather than "universal-socialist" interests, was tainted by nationalism and, therefore, beneath serious consideration. That does not mean that Deich did not care about the misfortunes of his "co-nationals."[77] But, as is obvious from his correspondence with Akselrod, Deich refused to deal with the pogrom question in any other context than prescripted by universal socialist principles. Thus, he also objected to Akselrod's suggestion, as spelled out in the brochure, that "the cosmopolitan idea of socialism" should not prevent Jews from upholding the legitimate interests of "the Jewish masses" and from being active in a Jewish environment.[78] This, Akselrod stated, ought to be the proper task of Jewish socialists, to which they must apply themselves immediately "by working among the masses to create, in alliance with Russian revolutionaries, the possibility of quick political and social change" – a change which best serves "a radical solution of 'the Jewish Question'," that is, the transformation of Jews into "productive elements" and their

amalgamation with "corresponding strata of the 'native' population."[79] All this did not sit well with Deich. In his opinion, a
socialist statement addressing Jews and their plight would have to be
devoid of national sentiment. He, as well as his Russian comrades,
had envisaged a brochure that was not concerned with the *Jewish*
tasks of socialist Jews, but merely with the tasks of explaining to Jews
in general the socioeconomic causes of the pogroms, the need to
cooperate with the revolutionary movement in its fight for universal
emancipation, and the necessity of merging with other nationalities
of Russia.[80] Anything that went beyond this framework of reference
was not only utopian, but also smacked of nationalist deviation – a
heresy which served neither the revolutionary cause nor the long-
term resolution of the Jewish Question.

In the meantime ideological disagreements were increasingly
overshadowed by political considerations which had been raised by
Lavrov in his letter to Akselrod. As we know, Lavrov thought it
inadvisable to publish an anti-pogrom brochure because of the
inherent dilemma of alienating precisely those people – the narod –
whom the Populists wanted to mobilize against the tsarist state.
While Akselrod was reluctant to comply with the demands of
political expediency, Deich fully accepted Lavrov's "realism."
Adding his own comments to the aforementioned letter, he told
Akselrod:

I agree fully with the thoughts expressed by Petr Lavrov. Realistically, in
practice, the Jewish Question is now almost insoluble for the revolutionaries.
What, for example, are they to do now in Balta where they beat up the
Jews? To intercede for them means, as Reclus says, "to call up the hatred
of the peasants against the revolutionaries who not only killed the Tsar but
also defend the Jews."...This is simply a dead-end avenue for Jews and
revolutionaries alike...Of course, it is our utmost obligation to seek equal
rights for the Jews...but that, so to speak, is activity in the higher spheres;
and to conduct pacificatory agitation among the people is presently very,
very difficult for the party. Do not think that this [situation] has not pained
and confused me...but all the same, I remain always a member of the
Russian revolutionary party and do not intend to part from it even for a
single day, for this contradiction, like some others, was of course not created
by the party.[81]

Exasperated by Akselrod's refusal to accept Lavrov's verdict, Deich,
in a highly emotional letter, appealed to him not to publish his
brochure for the sake of revolutionary solidarity. Replying to a
previous comment by Akselrod that not even the German Social

Democrats demanded "to such an extent the suppression of individual views in deference to party and personal ties," Deich brushed such a comparison aside and pleaded with him "not to write the brochure, not so much for party reasons as for *personal* considerations for a small group of former Chernoperedeltsy who find themselves in extraordinary circumstances where they need the tightest unity, a terrible solidarity, to have some influence [on the revolutionary movement]..." Hence, Deich, declared, "in view of precisely *such* a solidarity, we do not want your brochure."[82] Akselrod, in the end, yielded to Deich's reasoning and quietly shelved his brochure without ever again mentioning the pogroms of 1881 or raising the subject of a Jewish "going to the people."[83]

Was it simply an unimpaired belief in "socialist cosmopolitanism," buttressed by demands of solidarity, which compelled Deich and Akselrod, and so many others like them, to give in to the demands of political expediency? Why, in short, was their disillusionment superseded by a reaffirmation of revolutionary loyalty? A principal motive in all this was unquestionably their strong belief that any and all social problems could be resolved by a socialist restructuring of the world, and that therefore the Jewish Question as well must be answered with a revolution inaugurating "the dream of a happy, united humanity..."[84] But this was only half the story. An equally, if not more, important motif in their pro-Russian revolutionary choice was the existential-emotional attachment which claimed Jewish socialists to the movement – a motif which surfaced in Deich's letters to Akselrod, last but not least in his appeal for "terrible solidarity."

This "terrible solidarity" assumes a much more complex meaning in defining the relationship of Jews in the revolutionary movement than that of individual subordination to the will of the Gentile majority. It symbolizes their personal identification with a group of people that accepted them as equals and judged them according to their norms and values. What this meant in terms of "deserting" the movement because of pro-pogrom attitudes has been lucidly described by Abraham Cahan in his fictional rendering of Jewish–Gentile relations in Narodnaia Volia.[85] The heroine of his novel

was under the sway of two forces...One of these forces was...[personal loyalty to gentile friends in the movement]; the other was Public Opinion – the public opinion of underground Russia. According to the moral standard of that Russia everyone who did not share in the hazards of the revolutionary movement was a "careerist," a self-seeker absorbed exclusively in the feathering of his own nest; the Jew who took the special interests of his own race specially to heart was a narrow-minded nationalist, and the Nihilist who withdrew from the movement was a renegade. The power which this "underground" public opinion exerted over her was all the greater because of *the close ties of affection* which...bound the *active* revolutionaries to each other... The notion of these people thinking of her as a renegade was too horrible to be indulged in for a single moment.[86]

Ultimately, these emotions proved more powerful than "socialist cosmopolitanism." The latter was a necessary, but not sufficient cause in motivating Jews to remain loyal to their revolutionary calling. Without the bonds of friendship, common experience, and sentiment linking Jew and Gentile, there would have been little other than intangible ideological reasons to sustain a Jewish socialist in his "crisis of consciousness."

For the average revolutionary Jew the movement was more than just a political association seeking the millennium. It was for all practical purposes the only place where he felt "at home," where love and marriage between Jew and Gentile was the norm that foreshadowed the new world in the making. This was no abstract cosmopolitanism; this was a daily experience of "intimate comradeship and mutual devotion."[87] This was an existential experience that went much deeper than any formal sense of party loyalty. It permeated the whole being of those Jews who were deeply embedded in the social and spiritual world of revolutionary Populism. Thus, regardless of how much they may have suffered from witnessing the brutal persecution of their "own race," they suffered even more from the prospect of ostracism by "underground public opinion" – the opinion of people who meant more to them than anything else.[88]

This existential dimension of revolutionary loyalty did not, of course, apply to all socialist Jews equally. There were some like Gurevich who, while rendering invaluable service to the movement, had always been rooted more in a Jewish than Russian setting. Generally, they were active either in predominantly Jewish circles in Russia and abroad or else stood on the periphery of the movement.[89] Thus, their identity was never entirely rooted in the *Lebenswelt* of revolutionary Populism. Consequently, when the anti-Jewish riots erupted and touched off a general soul-searching, they were much less vulnerable than others to the pressures of "underground opinion" in reassessing their role within the movement. Peer pressure and "intimate comradeship" were not overriding factors in their deliberation whether or not to remain a Russian socialist. For them the issue was really that their gentile comrades had not lived up to the very principles of international socialism. Far from being the supranational spokesmen of all the disadvantaged people of Russia, in tolerating and abetting the pogroms, they had revealed themselves as narrow-minded socialists – or, even worse, as Russian chauvinists – who excluded the Jews from the brotherhood of international proletarians. In this they had violated precisely that universal humanistic premise of socialism which had motivated and sustained Gurevich and others in joining and serving the Russian revolutionary movement. Now, they felt deceived by its parties. Largely uninhibited by personal-existential considerations, they responded without moral qualms in trading in their erstwhile revolutionary loyalty for a return to the Jewish people. What they had lost in this "exchange of loyalties" was not, however, so much their "faith in socialist cosmopolitanism" (which, evidently, many retained since they remained socialists – albeit of "Jewish de-nomination"), but their faith in the Russian revolutionary move-ment as the guardian of socialist purity in Russia. Hence, the real reason for their change of allegiance was not disillusionment with socialism and its cosmopolitan ideals *per se*, but rather the absence of irrevocable existential ties to their erstwhile comrades-in-arms.

For those bound by these ties "socialist cosmopolitanism" remained the credo of the "socialist church" in Russia. As active members of revolutionary groups and Narodnaia Volia, they were wholly absorbed in the daily affairs of the revolutionary movement, a world which subsumed their whole mode of existence. Short of outright antisemitism, there was nothing persuasive enough to make them leave the "church." This option was available only to the Gureviches who, unlike the Deiches, were less embedded in the Russian revolutionary community – or to put it differently – much less well equipped to withstand the "nationalist challenge" of the pogroms.

Returning to the cosmopolitan-antisemitic paradigm that has governed much of historical scholarship on the Russian and Jewish response to the pogroms, it is safe to conclude that this conceptual framework suffers from serious shortcomings. "Socialist cosmopoli-tanism" was definitely not a defining characteristic which set "loyalists" and "deserters" apart. This "faith" was shared by all Jewish socialists and, therefore, cannot be considered a *decisive variable* in their choice to leave or remain in the revolutionary movement. More appropriately, it was a *constant* in the complex equation of factors which were at work in the "tortuous process" of choosing sides. At stake was really their faith in the Russian revolutionary movement – and here the *decisive variable* was the degree to which Jews identified themselves with the revolutionary community, which in itself was largely a function of their sociological embeddedness.[90] The only other variable which could have cancelled the existential attachment tying Jews to their Gentile comrades would have been antisemitism among the latter. But there was very little of it. Indeed, Jewish socialists themselves – including most "deserters" – denied the existence of "revolutionary antisemitism."

Few would have agreed with Tscherikower's statements that antisemitism was rife among the revolutionaries of the 1870s and that in the early 1880s its "symptoms boldly surfaced" with "the well-known antisemitic proclamation issued by Narodnaia Volia."[91] The first to object to this would have been the prominent Narodovolets Aron Zundelevich, whom Tscherikower called "the most Jewish of Jewish revolutionaries."[92] Taking his friend Deich to task for his partisan zeal in accusing Narodnaia Volia of antisemitism, Zundelevich wrote to him:

It does not please me that you have repeatedly stated in print that the pogrom proclamation of Romanenko was a manifestation of antisemitism...This was a distortion of revolutionary enthusiasm, a deformation of the idea of revolution which [some] were prepared to achieve by any means. As little as the golden charter proves that you were a monarchist, does this Romanenko proclamation prove that Narodnaia Volia was antisemitic... [Thus,] leave this theme alone.[93]

Zundelevich's opinion was probably shared by Gurevich, who in his explanation as to why he left the party does not refer to its supposed antisemitism or anti-Jewish prejudices. He was simply appalled by what Zundelevich called the "deformation of the idea of revolution," the unscrupulous implementation of the notion that the end justifies the means.[94] Moreover, both would have objected to the claim that "the antisemitic mood" was already felt in the 1870s.[95] There were certainly anti-Jewish prejudices, but these were generally equally prevalent among Jewish socialists. In any case, they did not equate these prejudices with traditional Judeophobia. Thus, as Isaak Gurvich said "[we] did not feel any antisemitism in the [radical] intellectual circles" of the 1870s.[96] Rather the contrary was the case, as Solomon Chudnovskii, for example, found during the Odessa pogrom of 1871. This "sad event" deepened his commitment to the revolutionary cause because his Gentile comrades, especially the future leader of Narodnaia Volia, Andrei Zheliabov, shared his indignation at what had happened and agreed with his conclusion that "the existing political and economic order of things" was to be blamed for the mob violence against the Jews. Their solidarity deeply impressed Chudnovskii and solidified his faith in the Russian revolutionary movement and its socialist goals of universal emancipation.[97]

As in 1871, the pogroms of 1881–2 ultimately had the same effect on Jewish socialists. They were gratified that the majority of their comrades responded to their disapproval of extremist anti-Jewish declarations designed to fuel a "pogrom-rebellion." In the end, the pogrom crisis actually cleansed the movement of its anti-Jewish prejudices, with the result that after 1884 it was no longer in good taste to greet popular antisemitic outbursts as manifestations of the "people's" revolutionary temperament. As for Jewish radicals themselves, the pogroms heightened their sense of Jewish self-awareness and made them more sensitive to the suffering of their "own race," which, in turn, drew them even closer to the revolutionary movement as the only alternative route to win Jewish political and social emancipation in Russia.

NOTES

1 J. Frankel, *Prophecy and Politics. Socialism, Nationalism, and the Russian Jews, 1862–1917* (Cambridge, 1981), 97–8, 107–8. See also: L. Greenberg, *The Jews in Russia*, 2 vols. (New York, 1976), II: 160–70; L. S. Dawidowicz, *The Golden Tradition* (Boston, 1968), 47–8; E. Goldhagen, "The ethnic consciousness of early Russian Jewish Socialists," *Judaism*, XXIII (1973), 490–2.

2 [E. Tscherikower], "Nationalist and revolutionary ideologies among Russian Jewry," in *The Early Jewish Labor Movement in the United States* (New York, 1961), 39–40. This work is a substantially revised and shortened edition of Tscherikower's original Yiddish version, *Geshikhte fun der yidisher arbeterbavegung in di fareynikte shtatn* (New York, 1945). For the cited statement of Tscherikower in this edition, see his much more detailed and unabridged chapter 3, 149 (hereafter cited as Tscherikower, *Geshikhte*). See also E. Tscherikower, "Yidn-revolutsionern in rusland in di 6oer un 7oer yorn," *Historishe shriftn*, III (Vilna, 1939), 172. This view has also been accepted by Stephen M. Berk in his article

"The Russian revolutionary movement and the pogroms," *Soviet Jewish Affairs*, vii, 2 (1977), 36. Jonathan Frankel, whom we have cited above as an exponent of the "revolutionary" nationalist response, qualifies his standpoint later on in accordance with Tscherikower's more cautious assessment (see *Prophecy and Politics*, 119–20).

3 Frankel, *Prophecy and Politics*, 98; Tscherikower, "Yidn-revolutsionern" 172; Berk, "Russian revolutionary movement," 36. For a good study on the cosmopolitanism of Russian Jewish socialists see the already cited article of Goldhagen, "Ethnic consciousness," 485–90.

4 Greenberg, *Jews in Russia*, ii: 163. Cf., Tscherikower, *Geshikhte*, 177–8; and Dawidowicz, *Golden Tradition*, 47.

5 Since this analysis is limited to the two principal parties of Russian revolutionary Populism in the early 1880s, Chernyi Peredel and Narodnaia Volia, some of my conclusion may not apply to the radical Jewish intelligentsia in general, but only to Jews who were organizationally associated with, or in some ways active in, these two revolutionary groupings.

6 V. S. Voitinskii and B. I. Nikolaevskii, eds., *Iz arkhiva P. B. Aksel'roda, 1881–1896* (Berlin, 1924), 215.

7 This characterization of the revolutionaries' pro-pogrom attitude is derived from: [V. Zhebunyev], "Iz derevni" and "Po povedu evreiskikh besporiadkov," *Listok Narodnoi Voli* (22 July 1881; 20 July 1883); [G. G. Romanenko], "Vnutrennee obozrenie," *Narodnaia Volia*, 6 (23 October 1881) – in *Literatura partii Narodnaia Volia* (n.p., 1905), 388–96, 622–6, 419–39. "Pis'mo s iuga" and "Iz Elizavetgradskogo uczda," *Chernyi Peredel*, 8–9 (September 1881) and 5 (December 1881), in *Chernyi Peredel. Organ sotsialistov federalistov. 1880–1881 g. Pamiatniki agitatsionnoi literatury*, 1 (Moscow, 1923), 303–7, 345–9.

8 Frankel, *Prophecy and Politics*, 113; M. Kiei, "The Jewish Narodnik," *Judaism*, xix (1970) 309; Tscherikower, *Geshikhte*, 174–6; A. B. Ulam, *In the Name of the People* (New York, 1977), 371. See also Berk, "Russian revolutionary movement," 25; and Dawidowicz, *Golden Tradition*. This view has also been accepted by M. Mishkinsky in his otherwise excellent article "The attitude of the Southern-Russian Workers' Union toward the Jews (1880–1), "*Harvard Ukrainian Studies*, vi (June 1982): see especially 209–10, where he contrasts the more qualified position of the Union, and by implication of the Chernoperedeltsy in general, toward the pogroms as a revolutionary phenomenon. The full text of Romanenko's proclamation ("Ispolnitel'nyi komitet ukrains'komu narodu") is cited by S. Valk in his article "G. G. Romanenko (Iz istorii 'Narodnoi Voli')," *Katorga i ssylka*, xlviii (1928): 50–2 (in Ukrainian).

9 [Romanenko], "Vnutrennee obozrenie," in *Literatura*, p. 439.

10 Greenberg, *Jews in Russia*, ii: 163; Cf. Berk, "Russian revolutionary movement," 35–6; E. Silberner, *Sozialisten zur Judenfrage* (Berlin, 1962), 277–8.

11 Tscherikower, *Geshikhte*, 174–5, and "Yidn-revolutsionern," 171–2;

Berk, "Russian revolutionary movement," 24–5, 36; Greenberg, *Jews in Russia*, II: 163–4. Of those who equate the Romanenko proclamation with "the official position of the Russian revolutionary movement," Frankel is the only one who does not "fortify" his interpretation with antisemitic explanations (*Prophecy and Politics*, 113).

12 V. S. Voitinskii, introduction to P. Akselrod's "O zadachakh evreisko-sotsialisticheskoi intelligentsii," in *Iz arkhiva Aksel'roda*, 215.

13 Greenberg, *Jews in Russia*, II: 162–3; Berk, "Russian revolutionary movement," 25, 35–6; Tscherikower *Geshikhte*, 176–78; Ulam, *Name*, 369–72.

14 [Romanenko], "Vnutrennee obozrenie," 425–31; [Zhebunyev], "Iz derevni," 390–2; "Iz Elizavetgradskogo uezda," 345–6; "Pis'mo s iuga," 303–4. For a good analysis of this prejudice, see Aksel'rod, "O zadachakh evreisko-sotsialisticheskoi intelligentsii," 222–4; and A. Linden [Leo Motzkin], "Prototype des Pogroms in den achtziger Jahren," in *Die Judenpogrome in Russland*, ed. Zionistische Hilfsfonds (Cologne, 1909), 46–66.

15 [Motzkin], "Prototype des Pogroms," 59.

16 Frankel, *Prophecy and Politics*, 101.

17 Without exception all historians, regardless of their views on "revolutionary antisemitism," have condemned the revolutionaries' attitudes in these terms. See especially: Greenberg, *Jews in Russia*, II: 162–3; Berk, "Russian revolutionary movement," 26–9; [Motzkin], "Prototype des Pogroms," 51–2, 53–5, 64; Goldhagen, "Ethnic consciousness," 492–4.

18 Cited in H. Rogger, "Government, Jews, peasants and land in post-emancipation Russia," in *Jewish Policies and Right-Wing Politics in Imperial Russia* (London, 1986), 143. In later pogroms the same concern was voiced in government circles (ibid., 163, 172).

19 What Solskii only predicted in case of government inaction had already been seen developing by the revolutionaries. They argued that there was evidence to show that the riots were not only directed against Jews, but also against Russian landowners and "private property" in general, and that moreover "the crowds [are heard saying] let's finish off the Jews and then we'll take care of the Russians." And when the government finally deployed troops to suppress the pogroms, the revolutionaries were quick to point out that "the people" reacted by attacking the police and soldiers as well ([Romanenko], "Vnutrennee obozrenie," 426–9, 434–7; [Zhebunyev], "Iz derevni," 390–2; "Iz Elizavetgradskogo uezda," 347–9; "Pis'mo s iuga," 304–6).

20 H. Rogger, "The Jewish policy of late tsarism: a reappraisal," in *Jewish Policies*, 28.

21 H. Rogger, "Russian ministers and the Jewish Question, 1881–1917," in *Jewish Policies*, 61. In this and the above cited articles, Rogger has finally laid to rest the myth that the tsarist authorities – directly or

indirectly – instigated the pogroms to diffuse popular hostility against the state. That the government itself was taken by surprise and quickly acted to bring the riots under control had already been documented in 1923 (see R. Kantor, ed., "Aleksandr III o evreiskikh pogromakh 1881–83 gg. [Novye materialy]", *Evreiskaia letopis'* 1 (Petrograd, 1923), 149–58). The spontaneous character of the pogroms has been clearly demonstrated by I. M. Aronson ("Geographical and socioeconomic factors in the 1881 anti-Jewish pogroms in Russia," *The Russian Review*, XXXIX (1980): 18–31). These findings invalidate the claim that, had it not been for the ingrained anti-Jewish prejudices of the revolutionaries, they should not have had "any difficulties at all... to see the hand of *politseyisher reaktsie*" in the making of the pogroms (Tscherikower, *Geshikhte*, 178).

22 Goldhagen, "Ethnic consciousness," 492–3.

23 Cited in Frankel, *Prophecy and Politics*, 98.

24 See his revolutionary rationale for supporting the pogroms in "Vnutrennee obozrenie," especially 438–9. On Romanenko and his role in *Narodnaia Volia*, see: S. Valk, "G. G. Romanenko," 35–59.

25 While it has never been explained how Romanenko was able to get his brochure printed, it is indisputable that once his proclamation came to the attention of all the other members of the Executive Committee it was unanimously rejected and withdrawn from circulation (see: A. P. Pribyleva-Korba, "*Narodnaia Volia*." *Vospominaniia o 1870–1880-kh gg.* (Moscow, 1926), 196–7; L. G. Deich, "Ia. V. Stefanovich sredi narodovol'tsev," *Gruppa*, III (1925): 110; V. Bogucharskii, *Iz istorii politicheskoi bor'by v 70-kh i 80-kh gg. XIX v.* (Moscow, 1912), 222–3; D. Shub, "Evrei v russkoi revolutsii," in *Politicheskie deiateli v Rossii* (New York, 1969), 359–64; Valk, "Romanenko," 52; S. S. Volk, *Narodnaia Volia, 1879–1882* (Moscow, 1966), 138n).

26 The case for this so-called "official position" rests primarily on the fact that shortly after the appearance of the proclamation (30 August, 1881) Romanenko was able to publish his views in an unsigned article, "Vnutrennee obozrenie," in the party's journal, *Narodnaia Volia* (23 October 1881) – note the proximity of these dates! The article itself, while extreme in tone, was largely typical of the mainstream pro-pogrom response (see Valk, "Romanenko," 49–50, 52). But Romanenko cleverly linked the article with his outrageous proclamation by adding a footnote to a concluding statement, declaring: "here the author [Romanenko] repeats only the view expressed by the [Executive] Committee in the proclamation to the Ukrainian people." This, of course, was a straight lie, since the Committee did not at all share his views. Thus, Romanenko simply confirmed his own proclamation which he had managed to get printed without the approval of the Committee. (The fact that both documents had been written by the same person – Romanenko – has escaped many historians who until recently simply attributed them to a collective authorship (see, for

example, Tscherikower, *Geshikhte*, 174–6; and [Motzkin], "Prototype des Pogroms," 52–60; Silberner, 278). That Romanenko was able to get away with making *his position* appear to be Narodnaia Volia's was made possible because, after March 1881, the Executive Committee had ceased to be an effective decision-making body. The party was in disarray and its remaining Committee members were dispersed all over Russia with only Tikhomirov and a few others (among them Romanenko) residing in Moscow – the party's "headquarters." It was in these circumstances that Romanenko, mainly active in the party's publishing enterprise (where he was also considered an "expert on the Ukraine"), was able to usurp the Committee's authority. In short, he was free to do as he pleased – at least until his mischief was revealed in print.

27 A. Cahan, *The White Terror and the Red. A Novel of Revolutionary Russia* (New York, 1905), 362–3.

28 The notion that a substantial number of revolutionaries was somehow involved in the pogroms was, initially, the government's explanation for the riots. This view was later retracted by the Minister of Internal Affairs, Count N. P. Ignatiev, who in a memorandum to Alexander III on 15 March 1882, stated: "Careful investigations of the popular vengeance... that occurred in the provinces show clearly that these disorders had no connection with the socialist movement"; P. A. Zaionchkovskii, *Russian Autocracy in Crisis, 1878–1882* (Gulf Breeze, FL, 1979), 241, 244, 361 n. 20; cf. Rogger, "Government, Jews, peasants, and land," 133–7, and "Russian ministers," 59–60. But that on rare occasions some radicals joined the pogromshchiki for revolutionary purposes seems to be true judging from two reports of provincial authorities (see Kantor, "Aleksandr III o evreiskikh pogromakh," 153). At least in one instance, revolutionaries actually managed to divert the mobs away from Jewish victims by screaming "beat the police and the rich, and not the poor Jews." When the pogromshchiki started to rummage in non-Jewish quarters, setting several Russian shops on fire, they clashed with patrolling Cossacks (V. I. Sukhomlin, "Iz epokhi upadka partii 'Narodnaia Volia,'" *Katorga i ssykla*, XXIV, 1926: 80).

29 "Po povodu evreiskikh pogromov," in E. Koval'skaia, *Iuzhno-Russkii Rabochii Soiuz, 1880–1881*. (Moscow, 1926). The Union did not belong organizationally to Chernyi Peredel, but its leaders were former Chernoperedeltsy who had left the party due to disagreements on the desirability of economic terror and their fundamental Populist opposition to political and social-democratic objectives which, in the person of Pavel Akselrod, had begun to influence the St. Petersburg Chernoperedeltsy (see E. Haberer, "The role of Jews in Russian revolutionary Populism" [Ph.D. dissertation, University of Toronto, 1987], 454–9). For a more detailed analysis of the Union and how its

members related to the pogroms, see M. Mishkinsky, "The attitude of the Southern-Russian Workers' Union toward the Jews," 191–216.

30 "Russian zhizn'." *Zerno: rabochii listok* (June 1881), 3, in V. Nevskii, ed., *Istoriko–revoliutsionnyi sbornik*, II (Leningrad, 1924), 360–1, cited by Frankel, *Prophecy and Politics*, 100.

31 Ibid. See the discussion of this article in 74–5.

32 Frankel, *Prophecy and Politics*, 100.

33 G. V. Plekhanov, "Neudachnaia istoriia partii 'Narodnoi Voli'," *Sochineniia*, XXIV (Moscow, 1927), 157–8.

34 Ibid.

35 L. G. Deich, *Rol' Evreev v russkom revoliutsionnom dvizhenii* (Berlin, 1923), 7–8; A. Yarmolinsky, *Road to Revolution. A Century of Russian Radicalism* (London, 1957), 310.

36 "P. L. Lavrov – P. B. Aksel'rodu," Letter, London, 14 April 1882, in *Iz arkhiva Aksel'roda*, 30.

37 Plekhanov, "Neudachnaia istoriia," 158 n.1. That Plekhanov had indeed written, or at least began writing the article, is proved by a reference to it in the Akselrod–Deich correspondence of 1883, where Deich enumerates the items of Plekhanov's intended publications for *Vestnik Narodnoi Voli* ("L. G. Deich – P. B. Aksel'rodu," Letter, 3 July 1883, *Gruppa "Osvobozhdenie truda,"* 1 [1925]: 171).

38 Berk, "Russian revolutionary movement," 36; Greenberg, *Jews in Russia*, II: 162.

39 Deich, "Stefanovich," 110 n.1.

40 Frankel, *Prophecy and Politics*, 113 (italics mine).

41 For a good analysis of what distinguished Romanenko from the Narodovoltsy and the mainstream pro-pogrom response, see: Valk, "Romanenko," especially 46–50, 52.

42 There can be no question that Tikhomirov was partly, if not solely, responsible for this affair because in March 1881 he had assumed the leadership of Narodnaia Volia and of what was left of the Executive Committee. He definitely sympathized with the pogroms, which may have encouraged Romanenko to go ahead with his proclamation. Yet, in a letter to Pribyleva-Korba, Tikhomirov disclaimed any responsibility for it and stated his own objection to it ("*Narodnaia Volia,*" 196–7). For Tikhomirov's pro-pogrom attitude, see: Plekhanov, "Neudachnaia istoriia," 157; Deich, "Stefanovich," 110; Shub, "Evrei v russkoi revoliutsii," 361–2.

43 [Motzkin], "Prototype des Pogroms," 62–3.

44 Tscherikower, *Geshikhte*, p. 175.

45 I. A. Hourwich, "Zikhroynes fun an apikoyres," *Fraye arbeyter shtime*, no. 1164 (New York, 23 June 1922), 3.

46 [A. Cahan], *The Education of Abraham Cahan* (Philadelphia, 1969), 182–4.

47 Ibid., 184–6; Hourwich, "Zikhroynes," 1163 (16 June 1922), 3.

48 Goldhagen, "Ethnic consciousness," 483–84.

49 Deich, *Rol'* 29; Goldhagen, "Ethnic consciousness," 483. One only needs to recall the memoirs of such well-known Jewish Narodovoltsy as Aron Zundelevich and Vladimir Iokhelson to appreciate the degree to which Jewish socialists had absorbed the Populist thinking in this respect (V. I. Iokhel'son, "Dalekoe proshloe. Iz vospominanii starogo narodovol'tsa," *Byloe*, 13 [1918]: 53–75; A. I. Zundelevich, letter, in B. Frumkin, "Iz istorii revoliutsionogo dvizheniia sredi evreev v 1870-kh godakh," *Evreiskaia starina*, 1 (January 1911): 221–24).

50 Kiei, "The Jewish Narodnik," 309.

51 Cahan, *The White Terror*, 342.

52 M. B. Ratner, "Evoliutsiia natsional'no-politicheskoi mysli v russkom evreistve," *SERP*, no. 2: 24, cited by Tscherikower, *Geshikhte*, 177.

53 Hourwich, "Zikhroynes," 1164 (23 June 1922), 3.

54 I. Getsov, Letter, in Deich, *Rol'*, 325–7.

55 Ibid. Compare the discussion of the episode, 76–7.

56 Ibid.

57 Bogucharskii, *Iz istorii politicheskoi bor'by*, cited by Pribyleva-Korba, "Narodnaia Volia," 196.

58 L. G. Deich, "Saveli Zlatopolski," *Tsukunft* 21 (June 1916): 512–14, and "Der ershter revolutsioner-'tsionist'," *Tsukunft*, xxi (September 1916): 779.

59 Pribyleva-Korba, "*Narodnaia Volia,*" 196.

60 Deich, "Zlatopolski," 513.

61 A local circle in Elisavetgrad even reproduced the proclamation on a hectograph (Yarmolinsky, *Road to Revolution*, 308–9). But, as Yarmolisnky points out, this was criticized in the lead article of *Narodnaia Volia*, vii–ix (February 1882).

62 Ulam, *Name*, 371.

63 I. Ruelf, *Drei Tage in Juedisch-Russland* (1882), 73–5, cited by A. Menes, "Di yidishe arbeter-bavegung in rusland fun onheyb 70-er bizn sof 90-er yorn," *Historishe shriftn*, iii (Vilna, 1939), 26–7.

64 Ibid., 27.

65 Cited by Yarmolinsky, *Road to Revolution*, 310.

66 The manuscript, entitled "O zadachakh evreisko-sotsialisticheskoi intelligentsii" (hereafter cited as "O zadachakh") was first published in *Iz arkhiva Aksel'roda*, with an introduction by V. S. Voitinskii, 215–27.

67 A. Ascher, "Pavel Axelrod: a conflict between Jewish loyalty and revolutionary dedication," *The Russian Review*, xxiv (1963): 249–65.

68 Cf. A. Menes, "The Jewish socialist movement in Russia and Poland," in *The Jewish People. Past and Present*, ii (New York: Marnsti Press, 1949), ii, 362–5.

69 G. Gurevich, "Sredi revoliutsionerov v Tsiurikhe," *Evreiskaia letopis'*, iv (1926), 98–103; Deich, *Rol'*, 246–53, and "Der ershter revolutsioner-'tsionist,'" *Tsukunft*, xxi (August 1916): 777–8. See also Ascher, "Pavel Axelrod," 252–3, and Frankel, *Prophecy and Politics*, 102–4, 107.

70 Deich, *Rol'*, 252–3, and "Der ershter revolutsioner-'tsionist,'" 779–81;
G. Gurevich, "Zikhroynes," *Historishe shriften*, III (Vilna, 1939), 224–55.

71 The correspondence in question was published by Deich ("L. G. Deich
– P. B. Aksel'rodu") in *Gruppa "Osvobozhdenie truda*," I (1925), 151–62
(hereafter cited as "Correspondence"). For a more detailed discussion
of the Akselrod brochure, "O zadachakh," see Frankel, *Prophecy and
Politics*, 104–7; Ascher, "Pavel Axelrod," 252–60; and *Pavel Axelrod and
the Development of Menshevism* (Cambridge, 1972), 69–78.

72 Deich, *Rol'*, 8, 251, and "Correspondence," 153n.; S. L. Tsitron
[Citron], *Dray literarishe doyres: zikhroynes vegn yidishe shriftshteler*, II
(Vilna, 1921), 137–8.

73 "Correspondence," 160 (Letter of 21 April 1882).

74 Gurevich, "Sredi revoliutsionerov," 99; "Correspondence," 153–4.

75 Gurevich, "Sredi revoliutsionerov," 99.

76 P. B. Aksel'rod, Letter to A. Lesin [Valt], *Tsukunft*, IX (1924), 550, cited
by S. Agurskii, "Der kharakter fun der sotsialistisher bavegung tsvishn
di yidishe arbeter bis onshteyung fun der R.S.D.A.P.," *Tsaytshrift*, IV
(Minsk, 1930), 249.

77 Deich himself had thought of writing on the pogroms and how this
affected Jews in the movement (*Rol'*, 5–6). Indeed, it had been the
pogroms which inspired him to write this unique work on the role of the
Jews in the Russian revolutionary movement. Later, when the task of
writing such a brochure was entrusted to Akselrod, he remained *very
active* in trying to have the latter's manuscript published in one form or
another. He favored its publication as late as May 1882; see
"Correspondence," 161. And when he felt that Akselrod suspected him
of being lukewarm about the whole enterprise, he wrote to him:
"Brother, it is wrong of you to think that we [Deich himself and the
Geneva Chernoperedeltsy] relate to this question less seriously than
others" (ibid., 154 [letter of 27 March 1882]).

78 Aksel'rod, "O zadachakh," 218.

79 Ibid., 225–6.

80 "Correspondence," 151–2 (letter of 17 March 1882), cf. also 159 (letter
of 21 April 1882).

81 Postscript of Deich to Lavrov's letter (14 April 1882), in *Iz arkhiva
Aksel'roda*, 31.

82 "Correspondence," 159–60 (letter of 21 April 1882). It should be noted
that the Chernoperedeltsy found themselves in difficult times indeed.
Being an already endangered species on the verge of transforming
themselves into Marxists and also locked into complex negotiations with
Narodnaia Volia – handled almost exclusively by Deich – they could
not afford any show of internal division that might harm their
bargaining position *vis-à-vis* the Narodovoltsy who were determined to
absorb them into their party. Even so no formal decision was ever made
regarding Akselrod's brochure. In a later letter (May 1882) Deich
again refers to the brochure and tells him to go ahead with it (ibid.,

162). In the meantime Deich was trying as best he could to get Narodnaia Volia's cooperation on the brochure which he and Lavrov thought absolutely essential to make the project a success and to prevent any worsening of the already strained relationship of the two parties (see ibid., 151–62).

83 Ascher, "Pavel Axelrod," 259–60, and *Pavel Axelrod*, 77–8.

84 Aksel'rod, cited in Ascher, "Pavel Axelrod," 262.

85 The novel in question is the already cited book of Cahan, *The White Terror and the Red*. In it Cahan provides a very perceptive and sensitive portrait of the emotional and ideological make-up of Jewish Populists and their interaction with Gentile revolutionaries. According to I. Gurvich, Cahan succeeded very well in "depicting the mood" of Jewish socialists at the time of the pogroms ("Zikhroynes," *Fraye arbeyter shtime*, 1158 [5 May 1922], 3n.).

86 Cahan, *The White Terror*, 395–6 (italics mine).

87 Ibid., 74–5, 341–3, 405–6. Sergei Kravchinskii makes the same point when in his characterization of Aron Zundelevich, he put the following words in his mouth: "there is nothing in... Russia worth caring for. But I knew the Nihilists, and I loved them even more than my own [Jewish] race. I joined them and fraternalized with them, and that is the only tie which binds me to [Russia]" (Stepniak [S. M. Kravchinskii], *The Career of a Nihilist. A Novel* (London, 1890), 42).

88 Cahan, *The White Terror*, 135. What this meant for some Jews is well expressed by one of Cahan's fictional Jewish characters by the name of Makar (most likely a characterization of Leizer Zukerman) who tells his comrades: "When I think of the moments of joy the movement affords me, of the ties of friendship with so many good people – the cream of the generation, the salt of the earth, the best children Russia ever gave birth to – when I think of the glorious atmosphere that surrounds me, of the divine ecstasy with which I view the future; when I recall all this I feel that I get a sort of happiness which no Rothschild could buy" (ibid., 74).

89 Although a member of both Zemlia i Volia and later Narodnaia Volia, Gurevich, for example, had been situated in his activity almost exclusively in a Jewish and German Social Democratic environment. All the circles he belonged to in Mogilev, Kiev, and Berlin were predominantly Jewish in membership, if not sentiment. Actually, he was already a *Jewish* socialist of sorts prior to the pogroms in his concerns and activity. For instance, in 1876–7, he and his Berlin circle of "Jewish Nihilists" (which was associated with Zemlia i Volia) readily responded to Aron Liberman's call to create a "Jewish section" and to publish a Jewish socialist journal in Hebrew. Even less embedded in the revolutionary movement were those Jews who flocked to the standards of Bilu (the Palestintsy) and Am Olam (the Amerikantsy). The vast majority of these people were merely socialist sympathizers, the so-

called "Jewish studying youth," who had no direct personal links with the movement.

90 For a lucid sociological analysis of the "embedding process" of Jewish revolutionaries in Russian Marxism and how this affected their ideological and political loyalties, see Robert Brym, *The Jewish Intelligentsia and Russian Marxism* (London, 1978).

91 Tscherikower, "Yidn-revolutsionern," 172, and *Geshikhte*, 174.

92 Tscherikower, "Yidn-revolutsionern," 159.

93 A. I. Zundelevich, "Pis'ma k L. G. Deichu," *Gruppa "Osvobozhdenie truda,"* III (1925), 211. The "golden charter" refers to Deich's and Stefanovich's attempt to cause an uprising of Ukrainian peasants with the help of a forged tsarist manifesto promising the peasants land and freedom if they were to attack landowners and local officials. For Zundelevich's own negative reaction to the pogroms to the point of losing all hope that Russia could be rid of antisemitism in decades to come, see A. Litvak [C. Y. Helfland], "Aron Zundelevich," *Royter pinkos*, II (1924), 105–6.

94 [G. E. Gurevich], Personal papers of Grigorii Evseevich Gurevich, Tscherikower Arkhives, YIVO Institute for Jewish Research (New York), file 1161, folio 86302–86303.

95 Tscherikower, *Geshikhte*, 174–5. One of the proofs which Tscherikower supplies to substantiate his claim is a manuscript that was found in the Archives of V. N. Smirnov entitled "Prejudices of our social revolutionaries against Jews" ("Predrassudki nashikh sotsial'nykh revoliutsionerov protiv evreev," in B. Sapir, ed., *Vpered! 1873–1877*, 2 vols. (Dortrecht, 1970), II: 497–510 [Appendix no. 4]). But actually this evidence proves the contrary. For what Tscherikower did not know is that Gurevich, who had received the manuscript in 1876 from unknown sources in Russia, advised the editors of *Vpered!* not to publish "Prejudices" because in his and his Jewish comrades' opinion the complaints of the author against Russian socialists were completely exaggerated (see letter of Gurevich to the editors of *Vpered!* [2 April, 1876], in Sapir, *Vpered! 1873–1877*, II: 346 (Document, no. 157)). It should be noted as well that the author of the manuscript has not been identified and was not necessarily a Jew (see Boris Sapir's comments, "On the history of 'Vpered'," in *Vpered! 1873–1877*, I: 280).

96 I. A. Hourwich, "Zikhroynes," *Fraye arbeyter shtime*, 1158 (5 May, 1922), 3.

97 S. L. Chudnovskii, "Iz dal'nikh let (Otryvki iz vospominanii, 1869–1872)," *Byloe*, X (1907) 232–6. For a detailed discussion of the revolutionaries' response, both Jews and Gentiles, to the Odessa pogrom of 1871, see Haberer, "The role of Jews in Russian revolutionary Populism," 97–104.

III

The impact of the first pogrom wave

The development of the Russian Jewish community, 1881–1903

Alexander Orbach

The last decades of the nineteenth century were critical ones in the history of Russian Jewry. From all external appearances, the community was not responding well to the devastating centrifugal forces associated with modernity that everywhere had shattered traditional societies. For Russia's Jews, the case was even more complicated because in addition to having to cope with the new circumstances ushered in as a consequence of major economic restructuring, they found themselves in an unfriendly environment. Unlike what had happened earlier in Western and Central Europe, the disintegration of traditional Jewish life in the Russian Empire did not occur in a milieu in which Jews saw possibilities for a new life in the larger society around them. Rather, the hostility expressed in verbal and at times even physical forms from both officials and from the surrounding population made it clear to Jews that they were not welcome in Russia. Hence, flight from the Jewish world in the Russian Empire meant quite literally flight from Russia itself. Thus, the primary question facing Jewish thinkers in Russia at the dawn of the twentieth century was this very issue of community cohesion. On what basis did a Jewish community currently exist or on what terms could one be founded given the realities of the situation were the key questions confronting those who attempted to lead or even to speak for Russia's 5 million Jews.

By the last years of the nineteenth century, a new group of leaders and spokesmen within both the secular and the religious spheres of Jewish life had emerged with tentative answers to these questions. Curiously, the year 1897 serves as a convenient point of departure for a review of these formulations as well as for an examination of Russia's Jews on the eve of the new century. That year saw the appearance of a number of significant movements, studies or public expressions on the Jewish future, which, when examined, reveal a common organizing theme for a coherent study of Russian Jewry at the time. The year 1897 also marked the completion of a systematic survey of the Empire's population, thereby establishing for the first time a clear picture of the Jewish population of the realm. In the past, all discussions of Jewish life had been based on fragmentary or even impressionistic data. Now, concrete information was available on the full spectrum of Jewish life, and such data would be the point of departure for all subsequent discussions of the Jewish Question. Thus, any serious discussion of Russia's Jews at the beginning of the twentieth century must necessarily begin with a review of that material generated by the census takers of 1897.

I

The census established that there were just over 5·2 million Jews, or nearly one-half of the world Jewish population, living in the Russian Empire. While this number constituted only 4 percent of the nearly 126 million people then living under tsarist control, a closer study of the report reveals a more significant Jewish visibility than that implied by the raw numbers alone.[1]

The first critical fact of Russian–Jewish life was the existence of the Pale of Settlement, an area of the country to which Jewish residence had been restricted since the end of the eighteenth century. Included within the Pale were the newer territories gained by Russia as a consequence of the successful military campaigns against Poland and the Ottoman Empire.[2] Initially, Russian rulers issued *ad hoc* directives in order to restrict Jewish life to these new territories. However, as part of the effort aimed at systematizing Russian domestic legislation in the reign of Nicholas I, Jewish rights, obligations, and limitations were clearly delineated in a series of directives and rescripts in the middle of the 1830s.[3] These regulations identified the geographical area of that zone now to be known as the Pale of Settlement as fifteen Russian provinces in the western part of the Empire. Jewish settlement was also permitted in the ten Polish provinces under Russian control. With 362,000 square miles of area covering less than 20 percent of European Russia or 4 percent of the total land mass of that which was the tsarist Empire, the Pale became home to Russia's Jewish population in the nineteenth century.

In the period of the Great Reforms of the 1860s certain categories of the Jewish population were permitted to leave the Pale in order to take up residence in the interior of the country, including also the capital cities, Moscow and St. Petersburg. However, by 1897 the census takers found that 94 percent of the Jewish population was still to be found within the confines of the Pale.[4] Living alongside the local people including the Poles, Ukrainians, Lithuanians, Russians, Moldavians and White Russians, the Jews of the Pale made up 11·6 percent of the population in those areas. However, these 4·8 million Jews were not distributed evenly throughout the region. In fact, the level of Jewish concentration diminished as one traveled from north to south and especially from west to east. In the older, northwestern region, six provinces in all, the Jewish population was 15 percent of the whole, while in the four southeastern provinces, areas opened to Jewish residence only at the close of the eighteenth century and then included in the borders of the Pale, the Jewish people contributed 9 percent to the total. In the ten Polish provinces, Jews numbered 14 percent of the whole.[5] Thus, the Jewish presence in the western border area was certainly quantitatively significant. But beyond these statistics, the concentration of Jewish residence in the urban areas of the Pale and the Jewish role within the local economy of the zone gave the Jewish population a qualitative importance far in excess of the numbers themselves.

Using the criteria by which the census takers measured urbanization, the Jewish presence in the urban zones of the western part of the Empire was overwhelming. With close to 2·4 million urban dwellers in the twenty-five provinces in which they were allowed to live,[6] Jews made up 55 percent of the urban population of White Russia, 50 percent of those counted as urban in Lithuania, and close to 38 percent of the urban mix in the Polish provinces.[7] While the Jewish population had always been an urban one, it became even more so in the last quarter of the nineteenth century.

The census figures show that the rate of Jewish population growth in the second half of the nineteenth century was significant. The numbers indicate that the Jewish population grew by about 20 percent in the decade and a half after the pogroms of 1881. Thus, with an expanding population base and shrinking area within which to live as a consequence of the stricter residential requirements imposed in 1882 as part of the so-called May Laws, the period 1881–97 saw the Jewish people being crowded even further into the confines of the Pale. Of course, this same period also saw the beginnings of a massive flight abroad. However, in spite of that exodus, the high birth rate led to very severe overcrowding especially

in the already congested urban areas.[8] Obviously, one way of
reducing that urban growth was for Jews to move to other areas of
the Pale with a lower population density. Thus, we should not be
surprised to learn that an internal migration, or resettlement, was
also taking place within Russia in those years. In this respect, Jewish
behavior conformed to a larger pattern as thousands of other
Russian residents, experiencing dislocations as a consequence of the
major economic transformations then taking place, were also moving
to newer areas of settlement within the country. However, unlike
some of those others, for whom mobility was less rigidly circum-
scribed, the Jews within the Empire were largely confined to the
Pale.[9]

The greatest growth in the Jewish population in the period
occurred in the southern provinces. The evidence indicates that the
numbers of Jews there nearly doubled in the last decades of the
century. The promise of greater economic opportunity there
attracted Jews to those underpopulated regions from the older, more
established sections of the Pale.[10] However this shift, undertaken
primarily for economic reasons, had important communal consequences, too. The flight from the established, structured, Jewish
world to virgin territories devoid of Jewish life was characterized not
by the transplantation of older institutions and patterns of life, but
by the effort to create new communities with new orientations that
would fit more comfortably into the locale in which the Jews found
themselves. Thus, the reconfiguration of Jewish residential patterns
did not bring with it an expansion of the traditional community with
its institutional frameworks, but marked instead the undermining of
the static community and its replacement by a new and dynamic
entity.[11]

In their reporting of Jewish occupational patterns, the census
takers caught the Jewish community in this transition from
traditional to modern economic life.[12] Nearly 70 percent of those
indicating their sources of income noted that they earned their
livelihood either through manufacture (38 percent) or commercial
enterprise (32 percent). An additional 3 percent of the Jewish
community stated that they were tied directly to the agricultural
sector of the economy, while another 25 percent of Jewish wage
earners reported that they earned their living through the sale of
their services, either personal (19 percent) or professional (6
percent).[13]

Breaking these numbers down even further, it is clear that in Lithuania and White Russia the industrial sector was gaining more and more Jewish workers as a rapid shift away from commercial activity tied to the traditional economy was in the process of transforming the Jewish way of earning a living.[14] In the main, it was the Jewish industrialist who was hiring his newly emerging class of Jewish laborers. One scholar has gone so far as to claim that "this group of industrialists created jobs for over 93 percent of Jewish industrial workers. And while acting in their own self-interest, they helped satisfy one of the greatest economic needs of the Jewish community – the need for gainful employment."[15]

While a small number of entrepreneurs with access to capital was in a favorable position to take advantage of the new outlets and incentives being made available to them, the overwhelming majority of Russia's Jews did not benefit materially as a consequence of Russian industrialization. This state of affairs becomes especially apparent when the data on Jewish poverty and increased Jewish hardship at the end of the century are examined. This evidence reveals that there was a dramatic increase in the number of Jewish loan associations and other social welfare societies operating within the Pale in the last decades of the century. For instance, data on Passover relief, money made available in order to purchase food for the holiday, indicate that as much as 20 percent of the Jewish community was getting this type of support.[16] From a purely economic perspective then, the Jewish community of tsarist Russia was not thriving: it was, in fact, struggling, with all indications pointing to the possibility of serious internal problems of cohesion and direction as a consequence of recent developments taking place in the surrounding society.

These social, economic, and demographic developments were directly related to the massive economic transformation then occurring in tsarist Russia. Intimately tied to the existing economy, the Jews could not help but be affected by this major restructuring of Russian economic life at the close of the nineteenth century. Of course, compounding the difficulties facing the Jews was the increased hostility in the form of legal and social exclusions that they had to confront. After the experience of 1881, the Jews realized that not only was the government reluctant to come to their aid and to deal effectively with rioters, but that, in its investigations of the pogroms, it had concluded that the Jews themselves were responsible for the violence directed against them. The government claimed that the very presence of the Jews in the area and the character of their relationship to the local population had incited those people against them. Thus, both the general conditions of Russian life, as well as the specific attitude to and treatment of the Jews, was threatening the continued viability of the community.

Certainly the Jews were not the only victims of tsarism at this time. However, they were that one minority toward whom patterns of discrimination were applied most relentlessly and consistently.[17] Firstly, the limitations imposed by the continued existence of the Pale precluded a real escape by Jews eager to participate fully in the growth of the Russian industrial or commercial sectors in both European Russia east of the Pale and in Central Asia. Secondly, within the Pale itself, the exclusions from government and public service and the quotas imposed on Jewish school enrollment meant that avenues of upward mobility generally exploited by an urban population in a time· of rapid modernization were closed off completely to them. Finally, the periodic expulsions of categories of Jews back to the Pale from areas of Russia opened to them only in the 1860s, together with the ever-present threat of violence directed at Jewish communities within the Pale, contributed to feelings of insecurity and reinforced the standing argument that they were a group of people alien to Russian life.

All of these forces came together to pose a crisis for Russian Jewry at the close of the nineteenth century. With diminished hope for their own and their community's ultimate integration into Russian life, contemporary Jewish activists began addressing themselves to the future needs of their people and the manner by which those could be met. These discussions invariably began with the premise that the Jews of Russia did in fact constitute a distinct community with its own culture, identity, economy, and decision-making structure, all of which distinguished it from neighboring ethnic and national entities. Thus, Jewish activists who voiced their views publicly on the future of Russian Jewry did so in collective and communal terms rather than with the individualistic approaches seen in Western and Central Europe.

Such proposals reflected yet another struggle then taking place within the world of Russian Jewry, that is, the campaign for group leadership. For if Jews were truly a national community, rather than a collection of individuals belonging to a faith community, that community then merited a nationally minded leadership able to organize and articulate its hopes and aspirations. Thus, the various programs developed and offered to Russian Jewry at this time reflected not only ideological perspectives on the future of that community, but also political credos articulated by those striving to fill what they perceived to be the leadership vacuum created as a consequence of the fire storm of 1881.

II

The impact of the pogroms of 1881 on Russian Jewry was considerable. Physical damage, including casualties and property damage, was extensive. An estimated 20,000 Jews had their homes destroyed and an additional 100,000 suffered major property loss. In addition, the pogroms also undermined the prevailing integrationist political ideology being pursued by the Jewish establishment. It is true that the St. Petersburg Jewish leaders, the champions of this course, were able to maintain their ascendancy over the community even after the riots and the ensuing governmental reaction.[18] However their argument, that a positive Jewish life could be lived in the Russian Empire and that Jews should put their trust in the government, was now challenged by a variety of radical, political orientations which completely rejected the basic premises of the integrationists.

This new form of Jewish politics, characterized by stridency and assertiveness, emphasized Jewish activism in an appeal directed to the Jewish masses. Using the press, organizing small cells of like-minded supporters and attempting to build large grass-roots type movements, these new ideologues recognized the events of 1881 as a significant turning point not only for Russian Jewry but for all of world Jewry. The spontaneous flight abroad by Jews in the aftermath of the pogroms became the starting point for the building of new political programs.[19]

Writing in the Russian–Jewish weekly, *Rassvet*, Moshe Leib Lilienblum called for a major shift in the destination of Russian Jews leaving the Empire. Instead of going to North America, he urged them to go to Palestine. He contended that only in Palestine would Jews be able to re-establish themselves as an independent and normal people, since only there could they set their own future course.[20] Lilienblum had come to the conclusion that antisemitism was fundamentally a problem of national confrontation between the Jewish people and those national communities on whose soil Jews were then living. In his view, the problem could only be truly resolved by addressing the question of Jewish homelessness. Passionately, he declared that only when the Jews were territorially rooted would their victimization cease. Breaking with his earlier reformist and acculturationist beliefs, Lilienblum was now convinced that there were no Jewish concessions which would be sufficient to those who deemed the Jews an alien people and therefore ineligible for full civic rights. Generalizing from this position, Lilienblum concluded that the Jew should aspire to the same goal as all other national groups, i.e., a free and independent home. Thus, Lilienblum focused on Jewish settlement in Palestine, the historic home of the Jewish people, as the means by which Jews could initiate the process of self-regeneration in the modern period.[21]

Independent of Moshe Leib Lilienblum, Dr. Leo Pinsker, twenty years Lilienblum's senior, came to similar views as he tried to make sense of recent events. A medical doctor and writer who in 1861 had coedited *Sion*, a Russian-Jewish weekly promoting Jewish acculturation, Pinsker found that the pogroms of 1881 shattered his worldview. He now admitted that he had never really understood the bases of antisemitism and had assumed that through education and general societal development this form of discrimination, along with all other residues of medieval intolerance, would disappear. Thus for Pinsker, Jewish emancipation had been part of that general process of reaching a higher level of human understanding and acceptance. After the events of 1881, Pinsker contended that antisemitism was not simply an anachronism that would vanish, but was an expression of national hostility, rooted in an incurable psychological illness. This conclusion emerged as a natural consequence of Pinsker's new vision of the Jewish community as a national one. Pinsker now argued that rather than focusing on emancipation, Jews first had to go through a process of self-confrontation whereby they would come to acknowledge their primary identity as a nation and begin their search for freedom from that starting point. This process Pinsker termed "autoemancipation" and he identified it as the next stage in the Jewish effort to resolve the dilemmas of modern Jewish life. Of central importance to Pinsker was the fact that this would be a process initiated by Jews themselves and not one which saw them still dependent upon the efforts or the good will of others. Pinsker rejected all Jewish programs of action which did not grasp the depth of these national antipathies toward Jews.[22]

While Lilienblum and Pinsker looked to Jewish leaders in order to organize and fund these efforts, both men also stressed the importance of mass action. They emphasized that an improvement in the status of Russian Jewry would not be attained simply by lobbying or through other forms of private negotiation with governmental leaders, but rather through the mobilization of the Jewish people themselves. The necessity of building a new movement which would generate its own leadership and delineate a new course of action was clear in each man's approach. An effort to organize the mass exodus and direct it to a Jewish territory rather than have it disperse around the world was, in their view, the first demand to be made of such new leaders. Thus, the role of the new leaders would not be confined to organizational or financial matters, but would of necessity be motivational and political too. Jews would now have to be organized communally along new lines. They had to be energized to the point of being convinced that not only immediate self-interest demanded their commitment to this objective, but that the fate of world Jewry would be served through the establishment of Jewish national life on that soil long identified with the Jewish people.

While Lilienblum and Pinsker agonized over the implications of the pogroms and tried to articulate a new course for Russian Jewry, others acted out their responses spontaneously. They fled the country. Hundreds of young Jews crossed the western border into the Austro-Hungarian Empire with the intention not only of avoiding violence, but also of quitting tsarist Russia forever. The overwhelming majority of these emigrants was headed to North America. However, a trickle of Jewish pioneers did not face west but turned south to Palestine. With utopian and altruistic intentions, these young people were convinced that by moving to Palestine in order to build a Jewish collective life there, they were taking the first steps in the ultimate redemption of their people.

In general, those who chose Palestine over other destinations shared a number of common characteristics. Products of Russian schooling, they had come to identify with Russian culture and especially its progressive literary tendencies of the 1860s and 1870s. This does not mean that they were completely estranged from the Jewish community and its way of life, rather, it is fair to say that the traditional world of the prayer house and the study hall no longer attracted them. Even though a good number of such young people joined the rest of the Jewish community in observing a national day of mourning in the synagogues of Russia in mid-January 1882, it should not be presumed that this marked for them a return to the religion of their forefathers. Instead, they came to the synagogue in order to express their solidarity with their fellow Jews with whose fate they now fully identified. Yet, the violence directed against the Jews, the indifference of Russian society to the victims, and the hostility of governmental officials to the Jewish masses estranged these Russophiles from their surroundings. Hence, they searched for a modern identity to which they could graft the progressive ideals garnered from that Russian culture they admired so much. That they could not construct such an identity in the Empire is understandable. That they denied the possibility of finding it in North America reflects the degree to which they had come to place their national concerns and ideology over all personal or individual matters. And, that they sought that identity among the sand dunes and swamps of Palestine confirms their dogged determination to solve the problems of modern Jewry in a manner never attempted before. Their own personal trek to Palestine or their organization of groups and associations intended to promote that effort stands as the first Jewish political response to the pogroms of 1881 and the first, groundbreaking, step in the movement that would reach its full development sixteen years later.[23]

Organizational needs brought together the various elements promoting a national emigration. The activists enthusiastically welcomed Pinsker's pamphlet and as a consequence prevailed upon him to assume a leadership role within their fledgling movement.[24] At least a dozen local societies had emerged within the Pale in the years 1882–3 committed to the goal of settling Jewish colonists in Palestine in order to build the base of a new society there. It soon became quite clear that a central organization was needed in order to coordinate the work of these disparate groups. In November 1884, some thirty delegates met across the Russian border in Germany in the town of Kattowitz, beyond the reach of tsarist officials, in order to create just such a group. To head their new society, called Hibbat Zion, the Lovers of Zion, the delegates chose Dr. Leo Pinsker, the most famous and most widely respected supporter of this approach. In order to communicate with the masses, they chose Moshe Leib Lilienblum as the secretary of the association. Lilienblum's ability to write in Hebrew and Yiddish in addition to Russian gave him access to a community broader than that of the disaffected Russian-Jewish youth.[25]

Hibbat Zion was created in order to raise money, facilitate the emigration process for those going to the Middle East, and promote that destination over America among Russian–Jewish emigrants. It was also to act as a central clearing house for all of the groups that had already sprung up as well as for subsequent organizations committed to the same goal. The movement was intended to be a grass-roots one as it appealed to the Jewish masses on behalf of a Palestinian solution to the dilemmas of modern Jewry.

The number of local chapters of Hibbat Zion grew steadily during the decade of the 1880s. By 1885, it is estimated that there were about 14,000 members in local chapters with the number of chapters exceeding 130 by the end of the decade.[26] While Hibbat Zion was the largest and best known organization promoting Jewish settlement in Palestine, it was not the only one doing so. The growth of Hibbat Zion was paralleled by the emergence of other contemporary movements, which while having somewhat different ideological orientations, nevertheless shared the common goal of returning the Jews to the ancient Holy Land.

Hibbat Zion grew and attained official and legal status in 1890 as the Society for the Support of Jewish Farmers and Artisans in Syria and Palestine, or as it was popularly called, the Odessa Committee. Yet the organization was not a success if measured in strictly material terms. It was never able to raise the necessary funds to purchase adequate lands and settle masses of Jews. Even those Jews whose transport and resettlement the Society did support found the level of aid inadequate for their needs. The leaders of Hibbat Zion had failed to penetrate the world of Jewish affluence in Russia and Europe or to rally Jewish philanthropists to their cause. Eventually, they did gain the support of Baron Edmund de Rothschild of the French branch of the family, and his contributions to the Palestinian colonies of Hibbat Zion saved them from collapse. However, in spite of this aid, the organization's effort to establish independent Jewish life in Palestine was not successful since the Baron's support was not motivated by ideological concerns but was an act of charity. Jews in Palestine under the care of the House of Rothschild were continuously made aware of their dependency upon their benefactor.

Also, the leaders of Hibbat Zion did not make the movement into a real political force within the Jewish world. Part of this is of course to be attributed to the fact that the movement toiled under the burden of illegality through the first seven years of its existence. Thus, during that period, the leaders could not organize, coordinate, or act politically in any open manner. Even after the Russian government extended legal recognition to Hibbat Zion, restraints on the organization continued to be considerable. Consequently, the leadership's primary objectives continued to be educational and cultural within Russia while all the while they were still committed to an activist settlement program.

On the other hand, the movement should not be dismissed as a failure. At a time when the idea of a secular Jewish national community was just emerging, Hibbat Zion gave organizational support to such an end. Through its various programs and efforts, Hibbat Zion promoted and even legitimated this new approach to Jewish identity and community structure. Thus, for a new generation of Russian Jews this idea was not only taken seriously, but was a welcome and even positive response to the traumatic impact that the pogroms had had on Jewish life in the Empire. In this, Hibbat Zion effectively prepared the ground, ideologically as well as organizationally, for Theodor Herzl's enthusiastic reception in Russia after his founding of the World Zionist Organization in 1897.[27] And, from the very start, the gravitation of Russian Jews to Herzl's Zionist organization and their impact on its ideologies and policies as well as its overall activities was profound.

III

Because economic change had the most significant effect in disrupting Jewish society, the group that initially had the most success in gaining popular support within the community was that group which offered direct answers to the immediate problems caused by industrialization and modernization – the socialists. In fact, beginning with the 1870s and continuing for the next twenty years, Jewish socialists of various tendencies became active propagandists within Jewish workers' circles in the Pale. At the time, these socialists were not at all committed to organizing a mass Jewish labor movement. Rather, their intent was to disseminate information, to raise consciousness among would-be laborers, and to begin building support for a true politically minded labor movement in Russia.[28]

As economic changes began to affect the Jewish community in the

1880s, the number of Jewish workers in the expanding industrial sector increased significantly. In addition, incidents of Jewish labor unrest also began to develop with strikes against working conditions in the textile and tobacco industries, industries dominated by Jewish workers and Jewish employers. While not seeing themselves as proletarians, either in class or political terms, these Jewish workers, nevertheless, began to attend the lectures and the classes sponsored by the Jewish socialists with greater frequency and in increased numbers.[29] These socialists, mainly Marxists with little in the way of a personal Jewish identity or positive feeling for the Jewish community or its history, nevertheless found themselves leading an all-Jewish movement.

A critical juncture in the history of this relationship between the propagandists and the workers can be noted with the publication of Arkadi Kremer's *Ob agitatsii* in 1894. In that pamphlet, Kremer called on his fellow socialists to shift their priorities and to begin emphasizing legal and economic issues to their "students" rather than to continue concentrating on educational and cultural activities.[30] Through this shift, Kremer wanted to link the activists and their disciples in a much stronger way than ever before. He thought that this new course would provide a new direction to the movement and would transform it into an energetic political force in its own right.

Kremer believed that the new focus on economic and legal matters would lead quite naturally to an examination of political realities and spark a call for real political change. With this new approach, a clear shift in the orientation of the organizers to their students also emerged. The new relationship was no longer to be that of teacher to student but rather that of organizer to party member in this new political web. Since these efforts were not focused exclusively on the Jewish workers of the Pale, it is clear that a new perception of that group had surfaced. Formerly, the effort had been to develop a proletarian consciousness among Jewish artisans and journeymen and to get them to identify themselves with the larger group that then constituted the Russian labor force. A universalist and cosmopolitan view had governed the earlier phase of the effort to organize Jewish labor. Now, specific objectives, economic, legal and strangely enough, national, were outlined with the expectation that confrontational activity would build a consciousness that would lead directly to the political organization of the Jewish workers of the Pale. As one writer has described these events, "The organized

Jewish labor movement...came about as a result of the intellectuals' decision to promote a mass movement."[31]

Iulii Martov [Tsederbaum], a political exile living in Vilna at the time, delivered the May Day speech in 1895 and used the occasion to call for a movement with a specifically Jewish character. Martov began his address with a standard Marxist analysis of the situation of workers in tsarist Russia. However, he then proceeded to introduce a Jewish component into that structure. "In the Russian Empire the Jew is able to improve his position only through his own activity...In the first years of our movement, we awaited the development of a Russian working-class movement...and because of this, we did not see the rudiments of a real Jewish movement."[32]

Not only was Martov using the occasion to justify the switch in tactics advocated by Kremer, he was also claiming that the embryo of an independent Jewish movement was in existence and that its birth should be encouraged. Martov went on to assert that such a movement would work side by side with future Russian and Polish labor movements in order to create a true pan-Russian proletarian organization. In that larger body, the Jewish movement would champion specific goals for the Jewish people, particularly equal rights and freedom of cultural life. Through his formulation, Martov was recognizing the contemporary Jewish community as a national one, and was placing it on a par with the other nationalities of the Empire. Furthermore, he was indicating that, in his view, a future Russian labor party would be multi-national with specific tasks being assigned to each of the constituent groups. Martov concluded his presentation by declaring that the biggest obstacle facing the Jewish socialists was the national passivity of the Jewish masses. He noted that "the awakening of national and class consciousness proceed hand in hand."[33] The implication here is clear – the stimulation of the first form of consciousness would lead directly to a heightening of the second one. Thus, by 1895, Jewish socialists in Vilna had come not only to recognize the existence of Jewish workers as a potentially valuable political entity in their own right, they had also come to associate them with specific tasks within the framework of that larger grouping which some day would represent all workers in Russia.

In 1896, socialist activists in Vilna produced an illegal Yiddish paper called *Di arbeiter shtimme*, and in October 1897, representatives of the editorial board together with delegates coming from Jewish workers' groups located in the major urban centers of the Pale met in Vilna in order to found the General Jewish Workers' Party of Russia and Poland, the Bund. Jewish laborers now had their own political party in order to represent both specific and general interests within the context of the Russian revolutionary movement. Delivering a key address at the founding meeting of the Bund, Arkadi Kremer outlined the priorities of the new organization:

A general union of all Jewish socialists will have as its goal not only the struggle for general Russian political demands; it will also have the special task of defending the specific interests of the Jewish workers, carry on the struggle for their civic rights and above all combat the discriminatory anti-Jewish laws.[34]

With this development, a Jewish national identity made its official appearance in left-wing and worker circles, and a Jewish agenda came to be part of the program being advanced by a section of a revolutionary movement in Russia.

The history of the Bund is well known.[35] Its role in the formation of the RSDLP in 1898 and its confrontations with Lenin in 1903 have been studied, analyzed, and fully described. All of these topics go far beyond our survey here and will not be addressed as they divert our attention from the critical theme, i.e., the efforts undertaken by a new generation of Jewish activists to deal with the crises of contemporary Jewish life.

While the leaders of the Bund were not the only Jewish socialist revolutionaries who recognized Jewish identity and a Jewish agenda as part of their broader political formulations, they were the most cosmopolitan and least national in their ideological framework. It is for this reason that so much attention has been focused on them. For if such individuals, coming from a Marxist ideological perspective which denied the legitimacy of Jewish national identity, could be brought to recognize such an identity as a valid one, then it is apparent that such a contention had come to penetrate the broadest sectors within contemporary Russian Jewry.

Our examination of the nationalist and socialist movements that appeared in the aftermath of the 1881 riots has revealed their divergent approaches to solving the Jewish Question in tsarist Russia. For the nationalists, the solution was to be found outside of the Empire and was to be achieved through the territorialization of the Jewish people in a land of its own. For the socialists, on the other

hand, the difficulties facing Jews would be resolved as part of the
larger process of liberating all of Russia and bringing true freedom
to all of her inhabitants. In spite of these differences though, the
nationalists and the socialists shared a common point of departure,
that being the recognition of Russian Jewry as a discernible national
group with interests and demands unique unto itself. In articulating
their respective positions and in developing their identities, both the
Jewish nationalists and the Jewish socialists reflected that mood of
separateness and distinctiveness which characterized the contemporary Jewish community of the Empire. However, not only did
these movements reflect the current mood within the Russian–Jewish
community, they also contributed substantially to developing this
orientation in a politically sophisticated manner for the next
generation of Jewish youth and in promoting this new identity
widely. While the major political activities of both the Jewish
nationalists and the Jewish socialists lay in the future, it is clear that
by 1897 both groups had reached a level of organizational maturity
and had built up sufficient support within the Jewish community to
be taken seriously by both Jews and non-Jews alike. If these leaders
were not yet among the primary decision-makers for Russian Jewry,
it was only because the old-line traditional leadership still held the
masses firmly in its grip. However, both the socialists and the
nationalists continued their organizational efforts so as to be in a
position to assert their claims to national leadership should the
occasion be forthcoming. Their prominence in Jewish life after 1903
reflected these years of growth and development.

IV

Other developments in the last decades of the nineteenth century
also contributed to the formulation of a distinctive Russian–Jewish
identity. Principally, the creation of literatures in both modern
Hebrew and Yiddish, as well as the fostering of a Russian-language
Jewish press, furthered this growing sense of Jewish self. While not
politically minded, these literary efforts did reach a wide audience
and implicitly supported the nationalization of Jewish life along a
number of distinctive cultural streams. Yiddishists and Hebraists
engaged in polemical exchanges with one another as each claimed to
be the authentic and legitimate voice of the people, and both
castigated the Russianists for their assimilationist tendencies.

Nevertheless, all three recognized their shared heritage which clearly separated them from the ethnic groups living alongside them.

While the Yiddishists and the Hebraists gravitated more naturally to the nationalist and socialist orientations when they offered political comments, the Russian-oriented writers faced a more problematic situation. Clearly, they could not champion the cause of emigration, and their moderate and generally middle-class world views precluded a revolutionary approach to the questions of the future of Jewish life. Hence, they needed to develop an integrationist view that would generate mass support and at the same time be both dignified and honorable. This new generation of integrationists had come to maturity since 1880. These men recognized that new relationships and attitudes had emerged within the Jewish community as well as within the general society. They realized that the personal lobbying and intercessionist efforts utilized by their predecessors would be neither effective with the Russian regime nor warmly received by the Jewish community. Hence, their first task was to develop a stance that would secure for them the respect of both the Jewish community they aspired to represent and the Russian government from whom they sought to gain status and rights for Jews.

These urbane, Russified, Jewish middle-class professionals generally lived outside the Pale. They were trained in law, medicine, or engineering and had the skills to express themselves publicly in both verbal and written forms on a variety of topics. Proud of their abilities and achievements and considering themselves an "aristocracy" of merit, individuals from this group began to play a more public and active role in Jewish affairs in the last decade of the nineteenth century.[36]

Their growing involvement with the Jewish community included representing the community in the pages of the Russian-language press, primarily *Voskhod*, or organizing a legal defense bureau to assist Jewish victims of Russian violence or Russian injustice, and participating in Jewish cultural or charitable organizations. These young men found themselves experiencing a real return to their people.[37] They found themselves drawn to the community, interested in its past, and committed to its future existence. For them, the community was not an artifact that had to be preserved, but a living organism that functioned and would continue to thrive under proper conditions. Furthermore, recent developments had shown them that the community was neither an endangered species that required especially tender care, nor a plant so delicate that it could exist only under the most ideal conditions. Rather, the community was tough and had the ability to withstand assault, persecution, and discrimination without losing either its character or its hopes for the future. As with the case of the Jewish nationalists who "returned" in the eighties, this return to the Jewish people did not bring with it any form of religious revival or greater religious commitment. While these individuals were now more sensitive to religious perspectives and perhaps did not flaunt so openly their own secular habits, they identified with a community that contained within it a broad spectrum of Jewish identities, and so had room in it for them, too.[38]

Public discussion of the theme of the Jewish community of Russia as a national or ethnic group in its own right and therefore deserving of more than civil liberties for its individual members was soon forthcoming. In a series of letters entitled *Pis'ma o starom i novom Evreistve* begun in 1897 and published in the Russian–Jewish weekly *Voskhod* over the next decade, the journalist-historian Simon Dubnow worked out the historical bases of the thesis of diaspora nationalism. In these essays, Dubnow addressed the question of Jewish national identity and its character as well as its particular needs in the present and for the future.[39]

Dubnow began by tracing the national idea through the various stages of its development. He concluded that the sense of national identity ultimately came to be a spiritual one, and once having attained this lofty status, the community would be free from all material needs in order to support and maintain its identity. Dubnow wrote: "We see that the decisive factor for the destiny of a nation is not its external power, but its spiritual force, the quality of its culture and the inner cohesion of its members."[40]

Assuring the reader that the Jewish people had already attained this plateau, Dubnow went on to assert that the Jewish nation did not require a territorial base in order to maintain itself. In his view, it only needed the strength furnished by unity and popular will. "[A people] which creates an independent existence, reveals a stubborn determination to carry on its autonomous development. Such a people has reached the highest stage of cultural-historical individuality and may be said to be indestructible, if only it clings purposefully to its national will."[41]

Dubnow argued that Jewish existence was not to be attributed to religion or territory but rather to the people's ability to establish an autonomous cultural existence in all the territorial settings in which they had found themselves. In emphasizing the continuous character of history, Dubnow concluded that that which had worked in the past continued to operate effectively today. Thus, for him, the future of Jewish life was still dependent upon the retention of Jewish cultural autonomy in the diaspora. Hence, all of the contemporary needs of the Russian–Jewish community could and would be satisfied through the guaranteeing of such cultural freedom to the community.[42]

The political ramifications of this analysis meant that in addition to pressing for civil rights for Jews, Jewish activists in Russia had also to call for national rights for the community. In affirming the viability of continued Jewish life in Eastern Europe, Dubnow was saying that a Jewish national identity with its own cultural integrity could be reconciled with individual civil liberties if, in addition to emancipation, Jews would also be granted the right of cultural autonomy in the lands where they were presently living. Since, in his view, the Jews had no need for territory in order to sustain themselves as a people and since they had no claim upon the lands they were living on, they would not be seen as a threat to the indigenous population. Dubnow feared forced acculturation and ultimate assimilation much more than any other possible physical dangers. In his writings, Dubnow tried to negate those aspects of Jewish existence which seemed to be most threatening to local nationalists in exchange for that level of autonomy which he believed was critical for continued Jewish national life.

By 1905, Dubnow's ideas on cultural rights became part of the platform of the newly formed League for the Attainment of Full Rights for the Jews of Russia. Bringing together Zionists, middle-class liberals, and autonomists, the League played an active role in securing the franchise for Jews in the vote for the state Duma, and in conducting the ensuing electoral campaign in February–April 1906.[43] Thus, here too, we are able to see the importance attached to community and the focus on the Jews as a national entity within the context of tsarist Russia, the epitome of the modern multi-national state.

For these liberals, the solution to the variety of problems besetting the community was to be found in Russia through the extension of civil liberties to the individual and the guaranteeing of cultural freedom, through autonomy, to the group. As with the nationalists and the socialists, for liberals too the definition of Jewish identity and that of Jewish community was never clearly delineated. However, while vague, the question of the future existence of the Jewish community was never in dispute. Here the experience of Russian Jews can be clearly distinguished from that of Jews in other countries in the modern period. With the absence in Russia of a serious assimilationist course, an option available to Western Jews in the wake of legal emancipation, the Russian Jews continued to be identified as a separate and distinct entity. And with the continuous biological growth of that community in the nineteenth century within the confines of the Pale, the visibility of the Jews became more and more apparent. The reality of Jewishness was noted by both Jews and non-Jews alike, and this reality was given explicit documentation with the publication of the 1897 census.

v

The Jewish Question was looming larger and larger for all Jews; even the religious community increasingly recognized that the new realities of life were calling for somewhat different approaches to the altered circumstances under which traditional life had to function. The rabbinical and lay religious heads of the Jewish community were quite conscious of the threat posed by modernity to the religious foundations of Jewish community life, and were fully prepared to respond to these challenges. In treating the world of religious Judaism, we are best served by focusing on the *yeshivot*, the schools of higher talmudic learning, in the last quarter of the nineteenth century. These schools not only produced the professional leadership of the community, the rabbis and the teachers, they also served as the model societies of piety to be emulated by all. As such, they played definitive roles in shaping the character of the traditional community.

Religious leaders, especially the heads of the yeshivot, were troubled by what they perceived to be the diminished role of the traditional educational institutions in contemporary Jewish life. Primarily, they recognized that religious teachings and especially Jewish religious law, *halakha*, were playing less and less of a critical role in the individual's private and personal behavior. The economic reorganization of the Empire, with its consequent negative impact on the Jewish community, was making it more and more difficult to fund this form of higher Jewish education. Finally, the reduced influence of religious leaders in decision-making positions and the shifts to secular educational systems or even technical schools by Jewish youth, as they sought those skills which they believed would be necessary in the new society, reduced the pool of potential students for the yeshivot and diminished their overall importance for that generation of Jews coming to maturity after 1880. In sum, these new realities moved the leaders of the yeshiva system to initiate a series of wide-ranging reforms in the system in the second half of the nineteenth century. These reforms included a restructuring of the relationship between the yeshiva and the community so as to give the school greater financial support, changes in the actual curriculum taught at the schools, and even pedagogical changes in the mode of instruction employed in the schools.

The first set of changes was addressed to the financial structure of the schools as administrators sought to assure the continuity of the system in an age of uncertainty. Working out arrangements with communal leaders, patrons, and benefactors throughout the Pale, the leaders of the yeshivot were able to stabilize their finances so that they could attract good students at minimal cost and pursue their mission with the confidence that bills would be settled and scholars and students would be sustained.[44] Since yeshiva leaders were committed to developing a cadre of students who would come to identify themselves as part of the communal elite and as spokesmen for what they believed was the authentic Jewish perspective, they concentrated on creating a close-knit society among the student body. This meant that the students who entered the yeshiva were being called on to move into a whole new world. Students received new names, lived in an all-male social setting, and were expected to study as much as twenty hours a day. Students were continuously reminded that they were engaged in a course of study that was part of a tradition that traced its origins back to biblical days. The yeshivot not only provided training and skills in forms of traditional hermeneutics, but also created individuals closely and passionately bound to an alternative system and world view.[45]

While the curriculum at the yeshiva continued to stress the Talmud with its continued relevance for contemporary issues, a new course of study introduced into the classroom at this time was the series of musar talks by the headmaster or a special instructor. These discourses, focusing on personal ethics, became the most important pedagogic innovation introduced into the Russian, mainly Lithuanian, yeshivot. However, the style of the musar talk and its impact did not remain restricted to Eastern Europe. Taken personally by the rabbi most widely identified with musar, Israel B. Z. Lipkin [Salanter] to both Germany and France, the movement also had a profound impact on modern Jewish education in the West.[46]

Musar talks, delivered in an emotional fashion, stressed personal ethics and piety and sought to base those exclusively on halakhic grounds. The focus on individual ethics and individual action was intended to personalize the educational process and force the student to undertake an introspective self-analysis, ultimately coming to the conclusion that all of his actions should be in conformity with Jewish law and not be influenced by local practice or secular custom. This Judaization of thought and action on the level of individual behavior was fundamental to the musar movement. In this, the founders of the movement intended to inculcate a positive attitude to halakha and to its continued relevance as a means of dealing even with the confused and ethically chaotic character of the contemporary world. It is clear that musar intended to establish once again the primacy of halakha and thereby re-establish the authority of the halakhist as the chief problem-solver or decision-maker for Jews under all circumstances. Rather than retreating to abstractions or philosophical and theological formulations, or even withdrawing into a spiritual asceticism that rejected the world in order to preserve the pristine character of a religious outlook, Lipkin and the musar preachers confronted head-on the challenges of modernity and affirmed that the age-old Judaic tradition of dealing with the world through halakha continued to be relevant. They believed that not only rabbis and scholars should be engrossed in the study of halakha, but also businessmen, as well as laborers, and students should turn their attention to the traditional sources and be bound by its insights.

Here we can identify an aggressive, even combative effort to sustain traditional Judaism, its values, world-view and structures by claiming that the tradition still had the power to shape the individual Jew and the modern Jewish community. The musar movement was not mass oriented, but rather was directed at the elite being trained in the yeshivot. It was intended as personal moral fortification for graduates of the yeshivot who were then dispatched directly into the maelstrom of the community as spokesmen for the authentic voice of the tradition. It was not contemplative – it was active and ultimately communal. The teaching of musar and its successful integration into the curriculum of the yeshivot at this time was a major accomplishment.[47]

By the 1890s, the yeshivot had not only regained their former exalted status within the traditional community, they had also come to be widely respected and looked to as centers of learning by the general community. By being able to attract serious and talented students, the yeshivot were able to train a new corps of traditional rabbis and teachers, and thus have a profound influence on the next generation of Jewish students. In this way, both traditional religious identity and the halakhic foundations of communal life received transfusions in the very same time period which saw the emergence of secular formulations of those same conceptions.

Within a few years, these rabbinic leaders and their lay supporters also came to recognize the critical importance of modern politics as the means by which they could promote their own vision as well as compete with others for communal leadership. Therefore, they, too, began the process of organizing politically and taking their case to the people. In doing so, they used all of the devices and tactics of modern political movements as they sought to disseminate their message and organize their supporters not only to protect their vision of the community, but to gain for themselves the recognition of the general society as the true representatives of the Jewish people. In this way, moral activism and religious energy initially aimed at the Jewish street made their way into the political arena as part of the same process of responding to the immediate crises confronting the community and seeking to organize its future course.

VI

We began this summary with a statistical analysis of Russian Jewry based on the census data collected in 1897. A closer study of that material indicates that the community was in the process of being dramatically transformed in the decades between the pogroms of 1881 and 1903. Given the hostile attitude of the government to the Jews and its negative response to Jewish requests for alleviations of discriminatory policies, it would have been reasonable to describe the community as being not only beleaguered, but also on the verge of disintegration. However, such a harsh assessment would be an incorrect one. While confronting change, social and economic dislocation, as well as enmity from the surrounding society, Jewish leaders did not despair; the community did not become paralyzed. Even though thousands of young people were fleeing their homes for either freedom in the West, or utopian dreams in the Middle East, or in pursuit of a better life elsewhere in the Pale, the Jewish community of tsarist Russia did not crumble. New spokesmen came to the fore and delineated scenarios or advanced programs that they believed would establish the community on firm foundations in the future. While some of these positions marked radical departures from approaches undertaken in the past, they nevertheless were not ephemeral in their conceptualization. Nor, for that matter, was the commitment on the part of the activists quixotic. The supporters of these movements applied themselves assiduously and built modern political movements addressed to the proposition that the Jews were a community whose present difficulties would be overcome and resolved through the tireless efforts of the people themselves.

This shift from a passive to an activist approach in order to solve the problems of Russian Jewry stands out as a common feature for all groups emerging in this period. The sense of Russian Jewry as a community, divided in the same ways that all national or ethnic groups were divided but all the same still an identifiable entity with characteristics unique unto itself, was accepted, recognized, and understood by all groups vying for its leadership. Finally, all looked forward optimistically to the new century as the time when significant and positive changes would take place.

The sequence of events triggered by the new wave of pogroms begun at Kishinev in April 1903 only accentuated and telescoped those views and programs already under discussion in the Jewish world. The violence in Kishinev initially released feelings of shame and revulsion that more was not done by the existing Jewish leadership in the defense of the community. For those who had been advocating a new course, the failure of the Jewish "establishment" to protect the Jews of Russia at this critical time documented their cry that a new approach to the problems of Russian Jewry was called for. The critics and the radicals moved dramatically to the center of Jewish life as they asserted their right to lead the community through this latest trial. Hence, the immediate responses to Kishinev, active self-defense, and the politicization of Russian Jewry, were not new responses which marked a new epoch in the history of the community, but were rather the fruits of more than twenty years of effort.

NOTES

1 The data collected by the census takers is available in I. M. Rubinow's *Economic Conditions of the Jews in Russia*, US Bureau of Labor Bulletin, no. 15 (1907) (reprinted New York, 1976). In addition to the government's census, the Jewish Colonization Association undertook a major study of the Jewish community at the close of the nineteenth century and published its findings in Russian, *Sbornik materialov ob ekonomicheskom polozhenii Evreev v Rossii* (St. Petersburg, 1904) and in French, *Recueil de matériaux sur la situation économique des Israélites de Russie* (Paris, 1906). Recent interpretations of these reports include S. W. Baron, *The Russian Jew under Tsars and Soviets*, 2nd edn (New York, 1984), 63–99; I. M. Dijur, "Jews in the Russian economy," in *Russian Jewry, 1860–1917*, ed. G. Aronson, et al. (New York, 1966), 120–43; Arcadius Kahan, *Essays in Jewish Social and Economic History*, ed. Roger Weiss (Chicago, 1986), 1–70 and 82–101; and Jacques Silber, "Some demographic characteristics of the Jewish population in Russia at the end of the nineteenth century," *Jewish Social Studies*, v (1980), 269–80.

2 See John D. Klier, *Russia Gathers Her Jews: The Origins of the Jewish Question in Russia, 1772–1825* (DeKalb, IL, 1986) and Richard Pipes, "Catherine II and the Jews: the origins of the Pale of Settlement," *Soviet Jewish Affairs*, v (1975), 3–20.

3 On Jewish policies and their impact during the reign of Nicholas I, see Michael Stanislawski, *Tsar Nicholas I and the Jews: The Transformation of Jewish Society in Russia, 1825–1855* (Philadelphia, 1983).

4 Just over 300,000 Jews lived outside the Pale of Settlement at the beginning of the twentieth century. Approximately 200,000 of these Jews lived in European Russia with about 15,000 Jews in the city of St. Petersburg. Just under 100,000 lived in Asiatic Russia, most of these in Georgia and the surrounding mountain regions.

5 Rubinow, *Economic Conditions*, 490–1.

6 Kahan, *Essays*, 52–6.

7 Rubinow, *Economic Conditions*, 493.

8 On Jewish birth rates and the general growth of the population, see Silber, "Demographic characteristics," 269–80. On Jewish emigration from Russia within the context of overall Jewish migratory patterns, see Mark Wischnitzer, *To Dwell in Safety: The Story of Jewish Migrations since 1800* (Philadelphia, 1948). See also Kahan, *Essays*, 101–28 for an assessment of the economic aspects of the 1881–84 emigration.

9 A study of internal resettlement at the close of the nineteenth century has been prepared by J. William Leasure and Robert A. Lewis, "Internal migration in Russia in the late nineteenth century," *Slavic Review*, XXVII (1968), 375–95.

10 Rubinow's data, *Economic Conditions*, 495–6, indicate that a significant number of Jews moved from the northwestern to the southeastern zone

of the Pale in the period after 1860. Patricia Herlihy's study, *Odessa: A History, 1794–1914* (Cambridge, MA, 1986) discusses the factors that contributed to the rapid growth of that region. See especially 202–63.

11 For instance, see Steven Zipperstein's discussion of the new forms of Jewish communal life in his study, *The Jews of Odessa. A Cultural History, 1794–1881* (Stanford, CA, 1985), 70–114. Jewish Odessa in the second half of the century should be contrasted to the character of the traditional community as depicted by Isaac Levitats in his *The Jewish Community in Russia, 1772–1844* (New York, 1943).

12 Kahan, *Essays*, 6–7.

13 Rubinow, *Economic Conditions*, 500 and Kahan, *Essays*, 6–8.

14 Rubinow, *Economic Conditions*, 502.

15 Kahan, *Essays*, 22–3.

16 Rubinow, *Economic Conditions*, 570–5.

17 Kahan, *Essays*, 34. For a thorough discussion of governmental policies and official attitudes to the Jewish population of the realm, see Hans Rogger, *Jewish Policies and Right Wing Politics in Imperial Russia* (Berkeley, CA, 1986).

18 I have traced the response of the Jewish establishment to the pogroms of 1881 in my essay, "The Russian-Jewish leadership and the Pogroms of 1881–82: the response from St. Petersburgh," *The Carl Beck Papers in Russian and East European Studies*, no. 308 (1984).

19 Jonathan Frankel's pioneering study, *Prophecy and Politics: Socialism, Nationalism and the Russian Jews, 1862–1917* (Cambridge, 1981), especially 51–90, has profoundly influenced the argument in this section of my presentation.

20 Lilienblum, "Obshcheevreiskii vopros i Palestina", *Rassvet*, Nos. 41 and 42 (1881).

21 This theme dominated the essays in Lilienblum's pamphlet *O vozrozhdenii evreiskogo naroda na sv. zemle ego drevnikh ottsov* (Odessa, 1903). An English-language edition of these essays appeared under the title *The Regeneration of Israel on the Land of Its Forefathers*.

22 An English-language version of *Autoemancipation* can be found in B. Netanyahu's *Road to Freedom* (New York, 1944), 7–93.

23 In addition to the discussion in Frankel's *Prophecy and Politics*, 90–7, see David Vital, *The Origins of Zionism* (Oxford, 1975), 65–74.

24 Vital, *Origins*, 144–7.

25 Ibid., 160–71.

26 Ibid., 155–8.

27 See the study by Joseph Goldstein assessing the reactions of the Russian Lovers of Zion to Herzl at the time of his growing involvement with Jewish nationalism. J. Goldstein, "Herzl and the Russian Zionists: the unavoidable crisis," *Studies in Contemporary Jewry*, II (1986), 208–10. Also of interest in conjunction with this theme is Goldstein's study, "Some sociological aspects of the Russian Zionist movement at its inception", *Jewish Social Studies*, XLVII (1985), 167–78.

28 E. Tcherikower, "Yidn revolutsionern in Rusland in di 6oer un 7oer yorn," *Historische schriften*, I, 60–172. See also Ezra Mendelsohn, *Class Struggle in the Pale* (Cambridge, 1970), 30–2.
29 Mendelsohn, *Class Struggle*, 37.
30 A. Kremer, *Ob agitatsii* (Geneva, 1897). See also Frankel, *Prophecy and Politics*, 173–200; Mendelsohn, *Class Struggle*, 53; and K. S. Pinson, "Arkady Kremer, Vladimir Medem and the ideology of the Jewish Bund," *Jewish Social Studies*, VII (1947), 233–64.
31 Mendelsohn, *Class Struggle*, 55.
32 Martov's speech was published as *Povorotnyi punkt v istorii evreiskogo rabochego dvizheniia* (Geneva, 1900), 17–18.
33 Ibid., 20.
34 Quoted by J. L. Keep, *The Rise of Social Democracy in Russia* (Oxford, 1963), 44.
35 Henry Tobias, *The Jewish Bund in Russia from its Origins to 1905* (Stanford, CA, 1972).
36 See the articles by J. G. Frumkin, "Pages from the history of Russian Jewry," 18–85, and Samuel Kucherow, "Jews in the Russian Bar," 9–56, in *Russian Jewry, 1860–1917*.
37 The recollections of one such individual, Henry B. Sliozberg, are especially revealing in indicating this growing attachment to the Jewish people. See G. B. Sliozberg, *Dela minuvshikh dnei*, I (Paris, 1933).
38 Gregor Aronson, "Ideological trends among Russian Jews," in *Russian Jewry, 1860–1917*, 144–72.
39 S. M. Dubnow, *Pis'ma o starom i novom Evreistve* (St. Petersburg, 1907). An English-language edition of these letters was published by K. S. Pinson under the title *Nationalism and History* (Philadelphia, 1958).
40 Dubnow, *Nationalism and History*, 79.
41 Ibid., 80.
42 "Autonomism, the basis of the national program," ibid., 131–42.
43 Sidney Harcave, "The Jews and the first Russian national election," *The American Slavic and East European Review*, IX (1950), 33–41.
44 See the dissertation by Shaul Stampfer, "Three Lithuanian Yeshivot in the nineteenth century" (in Hebrew, with English summary) (unpublished doctoral dissertation, The Hebrew University of Jerusalem, 1981), for a thorough discussion of these specific themes. The material offered here is based on that work and the essay by A. Menes, "Yeshivahs in Russia," *Jews in Russia, 1860–1917*, 382–408.
45 Stampfer, "Three Lithuanian Yeshivot," 87–98.
46 On Rabbi Lipkin (Salanter), see L. Ginzberg, *Students, Scholars and Saints* (Philadelphia, 1928), 145–94; Emmanuel Etkes, *R. Israel Salanter and the Beginnings of the Musar Movement* (in Hebrew) (Jerusalem, 1987) and *Encyclopedia Judaica*, XI, 279.
47 H. H. Ben Sasson, "Musar," *Encyclopedia Judaica*, XII, 536.

CHAPTER 7

Tsarist officialdom and anti-Jewish pogroms in Poland

Michael Ochs

In his introduction to a book of documents on pogroms in Russia, G. Krasnyi-Admoni posed the following rhetorical question: "Was there ever a case in the whole history of Jewish pogroms when the authorities -- if rumors arose of pogroms or ritual murders, as often happened before anti-Jewish disorders – openly and honestly came forth as a conciliator between Jews and the native population?"[1]

This chapter answers Krasnyi-Admoni's question in the specific context of Russian Poland[2] between 1881 and 1903. It then goes on to examine the broader question of whether the tsarist authorities instigated or tolerated anti-Jewish violence in Poland during that period.

Since most recent scholarship on the subject of pogroms argues convincingly against Russian government involvement or connivance,[3] one might wonder why it is worth singling out Russian Poland and asking the same old questions yet again. There are several good reasons. First, unlike Jews in the Pale of Settlement, Jews in Russian Poland in the second half of the nineteenth century have attracted relatively little scholarly attention.[4] Consequently, though there have been many studies of pogroms in the Pale, not much has been written on such events in Poland.

Second, such historiography as exists is often colored by anti-Russian prejudice deriving from various sources. For example, the idea of Polish–Jewish solidarity against Russian tyranny was popular among certain groups of Jews and Poles in the nineteenth and twentieth centuries. Jews who advocated assimilation to Polish culture were naturally loath to admit that Polish antisemitism could have grown out of native soil. Similar constraints influenced Poles who cherished assimilationist hopes for the Jews, particularly if these Poles were socialists, since they could accuse the "Moskale" of sowing discord between Polish and Jewish workers and splintering the unity of the proletarian cause. On the other hand, Poles who either rejected the idea of Jewish assimilation or were not sanguine about its feasibility or were completely indifferent to the issue also relished the opportunity to blame the Russians for provoking mob outbursts against the Jews. By contending that only "Asiatics" would behave so barbarously, they could mollify their national pride and indulge their contempt and hatred of their powerful neighbor to the east.[5]

The combined efforts of these groups produced historical and propagandistic works that, together with the strongly anti-Russian orientation of many Russian-Jewish historians[6] and publicists, point an accusatory finger at St. Petersburg. This finger-pointing has had a telling impact, both on specialized and general historical works of recent times.[7] Consequently, modern-day investigators must take into account the biases and preconceptions reflected in this secondary literature and see how accurately it corresponds with primary sources on the subject.

Third, Russian Poland merits studying because it was different from the Pale of Settlement in many respects. To begin with basics, the Jews living in this region enjoyed virtual civil equality, *Równouprawnienie*, as of 1862. In May of that year, Russian anxiety over Jewish attachment to Polish nationalist aspirations and the desire to keep Jews from backing the impending rebellion led Alexander II to annul almost all disabilities on Polish Jews accumulated over the centuries.[8] Though the greatest hope – or danger, depending on one's perspective – of Polish–Jewish solidarity waned after the defeat of the uprising, St. Petersburg thenceforth sought consistently to keep Jews and Poles from developing any shared interests or consciousness of shared interests.[9] At least one historian has suggested that concern about this threat led the Russians to organize a pogrom to set these two peoples against each other.[10] Any examination of possible Russian involvement in pogroms in Poland – as opposed to the Pale, where there was little history of, or potential for, such community of national-political interests between Jews and non-Jews – must therefore keep in mind the special circumstances obtaining in the Kingdom.

Post-1863 Poland, moreover, presented the sorts of problems and challenges that had already convinced the autocracy to resort to very radical policies. After crushing the uprising, the Russians reversed established patterns of reaching mutually beneficial terms with local elites. Furious at the Polish szlachta for having mounted a rebellion, St. Petersburg now systematically set about destroying its traditional partner, the landowning gentry, and staked its wager on the peasants.[11] Why would a regime that could embark on such a course flinch from provoking violence against Jews?

Finally, the Kingdom was special in yet another sense, for though the Russians undoubtedly viewed it as an integral part of the Empire, they could hardly help knowing that Congress Poland was indeed Poland, even if it was no longer so designated officially.[12] This might be one more reason they would have been tempted to test the effectiveness of tactics they would have been hesitant to employ when administering the "primordial Russian lands"[13] of the Pale.

In sum, to broaden and focus simultaneously Krasnyi-Admoni's question: were the differences between Russian Poland and the Pale of Settlement sufficiently great to invalidate the thesis of the non-involvement of tsarist officialdom in pogroms? Our answer to this question will be based primarily on unpublished archival documents from the chancelleries of the highest echelons of the Russian administration in Poland – the Governor-General of Warsaw, his assistant, and the governors of the Polish provinces. For the most part, these materials date from 1881–5 and 1903 (the year of the Kishinev pogrom), when the increased incidence of anti-Jewish violence generated large amounts of documentation.

At a later point, we will discuss the methodological problems involved in using these sources, and develop in greater detail the larger issue of their reliability. For now, let us turn to the pogroms in Russian Poland and let the sources speak for themselves.

If from 1881 on, the possibility of pogroms made the Jews' life anxious, the same was true, though naturally to a different degree, of the authorities. Before 1881, they would have noted a dispute between a Jewish shopkeeper and a Christian shopper and characterized it as a minor incident. Now such everyday occurrences could quickly turn into large-scale riots, an eventuality the authorities were under strict orders to avert. For the outbreak of pogroms in the Ukraine resulted in a flood of instructions and circulars from St. Petersburg to governors-general and governors all over the Empire about the necessity of preventing disorders in the areas under their control. These directives also came to the Governor-General of Warsaw. He forwarded them to his provincial governors, who, in turn, sent them on to their own subordinates.

On 8 April 1881, a secret circular from Minister of Internal Affairs M. T. Loris-Melikov empowered all governors "in extreme cases, where it seems drunkenness could lead to disorders" to close down drinking establishments. As justification for this extraordinary measure, Loris-Melikov cited the "current alarming events," which made "the prevention and suppression of any disorders the special concern of the police authorities."[14]

After receiving this directive, P. P. Albedynskii, the Governor-General of Warsaw, deluged his governors with circulars of his own. On 27 April, he wrote to them:

It has come to my attention that in certain localities of this region, a rumor is circulating among the lower classes that the Jews are expecting the advent of the Messiah and that attacks on them are expected...

At the present time, one of the homeowners in the city of Warsaw has received an anonymous warning about dangers which allegedly threaten the local Jewish population.

In view of the confrontations which have recently taken place in some southern [Ukrainian] cities between the Christian and Jewish populations, I most humbly beg Your Excellency to take appropriate measures to strengthen surveillance in order to prevent anything similar in the province entrusted to you.[15]

The governor-general followed up this communiqué with two more, on 15 May and 22 May, urging the governors to keep a careful eye on the mood of the populace during Eastertime and to ensure that disorders did not break out.[16] On 16 June a relieved but still concerned Albedynskii conveyed the following message:

The holidays passed quietly but it is nevertheless impossible to be completely sure that the future is secure. The peasants, with the onset of the busiest period of the season, will naturally devote themselves to their work and will avoid any excitement on the side. But the same cannot be said for factory workers who are most susceptible and inclined to passions [*uvlechenii*]...

Strict surveillance of the [popular] state of mind at this critical time constitutes the object of my special concern. Therefore, I ask you not to weaken vigilance.[17]

As is evident from this spate of directives, the Governor-General of Warsaw, the highest Russian official in the land, was determined that no anti-Jewish disorders would take place in Poland and he instructed his governors accordingly. Governor N. N. Medem of Warsaw province may serve as an example of how they responded.

On 1 May 1881, he sent a telegram to his district chiefs in which he repeated Albedynskii's message and also suggested that they use their personal influence with representatives of the Christian population and rabbis to remove all possible causes of misunderstandings. "And in case of disorders which cannot be put down by police, call the nearest army unit and report to me immediately."[18]

About one week later, one of Medem's district chiefs informed him about "a small disorder" in Zyrardów. "I immediately went there," he wrote, "and had those who threw stones at the Jews' shops arrested. To forestall any further trouble, observation by the police has been intensified, night patrols have been arranged, and I am here." He concluded that all was quiet and expressed the hope that it would remain so.

Despite these assurances, Medem himself visited Zyrardów on 13 May. Satisfied that the situation there was calm, and since the stone-throwing had not caused any property damage, he ordered the release of those arrested. However, he had his district chief tell them that they "would be the first to answer for the consequences of any new disturbances."[19]

The case just described was obviously a comparatively trivial matter. Yet the governor of the province went to Zyrardów to make sure that local officials had done everything possible to keep the peace. Indeed, Medem was in simultaneous contact with the military and police authorities. The former provided an extremely detailed, eight-page list of where troops were stationed and could most easily be called upon if needed. The Warsaw police chief, for his part, recommended measures to be followed in case of disorders. These included closing all drinking establishments; gathering at the scene all off-duty policemen; contacting him personally without delay; and, calling in the troops if the police forces were unable to handle the situation.[20]

Other governors acted likewise, and the events of 1881 and the experience gained in dealing with them prepared the authorities for similar outbreaks in the following years. On 2 April 1882, Albedynskii forwarded to his governors and the police chief of Warsaw a circular dated 26 March from the Minister of Internal Affairs Ignatiev to governors in the Pale of Settlement. Noting that holidays often coincided with anti-Jewish disorders, Ignatiev enclosed a list of measures used by officials in the southwest and New Russia the year before in order to help "protect social order and the personal safety of the Jewish population," and to standardize the administrative response to pogroms.[21]

The circular contained these general recommendations: closing drinking establishments for the duration of the disorders; fencing off, where possible, Jewish apartments and shops; forbidding workers in factories and large artisan enterprises to leave work; calling in troops. Nearly six supplementary pages of more specific suggestions followed.[22]

Finally, two Imperial ukazy of 10 May 1882 clarified Alexander's attitude to anti-Jewish disturbances: "let it be known to all that the government is firmly determined to prosecute undeviatingly any violence against the person and property of the Jews who, like all other subjects, are under the protection of His Majesty's laws applying to the entire population."[23] As for the provincial authorities, "it is their responsibility to take timely preventive measures to suppress disorders if they break out. Any negligence on the part of the administrative and police authorities – when they were able to but did not see to the suppression of violent acts – will result in their dismissal from their posts." They were also charged with explaining to local inhabitants the full criminality of violence against anyone's person or property.[24]

Given the quantity and tenor of all these decrees and circulars, it should not be surprising that from 1881 to 1885, the Governor of Warsaw kept special files entitled "on measures taken to prevent anti-Jewish disorders" or "on measures to prevent confrontations between the Christian and Jewish populations of Warsaw province." Other governors kept similar files, as did the governor-general and his assistant. These documents provide voluminous information on the state of Polish–Jewish relations. They contained detailed accounts of conflicts that took place, describing their origin, course, and methods used by the authorities to pacify the entire populace and bring to justice those held responsible for having disturbed the peace. The stream of reports from low echelon officials to their superiors and the instructions from the center to the provinces and districts demonstrate the importance placed by the Russian administration on *preventing* riots. Indeed, the maintenance of order was the paramount goal of the authorities.

Working on the reasonable assumption that the best way to prevent riots was to ensure that volatile situations did not even arise, the authorities carefully followed virtually anything that might

affect Polish–Jewish relations. The methods employed in their
"preventive medicine" approach were consequently quite varied.

For example, in May 1881, Albedynskii sent a circular to all his
governors noting that the recent pogroms in the Ukraine would
likely cause diminished production in factories in Poland, leading to
pay cuts and unemployment. He ordered them to inform him as soon
as possible of the plans of factory owners in their provinces, and to
make sure that any layoffs would affect foreigners rather than local
workers.[25]

More typical alarm signals, however, were rumors of impending
anti-Jewish riots. One motif of the rumors floating around the Polish
countryside was that the Jews had committed some heinous crime for
which they were to suffer retribution – with the government's full
approval. In a village of Łomża province in 1903, the alleged ritual
murder by Jews of a young girl in Białystok led to widespread
whispers of a forthcoming riot. It was further asserted that those
wishing to go and take part in the pogrom could travel there at no
cost to themselves. This rumor, however, was quashed when two of
the eager would-be avengers appeared at the train station
demanding free tickets and were promptly arrested.[26]

The chief of the Płock gendarmes informed the assistant to the
governor-general in June 1903 about the following rumor: "the
government itself wants to destroy the Jews but is afraid of other
countries and having to pay an indemnity [kontributsiia] for the
Jews, so through agents it has declared to all Poles that they should
attack the Jews."[27] According to another version of the same story,
"the Minister of Internal Affairs needs two million roubles and
doesn't know where to get the money so he has sent his agents into
the Kingdom of Poland to collect it. If [they are] unsuccessful, he has
instructed [them] to plunder Jewish property and slaughter the Jews
themselves. When they are annihilated, Poland will be returned to
the Poles."[28]

However bizarre these allegations may have sounded, the
authorities did not turn a deaf ear to them. Particularly if anti-
Jewish assaults had already occurred elsewhere in the Empire, they
quickly took steps to defuse tensions and disabuse the population of
any illusions concerning government support for pogroms.

When trouble seemed imminent, officials would travel to the
locale to read both Jews and Christians a lesson in civics, either
directly or through the mediation of their respective clergymen.

They would warn the Jews to "be restrained" in their contacts with Christians. In Łomża province in May 1903, rumors circulating that the Jews were "to be beaten" brought the district chief to the scene. He assembled all the Jews in the synagogue where he lectured them: "in view of the existing ferment [they] should not initiate any quarrels with the peasants and should in no way give any cause for any disorders."[29] Exactly what the Jews were to refrain from is not made clear, but we may assume care in business dealings was implied, along with avoiding more blatantly provocative acts.

The authorities would gather the Christians as well and would impress upon them that violence against the Jews would entail serious consequences. On 26 April 1882, Governor Medem notified his district chiefs that in Warsaw district they had found it very useful "to explain to village assemblies how illegal is any use of force."[30]

The authorities' desire to use the influence of local clergymen was more pronounced and standardized with regard to Catholics than Jews (presumably because Jews needed less persuading). Thus, priests often came under pressure to stress themes of order and brotherly love in their sermons, especially during Christmas and Easter, when experience indicated riots were most likely to occur. A 19 February 1882 circular from Albedynskii to all governors formalized this bit of common sense into routine procedure.[31]

Conversely, the Russians took action against priests whose behavior increased the dangers of a confrontation. On 8 May 1884, Governor-General Io. V. Gurko ordered Medem to investigate a priest in Radzymin district who apparently was stirring up his congregants against the Jews. Radzymin's district chief, instructed by Medem to find out what was going on, replied that he wanted this particular priest transferred elsewhere, where "his behavior would not harm the population and social order." On 22 June Medem advised the district chief that Gurko had asked the Archbishop of Warsaw to move the priest to a "lightly populated village parish."[32]

Transfer of priests or the threat of it was, of course, not resorted to lightly. Under other circumstances, Medem might have instructed a district chief to "invite [a troublesome priest] to change his manner of acting towards the Jews living in the *posad*," and fine him if he refused to cooperate.[33] In any event, however, the authorities were quick to take note of priests whose deeds or words risked inflaming anti-Jewish passions.[34]

Another example of the Russians' desire to keep tensions between Poles and Jews from boiling over into violence centered on *eruvs*. Broadly speaking, *eruvs* may be described as the perfect symbol of Jewish ingenuity when finding halakhically sanctioned ways of circumventing stringent religious proscriptions. More specifically, the type of *eruv* we are concerned with (there are various kinds) consisted of four poles connected by some sort of wire at the top. The poles would be placed in strategic areas around a settled district, thus making it seem as if the entire area was fenced in. The contrivance of an enclosure was necessary so that Jews could get around laws that forbade, for example, carrying an object between public and private domains or walking more than 2,000 cubits on the Sabbath or holidays.[35]

These *eruvs*, their location, and occasional change of location were a perennial source of unrest between Jews and their Gentile neighbors. In July 1882, the chief of Gostyn district wrote Medem about Jews who had moved an *eruv* from one place to another without permission. Upset by this, the local Christians began gathering in groups. The police averted a possible confrontation by arresting a drunk who was inciting the crowd against the Jews, restoring the *eruv* to its original place, and fining the Jews who had moved it.[36]

A similar, but more serious incident occurred in Płock in June 1903. In this case, the Jews had apparently used the city's barriers for an *eruv*. Enraged Catholics tore it down, precipitating a disturbance. The governor of Płock in his report to the governor-general, condemned the local authorities for having permitted the Jews to erect an *eruv*. The mayor was actually imprisoned for two days and another official was transferred.[37]

It was noted in the case above that Jews, who by building or somehow modifying an existing *eruv* undermined the authorities' attempts to maintain order, were fined. And indeed, Jews no less than Christians might wind up in prison because of the official resolve to maintain the inviolability of social peace. Any sort of behavior that threatened to result in disturbances was reported and generally penalized, regardless of whether the parties involved were Poles or Jews. This was particularly so during crisis periods of Jewish–Gentile relations, e.g., the early 1880s and after the Kishinev pogrom of 1903. At such times, the police intensified surveillance and punishments were correspondingly more severe.

For example, in an undated report from 1885, one district chief informed Medem that factory workers in his district were riled up because Jews were said to be spreading rumors about the alleged conversion [presumably to Judaism] of Pope Leo XIII. The local police were content to monitor the mood of the workers more carefully, but Medem demanded the incarceration of the Jewish rumor-mongers.[38]

On 30 May 1903, Warsaw's police chief apprised Governor-General M. I. Chertkov of the beating of several Christians by Jews who had accused them of giving poisoned candies to Jewish children. Chemical tests of the candies had shown the charges to be groundless. Still, given the post-Kishinev atmosphere and the attendant danger of disorders elsewhere, the police chief urged immediate action. He asked Chertkov to bypass the usual judicial procedures and act against the list of people (both Jews and Christians) provided.[39]

The authorities' anxiety to forestall even the possibility of disorders occasionally reached comical proportions. On 22 March 1882, the governor-general wrote Medem about "a very noisy Jewish wedding" in Grujec (Warsaw province) that had come to his attention and ordered an investigation. In his follow-up report, Medem explained, somewhat helplessly, that "all Jewish weddings are noisy." He quickly reassured Albedynskii that "the local population has become accustomed to these wedding celebrations and reacts to them quite indifferently; nonetheless, in view of the almost universal hostility to the Jews among the simple people... I have suggested to the district chiefs of the region entrusted to me that they pay special attention to this matter." Medem advised them to confer with the local rabbis and "if circumstances make it necessary, they should completely prohibit such street celebrations."[40]

This document is noteworthy not only for its amusing aspects. It illustrates what sorts of concerns animated the governor-general, the man, after all, responsible for all of Congress Poland, and how he monitored the vigilance and performance of his governors. Even more important, it shows how far governors were prepared to go to keep the peace.

The authorities were aware that under certain circumstances, preventive measures could backfire and produce results diametrically opposed to those intended. When possible, therefore, they used a low-key approach. In May 1881, for example, Medem notified his district chiefs of a directive he had received from Albedynskii in which the governor-general ordered the immediate arrest of any "sinister figures" caught stirring up the village population to rob and attack the Jews. In conveying this message, Medem added a discretionary note: "If you find someone and he is either a stranger or a Prussian citizen, arrest and interrogate him. But if he is from the locale and known, since the Jews are always frightened now and might give the police unfounded accusations, it could be dangerous to arrest local Christians." If the matter was not very important, Medem concluded, they were to be called in for a talk, told they were under suspicion, and warned they would be held accountable if disorders broke out.[41]

Such modifications of general instructions were not exclusive to governors or lower level officials more familiar with the situation on the scene than those in Warsaw. The governor-general himself occasionally rebuked subordinates for overzealously executing orders to keep the peace. On 22 May 1881, Albedynskii wrote to Medem that he had heard about the refusal of the district chief of Grujec to allow priests from other parishes to come to Góra Kalwaria for a church holiday, on the grounds that confrontations between Christians and Jews must be avoided. "I think not allowing a conference of priests [to take place] could have exactly the opposite effect," observed Albedynskii. He ordered the district chief to permit the conference to proceed as scheduled and intensify surveillance.[42]

Since the documents cited so far date from the 1881–5 era and from 1903, the reader may have had the impression that only after the outbreak of pogroms in the southwest region did Russian officials begin paying attention to the problem of anti-Jewish disorders, or that they did so only during crises, e.g., the Kishinev events. But it would be more accurate to say that while their concern was, of course, greatly heightened after the riots in the Ukraine, all indications are that the maintenance of order was a constant priority.

In September 1880, Medem wrote to the Procurator of the Warsaw District Court, mentioning parenthetically that he had also informed the governor-general, about two Jewish boys who had desecrated an image of Christ. "In the interests of pacifying the local Christian population... and preventing any possible confrontations between Christians and Jews, as well as protecting the Jewish boys from the population," Medem ordered an inquiry and the boys placed in custody. One week later, the governor-general wrote

Medem demanding to know what progress had been made in the case. The ensuing investigation revealed that the boys were quite young, not many Christians had witnessed the incident, and "no ferment has been observed among the local population." Noting that there was no evidence that older Jews had put the boys up to their prank, the procurator advised against strict measures and the entire matter was quietly dropped.[43]

Similarly, 1898 was a year of no special significance in the history of pogroms. Yet on 15 July, Governor-General A. K. Imeretynskii notified the Governor of Kalisz of anti-Jewish agitation and disorders in Austrian Galicia, adding that provocative underground literature had also surfaced in some of the Polish provinces. "I ask you to undertake a vigilant lookout for anti-Jewish agitational activity. If any such is uncovered in the province entrusted to you, take appropriate measures to put an immediate end to it and let me know of any such manifestations."[44]

As the authorities' preoccupation with preventing disturbances was continuous over time, so was it continuous over the entire area of the Kingdom. It should not be supposed that Warsaw, as the main city of Russian Poland and presumably the most closely watched by outsiders, received any special attention, apart from that which would naturally accrue to the city with the most Jews. The governors of other provinces as well kept a careful eye on Polish–Jewish relations and informed the governor-general of steps they had taken to ensure order. They sent copies of all circulars from Warsaw and St. Petersburg to their police chiefs and district chiefs, and ordered the latter to keep them posted of any ominous developments.[45]

Still, despite the governors' repeated urgings about the essentiality of maintaining order, reports would at times come in of local, low level officials either provoking or encouraging anti-Jewish feelings among Christians. In such cases, the center would assign officials to check on their veracity. For example, on 25 May 1881, the Senior Assistant of the Chancellery Board notified Medem that he had gone to Grujec district to determine whether a police constable had in fact permitted himself (or perhaps others – the text is unclear) to stir up the inhabitants against the Jews. He concluded that just the reverse was true: the constable had warned people *against* doing so.[46]

The results of such investigations, however, did not always present the local authorities in the best light. In a November 1883 report on disturbances caused by army recruits, the Chief of the Warsaw

Gendarmes noted that the officials from the recruits' villages failed to accompany them personally. They left them to the care of other officials who, with one exception, "did not take any measures to quiet the rowdies." When he appealed to his colleagues for help, "they laughed in his face and continued to look indifferently on the disorders taking place."[47]

The document does not say whether in this particular case the indifferent officials were in any way penalized for dereliction of duty. But we have already noted the imprisonment of a mayor for negligence leading to disorders, so we may assume that at least on occasion, local authorities suffered the consequences of ignoring the importunities of their superiors. And those who distinguished themselves in the battle to keep the peace were recommended for awards, such as the constable in Novo-Minsk district who quieted a crowd claiming that the Jews had poisoned a well by himself drinking a glass of water from it and forcing the Jews to do the same.[48]

When all other preventive measures proved unavailing, the authorities literally called out the big guns: the army. We have seen that circulars from the Ministry of Internal Affairs and the governor-general from 1881 on empowered local officials to do so if they and the police could not handle a given situation. The tense atmosphere and numerous disturbances of the period necessitated resorting to military assistance frequently during the first few years of the decade. For this purpose, detailed plans were drawn up of the army units in the area and emergency action was coordinated with the commanders of the military districts.[49]

In keeping with precautionary practice, the authorities would dispatch troops to a locale when trouble was anticipated, on the assumption that their very presence would ward off riots. On 29 May 1881, Medem asked the governor-general to send 200 Cossacks to Łowicz. They wanted to be prepared for the worst since the coincidence of Easter Day with the fair would bring a large number of people to the city and there were rumors that the Jews would be beaten and robbed.[50]

In some instances, relations between Jews and Christians were so volatile that troops had to be stationed in the area for extended periods. The major disturbances in Gąbin (Warsaw province) offer a good example of this role of the military. Violence had already erupted in mid-April 1882 when the soldiers were brought in. They remained in the city until at least the end of September, despite repeated requests from the military authorities that they be released for general levies.[51]

The hope that the mere sight of armed troops would be a sufficient deterrent usually was justified. But when situations got completely out of hand, soldiers were ordered to shoot at rampaging mobs. Occasionally, there were pitched battles between them, as in Częstochowa in 1902. There, troops trying to disperse the crowd were met by curses and rocks before they opened fire. The result was two dead and six wounded.[52] Of course, firing at rioters was the last resort, and it happened very rarely; but clearly, the authorities were prepared to take this step if all other options had been exhausted.

Examples of the authorities' attempts to prevent and suppress disorders could easily be multiplied, but enough have already been provided to permit an analysis of their significance. The following discussion is based on the obvious, fundamental question: if the authorities did in fact do all that the documents record they did to keep the peace, how does one explain those pogroms that did take place?

There are two ways to answer this question: the conspiratorial and the non-conspiratorial approaches. We will begin with the latter, which assumes the genuineness of the authorities' desire to forestall anti-Jewish pogroms. The fact that they nonetheless occurred must logically be attributable to the authorities' inability to carry out their desire or, alternatively, calls for a closer definition of the word "authorities."

To address the first possibility, there is some evidence that the police and military forces at the disposal of the governors were occasionally inadequate to the task of maintaining order. In his detailed report on the disturbances in Gąbin (1882), Medem bemoaned the insufficient number of police or their total absence in locales where disorders might flare up. As for the military, he wrote, if there were riots in places where troops were not already stationed, they always arrived after the crowd had finished ransacking Jewish property and scattered.[53] In October 1903, the Governor of Lublin echoed these complaints in his account of confrontations between Jews and recruits,[54] as did the Governor of Piotrków in May of the same year.[55] Still, if this factor is relevant to other cities and towns, it does not apply to Warsaw, where on 25 December 1881, a large-scale pogrom erupted that rocked the city for three days (see below pp. 181–3). For now, let us acknowledge that at various places and times, the authorities might simply have been incapable of preventing or putting down disorders, for reasons beyond their control.

As for what is meant by "authorities," it must be clarified that the assumption of an official desire not to allow attacks on the Jews by no means presupposes a friendly disposition towards them. Rather, it reflects the bureaucratic-police mentality of Russian administrators, whose job was to carry out orders and file a report on their successful implementation. Here, the orders concerned stopping pogroms, but this was not coincidental, because their concept of "governing" seems to have been limited to keeping the peace. *Political* considerations are strikingly absent from the documents of Russian officialdom in Poland. They are almost always couched in police phraseology and the primary goal of policemen is, after all, to prevent disorder. Given the powerful centralized tradition of the Russian autocracy, this generalization probably holds true for the administration of the entire Empire, so it is not surprising that it should be especially valid for a border region that had recently witnessed an uprising.

Since we cannot assume any Judeophilia on the part of Russian officials, we must ask whether there existed among them anti-Jewish animosities which might have affected their carrying out of peace-keeping duties. The documents do indeed reveal such sentiments, among both high and low level officials. Governor Miller of Piotrków is the best example of the former. His reports to the governor-general, unlike those of other governors, are replete with references to "yids."[56] His account of the disturbances in Częstochowa (1902) places all the blame for the antagonism between Poles and Jews on the latter, who "scandalously fleece and deceive them at every step."[57] The reports of other high officials display similar tendencies. In 1902, the Chief of the Kalisz Gendarmes accused the Jews of *wanting* a pogrom, "seeing in it a peculiar *gesheft*" [sic].[58] Conceivably, such an attitude might have led to perfunctory performance of duty. More likely, however, the very rank and attendant police responsibilities of higher level officials, along with the fact that their superiors had ways of checking up on them, would have inclined them to carry out, if perhaps sadly, their orders to protect Jews from the mobs.

Lower echelon officials, however, had less responsibility and they also had much more contact with the Jewish population. If relations were mutually hostile, such an official would have had ample opportunity to give vent to his anti-Jewish animus. There were cases when the Jews accused local officials of stirring up the Christians against them, such as in Kutno district in September 1884,[59] and we have already cited the negligent behavior of officials accompanying army recruits. It may be, therefore, that while higher authorities consistently urged their subordinates to prevent anti-Jewish violence, these instructions were indifferently carried out, ignored, or actually subverted.

There is one other vital consideration that might have inhibited the Russian authorities from doing everything possible to protect the Jews. The basis of Russian policy in Poland was to undercut the nobility and clergy while trying to win over the peasant masses. Acting against the latter by defending an increasingly unpopular minority could well have been seen as counter-productive.

To be sure, no unambiguous documentary evidence of such a political decision has surfaced. But there is no doubt the authorities on the scene were conscious of the general political implications. In 1882, Medem ordered that the troops stationed in Gąbin and environs be fed at the expense of the local inhabitants, justifying his decision as follows:

It allows us not to resort to more forceful, coarse methods and since it affects Jews and Christians alike, it does not have the exasperating influence on the Christians inherent in every other administrative action, the application of which [makes the authorities] look to the population like the defenders of the Jews.[60]

Some two decades later, Governor Miller of Piotrków voiced the identical concerns in his report on the pogrom in Częstochowa. He added that the Polish press outside Russian Poland exaggerated and played up such incidents, in order to intensify Poles' hatred of Russia.[61]

The need to court the Polish masses may also account for the relatively mild punishment meted out to those convicted of disturbing the peace in Gąbin. Medem considered such leniency the most important defect in the authorities' program of pacification:

In Gąbin the crowd was composed of thousands; only 68 were arrested and they got short terms. For these types, a two-week sentence is nothing. They are aware that they are committing very serious crimes and conscience tells them that for such serious crimes they should pay very serious penalties. But they are surprised to see that most go unpunished and those few who are detained are soon released. It is understandable that they explain their perplexity in their own way: they assume that the government does not prohibit the wrecking of Jewish homes and only, so to speak, to clear its conscience brings a few participants to justice.[62]

Medem's implied surprise and annoyance are instructive. Perhaps there was no room in the prisons for such large numbers of hooligans or backlogs in the courts precluded acting against them in a serious way.[63] But it is also possible that the light sentences reflected a political decision, perhaps made in St. Petersburg. If so, the Russian officials in Poland, who were basically policemen and carried out orders from the center, would have had little say in the matter. Indeed, they may well have resented such interference since, at least in the view of the Governor of Warsaw, by impeding their endeavours to keep the peace, it made their job harder.

The non-conspiratorial approach, in sum, absolves the higher levels of the Russian administration in Poland of conscious wrong-doing or negligence, but acknowledges doubts about lower level officials and leaves unanswered questions about the constraining influence of politics on the effective administration of justice. Even so, this latter consideration applies only to punishment of perpetrators of crimes already committed, not to the prevention of violence, a goal which, as we have seen, the Russians consistently pursued.

The conspiratorial approach, on the other hand, poses questions that are ultimately unanswerable. For the conspiracy theorist will argue as follows: first, looking for documentary evidence that any Russian authorities organized pogroms anywhere is fruitless and naive, since by its very nature, this kind of provocation would leave no paper traces. It would be arranged verbally, and, of course, secretly, all evidence dying with the provocateurs themselves. The absence of documents proving the existence of a conspiracy therefore means nothing.[64]

Second, even if we take at face value archival materials indicating that the Russians – either in St. Petersburg or Warsaw – did not want anti-Jewish violence to erupt, this too means nothing, for it is not at all surprising. No government wants riots in the streets; the maintenance of order is its principal domestic function. This is especially true of the Russian autocracy, whose outstanding historical characteristic was the attempt to stifle *any* public initiative not controlled from above. When we consider further that the area under discussion is Poland, where as recently as 1863 an uprising against Russian rule had been mounted, it becomes even less plausible that the Russians would have countenanced *spontaneous* disorders.

But it does not necessarily follow, continues the argument, that they would not have occasionally wanted to organize a pogrom, believing they could control it and put a stop to it when it had served its purpose. With regard to Russian Poland, such conspiracy theories center on the Warsaw pogrom.

There are different versions of how it began, but it is clear that on Christmas Day, 1881, a commotion broke out in Holy Cross church, which was filled to capacity. In the ensuing panic, over twenty people were trampled to death as the congregants rushed to the exits. Once they were outside, rumors apparently flew through the crowd that Jewish pickpockets had deliberately set the false alarm. A wave of beatings and plundering of Jewish homes and shops followed, which lasted until 27 December. Sources vary as to the number of fatalities.[65]

Sources also differ about the reaction of the authorities. In a cabled report to St. Petersburg, the Chief of the Warsaw District Gendarmes wrote: "Troops are unable to stop the destruction; when the military units approach, the crowds disperse."[66] But secondary literature on the pogrom, based on eyewitness accounts and the foreign and Russian–Jewish press, agrees that the police and troops did nothing to stop the mobs. Only on the third day were serious measures undertaken to suppress the disorder. Moreover, the police impeded Jewish efforts to organize self-defense.[67]

These are not the only suspicious aspects of the events of 25–7 December. According to press accounts, troops responded to pleas for help from Jews by replying that they had orders to become involved only if they themselves were attacked; it was alleged that the person whose actions apparently led to the tumult in the church subsequently gave a false name and address when questioned, and then disappeared; *Czas*, the influential Polish newspaper in Kraków, claimed the leaders of the mobs were primarily Russians, though there were Poles among them; no shops or homes of non-Jews were touched.[68]

Assuming that the accounts of the authorities' inactivity and the peculiarities noted above are accurate – and it must be remembered that much of this information comes from the Polish press in Galicia and Prussian Poland – why would the Russians have instigated a pogrom in Warsaw and let it continue for three days? The conspiratorial answer heard most often is the one offered tentatively by I. Gruenbaum,[69] and more confidently insinuated by Dubnow: "Evidently, someone had an interest in having the capital of Poland repeat the experiment of Kiev and Odessa, and in seeing to it that the 'cultured Poles' should not fall behind the Russian barbarians in order to convince Europe that the pogrom was not exclusively a Russian manufacture."[70]

Who would have had such an interest? Certainly not Alexander III; his notation on the margin of the cable mentioned above was: "all this is very nasty..." [*preskverno*].[71] Several days later, after learning that order had been restored in Warsaw, he commented: "God grant that it continue like this."[72] Who, then? The mysterious "someone" has never been identified. And even if such a person or persons existed, would such an internationally oriented, politically motivated provocation have been arranged without the Emperor's knowledge and consent? Would the highest Russian authorities, merely to blacken the Poles in Europe's eyes, have risked unleashing the masses in a country with so rebellious a history? Not likely; and there is not a shred of evidence to back up this hypothesis.[73]

Another conspiracy theory on the cause of the Warsaw pogrom implies that the Russians hoped to drive a wedge between Poles and Jews. Gruenbaum, for example, claims that the Russians wanted to organize pogroms in Poland and he rejects the possibility of Polish responsibility.[74] But he weakens his conspiratorial case by acknowledging that the period from 1863 to 1881 witnessed growing disillusionment among Poles with the idea of Jewish assimilation and the beginnings of modern Polish antisemitism.

Golczewski, the most recent historian of the Warsaw events, agrees that an "outside hand" was involved. Discussing previous incidents, in 1877 and earlier in 1881, when there were rumors of an impending pogrom, he says the authorities acted responsibly but that by December 1881, their interests had changed. He offers no reasons, however, as to why this should have been so. Nor does he ever explicitly propose a theory about what the Russians would have had to gain from a pogrom in Warsaw. In any case, since his particular focus is the history of Polish–Jewish relations, he places far more emphasis than Gruenbaum on the susceptibility of Poles to anti-Jewish agitation. He doubts that the tensions that had built up between the two communities could have been resolved without excesses, even if there had been no Russian provocation.[75]

Whether or not Golczewski is right about the likelihood of violence, it is certainly true that the glow of fraternal feelings born in 1861–3 had long since dimmed and relations between these two peoples were steadily worsening. The notion that the Russians would have felt it necessary to stage a pogrom in 1881 to counter the threat of Polish–Jewish solidarity is unsupportable. Even less credible is the first conspiracy theory, for if St. Petersburg was truly stung by international reaction to the pogroms in Ukraine and the haughty condemnation of the Polish press outside Kongresówka, there would at least have been a motive, however far-fetched.

What remain are suspicions and circumstantial evidence. Some of the latter can be explained away. For example, even if the story about the man in the church were true, it is not surprising that someone who might inadvertently have caused the death of over twenty people should have been reluctant to identify himself. Perhaps *Czas* and *Dziennik Poznański* had their own reasons to claim that the leaders of the mobs were Russians.

Still, the fact remains that a pogrom lasted three days in the capital of Russian Poland, where there were numerous troops and policemen. It is also curious that in Governor Medem's file on anti-Jewish disorders in 1881, which contains extremely detailed information on minor disturbances in small, distant towns, that there should be not a single page devoted to the Warsaw pogrom, which received international publicity. (Of course, it is quite possible – even likely, given the notoriety of the incident – that it would have been written up in a separate file, which might later have been lost or destroyed along with many other archival holdings in Poland.)

The conspiracy theorist will seize on this as proof of a cover-up: having arranged the riot and achieved their ends (whatever they might be), the Russian authorities then destroyed all evidence of their complicity and could afterwards return to peace-keeping as usual.

Everything is possible. But the historian cannot write on the basis of an absence of documents and circumstantial evidence. He is obliged to take note of both, evaluate them, and weigh the opposing evidence; in this case, masses of documents indicating that the Russians were careful to prevent pogroms and the absence of any convincing reasons for them to act any differently in Warsaw in December 1881. As for the behavior of the police and troops during that holiday season, he is constrained to admit that there are puzzling aspects to the story which the present evidence does not allow us to unravel.

The answer to Krasnyi-Admoni's question, therefore, depends on the definition of "conciliator." If understood merely as trying to prevent and suppress pogroms, then at least in the Kingdom of Poland before 1905, the answer is an unequivocal "yes." Though individual officials undoubtedly performed with varying degrees of diligence, the documents show that the tsarist administration in Poland did what it could to keep tensions between Poles and Jews from breaking out into acts of violence. There is no indication, in other words, that the considerable differences between the political situation of the Jews in Poland and in the Pale, and the Russians' perception of these differences, led tsarist officialdom to view pogroms in the Kingdom as any more attractive an option than in the Pale.

This does not mean, however, that the Russians sought to promote smooth relations between Poles and Jews. The subject exceeds the scope of this article, but the evidence leads to the no less unequivocal conclusion that the Russians consciously tried to check any blossoming of Polish–Jewish solidarity, and, to this end, helped create and nourished the very tensions which they then forbade to be expressed in the streets.[76]

The message sounds confused, and it was. But between 1881 and 1903, the situation was not conducive to official involvement in pogroms. Instigating or engaging in violence against its own subjects, inside its own borders, is a risky proposition for a government – especially in a country like Russia where, once long-suppressed social forces were released in brutal ways, there was no telling how far things might go. Taking such a weighty decision requires that the state either be very sure of itself or desperately terrified. Russia was neither during this period. The documents of the time reflect the psychology of a frightened, nervous state, but not one on the brink of panicky collapse, when it might well lash out in all directions. Until such time, in the minds of Russian officialdom, the state's monopoly on violence was sacrosanct. And its message to the Poles about the Jews can be reduced to the following: "You shouldn't like them or trust them. Neither do we. But keep your hands to yourselves."

Finally, an examination of tsarist documents on pogroms in Poland reveals a picture far more nuanced than that conveyed in anti-Russian diatribes of the nineteenth and early twentieth centuries. Such historiography has led to claims in modern historical works – often without even a footnote, much less a qualifier – that the Russian authorities routinely organized assaults on Jews. These careless assertions become generalizations that, once accepted as popular wisdom, hamper investigations of a highly emotional topic not only by spreading unproved allegations, but by implicitly dismissing the need for further research. It is hoped the above discussion demonstrates the complexity of the issue and the need for caution.

NOTES

1 S. Dubnow and G. Krasnyi-Admoni, eds., *Materialy dlia istorii anti-evreiskikh pogromov v Rossii*, 1 (Petrograd, 1919), xxii.

2 "Poland" here refers to the ethnically Polish rump territory carved out of the Polish-Lithuanian Commonwealth during the partitions of the late eighteenth century. Ruled first by Prussia and then by Napoleonic France, it came under Russian control in 1815 at the Congress of Vienna – hence "Congress Poland" and the more colloquial appellation "Kongresowka." It was officially known as the Kingdom of Poland from 1815 until 1874. In that year, as part of the ongoing process of administrative integration launched after the 1863 Polish uprising, the Russians, seeking to eradicate all traces of a Polish political entity separate from Russia, began calling it the "Region on the Vistula" (*Privislinskii Krai*). "Poland," "the Kingdom," and "Kongresowka" are employed interchangeably here.

There were ten provinces in Poland, each ruled by a governor. The highest Russian official in the land was a viceroy until 1874, when the post of Governor-General of Warsaw was created.

3 Hans Rogger, on the basis of extremely thorough and detailed study, has concluded that "It is... almost certain that pogroms were not manufactured, inspired or tolerated as deliberate policy at the highest level of government. The available evidence suggests rather that an important and continuous aim of policy was not to indulge but to control mob violence..." See his "Russian ministers and the Jewish Question, 1881–1917," in *Jewish Policies and Right Wing Politics in Imperial Russia* (Berkeley, CA, 1986), 109. Rogger concedes, however,

that at times – especially during the revolutionary years 1905–6 – this policy was not rigorously applied and was even violated by police and military officials. In addition to Rogger's work, see I. Aronson, "Geographic and socioeconomic factors in the 1881 anti-Jewish pogroms in Russia," *Russian Review*, XXXIX, 1 (January, 1980), 18–31.

4 Professor Artur Eisenbach is the premier historian of Jews in the Duchy of Warsaw and the Kingdom of Poland and all students of Polish–Jewish history are indebted to him for his many studies. However, his work has focused on the period up to 1862, when Alexander II granted the Jews of Poland civil equality, or "*równouprawnienie.*"

5 All these attitudes are discussed in Alina Cała, *Kwestia asymilacji Żydów w Królestwie Polskim, 1864–1897* (Warsaw, 1989).

6 Without question, the best known and most influential was S. Dubnow. See his *The History of the Jews in Russia and Poland – From the Earliest Times until the Present Day*, 3 vols. (Philadelphia, 1916–20).

7 As an example of the former, see R. F. Leslie, ed., *The History of Poland Since 1863* (Cambridge, 1980), 48: "The government manifested its black-hearted policy by the encouragement of pogroms of the Jews in the Ukraine, Byelorussia and Poland in an effort to divert discontent against an identifiable and often unpopular element in society." Paul Johnson, *A History of the Jews* (New York, 1987), 364, illustrates how allegations of Russian involvement in anti-Jewish violence, based on secondary sources, find their way into broad histories with a wide appeal.

8 The standard work on this subject is A. Eisenbach, *Kwestia równouprawnienia Żydów w Królestwie Polskim* (Warsaw, 1972).

9 See Michael Ochs, "St. Petersburg and the Jews of Russian Poland, 1862–1905" (unpublished doctoral dissertation, Harvard University, 1986), chapters 4–5.

10 The pogrom took place in Warsaw in 1881. We will examine it and the various theories about its origins in greater detail below.

11 There is a large literature on Russian policy in Poland after 1863. For a concise treatment, see Ochs, chapter 2.

12 See n. 2.

13 "Iskonnye russkie zemli," a term frequently used by Russian publicists to describe the Lithuanian, Belorussian and Ukrainian territories.

14 The document may be found in the archive of the Governor of Kalisz, in a file entitled "O priniatii mer k okhraneniiu obshchestvennogo poriadka i lichnoi bezopasnosti evreiskogo naseleniia," 1. I used a microfilmed copy of this file in the Central Archive for the History of the Jewish People, Jerusalem. It will henceforth be referred to as HM 7527, the identification number given to it by Israeli archivists.

15 Ibid., 6.

16 Ibid., 8–10.

17 Ibid., 13.

18 Kancelaria Gubernatora Warszawskiego (henceforth KGW)/I-1881/

156, "O priniatii mer k nedopushcheniiu stolknovenii mezhdu khristianskim i evreiskim naseleniiami v Varshavskoi gubernii," 3, Archiwum Główne Akt Dawnych (henceforth AGAD), Warsaw.

19 Ibid., 28–30.

20 Ibid., 33–7.

21 HM 7527, 28–30.

22 Ibid., 21–9.

23 *Sobranie uzakonenii i rasporiazhanii pravitel'stva – 1882* (St. Petersburg, 1882), 451–2.

24 Ibid., 41.

25 KGW/I-1881/156, 68.

26 Kancelaria General Gubernatora Warszawskiego (henceforth KGGW), 1893, "O proisshestviakh obshchestvennogo znacheniia v guberniiakh Privislinskogo Kraia," 155, AGAD, Warsaw.

27 Kancelaria Pomocnika General Gubernatora Warszawskiego (henceforth KPGGW), 347, "O stolknoveniiakh khristian s evreiami," 104, AGAD, Warsaw.

28 Ibid.

29 KGGW, 1932, "Po povodu trevozhnykh slukhov vyzvannykh kishinevskimi besporiadkami," 4.

30 KGW/I-1882/63, "O priniatii mer dlia preduprezhdeniia i prekrashcheniia novykh antievreiskikh besporiadkov," 92.

31 Ibid., 15.

32 KGW/I-1884/93, "O merakh k preduprezhdeniiu antievreiskikh besporiadkov," 11–27.

33 Ibid., 48.

34 A file in the KPGGW entitled "Po nabliudeniiu za rimskokatolicheskim dukhovenstvom" (1901), no. 119, is devoted to criminal and suspicious activities of priests and contains samples of such agitation.

35 *Encyclopedia Judaica*, VI, 849.

36 KGW/I-1882/128, "Ob antievreiskikh besporiadkakh v gorode Gombine, gostynskogo uezda," 125.

37 KGGW, 1932, 141.

38 KGW/I-1885/196, "O merakh k preduprezheniiu antievreiskikh besporiadkov za 1885 g." 35–6.

39 KGGW, 1932, 59–61.

40 KGW/I-1882/112, "Po predlozheniiu Varshavskogo General Gubernatora o shumnom ulichnym prazdnovanii evreiskoi svad'by v gor. Groits," 3–8.

41 KGW/I-1881/156, 77.

42 Ibid., 84.

43 KGW/I-1880/375, "Po raportu kutnovskogo uezdnogo nachal'nika ob oskarblenii i nadrugatel'stve evreiskikh mal'chikov nad izobrazheniem Spasitelia," 4–9.

44 HM 7527, 123.

45 Warsaw is the most heavily represented in the documents used because when doing research in Poland, I was based in Warsaw and had the easiest access to materials relating to that province. However, the same picture is conveyed in the reports of the governors of other provinces, which can be found in the KGGW, KPGGW, and in the Central Archive for the History of the Jewish People in Jerusalem, which has microfilmed archival holdings from all over Congress Poland.

46 KGW/I–1881/156, 144.

47 KGW/I–1883/133, "O merakh k preduprezhdeniiu antievreiskikh besporiadkov," 43.

48 KGW/I–1881/156, 114.

49 Ibid., 33–7. See also HM 7527, 64–88.

50 KGW/I–1881/156, 104.

51 KGW/I–1882/128. The entire file is devoted to the events in the city.

52 KGGW, 1893, 2–9.

53 KGW/I–1882/128, 68–80.

54 KGGW, 2108, "O besporiadkakh mezhdu evreiami i prizyvnymi v posade Kazimir," 6.

55 KGGW, 1932, 8.

56 For example, KGGW, 6481, "O gubernatore Miller i drugikh litsakh," (1894), 5, 7, 11.

57 KGGW, 1893, 1.

58 KPGGW, 270, (1902), "O stolknoveniiakh khristian s evreiami," 29.

59 KGW/I–1884/93, 62–86.

60 KGW/I–1882/128, 80.

61 KGGW, 1893, 2–9.

62 KGW/I–1882/128, 78–9.

63 The light sentences may also have been due to the lightness of the crimes committed, relative to the horrors that took place in the Ukraine. Gruenbaum has observed in his synthetic article on pogroms in Poland that both in number and scope, they cannot be compared to those in the Pale: fatalities were few and there was far less "bestiality." See "Die Pogrome in Polen," in *Die Juden-pogrome in Russland*, 1 (Cologne and Leipzig, 1910), 134–5. Damaging property and disturbing the peace would naturally have drawn shorter terms than rape and manslaughter.

64 See Dubnow and Krasnyi-Admoni, *Materialy*, xvii: "If direct proof of government participation cannot be found, it means they hid their traces."

65 According to Yakov Shatsky, two Jews were killed: *Di geshikhte fun yidn in Varshe*, iii (New York, 1953), 102. Gruenbaum says one Jew was killed: "Die Pogrome in Polen," 146. Golczewski claims that only one person perished and he was among the rioters; the apparent cause of death was an overdose of alcohol: F. Golczewski, *Polnisch–Juedische Beziehungen, 1881–1922* (Wiesbaden, 1981), 43. All agree that twenty-four Jews were wounded and that property damage was substantial.

66 R. Kantor, "Aleksandr III o evreiskikh pogromakh 1881–83 gg.," *Evreiskaia Letopis'* (Petrograd, 1923), 154.

67 Gruenbaum, *Die Juden-pogrome* 146, and Golczewski, *Polnisch–Juedische Beziehungen*, 41–51.

68 All these are listed in Golczewski, *Polnisch–Juedische Beziehungen*, and Gruenbaum, *Die Juden-pogrome*, 144–50.

69 Gruenbaum, *Die Juden-pogrome*, 145.

70 Dubnow, *The History of the Jews*, 283.

71 Kantor, "Aleksandr III," 152.

72 Ibid.

73 Apparently, Major General Polenov, a highly placed official in the Warsaw Police Department, told a Polish delegation after the pogrom had broken out that "the Polish plebs are not one whit better than the Russian plebs," Golczewski, 47. But even if he said so, this proves only that such was his opinion, not that the Russians had organized the riot to prove this point to the world.

74 Gruenbaum, *Die Juden-pogrome*, 134–7.

75 Golczewski, *Polnisch–Juedische Beziehungen*, 47–51.

76 See Ochs, *St. Petersburg*, chapters 3–5.

The pogroms of 1903–1906

The late nineteenth and early twentieth centuries saw a general increase of violence in Russian life. To the random violence of rural Russia, such as peasant vigilante justice (*samosud*) or resistance to the demands of landlords and police, was added the violence of the peasant-proletarian in the burgeoning industrial centers. Renewed political activism was an additional source. After a decade of quiescence following the assassination of Alexander II, revolutionary terrorism, albeit on an individual rather than a mass basis, reappeared. None of this violence was directed specifically against Jews, but as a group they proved to be particularly at risk when domestic order and controls weakened. Always in the background was the recent example of the pogroms of 1881–2 to serve as a reminder and a model.

The post-reform discontents of the rural village were exacerbated by the rise of capitalism and its destructive influences upon traditional peasant life. However one reads the debate among historians as to the actual condition of the peasantry at the turn of the century, there is no question that the peasants felt themselves abused and mistreated, and were consumed by an ever growing "land-hunger," strengthened by demographic pressures. The May Laws, as was predicted at the time, did nothing to decrease the danger of anti-Jewish violence among the peasantry. Many Jews remained, as before, in highly visible and vulnerable positions, especially as taverners and inn-keepers, as well as petty tradesmen. There were still large numbers of Jews living outside the Pale illegally or semi-legally, and particularly prone to official whims. Even legally settled Jews were the targets of periodic campaigns by local officials to encourage peasant communities to use the right which they possessed to expel "harmful individuals" against Jews and their families. Tavern brawls, robbery and violence against isolated Jewish inn-keepers, acts of arson, were constant features of Jewish–Gentile relations. These phenomena were generalized throughout the Pale, but they were especially marked in areas like Bessarabia and the Ukraine which were the locus for new outbreaks of mass violence before and during the Revolution of 1905.

Labor violence, occasionally organized but more often sporadic and non-ideological, was a common feature of Russian industrialization. When these disorders occurred in the Pale, they had a special propensity to turn against the Jews. A striking example is provided by the so-called cholera riot which took place in Iuzovka, a company town located in the Donets Basin in Ekaterinoslav province in 1892. Inchoate discontent over working conditions found an outlet in opposition to quarantine measures imposed upon workers who were suffering from the cholera. An attack on a cholera barracks, and its medical personnel, quickly escalated into a general assault upon nearby Jewish shops and property. The ease with which a confrontation with health inspectors could evolve into a pogrom demonstrates how thoroughly the pogrom paradigm was now in place.

The political climate was also inimical to the Jews. Jews were never disproportionately represented in the revolutionary movement, although the concentration of the Jews in the Pale of Settlement produced a concentration of Jewish revolutionaries in those same provinces. Moreover, even before the Jews had come to provide more than a minuscule number of active revolutionaries, conservative publicists, led by the Judeophobe newspaper *Novoe vremia*, had begun to attribute the whole revolutionary movement to a pernicious Jewish spirit. This stereotype became an integral part of both conservative and reactionary ideology in the early twentieth century, acquiring ever more bizarre and exotic forms, culminating in the fabrication and propagation of the notorious antisemitic forgery *The Protocols of the Elders of Zion*, with its paranoid vision of a Jewish world conspiracy. The accusation received further impetus with the foundation in 1897 of a successful Jewish social democratic party, the General Jewish Workers Union in Russia and Poland (The Bund). In response to pogroms in Częstochowa, Poland (1902) and Kishinev, Bessarabia province (1903), The Bund began to organize Jewish self-defense units. The activities of such units helped to raise Jewish morale and self-confidence, and on a few occasions, such as the pogrom in Gomel, Minsk province, served to limit damage and casualties. At the same time, the advisability of these activities was questioned by cautious communal leaders, especially when self-defense activities attracted violent responses from the police and the army. In any event, self-defense was overwhelmed by the scale of violence in 1905.

Just as certain professions, such as zemstvo schoolteachers, were viewed as collectively disloyal by reactionaries, or certain nationalities, such as the Poles, were branded as internal enemies, the Jews were reproached as anti-Russian and disloyal.

Whereas the Poles, at least, were concentrated in their own territory and enjoyed the safety of numbers, Jews were scattered and weak, even in the areas of their greatest concentration. This was a fatal situation when the cry "Beat the Yids, Save Russia!" became a profession of political loyalty by the agents of the counter-revolution.

In short, whenever the social and political fabric threatened to come unravelled – be it through peasant unrest, labor disorders, or anti-revolutionary political activity – the Jews presented a weak and poorly defended target, one which local authorities felt little incentive to protect. In a period of wholesale governmental collapse, as occurred throughout 1905 and 1906, the Jews were particularly menaced. The pogroms of 1881–2, despite the psychological terror which they induced, had claimed only scores of victims. In the period of revolutionary struggle, the toll of fatalities climbed into the thousands.

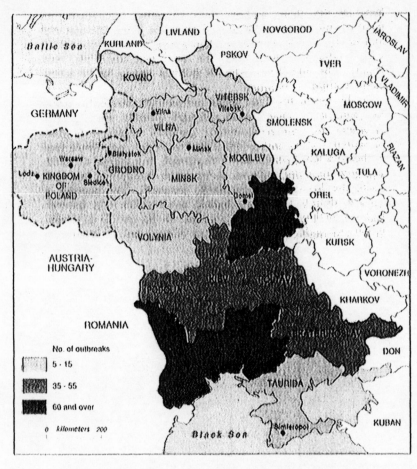

3 Major pogrom centers in Russia and Poland, 1903–1906

CHAPTER 8

The pogroms of 1903–1906

Shlomo Lambroza

I

Russia at the turn of the century was a country on a collision course with modernity. The historian Pavel Miliukov described it as "Two Russias": "One is a Russia of the future, as dreamed of by members of the liberal professions; the other is an anachronism, deeply rooted in the past, and defended in the present by an omnipotent bureaucracy." The Empire was experiencing modernization and the problems that accompany the industrialization of an economy and the urbanization of a people. Poor harvests in 1902–3 caused wide-scale violent unrest in rural areas. Urban areas also experienced their share of disorders. Unemployment was on the rise and workers found a vehicle for their frustrations in street demonstrations and political strikes. Political conditions were worsened by the disastrous Russo–Japanese War of 1904 and the massacre of innocents at the Winter Palace in January 1905.

The opening of the twentieth century found Russia with one foot in the twentieth century and the other mired in eighteenth-century absolutism: an unyielding autocracy face to face with inevitable change; an impoverished peasant and working class; a faltering economy; radical and violent political extremism. Manifestations of this conflict were chaos and anarchy in the countryside, demonstrations and rioting in the cities, and violent, anti-Jewish pogroms.

Violent antisemitism had not been in evidence since the 1881 pogroms but, the spring of 1903 reawakened fears Russian Jews had hoped lay buried with the victims of 1881.

In the late winter of 1903 a series of events began that led to the massacre of the Jewish community in Kishinev, a city in the southwestern province of Bessarabia. The massacre sent shock waves through the Jewish community and rekindled fears of the 1881 pogroms. Five months later, in September 1903, an equally violent pogrom occurred in Gomel, in Mogilev province.

Kishinev shocked world Jewry. It elicited outcries of indignation within Russia, Western Europe, and the United States. The concern of the Jewish community was to expose and punish the guilty. The government of Nicholas II, for its part, attempted to downplay and minimize the pogrom. The inherent conflict resulted in a mass of confusing and contradictory evidence.

The pogrom at Kishinev was caused by three converging factors: instigation by a local antisemitic newspaper, *Bessarabets*; irresponsibility, dereliction, and mismanagement by local officials (especially the governor and the chief of police); deep-seated antisemitic feelings among the non-Jewish population of Kishinev.

The groundwork for the pogrom was laid by strongly worded antisemitic articles in *Bessarabets*, a sensationalist tabloid published in the provincial capital of Kishinev. P. A. Krushevan, the reactionary publisher of *Bessarabets*, believed liberals, radicals, and Jews were a threat to the autocracy. Articles in *Bessarabets* were particularly antagonistic toward Jews. Prior to the pogrom the paper ran articles and editorials that were nothing more than anti-Jewish diatribes. Articles stated Jews should be fired from municipal jobs to make room for non-Jews and warned Jews to renounce Judaism and convert. Although never directly calling for pogroms the paper ran vituperative and provocative articles with headlines such as, "Death to the Jews!" and "Crusade Against the Hated Race!" Krushevan developed a small following and organized a group of people who shared his reactionary and anti-Jewish sentiments. Other important facts about the paper were that it had a circulation of approximately 29,000; it was the only daily paper in the province of Bessarabia; requests to begin a newspaper that might counter the political bias of *Bessarabets* were denied by Vice-Governor A. I. Ustrogov; the paper received funding from the central government.[1]

Compounding the anti-Jewish propaganda of *Bessarabets*, was the reappearance in Russia and Eastern Europe of the Jewish ritual murder legend. For the superstitious peasantry and unenlightened clergy, it was not outside the realm of reality that Jews would murder a Christian child and use his blood in the making of Passover *matzoh*. This was especially true if the charge was levied against obscure "Jewish sects," rather than Jews as a whole. The Greek Bishop of Kishinev was convinced that among some Jews ritual murder was still practiced and refused, when asked by the chief rabbi of Kishinev, to discredit the legend.[2]

Anti-Jewish sentiments simmered during the spring of 1903. The jingoism of the antisemitic *Bessarabets*, plus the coming of Passover and Easter, when the "Blood Accusation" was most commonly made, increased the possibility of conflict. The pre-conditions were in place, all that was needed was a spark to light the tinder.

In a small village, Dubossary, in the extreme western part of Kherson province (Kherson is bordered on the west by Bessarabia, and the town of Dubossary is about 40 km from Kishinev) on 11 February 1903 it was reported to the police that a young boy, Mikhail Rybachenko, had mysteriously disappeared. The proximity of Passover (which began on 11 April) led to accusations that the boy's disappearance was related to the holiday. Two days later, on 13 February, the boy's body was found. The police report stated that the body had twenty-four stab wounds and that the boy had been killed several days earlier. The report indicated no signs of ritual murder. An autopsy verified the initial police report.[3] But rumors and accusations, especially by *Bessarabets*, blamed Jews for the murder. Rejecting the police reports, *Bessarabets* claimed that the boy's wounds indicated a ritual murder. It also reported that an old Jewish woman testified that the child was abducted by Jews.[4] The latter accusation was given no credence by the authorities. To allay further suspicions, counter the spread of rumor, and avoid possible confrontation, the authorities consulted three physicians from Odessa who examined the body. Again it was concluded that there was no evidence of ritual murder. Government attorney, A. Pollan, who was part of the investigation, gave a speech indicating the fallacy of the ritual murder rumor and stated that a more likely motive for the murder was material gain.[5]

The evidence seemed unimportant to those intent on believing Jews were responsible; tirades from *Bessarabets* were more convincing than police reports. A Jewish delegation, fearing articles in *Bessarabets* would worsen an already sensitive situation, appealed to Vice-Governor Ustrogov to censor *Bessarabets*. It is unclear what the relationship was between Ustrogov and Krushevan, but Ustrogov had displayed favoritism toward Krushevan in the past and refused to take any action. A Jewish delegation also went to Governor R. S. von Raaben and pleaded that he do something to avert violence.

Plate 1. Morgue for victims of the Kishinev pogrom of 1903.

The governor did not act on their request. Requests were also made
to the Chief of Police I. D. Chezmenkov.[6]

One further incident aggravated the already volatile situation. A
few days before Easter a Christian girl in the employ of a Jewish
family committed suicide. She died after being rushed to the
hospital. Although the reports made it clear that the death was a
suicide, the rumor mill presented her death as another ritual
murder.[7]

As Jews celebrated the last day of the Passover holiday on Sunday,
19 April, Christians celebrated the first day of Easter. At dawn on
that Easter Sunday, probably sometime between six and eight
o'clock, after most Christians had left church following midnight
services, the pogrom began. It started with young boys throwing
rocks through windows of Jewish homes and shops. They were
followed by groups of men, mostly identified as laborers (stone
masons, carpenters, draymen, etc.) who roamed the Jewish business
quarter of the town looting and vandalizing shops.[8]

Initially, the crowd concentrated on Jewish homes and shops, but
as the pogrom gained momentum it became more violent. Violence
started when a group of Jewish workers and merchants armed with

Plate 2. Wounded victims of the Kishinev pogrom of 1903.

crude weapons confronted the mob. Jewish self-defense protected
property but also increased the level of violence. By the end of the
first day, twelve Jews were dead and nearly one hundred severely
injured. By the evening of the 19th, street rioting was over.

Governor von Raaben had 350 police and 8,000 troops at his
disposal during the first day of the riot, but no order was given to
stop the pogrom.[9] At 6 a.m. on Monday, 20 April, von Raaben
transferred the administration of the province to the commander of
the military garrison, General V. A. Bekman. It now became
Bekman's responsibility to re-establish control. Sometime after noon,
Bekman requested that von Raaben transfer authority to the
military and asked for written permission to use arms against rioters.
Between 3 p.m. and 4 p.m. that afternoon Bekman received
confirmation from von Raaben. According to Bekman, he dispatched
the order instructing his troops to use necessary force to end the
disturbances. The order reached the troops between 7 and 8 p.m. It
had now been more than thirty-six hours since the outbreak of the
pogrom.[10]

While von Raaben and Bekman were sending messages back and

גניזת ספרי תורה הנקרעים
בקעשנוב 18 מנחם אב' תר׳ סה.

די נשות מ׳ג די צוייטענע ספרי־תורות אין קישינעוו.

ומער מריינד 183 או/

Plate 3. Burial of Torah scrolls desecrated in the Kishinev pogrom of 1903
(from the Yiddish publication *Der Freynd*).

forth, rioting began again at 9 a.m. on the morning of 20 April. The
events of the 19th paled in relation to the nightmarish events of 20
April. In the hours before the renewed outbreak of violence peasants
from the surrounding countryside and hooligans from nearby towns
made their way to the city. What ensued was mass terrorization. The
litany of horrors recalled by observers and victims reflects the
brutality of the mob. The atrocities ranged from murder, to gang
rape, torture, and mutilations. It would not be hyperbole to indicate
that there was butchery at Kishinev. At the end of the two days, 47
Jews had been murdered, 424 wounded, 700 houses burned, 600
shops looted. Damage was estimated at 3 million roubles.[11]

Was Kishinev a planned pogrom? There is no direct evidence to
indicate that the outbreak on 19 April was premeditated. There is
strong circumstantial evidence that certain groups and individuals
acted as *agents provocateurs* encouraging the pogrom and inciting the

riot. There were those in Kishinev who sympathized with the inflammatory articles in *Bessarabets* and held similar beliefs to Krushevan's. It is also known that Krushevan had organized a group of these like-minded individuals. Although there is no direct evidence, members of this group figure high on the list of suspects.

If any part of the Kishinev pogrom was planned, it was the events of the second day. Letters, reports, and eye witness accounts document a far more concerted and significantly more intense attack on the morning of the 20th. The rioting did not begin slowly and build to a violent confrontation as on the first day. Instead, at 9 a.m. on the 20th, bands of rioters descended on different sections of the Jewish quarter.[12] This time rioters struck in greater numbers, many were armed and violence continued from the morning hours until the troops dispersed the crowd that evening. Two independent observers indicate that there were groups of red-shirted men directing the crowd.[13] There are also reports that the crowd was led and directed by seminarians.[14]

What role did the police play? Why did local officials not act more responsibly in stopping the pogrom? The documentation shows that no orders were given to the police to end the riot. Some historians who have written about Kishinev believe that the police conspired with the rioters and that "they [police] were among the organizers of the pogrom."[15] Articles and eye witness accounts also accuse the police of connivance in the pogrom.[16] Several accounts of the pogroms state that the police stood by and watched, some policemen participated in the looting and others exhorted the rioters. It is not surprising that misconduct by the police gave the appearance of culpability. On the other hand, evidence exists that the police acted to protect Jews. An account is given of a group of police officers and twelve of their men who saved the lives of many Jews by driving the mob away from a section of the Jewish quarter.[17]

As irresponsibly as the police acted, there were reasons why they did not attempt to stop the pogrom. First, they were clearly outnumbered by the mob. There were only 350 police in Kishinev and the rioters numbered from 1,500 to 2,000. Second, Governor von Raaben, out of fear that the destruction would spread to other parts of the city, ordered the police to defend the large factories and warehouses. Third, without clear orders from Chief of Police Chezmenkov, the police were unsure what to do. This is not to defend the inaction of the police, but rather to point out that there were no orders given by their superiors. The local police were left to guess at the appropriate action. Responsible policemen acted to protect Jews, while irresponsible policemen either took no action or participated in the pogrom.

The two men who bear direct responsibility for not stopping the pogrom were Chief of Police Chezmenkov and Governor von Raaben. Why did von Raaben not call out the troops and police on Sunday the 19th when the disorders started? Some historians speculate that von Raaben and Chezmenkov conspired with the pogrom organizers.[18] They charge that from the start the governor and the chief of police colluded with anti-Jewish groups to let the pogrom run its course without police or troop interference. Police complicity is further suggested because the only concerted police action during the 20th was the disarming of Jews who had organized a defense force.

There is strong evidence to convict both von Raaben and Chezmenkov for negligence and collusion. Both were negligent in not taking immediate steps to prevent the pogrom. Unlike the more responsible officials at Dubossary, where police and officials moved to avoid confrontation by making it clear that the death of the young murder victim had nothing to do with ritual murder, von Raaben and Chezmenkov turned a blind eye to the imminence of the pogrom. They were equally derelict in not ordering police or troops to stop the pogrom once it had started. The governor would have been well within the law to order police and troops into the city on the morning of 19 April. Had he acted immediately the pogrom would have been significantly less severe. But he chose not to. Why? There are several possible motives. First, von Raaben might have acted out of his own prejudice toward Jews. Major General Shostak, who contributed to the War Ministry's investigation of Kishinev indicated that von Raaben's antisemitism led him to take no action even though he had prior knowledge of the pogrom.[19] In von Raaben's mind, an anti-Jewish demonstration might be perfectly acceptable. Von Raaben probably thought the demonstration would be small, a few Jewish homes and shops would be looted, maybe some Jews would be hurt, but he did not expect a massacre.

Another possibility is that von Raaben believed that the central government condoned his actions. Anti-Jewish attitudes were prevalent at all levels of the government. In allowing the pogrom to run its course, von Raaben responded to the spirit of the regime rather than the letter of the law. The mistake von Raaben made in carrying out what he believed to be unspoken policy, was allowing the pogrom to go too far.

Problems began for von Raaben toward the end of the first day. The pogrom was already no small affair, twelve Jews had died and many more were wounded. He must have known that hostilities would resume the next day. Early next morning, hoping to rid himself of responsibility, von Raaben turned the city over to the military garrison. In a feeble defense, von Raaben blamed the military commandant, Bekman, to whom he handed over authority, for not suppressing the pogrom.[20] Bekman, before allowing his troops to use armed force, sought written verification of von Raaben's order. The transfer of authority created a power vacuum and it was at least ten to eleven hours before troops were given the direct order to stop all disorders. The delay between when von Raaben relinquished authority and when the troops took action appears more a matter of red tape and military inefficiency than a planned stalling tactic. On 20 April, Minister of the Interior V. K. Pleve, received a telegram from von Raaben describing the conditions at Kishinev. He ordered the city placed under martial law.[21]

Shortly after the pogrom the allegation was made that Minister of the Interior Pleve participated in the conspiracy. "There is no doubt whatsoever that Minister of the Interior Pleve was the instigator of the pogrom [in Kishinev]," wrote Louis Greenberg.[22] It was alleged that Pleve knew of the pogrom in advance and sent a dispatch to Governor von Raaben instructing him not to use arms against rioters. Copies of the dispatch were made public and printed in newspapers outside Russia. The dispatch was a forgery. There exists no evidence that Pleve had any prior knowledge of the pogrom or that he was part of a conspiracy.

Pleve's past activities showed that he was no friend of Jews. Sergei Witte characterized him as a Jew-hater and stated that "the guiding spirit behind the anti-Jewish laws under Ignatiev and Durnovo was Pleve."[23] Simon Dubnow labeled him the leader of the "bureaucratic inquisition."[24] Pleve had supported anti-Jewish legislation and was known for his anti-Jewish views. But, to condemn Pleve on his attitudes and past deeds is misguided. Pleve was a reactionary whose main objective as Minister of the Interior was to maintain order, not sponsor pogroms. If Pleve had prior knowledge of Kishinev, he might have taken steps to prevent the occurrence of violence. Pleve bears responsibility for Kishinev in that his own views on Jews encouraged antisemitism in others and that he allowed the province of Bessarabia to be administered by antisemitic, incompetent, and irresponsible bureaucrats.[25]

Who were the participants in the Kishinev pogrom? The city had a population of roughly 147,000 people: 50,000 Jews, 50,000 Moldavians, 8,000 Russians, and the remainder of the population composed of Bulgarians, Serbs, Greeks, Macedonians, Albanians, and Germans. From existing reports it is possible to put together a composite of the pogrom crowd. The crowd size at the height of the riot was estimated at 1,500 to 2,000.[26] No women participated in the pogrom. Of the men who participated, many were from the working class. Reports indicate that artisans, municipal workers, and day laborers were part of the crowd. Local peasants or *muzhiki* came into town on the second day of the pogrom and accounts show them as active participants. Students, especially seminarists, participated. The under class or the *lumpen* was represented: common criminals, "half-drunken loafers," hooligans, robbers. Soldiers and police were also known to have participated. Several reports mention Christian zealots, but these are not to be confused with the clergy. The crowd can also be divided by national origin. Most reports indicate that the largest segment of the pogrom crowd was made up of Moldavians (Krushevan, the publisher of *Bessarabets*, was a Moldavian). As a group they were a quarter of the city's population. Russians and Albanians are also mentioned as part of the crowd.

It is easier to identify the elements of the crowd than to establish their motives. What drove the crowd to participate in pogrom violence? As indicated earlier, articles in *Bessarabets* encouraged violence against Jews. One slogan associated with the newspaper was "Death to the Jews." An article in the paper indicated that Jewish corpses should be bound to cartwheels, for "the Jew is an abomination."[27] *Bessarabets* was also responsible for spreading the rumor of ritual murder and for asserting that revenge should be taken against Jews.

Two other rumors inspired rioters. First, a rumor that the Tsar had given permission to beat and rob Jews. This rumor became popular during the 1881 pogroms and reappeared in the months before Kishinev. A cable received by the *Jewish Daily News* on 25 April, 1903 reported, "Just as in the riots of 1880–1 [sic] there is a popular belief among the Russian peasants that the Czar decreed the slaughtering of Jews."[28] A letter received by the New York Relief Committee quoted a rioter saying "It is the Czar's will that the Jews be everywhere robbed," and "Poor brethren! We must kill you. It is so ordered."[29] Another letter stated; "In Kishineff on the first day of Easter the Vice-Governor [presumably Vice-Governor Ustrogov] read a paper to the people, in the name of the Czar, that the Jews of Kishineff and vicinity were to be killed and robbed."[30] The credibility of the latter two accounts is in some question. Whether the events described occurred or not is subordinate to the fact that the rumors circulated and acted as motivation for rioters.

The second rumor dealt with the Jewish role in the revolutionary movement. The rumor presented the Jewish community as disloyal subjects of the Tsar. Jews did participate in radical politics, but not all Jews were revolutionaries. Nevertheless, the association of Jews, as a group, with radical activities acted as further motivation for pogroms.

Religious issues were also a factor. It should be remembered that the pogrom began on the morning of Easter Sunday, directly after church services. What was said to the parishioners of Kishinev during the Easter service? Easter is the celebration of the death and resurrection of Christ, but Holy Week in the Russian Empire was also notorious for drunkenness and related violence. Were parishioners reminded that Jews were the killers of Christ? Did the Easter service provide a rationale for vengeance against those who were believed responsible for the death of Christ? Interestingly, the documentation indicates there existed several cases in which spikes were driven through the hands, legs, and into the heads of Jews; was this retribution for the crucifixion?[31]

The reason the riot became violent is that the authorities took no action against the rioters. In some instances police and troops participated, giving the appearance that the pogrom was somehow approved by the authorities. A telegram sent from Kishinev to the Minister of Justice indicated that many of the atrocities occurred during the "power vacuum" at which time, "crowds of people indulged themselves in robbery and slaughter in the presence of authorities without being punished."[32] A report to the Minister of Justice indicated that: "Assault and destruction happened in front of the military and police, while both refused to act properly. Utilizing the opportunity, the mob robbed entire houses and stores of Jews. Lack of action from the government during the 30 hours led the people to speak of permission from Petersburg to beat Jews."[33] The lack of immediate and effective action by authorities reinforced rumors and encouraged crowd violence.

The central government, for its part, acted irresponsibly throughout the ordeal. The government should have indicated that Kishinev was a tragedy, that local officials showed poor judgment and acted inappropriately, ordered the closing or minimally censoring of *Bessarabets*, enacted swift judgments against rioters, sympathized with victims through some form of aid, and condemned the entire act as an antisemitic incident that would not be tolerated. Instead of recognizing the riot as an outrage, the government attempted to soft-pedal the issue. By not condemning the pogrom immediately, the government laid itself open to accusations that it was following a pogrom policy. Suspicions about the government's role were heightened by the accusations made against Minister of the Interior Pleve.

At first, in an attempt to cover up the massacre, the government denied that the pogrom occurred.[34] The official police version indicated that the pogrom started when a Jew attacked a Christian woman who "fell to the ground, letting go her infant. This incident was the immediate cause of the outbreak." Why didn't the police act? According to the Director of the Police A. A. Lopukhin, the riot was "hindering the policeman's actions." On the following day, the police report states, "a group of armed Jews attacked Christians thus restarting the pogrom."[35] Why didn't police take action on the second day? The governor had handed over authority to the military garrison and therefore the police had no authority to suppress the riot.

The police report of the incident was riddled with half-truths and blatant fabrications. The report indicates that it was Jews who instigated the riot on the first and second day and insinuates that it was Jews who were responsible for the escalation of violence. Nowhere in the data was there corroborating evidence for this version of the events, nor was this report given credibility by the foreign press and the official government investigation that ensued.

To the government's credit it did act against local officials and rioters, but foolishly appointed an investigator whose background created a conflict of interest. The investigating magistrate assigned to the case was M. Davidovich, a known antisemite and contributor to *Bessarabets*. Davidovich was accused of impeding the course of justice and meting out lenient sentences.[36] The Ministry of Justice was careful to keep local officials free from involvement in court proceedings, and no criminal charges were brought against any Kishinev officials. Chief of Police Chezmenkov was dismissed for failing to take the appropriate measures to end the disorders. Governor von Raaben was also dismissed for the same reason and reassigned to the Ministry of the Interior. Vice-Governor Ustrogov was reassigned to the Caucasus. It was reported that between 700–800 rioters were arrested, 400 were convicted on various charges of rioting and 53 were charged with manslaughter, but only a handful were actually sentenced.[37]

In the months after the pogrom the Jews of Kishinev rebuilt their shattered lives. Funds were sent from Europe and the United States to aid Jewish victims. Count S. D. Urusov, a respected and thoughtful member of the bureaucracy, replaced von Raaben as Governor of Bessarabia. Count Leo Tolstoy and Maxim Gorky wrote damning letters in the foreign press about government culpability. To avert further incidents a Jewish delegation from Kishinev traveled to St. Petersburg to meet with Ministers Pleve and Witte.[38]

Despite the moral indignation of the public and the appearance of legal retribution, little was accomplished, especially towards forestalling future pogroms. The government held to its analysis that Jews bore responsibility for the violence committed against them: in an interview with the *New York Times*, Count Arthur Cassini, the Russian Ambassador to the United States stated: "the Jews ruin the peasants with the results that conflicts occur...But notwithstanding these conflicts the Jews continue to do the very things which have been responsible for the troubles which involve them."[39]

The myopic government of Nicholas II did not understand that Kishinev was not an isolated incident of local anti-Jewish violence, but rather a symptom of the social and economic tensions that festered in European Russia. Blaming the victims would not alleviate the need for wide-ranging reforms. By not sternly condemning pogroms, intentionally or not, the government encouraged future pogroms. They were not long in coming. Five months after Kishinev, a violent pogrom broke out in the town of Gomel, in Mogilev province.

The pogrom at Gomel marked the second, and only other major incident of antisemitic violence during 1903. Gomel was a city of

40,000, more than half of whom were Jews. (The 1897 census indicates 26,000 Jews. This is in contrast to Kishinev where Jews comprised one-third of the population). The town had strong and organized Bund and Zionist groups which, moved by the massacre at Kishinev, organized, armed, and trained self-defense squads numbering 200 men (*boevie otriady* or battle squads).[40]

On Friday, 11 September, a market day and a holiday in commemoration of the feast day of St. John the Baptist, an argument between a Jewish fishmonger and a peasant led to a brawl in the market place. Jewish merchants and members of the self-defense squads fought with local peasants and workers. By the end of the riot, several Jewish homes and businesses were destroyed. The Jewish defenders had beaten back the crowd and prevented the riot from reaching larger proportions. During the fighting many on both sides were injured and a peasant was killed. During the following Saturday and Sunday, 12 and 13 September, the town prepared for an inevitable confrontation. The Jews of Gomel organized and armed their self-defense units and appealed to the authorities for protection. In response, local authorities patrolled streets, placed drinking establishments off limits, and the police chief summoned an infantry regiment of 1,600 men.[41]

The pogrom began on noon Monday the 14th when a group of 400–500 railroad workers began a rampage through the Jewish neighborhood.[42] They were met with sturdy resistance by armed Jews: "Even women fought. Their physical ability and the correctness of their aim was not that at all of a race of cringing peddlars."[43] Peasants from the surrounding countryside arrived in town on the morning of the 15th, as did the 1,600 troops summoned by the chief of police. The riot worsened on the 15th, but Jewish self-defense held firm. By the following morning the rioting was over. Ten Jews and eight Christians were killed and dozens on both sides seriously wounded.[44]

A *New York Times* headline of 24 September read: "Russian Troops Aided the Slayers of Jews." The article quotes at length a letter from an eyewitness at Gomel asserting that police and troops openly sided with pogromists and participated in the looting and pillaging. A second report, however, indicates that police and troops were conscientious in suppressing the riot.[45] It is likely that both occurred. On Monday, 14 September, when the violence began, police were vastly outnumbered by both Jews and Christians. At the most liberal estimate, the Gomel police force did not constitute 100 men,[46] while the rioters numbered at least six times that and likely more, preventing any serious attempt to quell the riot. That certain members of the police acted capriciously or irresponsibly is possible and not surprising. That others acted conscientiously is also consistent with how the police acted at Kishinev.

The scene became more muddled the following day. On the morning of Tuesday the 16th, hundreds of peasants from the surrounding countryside came into town, as did the 1,600 troops called in by the chief of police. The military easily drove out the peasants and turned its attention to subduing the riot. Troops moved against armed Jews who had barricaded themselves in the streets of the Jewish section; to some this appeared as if the military attacked and disarmed Jews while allowing others to continue the pogrom. The reality is that police moved not only against Jews but also against pogromists. By the end of the day the military had killed five Jews and three pogromists in their attempt to end the disturbances.

The Gomel pogrom differed from Kishinev. At Gomel local administrators were more responsive to Jews, possibly because Jews made up 50 percent of the population. The chief of police of Gomel and the governor of Mogilev acted responsibly as conditions in the town deteriorated. Authorities patrolled the streets, closed down ale houses and called in troops; a sharp contrast to the indifference and irresponsibility of the local authorities at Kishinev.

Another striking difference between Gomel and Kishinev was the resistance of the Jewish community and the establishment of viable self-defense. Gomel might have been significantly worse were it not for aggressive Jewish defense measures. The traditional air of passivity that had marked the Jewish community was replaced by a militant spirit of self-defense leading one newspaper to indicate that Gomel was "more a fight than a pogrom."[47] One of those who participated in the defense at Gomel indicated that "despite the suffering it was good for the soul. There are no longer the former downtrodden, timid Jews. A new-born, unprecedented type appeared on the scene – a man who defends his dignity."[48] The spirit of self-defense displayed in Gomel contrasted sharply with the quiescence of the Kishinev Jews. The success of the Gomel defenders moved Jewish communities throughout the Pale to organize and train self-defense groups.

What was the relative impact of Kishinev on Gomel? Certainly, from the Jewish point of view, Kishinev represented the return of violent antisemitism. Organizers of defense were convinced that Jews could not count on local authorities, police, or the military to protect them. Kishinev sounded an alarm for Jews of the Pale.

The other side of the equation, the impact of Kishinev on pogromists, is more difficult to measure. Kishinev was shocking and dramatic and consequently received a great deal of attention in the local and national press. The inhabitants of Gomel knew of the massacre at Kishinev. Whether this encouraged them is impossible to know. What can be said is that Kishinev established a model of behavior. The pogrom became an acceptable means of registering social protest and animating latent antisemitism. The similarities between Gomel and Kishinev are also telling. Both pogroms were predicated or rationalized on the basis of revenge, in Kishinev the alleged murder of the boy at Dubossary and in Gomel the actual death of the peasant. Both occurred during religious holidays and there were analogous reports charging police and military culpability.

Most important, and the essential element for understanding the basis of future pogroms, is the position taken by the central government. Given the unfolding of events of Kishinev and Gomel the central government could not have stopped these pogroms. They happened too quickly (although this does not absolve local authorities from their lack of effort). The central government should have curtailed publication of inflammatory articles in the antisemitic press. The government's refusal to muzzle or censor these periodicals becomes a contributing factor in future pogroms. The ultimate in bad judgment was that after the pogrom, Nicholas II sent a letter to Krushevan complimenting him on his fine publication.[49] In addition, in the months following Kishinev, the government issued a new series of regulations that further restricted Jewish rights. This gave the appearance that Jews were being punished for their role in Kishinev.[50]

The government's lack of stern condemnation and its half-hearted approach to prosecuting pogromists was also damaging. At the closed-door trial for the Kishinev pogrom, requests that the ex-governor of Bessarabia (von Raaben) and ex-chief of police (Chezmenkov) testify were refused. Virtually no one who might have had a hand in the planning of the pogrom took the stand. Instead the government white-washed the issue by prosecuting ignorant peasants and workers. The harshest penalty handed down by the court was to two men sentenced to five years of penal servitude. Twenty-three others were sentenced from six months to two years.[51] Forty-seven people died, 700 houses burned, 3 million roubles worth of damage was done at Kishinev and the combined prison time served by all those convicted amounted to less than forty years.

The trial of the Gomel pogromists reflected the government's egregious attitude toward anti-Jewish violence. The evidence presented by the procurator (state's attorney) stated that the riot was an anti-Russian pogrom started by Jews. The government also charged that Jews destroyed Jewish houses to obtain wood as weapons to be used against the military and Christian population. The reason that the Jews began the attack against the Christians, stated the government's attorney, was in revenge for the Kishinev massacre. The government's case lacked both merit and substantive evidence. Jewish lawyers easily discredited the argument during the cross examinations.[52] The court hearing the trial of the Gomel pogrom handed down lenient sentences; twelve non-Jews and eighteen Jews were sentenced to up to one year in penal servitude and the court also petitioned the Tsar to mitigate the sentences. The leniency of the sentences levied against the rioters prompted the following from the law journal *Pravo*: "Who then is the real author of all the horrors that were perpetrated at Gomel?...[there] can only be one answer: besides the Christians and the Jews, there is still a third culprit, the politically rotten officialdom."[53]

Pravo was accurate in questioning the role of the central government, for the one issue that truly exacerbated relations between Jews and non-Jews was the attitude that Jews were at the root cause of pogroms. This is evident in the trial of the Gomel pogromists. By presenting the case as an anti-Russian pogrom, the government chose to prosecute the victims rather than the criminals. This was the traditional view espoused by the government on pogroms. It was articulated shortly after the 1881 pogroms when Minister of the Interior N. P. Ignatiev wrote a report that concluded that pogroms were caused by Jewish clannishness, religious fanaticism, prominence in the ranks of the opposition, and a Jewish propensity for exploiting the narod. Ignatiev concluded: "Their [the Jews] conduct has called forth protests on the part of the people, as manifested in acts of violence and robbery."[54]

Similar arguments were made by various Russian officials regarding the pogroms at Kishinev and Gomel. The viewpoint of many in the central government, including Nicholas II, was that the Jews bore responsibility for the violence that occurred against them. Often repeated, the official view was that Jews were a parasitic element in the Russian Empire who lived off the hard earned wages of the narod and secretly conspired in revolutionary cadres to overthrow the Romanov dynasty. Neither assessment was accurate. Jews throughout the Pale were as poor if not poorer than their Russian counterparts and only a small percentage of Jews participated in radical activity. Yet the reality was subordinate to the public perceptions shaped by the antisemitic press and reinforced by the attitudes of the central government.

II

The attack at Kishinev was barbarous, even by the standards of past Russian disorders, and its impact resounded deafeningly and violently at Gomel. The objective conditions that led to both pogroms remained substantively unchanged; the antisemitic press continued to publish unsubstantiated and libelous accounts against Jews; the action or lack thereof by the central government encouraged anti-Jewish attitudes; local bureaucrats, police, and the military could not be depended upon to protect Jews; and social tensions caused by economic hardships worsened. The only objective factor that changed was the catalyst or rationale for pogroms. (At Kishinev the rationale was an alleged ritual murder and at Gomel the death of a peasant.) Consequently, all that was necessary was the introduction of a new catalyst. This occurred on the evening of 27 January 1904 when a surprise naval attack by the Japanese destroyed two Russian battleships at Port Arthur, a Russian naval base on the Yellow Sea.

Russia stumbled into the Russo–Japanese War ill-prepared and ill-equipped. The war was a disaster. The Viceroy of the Far East, Admiral E. I. Alexeev, had allowed the Russian fleet in Port Arthur to deteriorate to the point of uselessness. In addition, the Trans-Siberian Railroad, the only artery for the transport of men and munitions, was still incomplete. If Nicholas and his ministers had been more thoughtful and less disdainful of the Japanese, they might have averted disaster. Instead they entered the war blinded by hubris, believing that the innate superiority of the Russian peasant/soldier led by an exemplary officer corps would triumph.

The Russians lacked good leadership, well-trained conscripts, and sufficient supplies to win the war. They were especially hampered by the inefficiency of the Trans-Siberian railroad, ignorance of the enemy, and a geriatric General Staff unfamiliar with new armaments and tactics. Russia had not yet learned to fight a twentieth-century war and her troops were led by officers who preferred the bayonet to the machine gun.[55]

The war served two purposes. If victorious, as the Russians believed they would be, it would establish Russia's imperial hold in the Far East. Second, a war might be a way to defuse anti-government sentiments and stabilize the Empire. The spirit of patriotism prevailed and the government was granted a respite from domestic troubles, but as the war proved less and less successful, public enthusiasm and patriotic zeal waned. Russian defeats and humiliations in the early months of the war highlighted the corruption and incompetence of the central government.

As the war deepened, conscripts became reluctant to leave their homes to fight in Manchuria. Discontented peasants and workers who had temporarily put aside anti-government protests renewed them with greater vigor. Even genuine patriots lost faith in the government's ability to win the war. The war worsened conditions at home, further alienated the narod, exposed government inefficiency, and supplied new justifications for pogroms.[56]

In 1904 forty-three pogroms occurred. At least twenty-four were in some way related to the war. (The remaining nineteen will be discussed later, pp. 216–18.) The first occurred in Bender (Bendery), a town 30 miles south of Kishinev, in the province of Bessarabia. Disturbances began on Saturday, 1 May, while most Jews were at synagogue. Reportedly, a mob attacked the Jewish quarter, killing five Jews (three men and two women), robbed Jewish homes and shops, and smashed windows. The mob was too large for the police to control and Cossacks were called to disperse the crowd. The military, using arms against the rioters, ended the pogrom.[57]

Bender is an interesting pogrom because it is the first to take place during the Russo–Japanese War. The war began in January and by May the Russians had suffered disastrous setbacks. During the same week as the Bender pogrom, the Russians lost between 3,000 and 4,000 men at the Battle of Yalu. The population of Bender had been moved to anti-Jewish violence by the writings of the antisemitic newspaper *Bessarabets*. This time it was not accusations of ritual murder that inspired the pogrom, but rather claims that Jews collaborated with the Japanese. Newspaper articles were supplemented by pamphlets that claimed Jews supplied the Japanese with funds and munitions, that Jewish soldiers were deserting the front, and that Japanese intelligence was receiving information from Jews. Articles and pamphlets encouraged Russians to fight the Jewish enemy at home.

One of these pamphlets, circulated around Easter, which fell on 3 April in 1904, was particularly vituperative. It reminded the reader that last year "our brethren settled accounts with the Jews [a reference to Kishinev], the murderers of our God. Brothers, it was a glorious time." It continued, building on the concept of "the enemy in our midst," by referring to Jews as "our foes at home." It restated the myths of Jewish ritual murder, "The peril is with the Jews, who drink our children's blood..." and that Jews were planning the destruction of the Empire, "[Jews] poison our youth with foul and pernicious ideas, and overthrow the pillars of our holy State and faith." Finally, it restated the rumor popular in 1881 that the Tsar favored violence against Jews and that citizens must rise against Jews in support of the government. This particular pamphlet also hinted at genocide, "the people must arise and help in this war of annihilation... Let us show the Jews our Russian might, and destroy them wherever they live. Kill them. No quarter. Every single one is a foe and a traitor... Death to the Jews. God is with us and the Czar is for us." As extreme and maniacal as this document is, it nonetheless captures the essential elements of the antisemitic/ pogromist mentality. It takes the standard antisemitic diatribes and puts them in the context of the Russo–Japanese War: "With their blood we will pay for the Japanese War," stated the closing lines of the pamphlet.[58]

Pamphlets and newspaper accounts contained a kernel of truth, as Jewish bankers did supply loans to the Japanese. Jacob Schiff, a prominent New York banker, underwrote and helped float a £5 million sterling bond issue to support the Japanese war effort. Schiff did not try to hide his attitude or his actions; he believed Russian Jews had suffered terribly under the tsarist regime. Schiff reasoned that a Russian defeat at the hands of the Japanese might force badly needed constitutional reforms, reforms that would benefit Jews.[59] But to extrapolate from this information that there existed an international Jewish banking scheme to destroy Russia or that the average Jew in the Pale was part of this scheme or that Jews were deserting to fight on the side of the Japanese was absurd. Although Schiff, a Jew, did help the Japanese raise money, Russia's war efforts were heavily subsidized by the Jewish Rothschild family. More important, the crucial link for continued French financial support for the Russian war effort was the confidential representative of the Russian government in Paris, Arthur Raffalovitch, an Odessa Jew.[60] Finally, 30,000 Jews, a disproportionately large number, served in Manchuria, fighting and dying in the name of Tsar and country, while in the towns and cities of the Pale their homes were burned and their wives and daughters violated by reservists in transport to the front.

Since the government was not winning the war through strategy and tactics, it decided to do so by overwhelming the enemy with numbers. Aggressive conscription for an unpopular war increased dissatisfaction among reservists, many of whom failed to report for duty, while those who reported did so unwillingly. As the men milled around in the small towns and cities waiting to leave for Manchuria, resentment towards the war led to riots and these riots led to pogroms. Jews, who according to the antisemitic press bore some responsibility for the war, became the target for the frustrated, alienated, hostile reservists.

Of the twenty-four mobilization pogroms, three occurred in Bessarabia, two in Kiev province, one each in Ekaterinoslav, Grodno, Lomzha (Lomza), Kherson, and Vitebsk. Fourteen took place in the province of Mogilev. Responses by local authorities varied. In Bessarabia, where *Bessarabets* continued to print anti-Jewish articles, Governor S. D. Urusov, who had replaced von Raaben after the Kishinev pogrom, moved to counteract the newspaper's influence by issuing an appeal through the clergy: "The Jews have shown their patriotism by those who have been killed and wounded in battle. So, the charges of the masses have no truth, it has only been said to provoke new agitation against Jews."[61]

Mobilization pogroms ended by December 1904, largely due to new conscription policies initially proposed by General A. N. Kuropatkin, the commander-in-chief of the armies of the Far East. Reservists had previously been drafted regardless of age, marital status, or number of dependants. Kuropatkin admitted in his memoirs that these men did not understand the reasons for the war and that they were fed "seditious proclamations."[62] The men being sent to the front were "physically and morally less reliable," and prone to rioting and desertion.[63] Instead of calling up untrained reservists, the army should have deployed soldiers serving in the reserves, but these men had been held back to respond to disturbances at home. Conscription policies were finally changed. Men with large families were given deferments when possible, and a greater effort was made to draft young, single men. The new policies coincided with the end of mobilization pogroms. No longer was the government pulling men away from their families to fight a war in which they had no interest. Those now being mobilized for the front were better trained and better disciplined troops, less likely to participate in riots or pogroms. It was also decided to transfer trained soldiers now in the reserve units at the rear to Manchuria. True to tsarist bureaucratic incompetence, action was taken too late: "These men were available for despatch [sic] to the front as drafts in the summer and autumn of 1904, but they only arrived a year later, after the Mukden battles, when they were too late. These splendid men saw no fighting at all."[64]

The Russo–Japanese War and the mobilization pogroms accounted for more than half of the pogroms occurring in 1904. There were an additional nineteen pogroms whose causes are not so easily determined. In looking at these pogroms some interesting patterns emerge. Five of the nineteen occurred in the towns of Poland, three in Kherson province, two each in Kovno, Volynia, and Kiev, and one each in Grodno, Bessarabia, and Vitebsk. Two occurred outside the Pale, in the cities of Smolensk and Samara. It is not surprising that a pogrom occurred in Smolensk, for it bordered the Pale, on Mogilev province, and 10 percent (4,650) of its population was Jewish. But that a pogrom occurred in Samara is remarkable. Samara is a good 800 miles east of the Pale and the entire province had only 2,500 Jews. Prior to 1904, no pogroms had occurred in this province. However, Samara was a stop on the Trans-Siberian Railroad that transported reservists to the front, and it is a plausible supposition that the pogrom here was caused by troops *en route* to Manchuria.[65]

The start of pogroms in September can perhaps be linked to the Jewish holidays *Rosh Ha Shannah* (New Year) and *Yom Kippur* (Day of Atonement) which fell on 10 and 19 September, respectively, during 1904. (Only three of the pogroms started before September.) There exists good evidence on only five of the nineteen pogroms. The details of these five provide interesting models for the outbreak of pogroms.

The so-called pogrom at Parchev (Parczew), a small town in Poland, started sometime at the end of July. The information on this pogrom is so conflicting that the truth is nearly impossible to discern. A local priest convinced a young Jewish girl to convert to Christianity. Her parents claimed that she was under age and could not act independently on such matters. At a subsequent trial, fighting started between Jews, who tried to abduct the girl, and Christians who tried to prevent them. This was not a typical pogrom by any means. There was no property destroyed, no attempt to attack Jews not directly involved in the initial incident and no aftershocks.[66]

In Ostrovets, also in Poland not far from Parchev (Parczew), at about the same time a more serious pogrom occurred. Again, the origins of the pogrom are unclear. One report indicates that Jewish boys threw stones at a Polish beggar, and in revenge factory workers attacked the Jewish quarter. Another report states that during a quarrel between a Jew and a Christian, the latter had an epileptic fit and fell to the ground. Rumor spread that the man was killed by a Jew. Two sources indicate that twenty Jews died during the pogrom and there was extensive property damage. The police acted responsibly in putting down the pogrom.[67]

The pogrom in Sosnovitsy began on the Jewish New Year. An unsubstantiated rumor that Jews had killed a Christian girl started the pogrom. At first the Jewish synagogue was stoned and wrecked and then the mob destroyed homes and shops in the Jewish quarter. One Jewish woman died from stab wounds and eight Jews were seriously injured. The police in Sosnovitsy did not take any immediate action to stop the pogrom. Eventually troops from the nearby garrison were called. They stopped the disorders and arrested several pogromists.[68]

In Smela (Kiev province), a pogrom began over accusations by a Christian woman that a Jewish merchant had abused her. Troops were called in by the governor-general, but not before 100 Jewish homes were burned, 150 shops looted, and two schools and two synagogues were destroyed. The well-organized Bund offered stiff resistance. Many of those who participated in the pogrom were arrested.[69]

Finally, in Rovno, another incident between a Jewish shopkeeper and Christian customers led to a dispute that turned into a pogrom. Jewish homes and shops were looted. The fire brigade put a stop to the pogrom by spraying the pogromists with water.[70]

The rise in the number of pogroms during 1904 was largely due to the increase in economic and political tensions, exacerbated by the Russo–Japanese War. Objectively, the external conditions that caused the pogroms remained unaltered while the precipitating variables, accusations of Jewish treachery in the war effort, accusations that Jews were at the forefront of radical activities, accusations that Jews were murdering Christians, became handy rationales for anti-Jewish violence. The response of local officials and the central government was, at best, inconsistent. While some officials denounced pogroms others looked away and still others covertly encouraged them. Because of the inconsistency of official-dom the masses were given mixed messages about participating in anti-Jewish violence. Since few were arrested for pogrom activity and even fewer convicted and since those convicted were given extremely lenient sentences, there existed minimal threat of reprisal from the authorities. Inconsistency of leadership extended to the police and troops. The action of troops and police usually depended upon the conviction of their superior officers. At times troops and police halted pogroms, at other times they joined in the looting and murdering.

Including the pogroms at Kishinev and Gomel, there were forty-five pogroms through 1903 and 1904. During these pogroms ninety-three Jews and thirteen non-Jews were killed; 4,200 people, mostly Jews, were severely injured. Total destruction of goods and property due to looting, burning, and vandalism was estimated in excess of 5·21 million roubles. Jews actively defended themselves in 34 percent of the pogroms, especially in areas where the Bund was most active. In only five cases (Kishinev, Gomel, Sosnovitsy, Vitebsk and Smela) were charges brought against pogromists. The maximum penalty was five years hard labor given to participants in the Kishinev pogrom. Others faced sentences of two months to one year, but in several cases the sentence was commuted or the accused were given clemency. In not one of these cases was a member of the police, or a reservist or member of the military, or government official charged with criminal activity.

Whatever the *de jure* prohibitions against the pogroms, *de facto* the government indicated that the Jews themselves, by their actions, helped instigate them. As a consequence stern repression of pogroms was not accepted policy, and they became a normal phenomenon of these troubled times. In April 1903, the brutality of Kishinev was a shocking display of violent antisemitism, but by 1904, little more than one year later, pogroms no longer elicited such surprise.

III

In December 1904, the Russian garrison at Port Arthur surrendered to the Japanese. The defeat discredited the already embattled central government. The following month, urban disorders reached unprecedented levels. In St. Petersburg, 12,500 Putilov workers walked off their jobs, followed by workers from the Neva Machinery and Ship Building factories. By mid-January, strikes closed 300 factories. At the height of strike activity in St. Petersburg, on 22 January, several thousand demonstrators led by a young prison chaplain, Father Georgii Gapon, were fired on by the military, and nearly 150 killed. The massacre on Bloody Sunday presented Nicholas and his ministers with a crisis that threatened the existence of the Romanov dynasty. The patriotism so evident only one year earlier, at the start of the Russo–Japanese War, turned to disillusionment and contempt.

The early months of the 1905 Revolution brought together Russia's disparate political, ethnic, and national groups. Students, workers, liberals, peasants, Jews, Armenians, and others formed a loose coalition supporting immediate and meaningful reforms. The liberal intelligentsia and political radicals went beyond the call for reform, demanding significant change in the existing political structure. In the face of imminent chaos, the central government failed to find the tactics necessary to end the wave of social upheaval and political unrest.

By February 1905, strikes became commonplace in major industrial areas. The workers' movement, initially economic, became politicized with the organization of soviets (councils of workers) in mid-April. Peasants, who at first responded hesitantly to urban disorders, also became disillusioned with government incompetence and economic instability. By the spring of 1905 rural disorders dotted the countryside. Attempts by Socialist Revolutionaries to organize and politicize the peasantry were marginally successful.

Plate 4. A Bund self-defense organization in Pinsk in 1905.

Peasants were too dispersed and their outlook too focused on land acquisition to develop sustained political awareness. Nonetheless, peasants understood the inherent commonality of the struggle faced by themselves and the urban workers. Whether or not they could articulate a political program was second to their ability to recognize that they were involved in a mass movement.

Along with workers and peasants, national minorities raised their voices in opposition to the central government. Even before the revolution there existed an uneasiness among national minorities who resented their inferior status, government policies of Russification, and discrimination. Believing that the first step to national autonomy was political freedom, Poles, Armenians, Transcaucasian Muslims, Georgians, Finns, Jews, and other religious and ethnic minorities joined the liberation movement.

While Jews were not at the core of radical activity, as was the claim of many Judeophobes, they nonetheless played an active and conspicuous role in the revolutionary movement. Moved by the desire to improve their political and material conditions and to achieve a minimal measure of civil liberties, Jews joined the Bund, the Social Democrats, Poale-Zion (Workers of Zion) and other left-wing organizations. While some Jews participated in radical activity, the majority were more concerned with eking out a living, surviving pogroms, and educating their children. At the very most, 100,000 Jews were members of left-wing groups. Given a community of 4 million and a working class of 1·53 million, the number of Jews participating in radical activity was a small percentage of the total Jewish population; but this small group was visible and active.[71]

At the center of Jewish radical activity was the Bund, a Marxist workers' group established in the 1890s. After the Kishinev pogrom, the Bund organized defense networks among Jewish workers and community members. It urged Jews to abandon their passive and accommodating policies and extolled the virtues of resistance. As successful as the Bund was, it did not constitute the nucleus of Russian radical activity in 1905. The Bund's effectiveness was inconsistent and varied geographically and chronologically. While extremely active in the northern provinces, the Bund was less organized and had fewer members in the southern and eastern provinces of the Pale. During the early months of the revolution, the Bund received strong support from members of the Jewish community and like-minded radical groups. But by the end of 1905 and the early months of 1906, the Bund had lost supporters in the Jewish community and among other Russian revolutionary parties. The Bund was merely one player in the general upsurge of political activity. Even at its height, the Bund's membership was less than 3 percent of the total Jewish working class.[72]

The statistical evidence was irrelevant to the central government which believed Jews constituted the core of radical activity. This long-standing attitude was articulated by Minister of the Interior Pleve as early as 1902 when he stated: "There is no revolutionary movement in Russia, there are only Jews who are the true enemies of the government."[73] Of course, the government refused to take the most obvious step to defuse Jewish participation in radical activity: repeal the May Laws and extend equal rights. Repression drove many Jews, especially the young, to anti-government activity. The government, whether meaning to or not, created a fatal cycle. The inability to actualize substantive reforms encouraged young Jews to join left-wing groups. Further persecution of Jews who joined these groups only strengthened their temerity and increased their numbers. As early as 1903, Theodor Herzl and Lucien Wolf, leading Jewish dignitaries, urged Minister of the Interior Pleve to rethink the government's Jewish policy. If Pleve wanted to end Jewish participation in revolution, Wolf stated, the government would have to begin eliminating the sources of political discontent. Wolf wrote the following after his meeting with Pleve: "I have always thought that it would have been in the interest of the Government to cultivate the innate conservatism of the Jews... I was certain that the only working remedy of revolution was to deprive it of its excuses."[74]

Some members of the government were keenly aware that discrimination encouraged Jewish participation in radical activities. In a conversation with Herzl, Count Witte indicated that while the Jews constituted only 7 million out of a population of 136 million, nearly half of the membership in radical parties was Jewish. When pressed by Herzl as to why he believed this to be the case Witte admitted: "I think that it is the fault of our government. The Jews are too oppressed."[75] But Witte was the exception, the government attitude was better articulated by Count Lamzdorf in a January 1906 report he sent to Nicholas II:

There is thus no room for doubt as to the close connection of the Russian revolution with the Jewish question in general... Nor can it be denied that the practical direction of the Russian revolutionary movement is in Jewish hands... it is precisely the Jews who are standing at the head of the revolutionary movement.[76]

Nicholas embraced this analysis, for at the top of the report in his own hand he wrote: "I share entirely the opinion herein expressed."[77]

The attitude of the government was not necessarily shared by other segments of the Russian population. In the early months of the revolution, there was a solidarity among Jews, workers, peasants, and national minorities. Pogroms were inconsistent with the general mood of the masses who supported the revolution and opposed the autocracy. *Voskhod*, the liberal Jewish newspaper, wrote: "Never before, perhaps, has the Christian population in the Pale felt so much solidarity with the Jews..."[78] and a correspondent for *Iskra* wrote: "The heroic behavior of Jews in clashes with police and army units arouses admiration everywhere..."[79] The Bund newspaper *Poslednie izvestiia* indicated that a change had taken place in the consciousness of the Russian masses, and attempts by either the government or right-wing supporters to stage pogroms would meet with failure: "Since Kishinev everything has changed."[80]

Regardless of the optimism of the liberal press and the apparent solidarity of the masses with the Jewish struggle, the *American Jewish*

Yearbook for 1906 reported that fifty-four pogroms occurred between January and the beginning of October 1905. In some measure, each of these incidents was affected, either directly or indirectly, by the development of the revolution.

Not all of the fifty-four incidents described in the *Yearbook* were typical pogroms. In some instances, what appears as a pogrom was actually police and troops intervening to disperse political demonstrations. This was especially true in April, May, and June when demonstrators clashed with authorities. Jews were among those who had taken to the streets to show their support for the revolution. In Warsaw on 2 April, a funeral march of 30,000 people was fired upon, 4 Jews were killed and 40 wounded.[81] In Lodz, during the turbulent "June Days", the Polish Socialist Party (PPS), the Polish Social Democrats, and the Bund challenged government troops after troops attacked a peaceful demonstration. The rioting in the streets of Lodz lasted for three days killing 561 people, 341 of whom were Jews.[82] The incidents of Warsaw and Lodz were clashes between demonstrators and the authorities, aimed more at dispersing radicals than pillaging Jewish homes or assaulting defenseless Jews.

More typical pogroms also occurred, the most serious in Zhitomir (11 May) and Kiev (23 July). At Zhitomir, rumors circulated that Jews had used the portrait of the Tsar for target practice and that Jews were planning a massacre of the Christian population. Rumors of an impending anti-Jewish pogrom mobilized the Bund's defense forces. Revolvers, knouts, homemade bombs, and daggers were passed out to the *kamf-grupe*, the core of the defense. Zhitomir became a legend among members of the Bund. One inhabitant of Zhitomir claimed: "If not for self-defense, Zhitomir would have been another Kishinev,"[83] while another Jewish contemporary stated: "in Zhitomir there was no pogrom but a war."[84] Even with a valiant self-defense, twenty-nine Jews were killed and 150 wounded.[85] The government claimed that the disturbances at Zhitomir were caused by Jews and Socialist Revolutionary agitators. The Minister of the Interior, Alexander Bulygin, directed the provincial governors to make it clear to the Jews, that in their own interest they should "warn their co-religionists against assuming a provocative attitude toward Christians."[86]

More interesting than the "blaming the victim" attitude of the government, was that the Zhitomir pogrom was planned and carried out by an amalgam of vigilante, pro-monarchist hooligans. It was during Zhitomir that the Black Hundreds, the terrorist arm of the Russian right, first began to gain prominence as the instigators of pogroms.

While the development of left-wing political movements began in the 1870s, there were virtually no right-wing political parties in Russia until 1900.[87] The Russian right opposed liberalization, firmly supported the Romanov troika of nationalism, autocracy, and Orthodoxy and many among their ranks were antisemitic. The deepening crisis of the autocracy through the early years of the 1900s mobilized the right to political action.

The first of these organizations, the Russian Assembly (Russkoe Sobranie), was formed as a cultural society and counted among its members government officials, military men, and publicists. Its membership also included Krushevan, the antisemitic publisher of *Bessarabets*, A. A. Suvorin, publisher of the conservative and anti-Jewish newspaper *Novoe Vremia*, and A. I. Dubrovin, V. M. Purish-kevich, and P. F. Bulatsel, the founding members of the more political and notoriously antisemitic Union of the Russian People (URP).[88]

The close association of government officials with the right has led to allegations that these organizations were merely an extension of the imperial government. Louis Greenberg wrote that: "This organization...was called into being by the government to save the tottering throne of Nicholas II,"[89] and Simon Dubnov characterized them as, "agents of the secret political police."[90] The fact that Nicholas II accepted a badge from a delegation of the URP in December 1905 and that in 1906 the government financially subsidized publications and activities of the URP, lends merit to the accusations.

The reality, though, is that while some in the government, especially Nicholas II, sympathized with the goals of the Russian right there existed no direct relationship between the two. The relationship was more subtle. There was a fine line between official and unofficial participation by the government in right-wing movements. For instance, Pleve was a member of the original Russian Assembly as were seven generals and twelve high-level government officials.[91] Individuals in the Interior Ministry were members of the URP as were some members of the police. In the provinces, local and provincial officials were known to have sympathized and at times conspired with members of the URP. In

Odessa, the commander of the Odessa Military Garrison, General A. V. Kaulbars, was the founder and organizer of the URP.[92]

Central to the organizational spirit of the right was a deep and hostile antisemitism. This antisemitism was vulgar and violent. A speech delivered by M. Dubrovin to 300 members of URP in Odessa stated: "The Holy Russian cause is the extermination of the rebels. You know who they are and where to find them...Death to the rebels and the Jews." His speech was greeted by wild enthusiasm with the crowd yelling "Death to the rebels. Death to the Jews."[93]

In the stormy spring and summer months of 1905 right-wing political organizations appeared throughout the provinces. They assumed a variety of names, but all represented the basic conservative policies articulated in the publications of the right. They identified as their enemy radicals and Jews and staged demonstrations and pogroms in opposition to the revolution and in support of the autocracy. These groups came to be known as the Black Hundreds.

The Black Hundreds were not themselves a political party, although the name later became associated with more defined right-wing political groups.[94] Rather, the Black Hundreds were an amorphous entity that acted as a semi-autonomous arm of the Russian right. The term Black Hundreds became a generic name for the many small right-wing groups ("Tsar and Order," "The White Flag," "People's Union," etc.) that instigated attacks against Jews. In reality, no one group can be identified as the Black Hundreds. These right-wing vigilantes were the terrorists of the right, the enforcement agents of reactionary politics. Under the guise of patriotism – carrying portraits of Nicholas and singing God Save the Tsar – the Black Hundreds organized pogroms. Their rallying cry was "Bei Zhidov" (Beat the Jews). The actions of these groups were encouraged by the antisemitic press, through pamphlets, by more established right-wing organizations (especially after the issuing of the October Manifesto), and at times by local and provincial officials. To their sympathizers, the actions of the Black Hundreds were interpreted as justified expressions of public indignation. Bertram Wolfe characterized them as the "extralegal armed forces, shock troops for the impending struggle."[95]

The "impending struggle" to which Wolfe referred developed in the autumn months of 1905. The revolutionary movement had gained momentum through the spring and summer and climaxed with the general strike of October 1905. What started as a strike of the Moscow rail workers evolved into a general strike that spread to almost every part of the country and involved millions of workers and peasants. The strike movement was given organization and direction by the Bund, the Social Democrats (SDs), and the Socialist Revolutionaries (SRs). The general strike closed down the economy of imperial Russia and led to violent clashes between strikers, police, and the Black Hundreds.

Until the general strike the government believed that it could withstand the crisis. The Empire was under martial law, the troops, with some exceptions, were still obedient, right-wing political groups remained loyal to the autocracy, and order had been restored in some areas. When the strike became total, the optimism of the government faltered. The government had to act decisively to preserve the autocracy. Instead the policy adopted by the government reflected an inconsistency that distinguished the reign of Nicholas II. V. I. Gurko in his memoirs stated: "The government was at a loss to know what to do. It was not ready to use strong measures, although there was still a possibility of doing so."[96]

Nicholas II called upon Count Witte, who had recently returned from negotiating the Portsmouth Treaty, for advice. Witte's analysis of the country's situation was contained in a report to the Tsar dated 22 October.[97] The report urged Nicholas II to take the initiative in creating a constitutional monarchy, extend the limits of civil liberties, eliminate exceptional legislation (such as the May Laws), and establish a body of ministers that would act to direct the government. The core of the report became the October Manifesto issued on 30 October 1905, which the Tsar reluctantly signed. With his signature affixed to the Manifesto, the entire essence of Russian autocracy was transformed. An extremely modest document, the October Manifesto was nonetheless a first step toward the dismantling of autocracy, even if, in the long run, it was a memorial to a failed revolution.

The days directly after issuing of the Manifesto were times of great uncertainty. The belief that the Manifesto would set Russia back on the road to tranquility and peaceful reform was erroneous. Unrest continued in urban and rural areas and the number of pogroms reached unparalleled proportions. Conservative estimates indicate that at least 650 pogroms occurred between the signing of the October Manifesto and September 1906.[98] The overwhelming

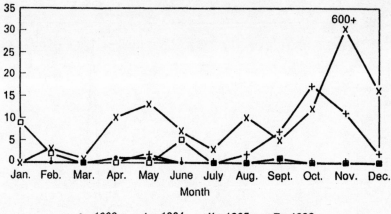

Figure 1. Number of pogroms by month.

majority occurred in the three months directly after the issuing of the Manifesto and only a small number in the months between February and September 1906.

It is difficult to know accurately how many pogroms occurred during the period following the October Manifesto. The most exhaustive survey, Leo Motzkin's *Die Judenpogrome in Russland*, estimated that 690 pogroms occurred in the two-week period following the issuing of the Manifesto.[99] Motzkin's count has become the accepted figure, and much of the scholarship since is based on his original estimate. Motzkin's 1910 study indicated that of the 690 pogroms, 666 occurred within the Pale of Settlement. He admits that his was not an exhaustive study, and indicated that there existed "essential gaps in the data collected."[100] Motzkin believed there were more pogroms than even his estimate reflects; this was especially true for pogroms occurring outside the Pale or what Motzkin identified as smaller, unreported pogroms.

Supporting Motzkin's estimate was a study carried out by the St. Petersburgh Aid Committee (an organization created to aid pogrom victims) that identified 638 pogroms.[101] Using the Motzkin and the St. Petersburgh studies and available resources from archives, contemporary accounts, correspondence, contemporary newspapers and journals, my own study identified 657 pogroms inside the Pale and an additional 17 outside the Pale.[102] One reason that Motzkin's estimate is higher than either the St. Petersburgh study or my own is that Motzkin included areas in which pogroms were attempted

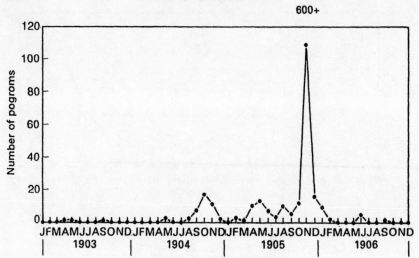

Figure 2. Number of pogroms: 1903–1906.

Table 2. *Number of pogroms and number of Jews killed during pogroms in the Pale of Settlement* 1905–1906

Gubernia	No. of pogrom	Jewish deaths
Chernigov	251	76
Kherson	82	371
Bessarabia	71	942
Poltava	52	53
Ekaterinoslav	41	285
Kiev	41	167
Podolia	37	35
Mogilev	15	48
Poland	15	452
Vitebsk	10	36
Grodno	10	356
Volynia	9	49
Taurida	8	131
Vilna	5	0
Kovno	5	2
Minsk	5	100
Totals	657	3,103

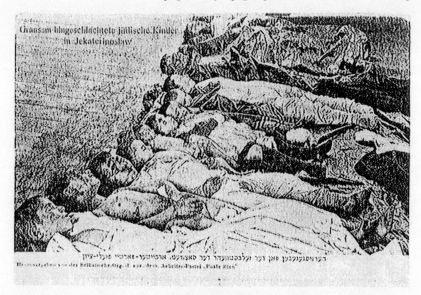

Plate 5. Child victims of the Ekaterinoslav pogrom of 1905 (postcard published by Poale-Zion, a socialist Zionist party).

but never actually occurred. It is also unclear as to what Motzkin meant when he reported that "insignificant pogroms" occurred.[103] The numerical disparity among the three studies is not as significant as the proximity of their findings. Clearly, they all corroborate that there was extensive antisemitic violence from October 1905 to January 1906.

More than 80 percent of the pogroms of 1905–6 occurred in the sixty days following the release of the Manifesto. The frequency of pogroms declined dramatically by the end of January 1906 (only six reported pogroms) and came to a virtual halt by February (four were reported in February). From the end of February to June 1906 there were no reported pogroms until the outbreak of the extremely violent Belostok (Bialystok) pogrom (Grodno province) of 14 June. There were several smaller pogroms in June, all in Grodno province, all likely an extension of Belostock. The last pogrom occurred in September 1906, in the town of Sedlits (Sedlets) in Poland.

Figure no. 1 shows the development of continuous pogrom activity from January 1903 through December 1906. The data for this graph represent all the known information on pogroms that included month and year. It is clear that while there was a low level of pogrom

Plate 6. Morgue in the city hospital for victims of the Ekaterinoslav pogrom of
1905.

activity throughout most of the four years, there is a dramatic rise
and equally dramatic decline of pogroms from October 1905
through January 1906. Even when years are compared on a month
by month basis the contrast is dramatic. (Figure no. 2).

The sheer number and ferocity of the pogroms overwhelmed the
Jews of the Pale. The modest self-defense forces established by the
Bund were insufficient to deal with the magnitude of the violence.
The northern provinces where the Bund was most active experienced
the fewest pogroms. The southern provinces of the Pale, where there
was only limited community organization and where the Bund had
not yet established significant self-defense units experienced the
greatest number and most violent of pogroms. Nearly 87 percent
(575) of all pogroms occurred in the southern provinces of
Chernigov, Poltava, Ekaterinoslav, Kherson, Podolia, Kiev, and
Bessarabia. The pogroms in these provinces accounted for 62 percent
(1,929) of Jewish fatalities in 1905. Surprisingly, 43 percent of all
pogroms in the southern provinces occurred in Chernigov. The
Chernigov pogroms are particularly interesting because while
numerous, they were not, comparatively speaking, violent. In the

251 pogroms that occurred in Chernigov only 76 Jews were killed. (See Table 1) The one anomaly among the southern provinces was Taurida (Taureda) which only experienced eight pogroms.

By the end of the pogroms the Jewish community was in shambles; over 3,100 Jews lost their lives, at least one-fourth of whom were women; the number of children left totally orphaned is estimated at 1,500; about 800 children lost one parent. In all it was reported that 2,000 Jews were seriously injured, and more than 15,000 wounded. The number of wounded reflects only those who sought medical attention; it is likely that the number of injured was higher. Total destruction of Jewish property is estimated at 57·84 million roubles within the Pale and an additional 8·2 million outside the Pale.[104]

The greatest destroyer of property was fire. Many reports and letters described entire towns being destroyed by fire. Although synagogues were usually the first to be burned, when this was not the case they were usually ransacked and pillaged. No one has estimated the value of the glass that was broken during pogroms, but virtually no pogroms occurred without all the windows of Jewish homes and shops destroyed.

The magnitude of violence during the 1905–6 pogroms far exceeded that of earlier years (see Table 1). For both 1903 and 1904 it is estimated that 93 Jews lost their lives in pogroms. The statistics for 1905 are sobering: in Odessa 800 Jews killed and 5,000 wounded;[105] in Kiev 100 Jews were killed and 406 wounded; in Minsk 100 Jews killed and 485 wounded; Simferopol 50 Jews killed; Kalarash (Bessarabia) 100 Jews killed and 80 wounded, the entire town was burned to the ground; Vitebsk 80 Jews killed; Belostok 200 Jews killed and 700 injured.[106]

How can the radical increase in number of pogroms be explained? As in earlier pogroms, a confluence of forces caused antisemitic disorders. The contributing factors to pogroms that have already been discussed (the antisemitic press, unresponsiveness by the central government, lack of coordination among local and provincial officials, and confusion among police and troops) were compounded by organized antisemitic right-wing political groups and their off-shoot, the Black Hundreds. In addition, the events and conditions surrounding the release of the October Manifesto contributed to the dramatic rise in pogroms.

Shortly after the issuing of the Manifesto, supporters of the revolution celebrated their victory over autocracy. Parades and demonstrations occurred in major cities. Crowds carrying red flags and singing the Marseillaise celebrated their triumph. The Jewish response was equally celebratory. Jews held parades in Odessa, Kiev, Minsk, took over government buildings and generally participated in what they believed was their long-due emancipation. Popular celebrations, Jewish or otherwise, reflected an overt hostility toward the government.

The government took no immediate measures to repress disorders. Local and provincial officials used their discretion in handling demonstrations. Some pursued their work responsibly, others did not. Out of concern that the central government was unable to defend itself and that the revolution had made a shambles of autocracy, counter-demonstrations were sponsored by pro-monarchist, right-wing political organizations. These groups saw themselves as the last line in the defense of Tsar and fatherland. Right-wing demonstrations were encouraged and at times organized by members of the clergy who interpreted the revolution as an attack on religion as well as autocracy. Support for pro-monarchist demonstrations also came from local and provincial officials who wanted to show their loyalty and support for the central government. It was inevitable that the forces of revolution and reaction were headed for violent confrontation.

Those of the right did not distinguish between Jews, liberals and radicals. The propaganda of the antisemitic press, the attitude of the government that Jews were to blame for the revolution and that Jews were active in radical politics made them a natural target for persecution. Throughout the Pale of Settlement, anti-revolutionary demonstrations turned into bloody anti-Jewish pogroms. The worst occurred in Odessa in the three days following the release of the Manifesto.

Odessa's history made it a prime target for a pogrom. The city had a large Jewish population (123,000 which was 32 percent of the total population), had a history of pogroms dating back to 1821 and was a center of radical activity in Novorossiia. The reactionary forces in Odessa (an unofficial branch of the URP) were well organized and courted local police and military officials. They enlisted into their ranks hooligans, miscreants and common criminals, the social dross of the right. The left was equally organized, staging strikes and demonstrations throughout the spring and summer of 1905. Revolutionaries and reactionaries gathered their forces for an imminent confrontation.

In the days directly after the issuing of the Manifesto, a confrontation between pro- and anti-government factions degenerated into a violent anti-Jewish pogrom. Jewish homes and apartments were ransacked, pillaged and set on fire. Jews in the streets were brutally murdered, raped, tortured. By the end of the pogrom 800 Jews were dead, 5,000 wounded, 463 children orphaned and 10,000 families ruined, property destruction was estimated at more than 100 million roubles. An emergency telegram sent by the Odessa Aid Committee to the Alliance Israelite, a Paris relief organization read: "The massacres at Odessa surpassed the cruelties of the rest of the world... 10,000 families without bread or roof – Indescribable miseries – Immediate aid needed on a large scale – Urgent!"[107] An official report on the pogrom labeled it as incredible savagery against Jews.[108]

The official investigation of the Odessa pogrom found that "in many cases police forces directed crowds of hooligans... and together with them took part in these acts of violence, robbing and beating and leading the crowd." It goes on to indicate that the City Governor, Dmitrii Neidhart was guilty of negligence, "by virtue of inaction."[109] The role of the Commander of the Odessa Military Garrison, Baron A. V. Kaulbars was also called into question. In an address to police and troops Kaulbars stated, "It is necessary that we call these things by their correct name. All of us intimately sympathize with the pogrom."[110] Kaulbars was later responsible for organizing the official Odessa branch of the URP, authorized the publication of two antisemitic journals that were distributed by his men and also claimed that anti-Jewish atrocities were actually the work of revolutionaries disguised as members of the Black Hundreds.[111] In the following year when Kaulbars was promoted to Commander of the Kiev District, it is known that he supplied arms to the combat unit of the URP.[112]

In another chapter, Robert Weinberg presents a significantly more detailed examination of the Odessa pogrom. His analysis explains how antisemitic propaganda, militant right-wing organizations like the Black Hundreds, and the collusion of local officials were the primary cause for the extreme violence in Odessa. Most importantly, Weinberg examines in detail the role of Neidhart and Kaulbars and concludes that although they did not plan the pogrom, they sympathized with the *pogromshchiki* and allowed the pogrom to run its course without taking appropriate measures.[113]

As the revolutionary movement lost support the pogrom movement gained momentum. As a backlash to the victory of October, hundreds of pogroms broke out throughout the Pale. Some spontaneous, others planned, some encouraged by officials and still others led by police and troops. Overwhelmingly, the outbreak of pogroms was rooted in the belief that the way to short circuit the revolution was by attacking Jews. Nicholas II in a letter to his mother the Dowager Empress expressed this belief most succinctly:

In the first days of the Manifesto the subversive elements raised their heads but a strong reaction set in quickly and a whole mass of loyal people suddenly made their power felt... the revolutionaries had angered people once more; and because nine-tenths of the troublemakers are Jews, the People's whole anger turned against them. That's how the pogroms happened. It is amazing how they took place simultaneously in the towns of Russia.[114]

The Manifesto made the Tsar a very unhappy man. It was possibly the despair that he felt at the issuing of the Manifesto that mobilized his efforts to regain control and re-establish authority. The height of pogrom activity coincided with the government's counter-offensive. Troops were deployed to rural areas to end agrarian disorders and General D. F. Trepov was given wide-ranging powers to bring an end to radical activity within cities. Trepov's appointment was specifically made to counter the more liberal ministers in the government. In January 1905, he was made Governor-General of St. Petersburg, by May his powers significantly increased when he was given the additional post of Assistant Minister of Internal Affairs and shortly after the issuing of the October Manifesto was promoted to Commandant of the Court. Trepov's appointments placed the police force of the Empire under his direct control and allowed him to exert enormous influence on government policy. Nicholas sustained a close relationship with Trepov, valuing his opinions and advice above that of Count Witte. In a letter to his mother he stated: "Trepov is absolutely indispensable to me... I give him Witte's bulky memoranda to read and he reports on them quickly and concisely..."[115] It was clear that in the closing months of 1905 Trepov held as much power, if not more power than Witte. In his memoirs Witte stated: "...I was the responsible premier without much influence...he [Trepov] was more or less the official dictator."[116]

The evidence against General Trepov presents the most compelling case that high level government officials encouraged pogroms. A. A. Lopukhin, Director of the Department of Police, in February 1906, reported to Witte that during October and November 1905, a secret printing press located at Police headquarters in St. Petersburg printed thousands of antisemitic pamphlets. The pamphlets proclaimed:

Do you know brethren, workmen and peasants, who is the chief author of all of our misfortunes? Do you know that the Jews of the whole world…have entered into an alliance and decided to completely ruin Russia. Whenever those betrayers of Christ come near you, tear them to pieces, kill them.[117]

A. A. Lopukhin's investigation indicated that Trepov had known about these pamphlets and that he had made editorial changes and marginal notations on the preliminary drafts. Lopukhin stated unequivocally that their existed "complicity of representatives of the Government in the organization of pogroms." The investigation indicated that the Chief of the Political Section of the Police Department, P. I. Rachkovskii, an advisor and confidant of Trepov, in collusion with other officials and members of the right (most notably, A. Dubrovin, organizer and leader of the URP and G. Gringmut, founder of the Monarchist Party) printed within the Ministry of the Interior, "thousands of proclamations" that urged individuals to "wage a war on Jews." Copies were distributed to the army, police and local and provincial officials. The chief of police at Vilna "telegraphed to the Police Department a request for additional copies in view of the great success which the appeal had had."[118]

In June 1906, Prince Urusov, delivered a speech to the Duma reaffirming the existence of the secret printing press and alleging government culpability in pogroms.[119] Urusov's speech followed a 17 May 1906 Duma report that stated: "Official documents…show that the Department of State Police was directly concerned in the mission of inflaming one section of people against the other, a mission that has concentrated hordes of assassins in the midst of peaceable citizens…proclamations drawn up by the same Department, incit[ed] the populace to massacre persons of other religions…"[120]

Whether officials in the Police Department acted on their own or with government approval is impossible to assess. The government was in disarray in the months following October. While part of the

Plate 7. Belostok haymarket, the site of the pogrom of 1906.

government under Witte argued for reforms and moderation, another part under General Trepov and the police used brutal methods to subdue the revolution and encourage pogroms. When Witte learned that individuals were using facilities at the Ministry of Interior to print antisemitic pamphlets he ordered that "the printing of the proclamations be immediately stopped."[121] His order was ignored and the publications by members of the Okhrana, under the charge of General Trepov continued. Lopukhin's statement to the Duma clearly indicates the schism within the government:

When in January and February I was collecting data relating to the organization of pogroms, I never encountered any member of the political or ordinary police who was not imbued with the absolute conviction that there are in fact two governments... one in the person of Secretary of State Count Witte, the other in the person of General Trepov who according to universal conviction, lays before the Tsar reports that represent the situation in the country in a different light from that in which it is represented by Count Witte, and thus exercises an influence on the direction of policy... This conviction is as firm as the belief that General Trepov is in sympathy with the *pogrom policy*.[122]

Lopukhin emphasizes that while there were officials in the

government who opposed pogroms, "they will assuredly recur as
long as the local police continues to believe in the powerlessness of
the Ministry and in the potency of other forces."[123] Lopukhin's
reference to "other forces" is an allusion to the right, officials of the
Political Section of the Police and others in the government who
supported what he termed a "pogrom policy."

Government officials who were complicit in instigating pogroms
did so with impunity. As late as September 1906 no charges were
brought against members of the Political Section of the Police.
M. S. Kommisarov, the officer responsible for running the secret
printing press was never brought up on charges. Nicholas II had
personally intervened to assure that Kommisarov would not be
punished. On the contrary, he retained his position within the
Ministry of Interior and was given a grant of 25,000 roubles from the
Tsar. D. M. Neidhart, City Governor of Odessa, was dismissed from
his position and brought to trial for his role in the Odessa pogrom,
but was cleared of all charges by the Senate in March 1906.[124]

As the central government continued to assert its control in late
December 1905 and early January 1906 the frequency of pogroms
diminished. The government moved to crush the last vestiges of the
revolution, re-establish order and bring to an end civil disturbances.
In February there was only the most minor of pogrom activity and
in March of 1906 there were no reported pogroms. In June, the
violent Belostok pogrom broke out killing 200 Jews and injuring 700.
The official report of the Duma on the Belostok pogrom indicated
that local officials, troops, and police colluded with members of the
Black Hundreds in organizing and staging the pogrom. The report
stated that troops and police were particularly brutal and bore
responsibility for some of the worst atrocities. It was also revealed
that proclamations printed at the Ministry of the Interior incited
"the extermination of the Jews" and that these proclamations were
distributed to "stimulate the patriotism of the troops." The report
concluded "that the pogrom against the peaceful Jewish population
arose... through the measures adopted by the authorities; that for
these acts not only the officials are responsible, but also the central
government which authorized an extensive propaganda for the
organization of an attack."[125]

The central government's response to the Belostok pogrom was
the release of a news item that gave "thanks" to the troops for their
"splendid service, and their glorious, self-sacrificing, untiring, just

and honest devotion to duty during the Belostok pogrom."[126] Police
Superintendent S. D. Sheremetev, who was identified in the Duma
report as one of the main organizers of the pogrom was transferred
and promoted.[127]

The final curtain on pogroms fell in September 1906. Reports
from Sedlits, in Poland, indicate that a pogrom was organized by
local officials and members of the Monarchist League. During the
pogrom 100 Jews were killed and 300 wounded.[128] A telegram from
Warsaw on the pogrom stated:

Evidence of the prearrangement of the pogrom at Sedlits by local
authorities and the monarchist league is accumulating ... when the massacre
was being planned, the officers of the Ostrolensky Regiment declared that
they would maintain order and fire upon the rioters. The regiment was
removed from the town and its place was taken by the Libau Regiment,
which distinguished itself so unenviably at Belostok.[129]

Sedlits brought to an end the drama of pogroms which began in
1903 at Kishinev. As the government continued to reassert its
authority in the months following the revolution, pogrom activity
abated. The central government was more interested in re-
establishing the *status quo ante* than in tolerating mass demonstrations.
The government had learned the painful lesson that mob rule, even
in the form of pogroms, potentially threatened the stability of the
autocracy. Had the government allowed pogroms to continue it
would reflect its own inability to maintain order. The government
refused to subsidize, tolerate, or encourage pogroms in the years after
the Revolution of 1905.

The right had also brought to an end its physical attacks against
Jews. Convinced that it was their efforts that aided in restoring the
power of the autocracy, the right went about establishing itself as a
legitimate political force. Subsidized by the central government and
encouraged by Nicholas II, the right's political influence had grown
in the months after 1905. From 1906 to 1917, the right became more
involved with pushing through its own political agenda rather than
instigating pogroms.

While there is very little hard evidence to show that the
government consciously pursued what Lopukhin referred to as a
"pogrom policy," the circumstantial evidence is damning. Within
the central government there were clearly officials who believed and
acted upon the concept that pogroms could be used to attack the

revolutionary movement. In league with members of the right, these officials acted to agitate, promote, and instigate pogroms in the misdirected belief that by attacking the Jews they would in some manner be attacking the core of the revolutionary movement. Some responsible officials within the government attempted to expose this antisemitic cabal, while others were clearly in sympathy. The sympathy of high-level officials, including Nicholas II, the Grand Duke Nikolai Nikolaevich, Assistant Minister of the Interior D. F. Trepov and other members of the Tsar's camarilla, must assume a certain responsibility for pogroms. They are as much to blame for their inaction and tacit approval as for their blatant antisemitic attitudes. While not pursuing a stated "pogrom policy," it was nonetheless "policy" among certain officials that pogroms would be tolerated and those who acted on this unstated policy did so without fear of reprisal. Quite the opposite, those officials associated with pogroms were frequently rewarded with promotions.

Sharing blame with the Tsar and his ministers were local and provincial officials. Possibly out of a misdirected sense of loyalty to the Tsar, or out of their own malevolence for Jews, local bureaucrats actively conspired to stage pogroms. It is also clear that officials within the Department of Police encouraged, participated and led pogroms. The same charge can be made against local police and military garrisons who were called in to control pogroms. The perception among local officials that excesses against Jews were tolerable and condoned, albeit unofficially, led them to carry out what they believed to be the Tsar's wishes.

IV

Antisemitism is a product of common mistrust, competition, jealousy, psychological habits, and religious antipathies. Motives for antisemitism, especially violent antisemitism, are not readily found by studying one time period or one phenomenon. The pogroms in Russia represented a complex manifestation of antisemitism. Their development must be understood within the social and political context of late Imperial Russia.

The arguments raised by the traditional historians regarding pogroms (Dubnow, Greenberg, Motzkin) focus on the tribulations of Russian Jews as caused by pogroms. By framing the argument in this way, these historians sought to establish the central government as

the culprit while neglecting to consider the sociopolitical conditions
in Russia during 1903-6. While correctly identifying the central
government's complicity, traditional historians nonetheless did not
provide an expose of the subtleties regarding government involvement. The fundamental point of the traditional analysis is that
the government used pogroms to channel the discontent of the
populace away from the autocracy and toward Jews and for this
injustice the government bears moral responsibility.

In substance I agree with this assessment. Nicholas II, his
ministers, provincial and local officials had the ability, even at the
height of revolutionary disturbances, to limit the excesses of pogroms.
For a variety of reasons they chose not to take appropriate actions.
Their reluctance to act makes the government, on a moral if not a
legal level, culpable. Where I disagree with the traditional view is its
emphasis on the action or more correctly the inaction of the
government, without adequate consideration of forces that contributed to pogroms.

Among these forces I would include the development of extremist
right-wing political organizations. It was through the publications,
propaganda and lobbying efforts of the right that violent antisemitism became an acceptable method for displaying loyalty to the
regime. The writings of the right-wing antisemitic press, the
establishment of right-wing political organizations in 1904 and 1905,
the recruitment of government officials to their cause and establishment of vigilante groups (Black Hundreds) were seminal in
encouraging violent antisemitism. Clearly, members of right-wing
groups had an agenda that went beyond encouraging pogroms, but
equally as clear is that a central component of their ideology was a
deep and abiding hatred of Jews. Because of this, the right
consciously attempted to foster antisemitic attitudes within the
narod and among government officials. Their persistent efforts
normalized and legitimized violence against Jews.

The right had a sympathetic ear among many in the government.
So much so, that there exists ample evidence that high level
members of the Political Section of the Police (the *Okhrana*),
members of the Ministry of the Interior, commanders of provincial
garrisons and local police officials colluded in the organization of
pogroms. The propaganda of the right fed upon the growing
discontents of the narod. Tutored at an early age that Jews were
pariahs, the narod were fertile ground for the cultivation of a

pogrom mentality. It was not difficult to convince the impoverished worker or peasant that the cause of their discontent rested on the shoulders of Jews. Embittered by economic conditions, and the unwillingness of the government to institute reforms, peasants and workers participated in popular and oftentimes violent demonstrations. The product of the frustrations of the narod included agrarian disorders, strikes and demonstrations in urban areas and anti-Jewish pogroms. Why attack Jews? It is difficult to account for the motivation of the narod. Certainly some participated merely for acquisitive purposes, that is, for loot and booty. Others might have participated in pogroms out of a misdirected belief that their action was supportive of the Tsar and in opposition to radicalism.

The narod might have also acted out of a belief that the extension of civil rights to Jews would somehow worsen their own socio-economic condition. Rising expectations among the narod and the inability of the government to meet those expectations led to the Revolution of 1905. When change did begin the narod might have been simply unwilling to share their gains with Jews. Possibly, they believed the extension of equal rights to Jews would in some way diminish their claims to economic reforms. This was especially true regarding the right of Jews to own land.

Finally, we arrive at the role of the government in pogroms. I feel it is beyond question that the attitude and actions of the government became the overwhelming contributive cause of pogroms. I do not believe that the central government (Nicholas, his ministers, and advisors) consciously set about implementing a policy that at its core encouraged violent attacks against Jews. There exists no documentary evidence to support this type of conclusion. What I believe occurred was a much more subtle manipulation of events whose end product, whether deliberate or not, was pogroms. The policy of the government was not to promote pogroms, but to promote anti-semitism. It seems quite clear from the May Laws through to 1906 the government consciously, deliberately, knowingly, and overtly supported antisemitic activity. The most obvious was the discriminatory May Laws of 1882. But the May Laws only begin the list: the participation of government officials in right-wing political movements; the subsidizing of these movements and their publications by the government; the willingness of the government not to prosecute officials who were clearly responsible for pogroms; the willingness of the government to promote individuals responsible for pogroms; the pernicious attitude that Jews bore responsibility for pogroms; the unwillingness of the government to compensate pogrom victims; all these factors point to a clear antisemitic policy by the central government.

It was the attitude of the government that created the conditions that allowed pogroms to occur. The government had an unspoken policy, a policy that rested on the erroneous belief that by persecuting Jews this would in some way neutralize the revolutionary movement. To this end the government turned its back, saw what it wanted to see, heard what it wanted to hear and disregarded the reality of its own situation. It was this disregard for the reality that caused many innocent lives and eventually the collapse of the Romanov dynasty.

NOTES

1 Michael Davitt, *Within the Pale* (London, 1903), 97–9; G. Ia. Krasnyi-Admoni and S. M. Dubnov (eds.), *Materialy dlia istorii anti-evreiskikh pogromov v Rossii* (Petrograd, 1919–23), 2 vols., 1; 7, n. 5; *New York Times*, 22 May 1903, 1:7 and 14 May 1903, 5:1. For more information see A. Linden [Leo Motzkin] (ed.), *Die Judenpogrome in Russland* (Cologne, Judischer Verlag, 1910).

2 The Blood Accusation, the accusation that Jews use the blood of a young Christian boy in making Passover matzoh can be dated back to the First Crusade. Young William of Norwich who died in 1144 was the first supposed victim. Maurice Samuels who wrote about the celebrated Beilis trial points out that the legend reappeared across the centuries and was particularly prevalent during the nineteenth century. The most famous accusations were those in Damascus (1860), Saratov, Russia (1857), Kutaiss Affair, Russia (1879) and Tisza-Eslar, Hungry (1882); for more information see Maurice Samuels, *Blood Accusations* (New York, 1966); Davitt, *Within the Pale*, 123.

3 *Materialy*, 1: 1 n. 1; *New York Times*, 14 May 1903, 5:1; Cyrus Adler in his introduction to *The Voice of America on Kishinev* (Philadelphia, 1904), states that the boy died on 16 February and that his body was found six days later on 22 February.

4 *Materialy*, 1: 7, n. 5; *New York Times*, 14 May 1903, 5:1.

5 *Materialy*, 1: 4–7, n. 4.

6 Ibid., 134–40, no. 12; S. M. Dubnow, *History of the Jews in Russia and Poland*, trans. I. Friedlaender (Philadelphia, 1918, 1920), 3 vols., III: 71–2; Davitt, *Within the Pale*, 123–4.

7 Davitt, *Within the Pale*, 122–3 and 176–7.

8 *New York Times*, 14 May 1903, 5:1.

9 Davitt, *Within the Pale*, 142.

10 *Materialy*, 1: 134–40, n. 12; William C. Fuller, *Civil-Military Conflict in Imperial Russia 1881–1914* (Princeton, 1985), 109.

11 For comprehensive accounts of Kishinev see *American Jewish Yearbook,* *1906–07* (hereafter cited *AJY*) (Philadelphia, 1907), 38–39; *Materialy,* I and II; Davitt, *Within the Pale.* Also, *Bulletin de l'Alliance Israélite Universelle* (hereafter cited *Bulletin*) (Paris, 1903), entire issue dedicated to Kishinev; the Archives of the Alliance Israélite Universelle (hereafter cited AAIU), USSR dossier Kishinev.

12 Davitt, *Within the Pale,* 126; *New York Times,* 14 May 1903, 5:1 and 19 May 1903, 2:3.

13 *New York Times,* 17 May 1903, 2:3 and 19 May 1903, 2:4.

14 Davitt, *Within the Pale,* 125.

15 Louis Greenberg, *The Jews in Russia. The Struggle for Emancipation* (New York, 1976), II: 51; Dubnov, *History of the Jews,* III: 71–5.

16 *New York Times,* 19 May 1903, 2:3 and 20 May 1903, 3:1.

17 Davitt, *Within the Pale,* 134–5.

18 Ibid., 126; Dubnow, *History of the Jews,* III: 71–5.

19 Fuller, *Civil-Military Conflict,* 109.

20 V. I. Gurko, *Features and Figures of the Past: Government and Opinion in the Reign of Nicholas II* (Stanford, 1939), 248.

21 *Materialy,* I: 130–2, no. 4 and 5.

22 Greenberg, II: 51.

23 S.Iu. Witte, *Vospominaniia: Tsarstvovanie Nikolaia II* (Berlin, 1922), I: 192; also, P. A. Zaionchovskii, *Rossiiskoe samoderzhaie v kontse XIX stoletiia* (Moscow, 1970), 27.

24 Dubnow, *History of the Jews,* 68.

25 For more on Pleve's role in Kishinev see Shlomo Lambroza, "Pleve, Kishinev and the Jewish Question: a reappraisal," *Nationalities Papers,* Spring 1984, XII, 1: 117–27; Edward H. Judge, *Plehve, Repression and Reform in Imperial Russia 1902–1904* (Syracuse, 1983), 93–101.

26 Davitt, *Within the Pale,* 170.

27 *New York Times,* 22 May 1903, 1:7.

28 Ibid., 28 April 1903, 6:2.

29 Ibid., 22 May 1903, 1:7.

30 Ibid., 19 May 1903, 2:3.

31 Ibid., 19 May 1903, 2:4 and 17 May 1903, 2:3.

32 *Materialy,* I: 132, no. 6.

33 Ibid., 137, no. 12.

34 The US Ambassador to Russia in 1903 cabled the State Department that the Russian government had denied that a massacre occurred in Kishinev. See *Papers Relating to the Foreign Affairs of the United States* (Washington, DC, 1903), 712.

35 *New York Times,* 6 June 1903, 3:2.

36 Ibid., 3:1.

37 *Bulletin* (Paris, 1903), entire issue dedicated to Kishinev.

38 *New York Times,* 27 May 1903, 3:3, Davitt, 207–17.

39 *New York Times,* 19 May 1903, 2:1.

40 Shlomo Lambroza, "Jewish self-defence during the Russian pogroms of

1903–06," *Jewish Journal of Sociology* (1981), 123–34. For more on the pogrom in Gomel see ΛΛIU, USSR dossier Mogilev no. 6713; B. A. Kraever, ed., *Gomel'skii prostess* (St. Petersburg, 1907); "Der protess fun der bundisher zelbstshuts in Homel in 1904," *Naye Folkstsaytung*, 19 September 1937; "Pogrom v Gomele," Bund Archives, New York.

41 *New York Times*, 23 September 1903, 7:2.

42 Ibid., 2 October 1903, 5:2.

43 Ibid.

44 *Naye Folkstsaytung*, 19 September 1937; Kraever, *Gomel'skii prostess*; *New York Times*, 2 October 1903, 5:2.

45 *New York Times*, 2 October 1903, 5:2.

46 Neil Weissman, "Regular police in Tsarist Russia, 1900–1914," *The Russian Review*, XLIV (1985), 45–68. Weissman indicates that the ratio of police to population before 1905 was 1:700 (p. 48). Given Gomel's population of 40,000 this would mean a police force of roughly sixty men.

47 *Der Freynd*, 20 September 1903, 1:4, no. 201.

48 *Poslednie izvestiia*, 6 October 1903.

49 Hans Heilbronner, "Count Aehrenthal and Russian Jewry, 1903–1907," *Journal of Modern History*, XXXVIII (1966), 396.

50 Lucien Wolf, ed., *The Legal Suffering of the Jews in Russia* (London, 1912), 97; Heilbronner, "Count Aehrenthal," 396.

51 *New York Times*, 22 December 1903, 5:3 and 19 May 1904, 5:4.

52 Ibid., 27 October 1904, 2:5; Dubnov, *History of the Jews*, 101–4.

53 Dubnow, *History of the Jews*, 103–4.

54 For N. P. Ignatiev's statement and his attitude toward the Jewish Question see Iu. I. Gessen, "Graf N. P. Ignat'ev i 'Vremennye pravila' o Evreiakh 3 maia 1881 goda," *Pravo*, 27 July 1908, no. 30, p. 1631–7 and 3 August 1908, no. 31, 1678–6. See also *The Times* (London), 13 January 1882, 4:2–3.

55 For more details on the Russo–Japanese War see F. B. Maurice, "The Russo–Japanese War" *Cambridge Modern History* (London, 1910), 576–601; also, A. N. Kuropatkin, *The Russian Army and the Japanese War* (London, 1909), I, II; David Walder, *The Short Victorious War* (London, 1973).

56 S. Iu. Witte, *The Memoirs of Count Witte* (Toronto, 1921), 250.

57 *AJY*, 38–9, *New York Times*, 4 May 1904, 1:6.

58 *New York Times*, 4 April, 1904, 2:4.

59 A. J. Sherman, "German-Jewish bankers in world politics, the financing of the Russo–Japanese War," *Leo Baeck Institute Yearbook*, XXVIII (1983), 68.

60 Sherman, "German–Jewish banker," 59–73.

61 *Bulletin*, 1904, 22–3.

62 Kuropatkin, *The Russian Army*, I: 281.

63 Ibid., 276–81.

64 Ibid., 285.

65 *AJY*, 42–3.

66 *Bulletin*, 1904, 31–2; *AJY*, 38–9; *New York Times*, 15 August 1904, 7:3 and 17 August 1904, 6:6. For more detailed information see *Berliner Tageblatt*, 5 August 1904.

67 *Bulletin*, 1904, 32–3; *AJY*, 38–9; *New York Times*, 15 August 1904, 7:3, 16 August 1904, 6:7 and 17 August 1904, 6:6; *Berliner Tageblatt*, 5 August 1904.

68 *Bulletin*, 1904, 28–31; *AJY*, 40–1; *New York Times*, 13 September 1904, 9:3 and 18 September 1904, 4:4.

69 *Bulletin*, 1904, 102–4; *AJY*, 38–9.

70 *Bulletin*, 1904, 104–5; *AJY*, 38–9.

71 For Jews in the Revolutionary Movement see, L. Schapiro, "The role of the Jews in the Russian revolutionary movement," *Slavic and East European Review*, no. 40 (1961), 148–67; S. Dimanshtein, "Di revolutsyonere bavegung tsvishn di yidishe masn in revolutsye fun 1905 yor," *Royte bleter*, 1 (Minsk, 1929), 1–42; L. Rubinov, "Yidishe zelbstshuts in dorem-rusland beys di yorn fun der ershter revolutsye," *Fun Noenten Ovar*, 1 (1938), 322–32 (YIVO Institute); Y. Leshchinsky, *Dos sovietische yidntum; zayn fargangenhayt un gegenvart* (New York, 1941), 22–4. J. Frankel, *Prophecy and Politics* (London, 1981), 143–58.

72 For a comprehensive account of the Bund see, H. Tobias, *The Jewish Bund in Russia: From its Origins to 1905* (Stanford, 1972).

73 *The Russian Correspondence*, 2 December 1905.

74 *The Times*, 6 February 1904, 6:3.

75 Schapiro, "The role of the Jews," 148.

76 The David Moslowitch Collection – The papers of Lucien Wolf, YIVO Archives, folder no. 53, no. 12892–12901, secret report from Count Lamzdorf entitled *On the Anarchists*.

77 Lamzdorf, *On the Anarchists*, no. 12892.

78 *Voskhod*, 29 June 1905, no. 26, 3; Frankel, *Prophecy and Politics*, 147.

79 *Iskra*, 15 June 1905, no. 102, 5; Frankel, *Prophecy and Politics*, 146.

80 *Poslednie izvestiia*, 18 May 1905, no. 231, 2; Frankel, *Prophecy and Politics*, 147.

81 *AJY*, 42–3; *Poslednie izvestiia*, 20 April 1905, no. 227, 1; Frankel, *Prophecy and Politics*, 146.

82 *AJY*, 46–7; *Poslednie izvestiia*, 27 June 1905, no. 239, 1–3 and 4 July 1905, no. 239, 1; Frankel, *Prophecy and Politics*, 146.

83 *Pogromen Blat*, 6 July 1905. See also AAIU, USSR, Dossier Zhitomir.

84 Quoted in Frankel, *Prophecy and Politics*, 147.

85 *AJY*, 44–45; *New York Times*, 10 May 1905, 5:3, 11 May 1905, 2:4 and 13 May 1905, 4:1; *The Times* (London), 11 May 1905, 5:3, 12 May 1905, 5:2, 13 May 1905, 7:2 and 15 May 1905, 5:2.

86 *The Times* (London) 13 May 1905, 7:2; *New York Times*, 13 May 1905, 4:1.

87 The earliest reactionary groups, The Holy Brotherhood, lasted only three years from 1881 to 1883. For a complete discussion of the

development of right-wing movements in Russia see Hans Rogger, "The formation of the Russian Right," *Jewish Policies*, 188–211.

88 Rogger, "Formation of the Russian Right," 191–2.

89 Greenberg, 54.

90 Dubnov, *Materialy*, 1: xii.

91 Rogger, "Formation of the Russian Right," 191.

92 "Vsepoddanneishii otchet senatora Kuzminskovo: o prichinakh besporiadkov proiskhodivshikh v gor. Odesse v oktiabre 1905 g., i o poriadke deistviia mestnykh vlastei," *Materialy k istorii russkoi kontr-revoliutsii*; I: *Pogromy po offitsial'nym dokumentam* (hereafter, Kuzminskii Report) (St. Petersburg, 1908); AAIU USSR Dossier in IC-I, Special Report to the Alliance Israelite Universelle by Maxim Vinaver, *The Situation in Odessa Since 1905* (hereafter, Vinaver Report) (Paris, 1907).

93 *The Times*, 10 October 1906, 3:3.

94 Rogger, "Formation of the Russian Right," 198.

95 Bertram Wolfe, *Three Who Made a Revolution* (New York, 1978), 327.

96 Gurko, *Features and Figures of the Past*, 394.

97 For complete text see S. Harvave, *The Russian Revolution of 1905* (Toronto, 1964), 289–92.

98 Shlomo Lambroza, "The Pogrom Movement in Tsarist Russia, 1903–06" (doctoral dissertation, Rutgers University, 1981).

99 Linden, *Die Judenpogrome*, 1: 189–92.

100 Ibid., 1: 189–91.

101 Findings of the St. Petersburgh study published in *Die Welt*, no. 43, 1905, 17.

102 Lambroza, The Pogrom Movement, 165–6.

103 Linden, *Die Judenpogrome*, 1, 189–92.

104 Lambroza, The Pogrom Movement, 156–62.

105 The police report indicated that 400 Jews were killed, and 300 people, mostly Jews were injured. But it is widely accepted that the police report underestimated the extent of the damage. Several sources, including the Kuminskii Report, clxvi-clxviii and 201; the Vinaver Report; Die Judenpogrome, II: 130, *Voskhod*, no. 44–5, 11 November 1905, 16, and *AJY*, 50–1, cite a higher figure for the number of dead and wounded.

106 *AJY*, "A table of pogroms from 1903–1906," 35–69.

107 AAIU USSR Dossier Odessa, no. 5269.

108 Kuzminskii Report, ccxiv.

109 Ibid., cli-cliii.

110 *Ost und West*, VIII, no. 1, January 1908.

111 Vinaver Report, 12.

112 Fuller, *Civil-Military Conflict*, 211.

113 Vinaver Report, 4–5.

114 E. J. Bing, *The Secret Letters of the Last Tsar* (New York, 1938), 187–8.

115 Bing, *Secret Letters*, 211.

116 Witte, *Vospominaniia*, II, 64–5, 71–2.

117 E. Semenoff, *The Russian Government and the Massacres*, translated by Lucien Wolfe (Westport, CT, 1972), for complete text of the pamphlet see pp. 98–109.

118 *The Times*, 28 December 1906, 8:2.

119 For complete text of Urusov's speech see, Maurice Baring, *A Year in Russia* (London, 1907), 250–7. Semenoff, *The Russian Government*, 149–60.

120 Semenoff, *The Russian Government*, 150–1.

121 *The Times*, 28 December 1906, 8:2.

122 Ibid.

123 Ibid.

124 Abraham Ascher, *The Revolution of 1905* (Stanford, 1988), 259. *The New York Times*, 28 September 1906, 5:1.

125 *AJY*, "Report of the Duma Commission on the Bialystok Massacre," 70–89.

126 *The Times*, 10 July 1906, 5:1.

127 Ibid., 19 June 1906, 5:1.

128 Ibid., 11 September 1906, 3:1.

129 Ibid., 13 September 1906, 3:1.

CHAPTER 9

The pogrom of 1905 in Odessa: a case study

Robert Weinberg

The wave of anti-Jewish pogroms that swept the Pale of Settlement after Tsar Nicholas II issued the October Manifesto in 1905 reflected the ethnic and political tensions and hostilities that characterized popular unrest and marred the social landscape of late Imperial Russia in that revolutionary year.[1] In the weeks following the granting of fundamental civil rights and political liberties, pogroms directed mainly at Jews but also affecting students, intellectuals, and other national minorities broke out in hundreds of cities, towns, and villages, resulting in deaths and injuries to thousands of people.[2]

In the port city of Odessa alone, the police reported that at least 400 Jews and 100 non-Jews were killed and approximately 300 people, mostly Jews, were injured, with slightly over 1,600 Jewish houses, apartments, and stores incurring damage. These official figures undoubtedly underestimate the true extent of the damage, as other informed sources indicate substantially higher numbers of persons killed and injured. For example, Dmitri Neidhardt, City Governor of Odessa during the pogrom and brother-in-law of the future Prime Minister Peter Stolypin, estimated the number of casualties at 2,500, and the Jewish newspaper *Voskhod* reported that over 800 were killed and another several thousand were wounded. Moreover, various hospitals and clinics reported treating at least 600 persons for injuries sustained during the pogrom.[3] Indeed, no other city in the Russian Empire in 1905 experienced a pogrom comparable in its destruction and violence to the one unleashed against the Jews of Odessa.

Despite the havoc wreaked by these pogroms, historians have only just begun to explore the origins, circumstances, and consequences of the October pogroms in an effort to evaluate their impact and connection with the general course of revolutionary events in 1905.[4] Even though the general contours of pogroms in Russia are known, detailed case studies are nonetheless required if historians are to offer

248

a more comprehensive and conclusive assessment of antisemitism and the pogromist phenomenon in late Imperial Russia. This chapter focuses on Odessa for several reasons. First, Odessa was the fourth largest city in the Russian Empire by century's end, boasting a Jewish population of approximately 138,000 in a city with 403,000 inhabitants. Second, the scope and breadth of the violence directed against Odessa Jewry merit special study. Third, since ethnicity often acted as a divisive force in labor movements in many parts of Western Europe and Russia during the nineteenth and early twentieth centuries, the ethnic heterogeneity of the Odessa work force provides an opportunity to study how ethnic and religious antagonisms affected worker solidarity and the capacity for collective action in 1905.[5] Finally, examination of the Odessa pogrom addresses the broader issues of the Revolution of 1905, particularly the character of worker unrest and protest and the dynamics of revolutionary politics. The fact that the pogroms followed quickly on the heels of major concessions offered by the autocracy strongly suggests that they were connected to the political crisis engulfing Russia in 1905 and should therefore be examined in the context of the social, economic, and political strains threatening the stability of state and society in late Imperial Russia.

Pogrom analysis raises two especially perplexing issues, namely how to identify pogromists and their motives and how to pinpoint the specific reasons for the outbreak and timing of pogroms. While members of various social and occupational groups often engaged in acts of anti-Jewish violence and behaved out of varying motives, is it possible to determine which residents of Odessa were particularly prone to pogromist behavior in 1905 and why they figured prominently in attacks on Jews and their property? Given the long heritage of antisemitism in Odessa that included periodic outbreaks of violent attacks against Jews, why did anti-Jewish violence surface only in the aftermath of the October Manifesto and not earlier in the year during other instances of social and political unrest? The October pogrom in Odessa also underscores the importance of studying popular and official attitudes toward Jews and assessing the extent to which the pogrom was a spontaneous display of popular antisemitism or the result of a carefully planned and premeditated strategy engineered by government officials.

The October 1905 pogrom in Odessa resulted from the conjuncture of several long-term and short-term social, economic, and political factors that produced conditions in the autumn of 1905 particularly ripe for an explosion of anti-Jewish violence. Among the long-term factors were economic competition between certain categories of Gentile and Jewish workers – unskilled day laborers in particular – long-standing ethnic and religious antagonisms, the prominence of Jews in the commercial affairs of Odessa, and the mistreatment of Jews as it was manifested by the central government and local authorities in discriminatory legislation and policies. More immediate factors include the general course of political events and developments in 1905, specifically the polarization of the political spectrum into pro and anti-government forces, the role of civilian and military officials in promoting an atmosphere conducive to a pogrom, and the visible position of Jews in the opposition movement against the autocracy. An examination of circumstances leading up to the pogrom and an analysis of the chain of events that triggered the attack on the Jews of the city underscore how the pogrom grew out of general developments in Odessa in 1905 and was an integral element in the trajectory of the revolution. The pogrom cannot be understood apart from the complex nature of social, economic, ethnic, and political life in Odessa.

Founded in the waning years of the reign of Catherine the Great, Odessa was a relatively new city that did not inhibit but rather encouraged all residents – Russians and non-Russians, foreigners and Jews – to participate actively in its economic development. Odessa was an enlightened city that tolerated diversity and innovation, welcoming persons of all nationalities who could contribute to the growth of the city. Greeks, Italians, and Jews helped set the tempo of commercial and financial life in Odessa and assumed active roles in the city's cultural and political affairs during much of the nineteenth century. Jews were especially welcome in Odessa and were exempt from many of the onerous burdens and restrictions that coreligionists in other areas of the Pale of Settlement endured.

But this tolerance did not mean that Jews in Odessa were accepted as social equals or that antisemitism did not exist in the city. Notwithstanding Odessa's well-deserved reputation as a bastion of liberal and enlightened attitudes toward its Jewish residents, the Jews of Odessa were no strangers to anti-Jewish animosity, which generally remained submerged but did assume ugly and violent forms several times before 1905. Serious pogroms in which Jews were killed and wounded and Jewish houses and businesses suffered substantial damage had occurred in 1821, 1859, 1871, 1881, and 1900. Anti-Jewish sentiment was common among Odessa's Russian population, as gangs of Jewish and Russian youths often engaged in bloody brawls. Every year at Eastertime rumors of an impending pogrom circulated through the city's Jewish community. Pogrom-mongering intensified after the turn of the century as militantly patriotic and pro-tsarist organizations emerged and engaged in Jew-baiting and other antisemitic activities.[6]

These pogroms stemmed in part from deep-rooted anti-Jewish feelings and reflected a Judeophobia prevalent among many non-Jewish residents of the city. Such was the case in the 1821 pogrom when Greeks attacked Jews, accusing them of aiding the Turks in killing the Greek Patriarch of Constantinople. After mid-century, however, religious fanaticism and hatred sometimes mixed with social and economic factors to heighten anti-Jewish sentiments. The increasing prominence of Jews in the commercial life of the city and structural changes in the economy played no small role in fueling antisemitism and leading to its expression in pogroms.

Until the Crimean War, Greeks controlled the export of grain from Odessa, while Jews dominated the roles of middleman and expediter. With the disruption of trade routes caused by the war, many of the leading Greek commercial firms either went bankrupt or decided to pursue other, more lucrative ventures. Jewish merchants and traders, who were accustomed to operating at smaller profit margins, filled the vacuum caused by the departure of Greek merchants and assumed prominent positions in the export business in Odessa, which was overwhelmingly dependent on the grain trade. Like other ethnic and religious communities in the city, Jewish merchants gave preference in employment practices to their coreligionists. Consequently, Greeks were supplanted by Jewish workers and fell into straitened economic circumstances.[7] These developments, along with rumors of a Jewish ritual murder in 1859 and desecration of the Greek Orthodox Church and cemetery in 1871, fanned the flames of antisemitism, driving many Greeks, sailors and dockworkers in particular, to participate in pogroms in these years.

Greeks were not the only residents of Odessa who perceived Jews as an economic threat. Russian resentment and hostility toward Jews came to the fore in the pogrom of 1871 as Russians joined Greeks in attacks on Jews. Thereafter, Russians filled the ranks of pogromist

mobs in 1881, 1900, and 1905. The replacement of Greeks by
Russians as pogromists reflects the decline of Greek influence in
Odessa and underscores the tension and hostility that also existed
between Russians and Jews in the city.[8]

According to some Russian inhabitants, exploitation by and
competition with Jews figured prominently as the causes of the 1871
pogrom. Some insisted that "the Jews exploit us," while others,
especially the unemployed, blamed increased Jewish settlement in
Odessa for reduced employment opportunities and lower wages.
One Russian cabdriver, referring to the Jews' practice of lending
money to Jewish immigrants to enable them to rent or buy a horse
and cab, complained: "Several years ago there was one Jewish
cabdriver for every 100 Russian cabdrivers, but since then rich Jews
have given money to the poor Jews so that there are now a countless
multitude of Jewish cabdrivers."[9]

The growing visibility of Jews enhanced the predisposition of
Russians to blame Jews for their difficulties. Like elsewhere in Russia
and Western Europe, many non-Jews in Odessa perceived Jews as
possessing an inordinate amount of wealth, power, and influence
and pointed to the steady growth of the city's Jewish population
during the nineteenth century – from approximately 14,000 (14
percent) in 1858 to nearly 140,000 (35 percent) in 1897 – as an
indication of the Jewish "threat."[10] The increasingly prominent role
played by Jews in the commercial and industrial life of the city after
mid-century also contributed to resentment against Odessa's Jewish
community. In the 1880s, for example, firms owned by Jews
controlled 70 percent of the export trade in grain, and Jewish
brokerage houses handled over half the city's entire export trade.
Jewish domination of the grain trade continued to expand during
the next several decades; by 1910 Jewish firms handled nearly 90
percent of the export trade in grain products. In addition to their
activities as merchants, middlemen, and exporters, Jews in Odessa
by century's end also occupied prominent positions in the manufacturing, banking, and retail sectors. In 1910 Jews owned slightly
over half the large stores, trading firms, and small shops. Thirteen of
the eighteen banks operating in Odessa had Jewish board members
and directors, while at the turn of the century Jews comprised
approximately half the members of the city's three merchant guilds,
up from 38 percent in the mid-1880s. Jews virtually monopolized the
production of starch, refined sugar, tin goods, chemicals, and

wallpaper and competed with Russian and foreign entrepreneurs in the making of flour, cigarettes, beer, wine, leather, cork, and iron products. Even though Jews in 1887 owned 35 percent of all factories, these firms produced 57 percent of the total factory output (in roubles) for that year.

Despite the outstanding success of some Jews in economic pursuits, the common perception that the growing Jewish presence threatened to result in total Jewish domination had little basis in reality. The proportion of Jews in the city's population, which had risen from about a quarter to a third during the last quarter of the century, leveled out after 1897, with the percentage of Jews somewhat dropping by the eve of 1905. According to data assembled by the city governor, the number of Jews living in Odessa in 1904 was approximately 140,000, or just over 28 percent of the city's total population. The reasons for this decline are difficult to ascertain but may be due to imprecise census-taking by local officials, since other studies state that the percentage of Jews in Odessa still remained above 30 percent in 1904.[11] Regardless of slight variations in estimates of the size of the Odessa Jewish community at the turn of the century, non-Jews continued to hold their own in the economic sphere and were in no danger of being eliminated by Jewish entrepreneurs and industrialists. According to the 1897 census, thousands of Russians and Ukrainians were engaged in commercial activities of some sort, especially the marketing of agricultural products, and comprised approximately a third of the total number of individuals listed as earning livings from trade. Moreover, on the eve of 1905 approximately half the licenses granting permission to engage in commercial and industrial pursuits were given to non-Jews, and in 1910 non-Jews owned slightly under half the large stores and trading firms and 44 percent of small shops. Forty percent of manufacturing enterprises in 1887 were owned by foreigners, with Russians owning another 25 percent. On the eve of the First World War foreigners and Russians, many of whom employed primarily Russian workers, owned the majority of enterprises under factory inspection in Odessa. Lastly, Jews in 1910 owned only 17 percent of real estate parcels in the city, down from 20 percent a decade earlier, while Gentiles controlled about half of all large commercial enterprises. The bulk of the wealth in Odessa still remained in the hands of non-Jews.[12]

Furthermore, wealthy Jews could not enter the leisured propertied

class or translate their wealth into political influence and power.
Contrary to popular perceptions prevalent among non-Jews in both
Odessa and throughout Russia, Odessa was not controlled by its
Jewish residents. Only a handful of Odessa's Jews lived from
investments in land, stocks, and bonds, and even fewer – 71 in a staff
of 3,449 – worked for the imperial government, the judiciary, or the
municipal administration. This was due in part to the 1892
municipal reform which made it more difficult for Jews to occupy
government posts and disenfranchised Russian Jewry, who no longer
enjoyed the right to elect representatives to city councils. A special
office for municipal affairs was assigned the responsibility of
appointing six Jewish members to the sixty-man Odessa city
council.[13]

In contrast to the wealthy and influential stratum of Jews, which
never constituted more than a fraction of the total Jewish population
of Odessa, the vast majority of Jews eked out meager livings as
shopkeepers, second-hand dealers, salesclerks, petty traders, domestic servants, day laborers, workshop employees, and factory hands.
Poverty was a way of life for most Jews in Odessa, as it undoubtedly
was for most non-Jewish residents. Isidor Brodovskii, in his study of
Jewish poverty in Odessa at the turn of the century, estimated that
nearly 50,000 Jews were destitute and another 30,000 were poverty-
stricken. In 1905 nearly 80,000 Jews requested financial assistance
from the Jewish community in order to buy matzoh during Passover,
a telling sign that well over half the Jews in Odessa experienced
difficulties making ends meet.[14]

Despite the disparity between popular perception and the reality
of Jewish wealth and power, a reversal in Odessa's economic fortunes
at the turn of the century strengthened anti-Jewish sentiments
among its Russian residents. Russia entered a deep recession as the
great industrial spurt of the 1890s faltered. In turn, Odessa's
economy suffered a setback due to the decrease in the demand for
manufactured goods, the drop in the supply of grain available for
export, and the drying up of credit. Weaknesses and deficiencies in
Odessa's economic infrastructure complicated matters. Conditions
continued to deteriorate as the year 1905 approached, due to the
outbreak of war between Russia and Japan in 1904. Trade, the
mainstay of Odessa's economy, declined even further and the city's
industrial sector entered a period of retrenchment.[15]

Although anti-Jewish sentiments in Odessa usually remained

submerged, many residents feared that Russian–Jewish hostilities could explode in a matter of hours given the right combination of factors. During major labor demonstrations or strikes, organizers often felt compelled to exhort workers not to direct their anger at Jews, but to present a united front of Jew and Russian against employers. More important, organizers had to allay fears among the general public that demonstrations and strikes might develop into pogroms. As one Russian worker assured the Odessa Jewish community in early 1905, Russian workers were not "wild animals ready to unleash a pogrom."[16] The fear that strikes and demonstrations would degenerate into antisemitic violence even served to curb labor militancy. For example, the 1903 May Day rally never materialized because many potential participants, Jews and Russians alike with the memory of the recent Kishinev pogrom fresh in their minds, feared that a march through Odessa would spark a pogrom. In fact, a group of Jewish shopkeepers and property owners, upset by workers gathering in a field to celebrate May Day, informed the police, who arrested some thirty workers.[17] Employers also understood that religious animosities could be used to hinder worker solidarity; owners of the few enterprises with ethnically mixed labor forces sometimes encouraged Russian workers to direct their anger at Jewish coworkers.[18] Ethnic loyalties and hatreds of Russian workers sometimes overshadowed their affinities to Jewish workers based on the common exploitation and oppression both groups experienced as wage laborers and permitted ethnic tensions to surface.

During the first half of 1905 tensions between Jews and Russians ran particularly high. Fomented in part by the popular belief that Jews were not contributing to the war effort against the Japanese, anti-Jewish hostility nearly reached a breaking point in the spring.[19] As in previous years rumors of an impending pogrom circulated among the Jewish community during Orthodox Holy Week in April. Yet unlike the past, when Jews did not take precautions, in 1905 they mobilized.

Building upon the self-defense groups they had formed in the aftermath of the 1903 Kishinev pogrom, Odessa's Jews armed themselves and issued appeals, calling upon the non-Jewish residents of Odessa to show restraint and not engage in violence against Jews. Just before Easter the National Committee of Jewish Self-Defense distributed a series of leaflets threatening non-Jews with armed retaliation in the event of a pogrom. The committee urged all Jews to join self-defense brigades and prepare to counter any attack on Jews and their property. Men were told to arm themselves with guns, knives, clubs, and whips, and women were encouraged to prepare solutions of sulfuric acid. Bundists, Bolsheviks, and Mensheviks joined in these efforts by also reorganizing self-defense brigades established the year before and taking up collections for weapons and ammunition. Despite the circulation of pogromist literature inciting Russians to attack Jews, local officials and a Bundist correspondent concluded that rumors of a pogrom were unfounded. In fact, the Bund's correspondent wrote that "a pogromist mood was...unnoticeable."[20]

Yet fear of an impending pogrom resurfaced in June in the aftermath of a general strike and disorders occasioned by the arrival of the battleship *Potemkin*. On 13 June Cossacks shot several workers from metalworking and machine-construction factories who had been on strike since the beginning of May. Workers retaliated on 14 June by engaging in massive work stoppages and attacking the police with guns and rocks, but the arrival of the *Potemkin* that night diverted the workers from further confrontation with their employers and the government. On 15 June instead of intensifying the strike, thousands of Odessans jammed the port district in order to view the battleship and rally behind the mutinous sailors. By late afternoon some members of the crowd began to ransack warehouses and set fire to the harbor's wooden buildings. Although available sources do not allow a precise determination of the composition of the rioters, partial arrest records reveal that non-Jewish vagrants (*liudi bez opredelennykh zaniatii*), dockworkers, and other day laborers comprised the majority. To suppress the unrest, the military cordoned off the harbor and opened fire on the trapped crowd. By the next morning well over 1,000 people had died, victims of either the soldiers' bullets or the fire which consumed the harbor.[21]

During these disorders rumors of an impending pogrom once again surfaced, as right-wing agitators attempted to incite Russian workers against the Jews.[22] On 20 June, only a few days after the massacre, a virulently antisemitic, four-page broadside entitled *Odesskie dni* appeared. The tract blamed the Jews, in particular the National Committee of Jewish Self-Defense and secondary school students, for the recent disorders and the tragedy at the port.

Accusing the Jews of fomenting the unrest and enlisting the support of unwitting Russians, the author of the broadside stated that Jews initiated the shootings on 14 and 15 June and were responsible for setting fire to the port. The tract ended with a call to hold the Jewish community of Odessa collectively responsible for the destruction and demanded that Jews compensate Gentiles who suffered property damage and personal loss. In addition, *Odesskie dni* called for the disarming of all Jews and suggested a general search of all Jewish apartments in the city. Failure to carry out these proposals, the tract concluded, would make it "impossible for Christians to live in Odessa" and result in the take-over of Odessa by Jews.[23]

While *Odesskie dni* did not call for acts of anti-Jewish violence, its appearance underscores the tense atmosphere existing in Odessa and highlights how in times of social unrest and political crisis ethnic hostility could come to the fore and threaten further disruption of social calm. In the week or so following the massive disorders of mid-June, scattered attacks against Jews were reported as antisemitic agitators tried to stir up Gentiles into a pogromist mood.[24] Moreover, the belief that Jews were responsible for the June unrest was evident in the reports of some government officials. Gendarme chief Kuzubov wrote that the instigators of the disorders and arson were "exclusively Jews" and Count Aleksei Ignatiev, in his report on the disorders in Kherson and Ekaterinoslav provinces, also accused Jews of setting fire to the port but did not furnish any hard evidence or substantiation.[25] Though no pogrom occurred in June, the sentiments expressed in both *Odesskie dni* and official reports indicate the emotionally charged atmosphere of Russian–Jewish relations in Odessa and the extent to which government officials, who in their search for simple explanations and unwillingness to dig deeper into the root causes of the social and political turmoil engulfing Odessa, were prepared to affix blame to the Jews.

Jews found it difficult to dispel the accusations expressed in *Odesskie dni*. While many reports of Jewish revolutionary activity were exaggerations or even fabrications, Jews *were* behind some – though certainly not all – of the unrest in Odessa. During the summer the police arrested several Jews for making and stockpiling bombs. Jews also figured prominently among the 133 Social Democrats and Socialist Revolutionaries either considered politically unreliable, arrested or exiled after the June Days. In addition, a leaflet distributed throughout the city, apparently by a

Plate 8. Group portrait of the Odessa Bund self-defense group, posing with victims of the 1905 pogrom at the cemetery. The banner, in Yiddish and Russian, reads: "Glory to those who have fallen in the struggle for freedom!"

Plate 9. Members of the Odessa Bund killed in the pogrom of 1905

Bundist organization, urged Jews to arm themselves, struggle for civil and political freedom, and overthrow the autocracy.[26] Jews also helped organize rallies at the university and direct student strikes and public demonstrations. Like others throughout the Empire, Odessa's university became the locus of anti-government activity after August when the Tsar granted administrative autonomy to Russia's universities, thereby removing these institutions from the jurisdiction of the police. Jewish youths, students, and workers filled the ranks of the crowds that attended the rallies at the university in September and October, and Jews actively participated in the wave of work stoppages, demonstrations, and street disorders that broke out in mid-October. On 16 October, a day of major disturbances, 197 of the 214 persons arrested were Jews.[27] Moreover, Jews eagerly celebrated the political concessions granted in the October Manifesto, seeing them as the first step in the civil and political emancipation of Russian Jewry.

These events confirmed many high-ranking police and other officials in the belief that Jews were a seditious element. As we have seen, many government officials blamed Jews for the June unrest. In doing so they were following a tradition of accusing Jews for fomenting trouble in Odessa. At the turn of the century, for example, the city governor even asked the Ministry of the Interior to limit Jewish migration to Odessa in the hope that such a measure would weaken the revolutionary movement.[28] Such attitudes, along with the legacy of discrimination against Russian Jewry and governmental tolerance and at times sponsorship of anti-Jewish organizations and propaganda, signaled to antisemites that authorities in Odessa would probably countenance violence against Jews.[29] When combined with economic resentments and frustrations as well as timeworn religious prejudices, the perception that Jews were revolutionaries provided fertile ground for a pogrom. To those residents of Odessa alarmed by the opposition to the Tsar and government, Jews were a convenient target for retaliation.

Politics in Odessa polarized during 1905 as anti and pro-government forces coalesced and mobilized. Militant right-wing organizations like the Black Hundreds and patriotic student groups consolidated their ranks, and radical student groups emerged as significant political forces, joining the organized revolutionary parties already active in Odessa. Indeed, the stage was set for confrontation between the forces of revolution and reaction and the pogrom occurred in the context of this unrest and Odessa's feverish atmosphere. During the week before the October pogrom, public calm was disturbed by bloody confrontations pitting the populace against soldiers and police. The crucial question is why this unrest degenerated into one of the worst anti-Jewish progroms ever experienced in imperial Russia.

On 15 October, a day after the police injured several high school students who were boycotting classes in sympathy with striking railway workers, radical students and revolutionaries appealed to workers to start a general strike. They collected donations for guns and ammunition and representatives of the city's three Social Democratic organizations visited factories and workshops. Reports also circulated that students and revolutionaries were forming armed militias. On 16 October students, youths, and workers roamed the streets of Odessa, building barricades and engaging the police and military in pitched battles. The troops summoned to suppress the demonstrations encountered fierce resistance, as demonstrators behind the barricades greeted them with rocks and gunfire. Military patrols were also targets of snipers. The troops retaliated by opening fire, and by early evening the army had secured the streets of Odessa. The police disarmed and arrested scores of demonstrators, systematically bludgeoning some into unconsciousness.[30]

The 17th of October passed without any public disturbances or confrontations, but life did not return to normal. The military continued to patrol the city, schools and many stores remained closed and, even though not all workers responded to the appeal for a general strike, at least 4,000 workers – many of whom were Jewish – walked off their jobs either voluntarily or after receiving threats from other workers already on strike. Groups of workers congregated outside stores that opened for business, singing songs and drinking vodka. At the university, professors and students, along with representatives of revolutionary parties, redoubled efforts to form armed militias.[31]

The storm broke on 18 October. News of the October Manifesto had reached Odessa officials the previous evening and by the next morning thousands of people thronged the streets to celebrate. As one university student exclaimed, "a joyous crowd appeared in the streets – people greeted each other as if it were a holiday."[32] Jews, hoping that the concessions would lead to the end of all legal disabilities against them, were joined by non-Jews in vigorously and enthusiastically celebrating the granting of civil and political liberties.

At first the crowds were peaceful, but the quiet did not last long. Soon after the demonstrations began, several individuals began to unfurl red flags and banners with anti-government slogans. Others shouted slogans like "Down with the Autocracy," "Long Live Freedom" and "Down with the Police." Apartment dwellers draped red carpets and shawls from their balconies and windows, while groups of arrogant demonstrators forced passersby to doff their hats or bow before the flags. In the city council building, demonstrators ripped down the portrait of the Tsar, substituted a red flag for the imperial colors and collected money for weapons. The city governor also reported that one group of demonstrators tied portraits of Nicholas II to the tails of dogs and then released them to run through the city.[33] The mood of the demonstrators grew more violent as the day wore on. Groups of celebrants – primarily Jewish youths according to official accounts – viciously attacked and disarmed policemen. By mid-afternoon the office of the civil governor had received reports that two policemen had been killed, ten wounded and twenty-two disarmed, and that many others had abandoned their posts in order to avoid possible injury.[34]

The clashes were not limited to attacks on policemen by angry demonstrators. Toward the end of the day tensions between those Odessans who heralded the Manifesto and those who disapproved of the concessions granted by Nicholas had reached a breaking point. Angered over being forced to doff their caps and outraged by the sight of desecrated portraits of the Tsar, supporters of the monarchy gave vent to their anger and frustration. They demonstrated their hostility not by attacking other Russians celebrating in the streets, but by turning on Jews, for they viewed them as the source of Russia's current problems. Clashes occurred throughout the day as groups of armed demonstrators, chiefly Jewish students and workers, scuffled with bands of Russians. These outbreaks of violence marked the beginning of the infamous pogrom and were the culmination of trends that had been unfolding in the city for several weeks.

Armed confrontations between Jews and Russians originated near the Jewish district of Moldavanka in the afternoon and early evening of 18 October. The clashes apparently started when a group of Jews carrying red flags to celebrate the October Manifesto attempted to convince a group of Russian workers to doff their caps to the flags. Harsh words were exchanged, a scuffle ensued and then shots rang out. Both groups scattered, but quickly reassembled in nearby streets and resumed fighting. The clashes soon turned into an anti-Jewish riot, as Russians indiscriminately attacked Jews and began to vandalize and loot Jewish homes, apartments, and stores in the neighborhood. The rioters also turned on policemen and troops summoned to quell the disorders, actions suggesting that pogromists were not yet fully focused on Jews in their attacks. The military on October 18 was equally vigilant in its efforts to restrain both Russian and Jewish rioters, vigorously suppressing these disturbances and restoring order by early evening. Four Russians were killed, dozens of Russians wounded – including policemen – and twelve Russians arrested as a result of the unrest. The number of Jews who were injured or arrested is unknown.[35]

The pogrom began in full force the next day, 19 October. In the mid-morning hundreds of Russians – children, women, and men – gathered in various parts of the city for patriotic marches to display their loyalty to the Tsar. Day laborers, especially those employed at the docks, comprised a major element of the crowd that assembled at the harbor and were joined by Russian factory and construction workers, shopkeepers, salesclerks, workshop employees, other day laborers, and vagrants.[36]

These patriotic processions had the earmarks of a rally organized by extreme, right-wing political organizations like the Black Hundreds. The main contingent of marchers assembled at Customs Square at the harbor, where the procession's organizers distributed flags, icons and portraits of the Tsar. The marchers passed around bottles of vodka, and plainclothes policemen reportedly handed out not only vodka but also money and guns.[37] Onlookers and passersby joined the procession as the demonstrators made their way from the port to the city center. Singing the national anthem and religious hymns and, according to some reports, shouting "Down with the Jews" and "It's necessary to beat them," they stopped at the city council building and substituted the imperial colors for the red flag that demonstrators had raised the previous day. They then headed toward the cathedral located in central Odessa, stopping en route at the residences of Neidhardt and Baron Aleksandr Kaulbars, Commander of the Odessa Military District. Kaulbars, fearing confrontation between the patriotic marchers and left-wing students and revolutionaries, asked them to disperse. Some heeded his request, but most members of the procession continued their march. Neidhardt, on the other hand, greeted the patriots enthusiastically and urged them to hold their memorial service at the cathedral. After a brief prayer service, the procession continued to march through the streets of central Odessa.[38]

Suddenly, shots rang out and a young boy carrying an icon lay dead. Most accounts of the incident assert that the shots came from surrounding buildings, probably from the offices of *Iuzhnoe obozrenie*. No one knows for certain who fired first, but evidence strongly suggests that revolutionaries or members of Jewish and student self-defense brigades were responsible.[39] In any case, the crowd panicked and ran through the streets as more shots were fired from rooftops, balconies, and apartment windows, prompting some to plead for police protection. Revolutionaries and self-defense units organized by students and Jews threw homemade bombs at the Russian demonstrators. These actions suggest that they, along with pro-government forces, were itchy for confrontation and ready to instigate trouble. The shootings triggered a chain reaction: convinced that Jews were responsible for the shootings, members of the patriotic demonstration began to shout "Beat the Yids" and "Death to the Yids" and went on a rampage, attacking Jews and destroying Jewish apartments, homes, and stores.

The course of events was similar in other parts of the city, as members of student and Jewish self-defense units fired on other Russians holding patriotic services and provoked similar pogromist responses. However, in Peresyp, a heavily Russian working-class district where no patriotic procession took place, the pogrom started only after pogromists from the city center arrived and began to incite local residents. By mid-afternoon a full-fledged pogrom had developed and it raged until 22 October.[40]

The lurid details of the pogrom can be found in several eyewitness and secondary accounts. Although the list of atrocities perpetrated against the Jews is too long to recount here, suffice it to say that pogromists brutally and indiscriminately beat, mutilated, and murdered defenseless Jewish men, women, and children. They hurled Jews out of windows, raped and cut open the stomachs of pregnant women, and slaughtered infants in front of their parents. In one particularly gruesome incident, pogromists hung a woman upside down by her legs and arranged the bodies of her six dead children on the floor below.[41]

The pogrom's unrestrained violent and destructive excesses were in large measure made possible by the failure of authorities to adopt any countermeasures. Low-ranking policemen and soldiers failed to interfere with the pogromists and in many instances participated in the looting and killing. At times, policemen, seeking to avenge the attacks of 16 and 18 October on their colleagues, went so far as to provide protection for pogromists by firing on the self-defense units formed by Jews, students, and revolutionaries. For their part, soldiers, concluding from the actions of the police that the pogrom was sanctioned by higher authorities, stood idly by while pogromists looted stores and murdered unarmed Jews. Some policemen discharged their weapons into the air and told rioters that the shots had come from apartments inhabited by Jews, leaving the latter vulnerable to vicious beatings and murder. Eyewitnesses also reported seeing policemen directing pogromists to Jewish-owned stores or Jews' apartments, while steering the rioters away from the property of non-Jews. As the correspondent for *Collier's* reported, "Ikons and crosses were placed in windows and hung outside doors to mark the residences of the Russians, and in almost every case this was a sufficient protection." Indeed, *Odesskii pogrom i samooborona*, an emotional account of the October tragedy published by Labor Zionists in Paris, argues that the police more than any other group in Odessa were responsible for the deaths and pillage.[42]

The evidence indicates that policemen acted (or failed to act) with the knowledge and tacit approval of their superiors. Neither Neidhardt nor Kaulbars took any decisive action to suppress the pogrom when disorders erupted. In fact, the head of the Odessa gendarmes admitted that the military did not apply sufficient energy to end the pogrom and stated that pogromists greeted soldiers and policemen with shouts of "Hurrah" and then continued their rampage and pillage without interference.[43] It was not until 21 October that Kaulbars publicly announced that his troops were under orders to shoot at pogromists as well as self-defensists. Until then soldiers and police had shot only at self-defensists. Whether the 21 October directive ordering troops to shoot at pogromists helped to restore order is unclear. While it is difficult to discount entirely the effect of the directive, particularly since the pogrom petered out the next day, it bears noting that the return to calm may have been due more to the exhaustion of the pogromist mobs than to any military directive and action. Yet it is also important to stress that when the military did act to stop public disorders, as they did on 18 October and again on 21 and 22 October, pogromists generally did desist and disperse. Considering that the pogrom ended on 22 October, one cannot help but conclude that more immediate and effective action by the military could have prevented the pogrom from assuming such monstrous dimensions.

Kaulbars, defending his inaction before a delegation of city councillors on 22 October, stated that he could not take more decisive measures since Neidhardt had not made a formal determination that armed force be used to stem the disorders. Relevant regulations permitted civil authorities to request the assistance of military units when the police concluded that they were unable to maintain control; the prerogative to determine whether force should be employed resided with the city governor, but once he made such a decision, then the military commander assumed independent control until the end of operations.[44] Thus, Kaulbars believed that he lacked authorization to deploy his troops against the pogroms since Neidhardt had not followed procedure, a conclusion also reached by Senator Aleksandr Kuzminskii, head of the official government inquiry into the pogrom.

Kaulbars discounted reports that his troops were participating in the disorders, terming them unfounded and unsubstantiated rumors. He issued his directive only after Neidhardt visited him on 20 October and reiterated a request made on 19 October to adopt measures to prevent the outbreak of a pogrom. More importantly, the fact that the 21 October order was signed by chief-of-staff Lieutenant-General Bezradetskii and only issued by Kaulbars's office strongly suggests that the military commander was compelled by his superiors to suppress the pogrom. Neidhardt and Kaulbars defended their individual actions (or inactions) and bitterly accused each other of dereliction of duty, claiming the other was responsible for maintaining order. The sad truth of the matter is that police and troops were in a position to act but failed to due to the absence of instructions, rendering irrelevant the claims of Neidhardt and Kaulbars that the other possessed authority to suppress the pogrom.[45] Consequently, pogromists enjoyed almost two full days of unrestrained destruction.

Senator Kuzminskii castigated the city governor for withdrawing all police from their posts in the early afternoon on 18 October, an action he believed to warrant criminal investigation. The reasons for Neidhardt's action are unclear, since his reports are contradictory

and conflict with accounts of other informed police officials and
civilian leaders. Neidhardt claimed that he was seeking to protect
the lives of policemen who were subject to attack by celebrants of the
Manifesto, but close examination of the testimony indicates that the
bulk of attacks on policemen occurred after they were removed from
their posts. Indeed, many had abandoned their posts before trouble
erupted. Nonetheless, the possibility remains that the city governor
was acting to protect his men, since several of them had been
victimized prior to his directive. Having removed policemen from
their posts, Neidhardt instructed them to patrol the city in groups.
Strong evidence also suggests that Neidhardt tacitly approved the
student militias and hoped they could maintain order in Odessa in
the absence of the police.[46] Kuzminskii concluded that Neidhardt
was guilty of dereliction of duty because he had left Odessa
defenseless by not ordering the police patrols to take vigorous action
to prevent trouble and suppress the disorders.[47] The absence of
police ready to maintain law and order on 18 and 19 October made
for an explosive situation, signifying the surrender of the city to
armed bands of pogromists and self-defensists.

Both Neidhardt and Kaulbars defended the behavior of the police
and military. Referring to the intensity of the shooting and bombing,
the city governor and military commander argued that attacks by
student and Jewish militias hampered efforts of policemen and
soldiers to contain the pogrom. They also accused self-defense
brigades of shooting not only at pogromists, but also at police,
soldiers, and Cossacks. The police and military, according to
Neidhardt and Kaulbars, had to contend first with the self-defense
groups before turning their attention to the pogromists.[48] Konstantin
Prisnenko, commander of an infantry brigade, supported Neidhardt
and Kaulbars when he told Kuzminskii that "it was hard to stop
pogromshchiki because the soldiers were diverted by revolutionaries
who were shooting at them."[49]

The police and military undoubtedly were targets of civilian
militias and were rightly concerned about their safety and security.
Yet as the pogrom gathered momentum, one can hardly blame
members of self-defense brigades for shooting at soldiers and
policemen, for many of them were actively participating in the
violence. Moreover, Neidhardt and Kaulbars acted as though
civilian militias were the only groups involved in the violence,
conveniently ignoring how the actions of policemen and soldiers

after the pogrom began were provocative and might compel Jews to defend themselves. Despite Neidhardt's 19 October request to Kaulbars to help forestall disorders, it was not until the pogrom was in full swing that any official made an effort to stop it. Neither Neidhardt nor Kaulbars gave immediate orders to their staffs to subdue pogromists and restore order. Had the police and military genuinely applied their energies to halting the pogrom, the need for self-defense would have been reduced and attacks on soldiers and policemen would have dropped accordingly. The explanations offered by Neidhardt and Kaulbars were self-serving attempts to shift the blame for the failure of the police and military to perform their basic law enforcement functions to the victims of the pogrom.

How then are we to explain the outbreak of the pogrom? Was any one individual or group responsible for conceiving and directing the pogrom or was the orgy of violence against Jews spontaneous in origin and execution? Like many government officials, Kuzminskii concluded that the Odessa pogrom was a spontaneous display of outrage against the Jews whose political activity had elicited the pogromist response. Despite his criticism of Neidhardt, Kuzminskii joined the city governor, Kaulbars, and other authorities in Odessa in blaming the pogrom on its victims, since the Jews played a visible role in the revolutionary movement and events of 1905. Such tortuous reasoning dated back to the 1880s when government apologists seeking to explain the pogroms of 1881 argued that Jews, not pogromists, bore responsibility for anti-Jewish violence.[50] Unlike previous pogroms, which Kuzminskii attributed to national hatred and economic exploitation, the October disorders occurred as a result of the scandalous public behavior of Odessa's Jews, especially after the announcement of the October Manifesto. Okhrana chief Bobrov, for example, concluded that Jews were responsible for provoking pogromist attacks because they were spearheading a revolutionary attack on the autocracy in an effort to establish their "own tsardom." For government officials, then, patriotic Russians were justified in seeking punishment of Jews for such treasonous behavior as desecrating portraits of the Tsar and forcing bystanders to pay tribute to revolutionary flags. They could also point to the stockpiling of weapons and medical supplies at the university and the organization of student militias in the days immediately before the issuance of the October Manifesto as evidence of a revolutionary conspiracy to overthrow the government. Fears that Jews were prepared to use the concessions of the manifesto as a springboard for the subjugation of non-Jews created a situation fraught with frightening prospects. Kuzminskii defined the pogrom as an offshoot of the patriotic procession and blamed its excesses on the failure of Neidhardt to adopt adequate countermeasures.[51]

The legacy of discrimination against Russian Jewry and governmental tolerance and at times sponsorship of anti-Jewish organizations and propaganda provided fertile ground for a pogrom.[52] When combined with economic resentments and frustrations, timeworn religious prejudices and the political polarization of Odessa society during 1905, the belief that Jews were revolutionaries and fears that they were prepared to use the concessions of the manifesto as a springboard for the subjugation of non-Jews helped to create a situation fraught with frightening prospects. To those residents of Odessa alarmed by the opposition to the Tsar and government, Jews were a convenient and obvious target for retaliation.

It is questionable, however, whether the pogrom was purely spontaneous. Even though the work of Hans Rogger and Heinz-Dietrich Löwe has done much to absolve many high-ranking government ministers and officials in St. Petersburg of engineering the pogroms and giving a signal to mark their start, the culpability of certain local officials is less easy to dismiss.[53] The standard view of the Odessa pogrom places much of the blame on the encouragement and connivance of local officials, though not all the sources agree on whether the police and military actually planned the pogrom. Many contemporaries blamed civilian and military authorities, especially Neidhardt, for fostering a pogromist atmosphere and not taking measures to suppress the pogrom. Members of the city council and the newspaper *Odesskie novosti*, for example, placed full responsibility for the bloodletting on Neidhardt by stressing that his decision to remove the police from their posts gave free reign to pogromists. and *Khronika evreiskoi zhizni* called for a judicial investigation in order to reveal the city governor's "criminal responsibility."[54]

Kuzminskii himself collected evidence that points to the involvement of low-ranking members of the police force in the planning and organization of the patriotic counter-demonstration and pogrom. He stopped short, however, of suggesting that either Neidhardt or other local civil and police officials planned the pogrom.[55] According to the testimony of L. D. Teplitskii, an ensign in the army, as early as 15 and 16 October policemen were proposing to use force against Jews as punishment for their role in instigating the current wave of strikes and disorders in Odessa. As one policeman told Teplitskii, "Jews want freedom – well, we'll kill two or three thousand. Then they'll know what freedom is." Teplitskii also testified to meeting a group of day laborers on the morning of 18 October who told him they had just received instructions at a police station to attack Jews that evening.[56] In working-class neighborhoods policemen and pogromist agitators went from door to door, spreading rumors that Jews were slaughtering Russian families and urging Russian residents to repel the Jews with force. Policemen reportedly compiled lists of Jewish-owned stores and Jews' apartments to facilitate attacks, and one Jewish newspaper reported that documents existed revealing how plainclothes policemen paid pogromists from 80 kopecks to 3 roubles per day upon instructions of their superiors.[57] Other evidence even suggests that policemen were instructed not to interfere with pogromists. An army captain informed Kuzminskii that a policeman had told him that his superiors had given their permission for three days of violence because Jews had destroyed the Tsar's portrait in the city council.[58]

Unfortunately, no evidence has surfaced indicating which police officials were responsible for these directives. Nor is there conclusive evidence linking Neidhardt to the planning and approval of the pogrom or even pogrom agitation. Considering Neidhardt's efforts prior to October to avert unrest and disorders through patient negotiation and timely compromise with workers and employers, it would have been out of character for him to have approved, let alone planned, a major public disturbance. We have already seen how he behaved when rumors of a pogrom circulated earlier in the spring. Like most government officials entrusted with the responsibility of maintaining law and order, Neidhardt possessed a strong disciplinarian streak and would have been hesitant to sanction any kind of public unrest for fear of events getting out of hand.[59] To be sure, Neidhardt knew about the patriotic procession and even welcomed it, but this does not warrant the conclusion drawn by many Odessa residents that the city governor had advance knowledge of the pogrom. In fact, Neidhardt so feared an eruption of violence on 19 October that he requested Kaulbars to withdraw permission for a funeral procession planned for that day to commemorate the

students killed on 16 October in order to avoid confrontation
between funeral marchers and the patriotic counter-demonstration.
He also called upon the military commander to adopt measures to
prevent the outbreak of anti-Jewish violence.[60] The quickness with
which the authorities cooperated on October 16 to suppress street
disorders clearly suggests that Neidhardt and Kaulbars were
genuinely trying to prevent a serious breach of social peace.

Yet questions remain. Why were the police and military derelict
in their duty once the pogrom began? What accounts for Kaulbars's
failure to order his troops, who were in position, to restore order?
Why did Neidhardt not prevent individual policemen from
participating in the looting and pillaging and wait until 21 October
before ordering his staff back to work? And how can we explain his
failure to request vigorous action by the military as well as his callous
refusal to heed the pleas of pogrom victims, including a rabbi and
bank director, who begged him to intercede?[61] The truth of the
matter may simply have been that Neidhardt had few options.
Individual policemen were already abandoning their posts even
before he issued his directive of 18 October and civilian attacks had
begun. Furthermore, the police refused to return to their posts on 21
October, despite the city governor's order to do so. Neidhardt may
have realized that he could not depend on a severely underpaid,
understaffed, and disgruntled police force to maintain order in the
city. The Odessa police, like most municipal police forces throughout
the Empire, not only had a long-standing reputation for corruption
but, unlike many others, often failed to obey orders and directives.
Neidhardt was aware of the low morale among his police force,
attributing it to low wages and inadequate training.[62] The city
governor may also have realized that he could no longer control the
actions of most members of the police force and turned to Kaulbars
for help only after the pogrom had reached such dimensions that it
became clear that student self-defense brigades were an ineffective
check on the violence and destruction. Another possible scenario is
that he may simply have reasoned that the police and military were
powerless to control the pogromist mobs in light of their failure to
contain popular unrest earlier that week.

His sense of helplessness notwithstanding, Neidhart's behavior
certainly was not blameless, and there is no doubt that his sympathies
lay with the pogromists. He was a virulent antisemite who, in the
midst of the pogrom, reportedly told a delegation of Jewish leaders,

"You wanted freedom. Well, now you're getting 'Jewish freedom'."[63] From Neidhardt's perspective, Jews were responsible for the disorders and the pogrom was retribution. Thus, although Neidhardt did not plan the pogrom or even, it would seem, possess prior knowledge of it, he generally sympathized with the actions of pogromists and may have viewed attacks on Jews, once he realized that he was unable to prevent them, as an effective method of squelching the revolution. Neidhardt's actions, then, support in a very limited and modified way the notion that officials hoped pogroms would deflect popular resentment from the government. However, in the case of the Odessa pogrom, the anti-Jewish violence was not the result of plotting by high-ranking local authorities: the willingness of Neidhardt as well as Kaulbars to tolerate the pogrom and delay ordering their men into action evidently occurred *after* the violence erupted but nonetheless underscores their culpability and negligence.

Kaulbars also shares the burden of responsibility for not acting more promptly to restore order. The military commander, who was curiously not censured by Kuzminskii, was derelict in the performance of his duty since his troops were already in position to act against pogromists. Despite confusion over whether he or Neidhardt possessed jurisdiction to issue orders to stem the disorders, Kaulbars certainly had the authority to order his men to subdue the pogromists, especially since Neidhardt had requested on the 19th that he take measures to prevent a pogrom. Thus, Kaulbars's defense that he could not interfere in "civilian administration" since Neidhardt had not explicitly determined that armed force was needed to restore order is a feeble excuse for his lack of action and direction, as was the mud-slinging, so evident in Kuzminskii's final report, between Kaulbars and Neidhardt over who possessed authority to suppress the pogromists.

Kaulbars not only ignored reports that his troops were participating in the pogrom and waited several days before ordering them to combat pogromists, but he even remarked to an assembly of Odessa policemen on 21 October that "all of us sympathize in our souls with the pogrom." Yet Kaulbars, who somewhat later openly patronized and even supplied arms to the right-wing Union of Russian People, tempered his remarks by acknowledging that neither his personal sympathies nor those of policemen and soldiers relieved them of the responsibility to maintain law and order.[64] This

conflict between personal values and official duty, between sympathy
for the pogromists and obligation to preserve social peace, helps to
account for the failure of Kaulbars and Neidhardt to act more
decisively. Undoubtedly they were galled at the prospect of ordering
their men to interfere with the pogromists, who, in their eyes, were
the only loyal subjects of autocracy in Odessa. How can one justify
shooting defenders of the Tsar and the autocratic order? Such logic
and attitudes led both men to be derelict in their duties to preserve
law and order and suppress the pogromist mobs.

Kuzminskii was essentially correct to explain the timing of the
pogrom in terms of the political crisis facing the regime in October
1905. But politics alone do not explain the motives of many
pogromists. Aside from the police, who were the other participants
in the pogrom and why did they join the police in viciously attacking
Jews? While not discounting the impact of political events in
triggering the pogrom, certain social and economic characteristics of
life in Odessa also must be considered in a complete account of the
pogrom.

Available sources do not allow a precise determination of the
composition of the pogromist crowds, but they do reveal that
unskilled, non-Jewish day laborers, more than any other group
(including the police), filled the ranks of the mobs which attacked
Jews and destroyed property. Since these workers were especially
prone to anti-Jewish violence and, as we have already seen, played
a significant role not only in the patriotic procession but in other
popular disorders earlier in the year as well, a closer examination of
their lives might provide insight into their motives.

Day laborers in Odessa led a precarious social and economic
existence, suffering from irregular impermanent work and low
wages. Many were unmarried male migrants to Odessa who lacked
marketable skills and work experience. Large numbers of these day
laborers came from the countryside, where rural poverty and
overpopulation were driving many young peasants to the cities in
search of work. Other day workers were Jews who moved to Odessa
in order to escape the destitution of life in the *shtetlekh* and small
towns of the Pale of Settlement.

Competition for employment between Jewish and gentile day
laborers assumed special importance at docksides and in the railway
depots, where thousands of unskilled workers vied for employment

during the peak season of commercial activity, which began in spring and lasted well into the autumn. According to the 1897 census, slightly over 16,000 workers were unskilled day laborers without permanent jobs and specific occupations, but who supplemented the city's sizable work force of dockworkers, porters, and carters during the busy season. Precise data do not exist, but most estimates of the number of dockworkers in Odessa at the turn of the century range from 4,000 to 7,000, with one estimate placing the number of dockworkers at 20,000. Approximately half these workers were Jews and close to 10,000 other Jews found employment as unskilled laborers elsewhere in the city by century's end.[65]

Even during peak periods of port activity, operators of shipping lines, brokerage firms, and warehouses did not require the services of all dockworkers looking for work. In the summer few dockworkers worked more than fifteen days a month; job competition acquired even larger dimensions during the off-season or periods of slump and recession, when over half of all dockworkers were unemployed. It is estimated that between 1900 and 1903 at least 2,000 dockworkers were unemployed at any given time[66]. More specifically, unemployment for longshoremen increased dramatically in the late 1890s and early 1900s when the labor market began to constrict as a result of crop failures, economic recession, the Russo-Japanese War, and Odessa's declining share of the export trade in grain. The last factor was due in part to the failure of Odessa to keep pace with the more modern and better-equipped harbors of other port cities in southern Russia. The use of conveyor belts at docksides, first introduced on a limited basis in the 1870s to facilitate port operations, reduced employment opportunities for stevedores and exerted downward pressures on wages by the century's end. The constricting labor market heightened job competition between Jewish and Gentile dockworkers, culminating in 1906 and 1907 with shipowners, city authorities, and longshoremen setting up a hiring system that established quotas for the number of Jewish and non-Jewish dockworkers. Evidence exists indicating that tensions among dockworkers of different nationalities – primarily between Russians and Jews, but to a lesser extent also among Russians, Georgians, and Turks – influenced the decision to establish this quota system.[67]

Some day workers belonged to work gangs or artels which were either hired by subcontractors on a regular basis or employed directly by the shipping lines. Each company generally used the

services of different work gangs, whose members were hired by the
month or day. Yet the vast majority of day laborers lacked
permanent work, a situation that the hiring process made even more
difficult. In order to work on a given day, day laborers not belonging
to work gangs placed their names on sign-up sheets that subcontractors for shipping lines and import-export firms posted at
different taverns throughout the city. The prospects of finding work
in this manner were slim, however. Prospective laborers had to
arrive between 2 and 3 am in order to ensure themselves a place on
the lists, and those fortunate to find employment for a day had to
give the subcontractor approximately a third of their earnings,
leaving them with barely a rouble to take home. According to 1904
data, day laborers earned an average daily wage of 60 kopecks to a
rouble. After a long day's work, they returned to await payment at
the tavern where their subcontractor conducted business; settling up
often took until 10 pm[68] Given the extraordinary number of wasted
hours, it is not surprising that many day laborers lacked the
inclination to work every day. Even if they so desired, competition
from other job seekers reduced their chances of finding work.

Although some day laborers lived in apartments with their
families or other workers, many found their wages inadequate to rent
a room or even a corner in an apartment and were forced to seek
shelter in one of the crowded flophouses (*nochlezhnye doma*) that
speckled the harbor area and poor neighborhoods of Odessa. At the
turn of the century several thousand people – mostly Great Russian
by nationality – slept in flophouses, with a sizable majority of them
living in such accommodations for over a year and nearly half for
over three years. In other words, many day laborers had become
permanent denizens of night shelters. Indeed, many frequented the
same flophouses day after day and even had their favorite sleeping
corners.[69]

Conditions in the night shelters were abominable. Night shelters
were breeding grounds for infectious diseases and offered the lodger
only a filthy straw mattress on a cold, damp, and hard asphalt
floor.[70] Often they lacked heat and washing facilities. Their patrons
usually bathed in a canal filled with the warm, runoff water from the
municipal electric plant, since no public baths existed in the port
district.[71] Of the nine night shelters located in the harbor district,
seven were privately owned and two were operated by the city.
Conditions in the city-run shelters were better than those found in

privately owned flophouses, since city shelters generally provided bathing facilities and free medical care and operated cafeterias. In addition, the city ran a day shelter that attracted daily up to 500 persons who took advantage of its showers, kitchen, and lending library.[72]

Alcoholism was another contributing factor in the entry of day workers into the world of flophouses. As one twenty-year-old explained, he began sleeping in night shelters "because of vodka."[73] Contemporary observers often characterized residents of flophouses as lacking the resolve to lift themselves out of these degrading surroundings. Like many other workers, they drowned their sorrows in drink. Observers also commented that many day laborers worked only in order to earn enough money to get drunk. The system of subcontracting encouraged heavy drinking since it invariably took place in taverns.[74] Drinking not only diminished the chances of finding work, but also robbed day workers of the motivation to work on a permanent basis. Consequently, many of them could not disengage themselves from the crippling world of vodka and were content to work one or two days a week, spending the rest of the week drinking. As one observer noted: "Hope has died in their hearts – apathy has replaced it."[75]

Dependent on the activity of the port for their livelihood, day laborers in general and dockworkers in particular were usually the first workers to feel the impact of downturns in the economy. During such times, lacking even the few kopecks that night shelters charged, they often slept under the night-time sky or in open barrels at dockside.[76] Hunger was such a constant factor in the day laborers' lives that they used a broad range of colorful phrases to express its intensity. For example, "simple hunger" (*gekokht prostoi*) referred to hunger caused by not eating for one day. "Deadly hunger" (*gekokht smertel'nyi*) lasted somewhat longer, and "hunger with a vengeance" (*gekokht s raspiatiem*) was of "indeterminate length, whole weeks, months, in short, hunger which has no foreseeable end."[77]

Many day laborers never established secure family and social roots and were never fully integrated into urban, working-class life. Even though many had lived in Odessa for years, their lives had a marginal and rootless quality. The faces of their workmates, employers, and those who slept near them in the night shelter changed frequently, even daily, and the lack of fulltime employment and permanent lodgings limited their opportunities to form friendships and establish bonds either at home or at work. Even for day laborers who enjoyed the comforts and security of steady work through membership in a work gang and apartment living, life in Odessa had an ephemeral quality, since many of them were seasonal migrants who never settled permanently in Odessa. Day laborers found it difficult though not impossible under such circumstances to promote and defend their interests in an organized and sustained manner.

Observers referred to day laborers as "peaceful" and believed that the "day laborer is not terrifying when he's had his fill; when the port is busy, this Odessan is calm."[78] This comment's implication is clear, however: day laborers could be less than law-abiding and peaceful during times of economic hardship. An undercurrent of tension and discontent was clearly visible among day laborers, and there were times when they gave vent to their frustrations and anger in fits of rage and fury. At the height of the Boxer Rebellion in 1900, for example, resentful that soldiers were assigned the task of loading ships destined for the Far East, day laborers reacted to their displacement by attacking Jews and stores owned by both Jews and Gentiles.[79] In 1905 day laborers exploded twice, first in June, when Jews were not singled out as targets of their wrath, and then again in October, this time however with anti-Jewish violence reaching alarming proportions. Quite clearly, then, day laborers did not follow a preordained path that inevitably led to pogromist actions, and their occupation and social characteristics lack foolproof predictive values of behavior. Day laborers did not always direct their ire toward Jews; sometimes they channeled their anger toward those possessing wealth and property regardless of ethnic or religious background. Day laborers did not consistently follow a conservative pro-government line. To be sure, members of the Moscow Customs Artel took part in the patriotic procession and pogromist violence, but they also were caught up in the movement to challenge employers for improved working conditions. For instance, in May several hundred of them conducted an orderly and successful strike for higher wages and shorter workdays, and in November they again struck over low pay, hours, housing allowance, and the right to select deputies who would be empowered to have final say in the levying of fines. This labor activism continued into 1906.[80] It took a conjuncture of certain social, economic, and political factors to transform a riot into an anti-Jewish pogrom.

In Odessa pogromist behavior had both an ethnic and a class basis that reflected the complex relationship of long-term ethnic antagonisms, the structure of Odessa's economy, and short-term political catalysts. The heritage of antisemitism made Odessa particularly ripe for a pogrom: the legal disabilities and mistreatment endured by the Jews of Russia engendered an attitude that accepted antisemitism and tolerated anti-Jewish violence. The domination of the grain trade by Jewish merchants predisposed many dockworkers against Jews, whom they conveniently saw as the source of the troubles, particularly the lack of jobs, besetting the city and themselves. Consequently, when day laborers sought an outlet for their frustrations and problems, they focused on Jews. Without taking into account the hostile, anti-Jewish atmosphere in Odessa, we cannot understand why Russian day laborers at times of economic distress chose not to attack other Russian workers who competed with them for scarce jobs or Russian employers, but instead indiscriminately lashed out at *all* Jews, regardless of whether they were job competitors.

Similarly, the depressed state of the Odessa economy also helped set the stage for the outbreak of the pogrom. The straitened economic circumstances of 1905 produced a situation especially ripe for anti-Jewish violence. Many day laborers were out of work and, owing to their lack of skills, unlikely to find employment. Unemployment and economic competition contributed to a growing sense of frustration and despair among many pogromists and helped channel their anger against Jews. Yet economic problems alone do not explain why Russian day workers decided to attack Jews in October 1905. In June, for example, dockworkers and day laborers exploded in a fit of wanton rage, but chose to challenge established authority by destroying the harbor. In October these same workers directed their hostility and frustration toward Jews, although material conditions had not substantially changed.

What had changed since the June disorders was the political atmosphere which had become polarized and more radicalized. The heated revolutionary climate of mid-October precipitated the pogrom. Many participants in the patriotic procession of 19 October, especially members of the Black Hundreds and other organized right-wing groups, undoubtedly marched in order to express their support of the autocracy and disapproval of the October Manifesto. They even tried to recruit other Odessans, particularly day laborers

and dockworkers, by appealing to age-old fears and suspicions that
Jews threatened the purity of Russian Orthodoxy and contaminated
the social fabric. Some workers, as one Social Democratic activist
speaking about the labor movement in 1903 stated, feared that
"they would be replaced by Jews and be left without work" in the
event of political revolution.[81] And still others undoubtedly seconded
the opinion of one Odessan who said the 18 October celebrations
brought "tears to his eyes" as he regarded them as insulting and
disgraceful.[82]

Yet many others, day laborers and dockworkers in particular,
were less enticed by politics than by the vodka and money that the
police reportedly offered. Certainly not all members of the procession
and pogromists necessarily stood on the extreme right of the political
spectrum, as the dockworkers' and day laborers' riot in June strongly
suggests. For the politically apathetic and unaware, the struggle
between revolution and reaction which inspired the more politically
conscious played a secondary if not negligible role. Many may not
have intended to assault Jews and destroy their property, but were
provoked by the shooting and bomb-throwing of the revolutionaries
and self-defense brigades. These actions help to explain the virulence
and intensity of the pogromists' attack – especially by the police – on
their victims. They were simply caught up in the general tenor of
events and, while not being dupes or pawns manipulated by Black
Hundred agitators, found themselves attacking Jews and their
property in much the same way that they destroyed the harbor in
June. In fact, pogromists looted drinking establishments, after which
they indiscriminately trashed non-Jewish houses, thereby dem-
onstrating that popular violence was not always directed against
Jews, even in the midst of a pogrom.[83] These pogromists were not
acting with the malice of forethought but responding to immediate
events that channeled their anger and ire against the Jews. Still
others may have welcomed the pogrom because it afforded them the
opportunity to vent some steam and, perhaps, acquire some booty.
Thus, whatever the specific motivations of the various individuals
involved in the pogrom, popular and official antisemitism and
depressed economic circumstances set the stage by providing the
necessary psychological and material preconditions, while the
hothouse political atmosphere of Odessa in 1905 helped trigger the
pogrom. Violence often lacked political import and significance and
served the cause of revolution or counter-revolution only when it
appeared in conjunction with other factors.

By no means did all Russian workers participate or even sympathize with the bloodletting. Many Russian workers enlisted in self-defense units, while others sheltered their Jewish neighbors and friends during the terror. For example, members of the sailors' union armed themselves and patrolled the harbor to protect Jewish property. After the pogrom Russian self-defensists provided financial aid to pogrom victims and took vigorous action to punish pogromists and ensure that another round of anti-Jewish violence would not occur.[84] Significantly, many of the Russian self-defensists were skilled workers from the same metalworking and machine-construction plants that supplied the workers active in the organization of strikes and the formation of district and city strike committees, trade unions and, in December, the Odessa Soviet of Workers' Deputies.

Two reasons can be adduced to explain the reluctance of these workers to join ranks with pogromists. First, skilled metalworkers and machinists did not face serious employment competition with Jews, who rarely worked in these industries. Despite the fact that Jews comprised a third of Odessa's population, Jews and Russians rarely worked in the same factory or workshop, or even as members of the same work gang at the dockside. In fact, Jews and Russians were generally not employed in the same branch of industry. The exception, as we have seen, was unskilled day labor. Most factory workers were Russians and Ukrainians; Jews formed a small minority. One estimate placed the number of Jews employed in factory production at between 4,000 and 5,000 with most working as unskilled and semi-skilled operatives in cork, tobacco, match, and candy factories.[85]

In addition, many of the factories employing skilled workers had a history of labor activism and a tradition of political organization and awareness. As Ivan Avdeev, a Bolshevik organizer in the railway workshops, told a meeting of his co-workers, the railway workshops formed a self-defense group during the pogrom to demonstrate that "the Russian worker values civil freedom and liberty and does not become a Black Hundred or a hooligan. On the contrary, he is capable of not only protecting his own interests but those of other citizens."[86] One Menshevik concluded that the pogrom and other outbursts of anti-Jewish violence was part of the government's effort to stem the tide of revolution by enlisting the support of "the wild, dark, ignorant masses of the dregs of society ... the hungry throngs of *bosiaki*."[87] Workers in the railway repair shops and the Henn

agricultural tool and machinery plant organized self-defense groups
and both enterprises had a long heritage of labor radicalism and a
close association with Zubatovism and Social Democracy. The
presence of political organizers and propagandists may have muted
the anti-Jewish sentiment of the Russian workers in these plants and
imparted an appreciation of working-class solidarity that tran-
scended ethnic and religious divisions.

To sum up, the social composition of the work force helped
determine the form and content of popular unrest. At one end of the
occupational spectrum stood the unskilled day laborers who were
wont to engage in campaigns of violence and destruction. At the
other end were the skilled, more economically secure Russian
metalworkers and machinists who tended not to participate in the
pogrom and were more inclined than the unskilled to channel their
protest and discontent in an organized fashion. Even though skilled
and unskilled workers in Odessa frequently resorted to violence as a
way to achieve their objectives, they used violence differently. The
violence and public disorder that often accompanied strikes by
skilled workers, as in June, could radicalize the participants and pose
a revolutionary threat. But worker militance and social unrest also
had reactionary consequences when Jews became the object of the
workers' outrage and hostility. It is a commonplace that the most
politically militant and radical of workers in both Western Europe
and Russia during the late nineteenth and early twentieth centuries
were generally not found among the poorest and most disadvantaged
segments of the work force. Yet the unskilled and least integrated
workers were very prone to violence – perhaps to a much greater
extent than the better skilled and politically aware and mobilized
workers – and this violence could contribute to or impede the
revolutionary cause. In June a riot by the unskilled posed a serious
threat to the authorities, but in October protest by these same
workers effectively undercut the force and power of the revolution.
The pogrom served the cause of political reaction and counter-
revolution by revealing how a potentially revolutionary situation
could be defused quickly when the target of the workers' wrath was
no longer a symbol of the autocracy. The October 1905 pogrom in
Odessa illustrates how ethnic hostility was a potent force in workers'
politics and served as a centrifugal force that diminished the capacity
of Odessa workers to act in a unified fashion. The pogrom defused
the revolutionary movement in Odessa by dampening the workers'

militancy, and despite a resurgence of labor unrest in December, the fear of more bloodletting dissuaded workers from vigorously challenging their employers and the government like workers in Moscow.

NOTES

1 This essay first appeared in *The Russian Review* XLVI, 1 (January, 1987) in slightly different form.
2 Excellent treatments of the late 1905 pogroms can be found in Shlomo Lambroza, "The pogrom movement and antisemitism in Russia, 1903–1906" (Ph.D. dissertation, Rutgers University, 1981); E. Maevskii, "Obshchaia kartina dvizheniia," in Iu. Martov, P. Maslov, and A. Potresov, eds., *Obshchestvennoe dvizhenie v Rossii*, II, pt 1 (St. Petersburg 1909), 96–104; *Die Judenpogrome in Russland*, 2 vols. (Cologne and Leipzig, 1910); Heinz-Dietrich Löwe, *Antisemitismus und reaktionäre Utopie: russischer Konservatismus um Kampf gegen den Wandel von Staat und Gesellschaft, 1890–1917* (Hamburg, 1978), 87–103; John Thompson and Howard Mehlinger, *Count Witte and the Tsarist Government in the 1905 Revolution* (Bloomington, 1972), 57–65.
3 On estimates of casualties and property damage, see A. Linden (L. Motzkin), "Die Dimensionen der Oktoberpogrome (1905)," in *Die Judenpogrome in Russland*, II: 130; *Voskhod*, 44–45, 11 November 1905, 16; *Materialy k istorii russkoi kontr-revoliutsii*, I, *Pogromy po offitsial'nym dokumentam* (St. Petersburg, 1908), clxvi–clxvii and 201 (hereafter cited as Kuzminskii Report); S. Iu. Witte, *Vospominaniia*, III (Moscow, 1960), 615; Maxim Vinaver, "La Situation à Odessa," Archives of the Alliance Israélite Universelle, Dossier: URSS IC-1, Odessa; Viktor Obninskii, *Polgoda russkoi revoliutsii*, I (Moscow, 1906), 44.
4 In addition to the contributions to this volume, other major exceptions are Löwe, *Antisemitismus*, Lambroza "Pogrom movement," and *Die Judenpogrome in Russland*, the massive two-volume study prepared by Zionist organizations and cited in note 2. See also Charters Wynn, "Russian labor in revolution and reaction: the Donbass working class, 1870–1905" (Ph.D. dissertation, Stanford University, 1987).
5 See Ronald G. Suny, *The Baku Commune, 1917–1918: Class and Nationality in the Russian Revolution* (Princeton, 1972) for an excellent study of how class and nationality affected the labor movement in another ethnically mixed region of the Russian Empire.
6 The best and most thorough English-language accounts of the early pogroms in Odessa are provided by Steven Zipperstein, *The Jews of Odessa: A Cultural History, 1794–1881* (Stanford, 1985), 114–28 and Lambroza, "Pogrom movement," 275–7. For accounts in Russian, see D. Kogan, "Pervye desiatiletiia evreiskoi obshchiny v Odesse i pogrom 1821 goda," *Evreiskaia starina*, III (1911): 260–7; M. Morgulis, "Bespo-

riadki 1871 goda v Odesse," *Evreiskii mir*, II (December 1910), 42–66; *Opisanie odesskikh ulichnykh besporiadkov v dni sv. Paskhi 1871 goda* (Odessa, 1871). The 1900 pogrom is described in "Khronika vnutrennei zhizni," *Russkoe bogatstvo*, no. 8 (1900), 159–62 and *Budushchnost'*, nos. 30, 28 July 1900 and 34, 25 August 1900. For material on the activities of antisemitic political organizations, see *Voskhod*, no. 5, 5 February 1904, 26–7 and no. 11, 17 March 1904, 25–6; *Iskra*, nos. 59, 10 February 1904 and 65, 1 May 1904; *Poslednie izvestiia*, no. 156, 3 December/20 November 1903, 4, no. 159, 17 December 1903, 2–3, no. 174, 6 April/24 March 1904, 1, and no. 179, 5 May/22 April 1904, 1; Tsentral'nyi gosudarstvennyi istoricheskii arkhiv SSR (TsGIA), f. 1284, op. 194, d. 69, 202 ob. and 1405, op. 530, d. 110, 60–61 ob.

7 On the displacement of Greeks by Jews in the commercial life of Odessa, see G. Bliumenfel'd, "Torgovo-promyshlennaia deiatel'nost' Evreev v Odesse," *Voskhod*, nos. 4 (April 1884), 5–6 and 5 (May 1884) 2–3.

8 By the end of the century only 5,086 Greeks (based on native language) lived in Odessa, or about 1 percent of the population. Compare these figures with those from 1816 when there were twice as many Greeks living in Odessa, comprising about two-fifths of the city's total population. See *Pervaia vseobshchaia perepis' naseleniia Rossiiskoi Imperii, 1897g.*, XLVII *Gorod Odessa* (St. Petersburg, 1903), vi; Patricia Herlihy, "Greek merchants in Odessa in the nineteenth century," *Harvard Ukrainian Studies*, III–IV, 1 (1979/80), 399; *Odessa, 1794–1894* (Odessa, 1895), 56.

9 *Opisanie odesskikh ulichnykh besporiadkov v dni sv. Paskhi 1871 goda*, 10–11.

10 A. A. Skal'kovskii, *Zapiski o torgovykh i promyshlennykh silakh Odessy* (St. Petersburg, 1865), 12; *Pervaia vseobshchaia perepis' naseleniia Rossiiskoi Imperii, 1897 g.*, 2–3.

11 *Obzor Odesskago gradonachal'stva za 1904 g.*, 25. A government publication published in 1914 but relying on data from 1904 places the number of Jews in Odessa at 152,364, or 30.5 percent of the population. Patricia Herlihy estimates the number of Jews at 160,000, or 31·3 percent of the population. The discrepancies are evidently due to different data bases. *Goroda Rossii v 1910 god* (St. Petersburg, 1914), 530 and 558–9 and Patricia Herlihy, *Odessa: A History, 1794–1914* (Cambridge, MS, 1986), 251.

12 A. P. Subbotin, *V cherte evreiskoi osedlosti* (St. Petersburg, 1890), 212–30; "Odessa," *Evreiskaia entsiklopediia*, XII (St. Petersburg, 1910), 59–62; Bliumenfel'd, nos. 4, 1–14 and 5, 1–14; Herlihy, "Greek merchants," 419; "Odessa," *The Jewish Encyclopedia*, IX (New York, 1905), 378–80; *Pervaia vseobshchaia perepis'*, 134–49.

13 *Pervaia vseobshchaia perepis'*, 134–49; *Voskhod*, no. 4, 29 January 1904, 23–26, no. 5, 5 February 1904, 1–5 and no. 4, 27 January 1905, 15–16.

14 I. Brodovskii, *Evreiskaia nishcheta v Odesse* (Odessa, 1902), 5–6: *Iuzhnoe obozrenie*, no. 2784, 22 March 1905.

15 See Robert Weinberg, "Worker organizations and politics in the

Revolution of 1905 in Odessa" (Ph.D. dissertation, University of California, Berkeley, 1985), 36–45.

16 *Kommercheskaia Rossiia*, no. 47, 19 February 1905.

17 *Poslednie izvestiia*, no. 129, 3 June/21 May 1903, 1–2; *Revoliutsionnaia Rossiia*, no. 24, 15 May 1903, 14, no. 25, 1 June 1903, 16–17 and no. 27, 1 July 1903, 19. In 1904 the Odessa factory inspector observed that workers refrained from striking because they feared worker militance "could lead to a Jewish pogrom." TsGIA, f. 23, op. 29, d. 80, 14–14 ob.

18 *Kommercheskaia Rossiia*, no. 241, 2 November 1905; *Proletarskoe delo*, no. 5, 10 October 1905.

19 *Iskra*, no. 75, 5 October 1904 and no. 97, 18 April 1905; *Poslednie izvestiia*, no. 174, 6 April/24 March 1904, 1; *Iuzhnoe obozrenie*, no. 2805, 13 April 1905.

20 The National Committee of Self-Defense first appeared in 1904, along with the self-defense group called "An Eye for an Eye" and others set up by the various revolutionary parties. Tsentral'nyi gosudarstvennyi arkhiv oktiabr'skoi revoliutsii SSR (TsGAOR), f. 124, op. 43, d. 298, 1905, 1–2; Kuzminskii Report, 102; *Poslednie izvestiia*, no. 179, 5 May/22 April 1904, 1 and no. 240, 10 July/24 June 1905, 1; J. Sh. Hertz, "Di ershte ruslender revolutsye," in G. Aronson, S. Dubnow-Erlich, and J. Sh. Hertz, eds., *Di geshikhte fun Bund*, ii (New York, 1962), 74; *Khronika evreiskoi zhizni*, no. 14, 10 April 1905, 24 and no. 17, May 8, 1905, 25–27; *Vedomosti Odesskago gradonachal'stva*, no. 92, 28 April 1905.

21 See Weinberg, "Worker organizations," chapter 5, for details of the June unrest. See *Odesskii listok*, no. 161, 2 July 1905, for the names of people arrested during the 15 June disorders.

22 *Poslednie izvestiia*, no. 241, 17/4 July 1905, 2 and no. 242, 25/12 July 1905, 4–5; *Proletarii*, no. 7 10 July/27 June 1905, 12; *Iskra*, no. 104, 1 July 1905.

23 *Odesskie dni* can be found in the Bakhmeteff Archives at Columbia University, Zosa Szajkowskii Collection, Oversized Folders.

24 *Proletarii*, no. 9, 20 June/3 July 1905, 11.

25 One exception to this official view was offered by the procurator of the Odessa Circuit Court, who wrote that the disorders were due to hostility harbored by "a significant portion of the Odessa populace" toward the police and government. TsGAOR, f. 102, 7th delopr., d. 3769, 1905, 16 ob. and 24 and f. 124, d. 3115, 80; TsGIA, f. 1101, op. 1, d. 1033, 4.

26 At the empirewide level, Jews by 1900 constituted 30 percent of persons arrested for political crimes. See the 1986 University Lecture at Boston University by Norman Naimark, "Terrorism and the fall of Imperial Russia," 4. See *Otvet na odesskie dni i g.g. Odessity* (Odessa, 1905) for one attempt to refute *Odesskie dni*. For the leaflet see TsGAOR, f. 102, oo, d. 5, ch. 4, 1905, 193–4. On the role of Jews in the revolutionary movement, see TsGAOR, f. 102, oo, d. 106, ch. 2, 1905, 54–61, 68–9

ob., 76–8 ob., and 80–1; *Kommercheskaia Rossiia*, no. 167, 26 July 1905; *Iuzhnye zapiski*, no. 29, 17 July 1905, 61–2; Kuzminskii Report, cvii.

27 Kuzminskii Report, cxxv.

28 TsGIA, f. 1284, op. 194, d. 68, 1902, 4 ob. See also Frederick W. Skinner, "Odessa and the problem of urban modernization," in Michael F. Hamm, ed., *The City in Late Imperial Russia* (Bloomington, 1986), 228.

29 This viewpoint is developed more fully in the work of Hans Rogger. See especially "The Jewish policy of late tsarism: a reappraisal," in Hans Rogger, *Jewish Policies and Right-Wing Politics in Imperial Russia* (Berkeley and Los Angeles, 1986), 33.

30 Some of the relevant sources are: Kuzminskii Report, passim; TsGAOR, f. 102, op. 5, d. 3, ch. 49, 1905, op. 5, d. 3, ch. 56, 1905, d. 1350, ch. 30, lit. A, 1905, and op. 233, d. 1350, ch. 20, 1905; *Revoliutsionnoe gnezdo. Iz istorii Novorossiiskogo universiteta* (St. Petersburg, 1909); *Odesskie novosti*, no. 6767, 15 October 1905, no. 6769, 26 October 1905; *Iuzhnoe obozrenie*, no. 2948, 15 October 1905, no. 2950, 26 October 1905.

31 TsGAOR, f. 102, oo, d. 1350, ch. 30, lit. A, 1905, 36 and 40 and op. 5, d. 3, ch. 49, 1905, 63, 64 ob. and 123; Kuzminskii Report, cxxviii–cxxix, cxxxii and 58; *Revoliutsionnoe gnezdo. Iz istorii Novorossiiskogo universiteta*, 16.

32 Kuzminskii Report, 97.

33 The incident about the dogs is disputed in *Voskhod*, no. 51–2, 30 December 1905, 27. Some of the more relevant sources on the events of 18 October are: Kuzminskii Report, cxxxiv–cxxxv, 110–11, 138–9, 186, 196–8; TsGAOR, f. 102, oo, d. 1350, ch. 30, lit. A, 1905, 42, 45 ob. and 83, op. 233, d. 1350, ch. 30, 1905, 60–61 and op. 5. d. 3, ch. 49, 1905, 63 ob. and 123 ob.–124.

34 TsGAOR, f. 102, oo, d. 1350, ch. 30, lit. A, 1905, 45 ob.; Kuzminskii Report, 126, 168, 177–80, 198.

35 TsGAOR, f. 102, oo, d. 1350, ch. 30, lit. A, 1905, 42 ob.; Kuzminskii Report, cxlvii, 104; *Izvestiia Odesskoi gorodskoi dumy*, no. 3–4 (February, 1906), 312.

36 On the large number of dockworkers, day laborers, and vagrants in the procession, see N. N. Lender (Putnik), "Revoliutsionnye buri na iuge. ('Potemkin' i oktiabr'skaia revoliutsiia v Odesse)," *Istoricheskii vestnik Kommercheskaia Rossiia*, no. 261, 25 November 1905; S. Semenov, "Evreiskie pogromy v Odesse i Odesshchine v 1905 g.," *Puti revoliutsii*, no. 3 (1925), 119–20.

37 Kuzminskii Report, 105.

38 Kuzminskii Report, cxlviii–cl, 105, 111, 129; Tsentral'nyi gosudarstvennyi voenno-istoricheskii arkhiv SSR (TsGVIA), f. 400, 16th otd., op. 15, d. 2641, 1905, 35–5 ob., TsGAOR, f. 102, oo, op. 5, d. 3, ch. 49, 1905, 59 and 64 ob., op. 233, d. 1350, ch. 30, 1905. 60 ob.–61

and d. 1350, ch. 30, lit. A, 1905, 47; *Khronika evreiskoi zhizni*, no. 43–4, 11 November 1905, 19.

39 One eyewitness testified, however, that the first shots came from the crowd of patriotic demonstrators. Another eyewitness reported that he saw members of the patriotic procession discharge their revolvers into the air, but whether he is referring to the shootings in which the boy was killed cannot be determined. Kuzminskii Report, 129, 158; A. S. Shapovalov, *V podpol'e*, 2nd edn (Moscow–Leningrad, 1931), 122.

40 See the reports of Kaulbars and the head of the Odessa Okhrana. TsGVIA, f. 400, 16th otd., op. 15, d. 2641, 1905, 35 ob.; TsGAOR, f. 102, 00, op. 5, d. 3, ch. 49, 1905, 125 ob. and f. 124, op. 49, d. 294, 1911, 58 ob.; Kuzminskii Report, cl–cli, 152–3 and 170–1; *Odesskii pogrom i samooborona* (Paris, 1906), 46–7.

41 Semenov, "Evreiskie pogromy," 115–35; D. Hurvits, *Der blutiger pogrom in Odessa* (Odessa, 1905); A. Malavich, *Odesser pogrom* (London, 1906); *Khronika evreiskoi zhizni*, no. 41–2, 28 October 1905, 11–14, no. 43–4, 11 November 1905, 20; *Voskhod*, no. 42–3, 27 October 1905, 29, no. 44–5, 11 November 1905, 16–29 and no. 6, 9 February 1906, 14–15.

42 Kuzminskii Report, cliii–clvi, 4, 10, 112, 115, 137; N. Osipovich, "V grozovye gody," *Kandal'nyi zvon*, no. 3 (1926), 66; TsGVIA, f. 400, 16th otd., op. 15, d. 2641, 1905, 38; Semenov, "Evreiskie pogromy," 118 and 123; TsGAOR, f. 102, 00, d. 2540, 1905, 94; T. Forre, "Vospominaniia sestry miloserdiia ob oktiabr'skikh dniakh 1905 goda," in *1905 god. Revoliutsionnoe dvizhenie v Odesse i Odesshchine* (Odessa, 1926), II: 233–4; *Odesskii pogrom i samooborona*, 64–5; *Collier's*, no. 11, 9 December 1905, 13.

43 TsGAOR, f. 102, 00, op. 5, d. 3, ch. 49, 1905, 65–5 ob.

44 See Richard Robbins, *The Tsar's Viceroys: Provincial Governors in the Last Years of the Empire* (Ithaca, 1987), 196–97.

45 TsGAOR, f. 102, 00, d. 1350, ch. 30, lit. A, 1905, 71; TsGVIA, f. 400, 16th otd., op. 15, d. 2641, 1905, 37; Semenov, "Evreiskie pogromy," 125 and 130; Kuzminskii Report, clvi–clix, clxi–clxii, clxxix, clxxxi, cci, 9–11, 27, 31, 39, 43–4, 47, 68, 82–90, 115, 123–4, 175–6, 191–2, and passim.

46 Kuzminskii Report, cxxxviii, cxli, cxliii, clxxv–clxxvii, clxxxviii–clxxxix, cxcv–cxcvi, 7, 40, 42, 129–30, 170, 172, 182–3, 185–6, and passim; TsGAOR, f. 124, op. 49, d. 294, 1911, 81 ob. and 167–7 ob.

47 Ibid., cxxxviii–cxli, clxxiv–clxxvii, clxxix–cxl, cxcvi–cci, 6–13, 18–22, 40–4, 120–1, 169–70, 177. See also TsGAOR, f. 124, op. 49, d. 294, 1911, 81 ob.

48 TsGAOR, f. 102, 00, d. 2540, 1905, 90, d. 1350, ch. 30, lit. A, 1905, 85 and op. 5, d. 3, ch. 49, 1905, 65; TsGVIA, f. 400, 16th otd., op. 15, d. 2641, 1905 35 ob.; Kuzminskii Report, cxciv and 191; *Pravitel'stvennyi vestnik*, no. 245, 12 November 1905.

49 TsGAOR, f. 124, op. 49, d. 294, 1911, 58 ob.

50 See Shlomo Lambroza, "Jewish responses to pogroms in late Imperial Russia," in Jehuda Reinharz, ed., *Living with Antisemitism: Modern Jewish Responses* (Hanover and London, 1987), 258.

51 TsGAOR, f. 102, 00, op. 5, d. 3, ch. 49, 1905, 66 ob. and 124 ob. and d. 1350, ch. 30, lit. A, 1905, 85 ob.; TsGVIA, f. 400, 16th otd., op. 15, d. 2641, 1905, 35; Kuzminskii Report, cv–cvi, ccxv, cxlviii, 4, 17.

52 This viewpoint is developed more fully in the work of Hans Rogger. See especially his "Jewish policy of late tsarism," 33.

53 See Rogger, "Jewish policy of late tsarism"; Löwe, *Antisemitismus*.

54 Soviet and Western authors also accuse Neidhardt and the police of planning and executing the pogrom. See *Odesskie novosti*, no. 6775, 2 November 1905 and no. 6787, 16 November 1905; *Voskhod*, no. 47–8, 1 December 1905, 39 and no. 51–2, 30 December 1905, 25–7; *Die Judenpogrome in Russland*, passim; Louis Greenberg, *The Jews in Russia: The Struggle for Emancipation*, 2 vols. (New York, 1978), II: 76–88; *Khronika evreiskoi zhizni*, no. 43–4, 11 November, 1905, 19–20 and 22 and no. 48–9, 23 December 1905, 44; Kuzminskii Report, cxlv, clxi, clxxi; G. Achkanov, "Vospominaniia o revoliutsii 1905 goda," in *1905 god. Revoliutsionnoe dvizhenie v Odesse i Odesshchine*, 2 vols. (Odessa, 1925), II: 198; Semenov, "Evreiskie pogromy," 130.

55 Kuzminskii Report, cxlviii–cxlix, clxxi, 3–4.

56 Ibid., 100–1.

57 *Khronika evreiskoi zhizni*, no. 43–4, 11 November 1905, 22; Achkanov, "Vospominaniia o revoliutsii 1905 goda," 199–200; Semenov, "Evreiskie pogromy," 116–17.

58 Kuzminskii Report, cliii–cliv; *Khronika evreiskoi zhizni*, no. 43–4, 11 November 1905, 22.

59 Neidhardt had been an active labor mediator since assumption of his post as city governor in 1903 and pursued various strategies and tactics to avert work stoppages and end strikes. See Weinberg, "Worker organizations," 205–7.

60 Kuzminskii Report, 3–4, 39, 47, 189–90.

61 Ibid., 123 and 156–7.

62 Neidhardt emphasized in his annual reports that the police were poorly paid and inadequately trained. According to recently appointed Chief of Police Aleksandr von Hessberg, the police were striking for higher wages. TsGIA, f. 23, op. 20, d. 1, 174; Kuzminskii Report, cxlv–clxvi, 69–71, 74, 128, 155, 186.

63 S. Dimanshtein, "Ocherk revoliutsionnogo dvizheniia sredi evreiskikh mass," in M. N. Pokrovskii, ed. *1905: Istoriia revoliutsionnogo dvizheniia v otdel'nykh ocherkakh*, III, *Ot oktiabria k dekabriu. Revoliutsionnoe dvizhenie natsional'nostei i okrain* (Moscow–Leningrad, 1927), 171. Neidhardt's right-wing sympathies were clearly revealed when he welcomed in 1903 the formation of a monarchist student organization at the university as "a favorable event in the life of the students." TsGIA, f. 1284, op. 194, d. 69, 1904, 2 ob.

64 See note 45 above; Kuzminskii Report, clxv, 123–5; William C. Fuller, Jr., *Civil–Military Conflict in Imperial Russia, 1881–1914* (Princeton, 1985), 211; Vinaver, "La situation à Odessa," passim. In his report on the October disorders, Kaulbars admitted that men wearing military uniforms were part of the pogromist mobs, but he insisted that they already had been discharged from service. TsGVIA, f. 400, 16 otd., op. 15, d. 2641, 1905, 38.

65 By 1884 there were over 1,700 Jewish dockworkers in Odessa; in some categories, such as those who weighed sacks of grain, Jews filled a majority of positions. Zvi Halevy, *Jewish Schools under Czarism and Communism : A Struggle for Cultural Identity* (New York, 1976), 21; TsGIA, f. 23, op. 20, d. 1, 173; TsGAOR, f. 102, d. 2409, 1903, 74 and 4th delopr., d. 84, ch. 12, t. 12, 1907, 279; *Pervaia vseobshchaia perepis'*, xlvii, 88–131, 134–49; I. A. Adamov, "Rabochie i moriaki odesskogo porta v revoliutsionnom dvizhenii xix i nachala xx stoletii" (Candidate of Historical Science dissertation, Odessa University, 1940), 59; Ia. M. Shternshtein, *Morskie vorota Ukrainy* (Odessa, 1958), 19; V. K. Vasil'evskaia, "Polozheniia portovykh rabochikh v Odesse," *Trudy Odesskogo otdela Russkogo obshchestva okhraneniia zdraviia*, iv (1904), 37; M. Tsetterbaum, *Klassovye protivorechiia v evreiskom obshchestve* (Kiev, 1905), 27; Subbotin, *V cherte evreiskoi osedlosti*, 230; N. Vasil'evskii, *Ocherk sanitarnogo polozheniia g. Odessy* (Odessa, 1901), 6.

66 One observer of the Odessa port stated that dockworkers worked an average of 120 days per year. N. Shelgunov, *Ocherki russkoi zhizni* (St. Petersburg, 1895), 470. See also Adamov, "Rabochie i moriaki odesskogo," 70; Vasil'evskaia, "Polozheniia portovykh rabochikh v Odesse," 44; *Opisanie odesskogo porta* (St. Petersburg, 1913), 40.

67 Day laborers had not always found it difficult to find work. From the 1860s until the 1890s workers often preferred employment at the docks as longshoremen and porters because such work paid more than factory labor and was more available than after the turn of the century. "Polozheniia portovykh rabochikh v Odesse," 41 and 44; *Opisanie odesskogo porta*, 40; *Kommercheskaia Rossiia*, no. 226, 7 October 1905 and no. 232, 14 October 1905; *Iuzhnoe obozrenie*, no. 2747, 12 February 1905; *Otchet Odesskogo komiteta torgovli i manufaktur za 1906 g.* (Odessa, 1907), 31; Brodovskii, *Evreiskaia nishcheta v Odesse*, 13; TsGAOR, f. 102, 4th delopr., d. 84, ch. 12, t. 2, 1907, 273, 275, 279 and 4th delopr. d. 84, ch. 12, t. 3, 1907, 147–7 ob., 224 and 349; *Odesskie novosti*, no. 6634, 4 May, 1905; N. P. Mel'nikov, *O sostoianii i razvitii tekhnicheskikh proizvodstv na iuge Rossii* (Odessa, 1875), 12; D. S. Bronshtein, *Mery k uluchsheniiu fabriochnoi i zavodskoi promyshlennosti g. Odessy* (Odessa, 1885), 16.

68 TsGAOR, f. 102, oo, d. 4, ch. 10, lit. G., t. 1, 1898, 6; L. O. Narkevich, "K voprosu o polozhenii bezdomnykh rabochikh v odesskom portu," in *Trudy Odesskogo otdela Russkogo obshchestva okhraneniia zdraviia*, iv (1904),

111–13; Shternshtein, *Morskie vorota Ukrainy*, 26; *Odesskie novosti*, no. 6565, 17 February 1905; *Goroda Rossii v 1910 godu* (St. Petersburg, 1914), 605; *Kommercheskaia Rossiia*, no. 67, 12 March 1905.

69 On day laborers in flophouses, see Narkevich, "K voprosu...," 103–31; Vasil'evskaia, "Polozheniia...," 36–49; *Otchety rasporiaditel'nogo komiteta nochlezhnykh priiutov* (Odessa, 1880–1904).

70 For descriptions of the appalling conditions, see Vasil'evskaia, "Polozheniia...," 47–8; S. Lazarovich, "Materialy k voprosu o nochlezhnykh domakh v g. Odesse," *Otchet o deiatel'nosti Petropavlovskogo sanitarnogo popechitel'stva goroda Odessy za 1898–1899 gg.* (Odessa, 1900), 214–17; Narkevich, "K voprosu...," 104–5; Chivonibar (A. Rabinovich), "Dikari" in *Bosiaki. Zhenshchiny. Den'gi.* (Odessa, 1904), 32–48; *Odesskii listok*, no. 267, 1 December 1885; *Odesskii vestnik*, no. 295, 16 November 1892.

71 L. O. Karmen, *V rodnom gnezde* (Odessa, 1900), iii.

72 *Putevoditel' po Odesse i ee okrestnostiam* (Odessa, 1907), 219.

73 Chivonibar, "Dikari," 46.

74 The lyrics of popular day laborers' songs underscore the importance of drink in their lives. See Andrei Tiazheloispytannyi, *Pesni odesskikh bosiakov* (np, nd). See also Chivonibar, "Dikari," 34; Vasil'evskaia, "Polozheniia...," 48; *Kommercheskaia Rossiia*, no. 36, 8 February 1905.

75 Another observer wrote that unskilled day laborers "perpetually curse and are dirty, ragged, drunk, and have almost lost a human appearance... Life has passed them by; they have no hope for a better future and are concerned only with finding a piece of bread and a corner in a flophouse." Grigorii Moskvich, *Illiustirovannyi prakticheskii putevoditel' po Odesse* (Odessa, 1904), 177. See also *Odesskii listok*, no. 267, December 1, 1885; Narkevich, "K voprosu...," 107.

76 Z. V. Pershina, "Nachalo rabochego dvizheniia. Pervye marksistskie kruzhi v Odesse (1883–1895 gody)," in K. S. Kovalenko, ed., *Iz istorii odesskoi partiinoi organizatsii. Ocherki* (Odessa, 1964), 9.

77 *Kommercheskaia Rossiia*, no. 36, 8 February 1905. It is unknown whether these expressions, which are a mixture of Yiddish and Russian, were used exclusively by Jewish day laborers.

78 *Peterburgskii listok*, no. 166, 29 June 1905. I thank Joan Neuberger for this reference.

79 *Iskra*, no. 1 (December 1900); "Khronika vnutrennei zhizni," *Russkoe bogatstvo*, no. 6 (August 1900), 159–62.

80 TsGAOR, f. 102, oo, d. 4, ch. 19, lit. A, 1905, 213–14; *Kommercheskaia Rossiia*, no. 263, 27 November 1905 and no. 266, 1 December 1905; TsGIA, f. 1405, op. 530, d. 400, 52; *Iuzhnoe obozrenie*, no. 3136, 29 June 1906 and no. 3144, 9 July 1906; M. I. Mebel', ed., *1905 god na Ukraine. Khronika i materialy* (Kharkov, 1926), 113.

81 Godlevskii, "Kishinev, Odessa, Nikolaev. (Iz istorii s.-d. dvizheniia 1895–1903 gg.) Vospominaniia," *Letopis' revoliutsii*, no. 3(8) (1924), 131.

82 TsGAOR, f. 102, 00, op. 233, d. 1350, ch. 30, 1905, 60–1.

83 See the account published in *Collier's*, no. 11, 9 December 1905, 13.

84 Kuzminskii Report, 130–1; *Kommercheskaia Rossiia*, no. 237, 28 October 1905; no. 239, 30 October 1905; no. 240, 1 November 1905; no. 242, 3 November 1905; no. 244, 5 November 1905; no. 246, 8 November 1905; no. 251, 13 November 1905; no. 270, 6 December 1905; *Odesskii listok*, no. 252, 29 October 1905; no. 269, 18 November 1905; no. 270, 26 November 1905; *Odesskie novosti*, no. 6775, 2 November 1905; no. 6776, 3 November 1905; no. 6779, 6 November 1905; no. 6801, 2 December 1905; and no. 6804, 6 December 1905; *Iuzhnoe obozrenie*, no. 2954, 30 October 1905, no. 2964, 11 November 1905.

85 TsGIA, f. 23, op. 29, d. 80, 23.

86 *Odesskii listok*, no. 255, 2 November 1905.

87 *Kommercheskaia Rossiia*, no. 239, 30 October 1905.

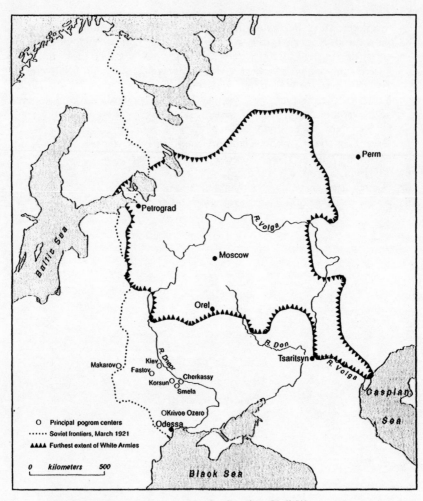

Map labels:

Perm

Baltic Sea

Petrograd

R. Volga

Moscow

Orel

R. Dnepr

Makarov   Kiev
Fastov
Korsun   Cherkassy
Smela

Krivoe Ozero
Odessa

R. Don

Tsaritsyn   R. Volga

Caspian Sea

○   Principal pogrom centers
·····   Soviet frontiers, March 1921
▲▲▲▲   Furthest extent of White Armies

0   kilometers   500

Black Sea

4 Major pogrom centers during the Russian Civil War, 1918–1921

V

The pogroms of 1919–1921

It was not immediately apparent in 1914 that the Russian Empire was about to enter its death throes. An outpouring of support followed the declaration of war against the Central Powers, and the political mainstream rallied to the slogan of "war to a victorious end." Yet the internal weaknesses of the late Empire – the absence of a broad political consensus, ethnic and national rivalries, uneven economic development, and obsolete political institutions – were accentuated rather than resolved by the stresses of total war. Collectively they crippled the war effort and helped bring on revolution in 1917.

The military crisis was not long in coming. The Russian army suffered two disastrous reverses in East Prussia in the opening weeks of the war. In 1915 much of Russian Poland and the province of Kurland were lost to the Germans. Russia's military position continued to deteriorate, despite a series of costly offensives, throughout 1916. The disasters of war engendered political discontent. Moderates, aware of the strength they had gained as a consequence of participation in autonomous relief and supply organizations, demanded political reform through appointment of a "ministry of public confidence," one dominated by liberals and responsible to the Duma rather than to the Tsar. The right feared for the survival of the dynasty under the uncertain leadership of Nicholas II and cautiously bruited plans for the deposition of the Tsar in favor of his son. The murder of Grigory Rasputin, the royal family's "friend" and adviser in 1916 was tangible evidence of this discontent. The discontent of the revolutionary left was disorganized, but possessed great potential strength, as events were soon to show. In society at large, worker and peasant discontent grew with each passing year.

The war had an immediate and dramatic effect upon the Jews of the Empire. Much of the military action took place within Russian Poland and the Pale of Settlement. The Russian military high command was very distrustful of the Jews, and in March of 1915 began the precipitous evacuation of Jewish communities away from the front. As many as 600,000 Jews were ultimately displaced. In the absence of any better plan, the Council of Ministers was forced to agree to the relocation of these refugees into the Russian interior, thus affecting the *de facto* abolition of the Pale. The evacuation was poorly planned and executed, however, and refugee Jews enjoyed no rights and an unclear legal status in their new homes. Despite the fact that almost half a million Jews served in the tsarist army, there were widespread rumors and charges that the Jews were evading military service. The military was especially prone to question the loyalty of the Jewish population, and a number of Jews were the victims of summary, and well-publicized, executions for acts of treason. Typically, and after the fact, most of these accusations were shown to be false. This ambiguous status of the Jewish population was strengthened by the efforts of German occupation troops to enlist the cooperation of the Jews. Even under the Germans, however, the Jews were targets for forced requisitions and labor services.

The monarchy collapsed in February of 1917, and the new Provisional Government set about abolishing all the restrictive legislation that touched the Jews. As a consequence, Jews became free and equal citizens. Events soon overtook this brief interlude of political emancipation. Within the year the Provisional Government was overthrown by the Bolsheviks, and the Empire itself dissolved into a battleground where political and national rivalries surfaced, and old scores were settled. All subjects of the old Empire suffered, but the Jews were again an exceptional case because much of the ensuing Civil War was conducted in the Ukraine, where the Jewish population was most densely settled.

The Empire had been brutalized by four years of total war. Extensive quantities of military equipment fell into the hands of various irregular military forces. Life was reckoned cheap, and no quarter was asked or given. Civil authority, insofar as it existed at all, was weak and diffuse. As all traditional constraints weakened, the Jews were especially vulnerable, especially given the example of past pogroms. Traditional anti-Jewish enmities and fears were joined by new, modern strains of antisemitism, exemplified by the *Protocols of the Elders of Zion*, and its claim that the Jews sought domination of the world. The visibility of Jews like Trotsky, Zinoviev, and Kamenev among the Bolshevik leadership offered whatever confirmation skeptics might require. As many as a quarter of a million Jews perished in the Russian Civil War and the Soviet–Polish War, a time of Jewish suffering which was unparalleled in Eastern Europe before the Holocaust itself.

CHAPTER 10

Pogroms and White ideology in the Russian Civil War

Peter Kenez

Civil wars are cruel: there is no easy way to fight the enemy when it is not even clear who the enemy is and those who take sides in the conflict cannot forgive their compatriots who see matters differently. But even compared to other civil conflicts the Russian Civil War was unusually bitter.[1] The preceding war and the unparalleled misery of the survivors cheapened the value of human life: revolutionary mobs murdered innocent people randomly and the Cheka used terror with little restraint; incensed landlords, who succeeded in reclaiming their property and power with the aid of counter-revolutionary armies, were determined to take revenge for their sufferings and for their fear on the rebellious peasants. Even the earliest period of the Civil War is full of blood-curdling episodes of inhumanity. For example, combatants on occasion put their captured enemies in buildings and then set fire to them.[2] In this respect there was not much to choose between Whites and Reds; both sides behaved abominably.

Under the circumstances it could hardly be considered surprising that a particular form of beastliness, pogroms, which had a long history in the Russian empire, reappeared during the Civil War. Indeed, in the Ukraine in 1919 and 1920 mass murder of Jews took place on a scale that was surpassed only during the Second World War. The majority of Jews (1·6 million out of 2·6 million) who remained in the territory that was to become the Soviet Union, lived in the Ukraine. It was this part of the defunct tsarist Empire that had by far the richest history of pogroms. It is safe to say that up to this time no nation on earth had a record comparable to the Ukrainians in killing and abusing Jews. During every social upheaval, be it a murder of the Tsar, famines, revolutions, the Jews suffered. Furthermore, nowhere was the Civil War more bitter and more confusing than in the Ukraine. Germans, various shades of

Ukrainian nationalists, anarchist peasant bands, and of course, Red and White armies, at different times occupied larger or smaller territories in the country.[3]

All armies involved in the Civil War, including the Bolshevik, were responsible for some of the anti-Jewish violence.[4] The pogroms, no matter which army was responsible, had a great deal in common. The killings were done mostly by ill-disciplined soldiers and the peasants usually participated in looting. In the past pogroms were largely restricted to cities; during the Civil War most of the killings occurred in villages. During peace-time periods of violence had been relatively brief; now they became chronic. All antisemites operated on the basis of the pernicious doctrine of collective guilt. The pogromists managed to project the picture of the enemy on the face of the Jew, and then held every one responsible for the real or imagined guilt of the few. Ukrainians believed Jews to be pro-Russian; socialists saw them as capitalist exploiters; and conservatives blamed them for being socialists.

The character of the pogroms carried out by anarchists, Ukrainian nationalists, and counter-revolutionary Whites also varied. Of the belligerents the anti-Bolshevik Volunteer Army, which occupied the Ukraine between June and December 1919, was responsible for the largest number of victims. In order to put the White pogroms into proper perspective, it is necessary first to examine the pogroms carried out by the followers of Petliura and by the anarchists. On the one hand, these pogroms were only preparations for what was to follow. Repeated killings dulled the sensibility of human beings. On the other, a comparative approach will allow us to see best the peculiarities of the pogroms carried out by the troops of General Denikin.

I

The beginning of antisemitic agitation cannot be dated, for the Ukraine had not been without it for centuries. During 1918, however, when the country was occupied by the Germans and the Austrians, agitation accelerated. The occupying authorities contributed to antisemitism by their proclamations, which singled out the Jews. These proclamations attacked the Jews for black marketeering and for the spread of anti-German rumors. An Austrian commander, for example, forbade Jews under pain of death to have any contact with his soldiers; he was afraid that the Jews would somehow corrupt them.[5]

The Germans, however, maintained order. As long as they remained in occupation, they prevented the outbreak of random violence. The situation immediately deteriorated when, according to the terms of the armistice, they were forced to evacuate the Ukraine. The country was plunged into unparalleled anarchy. At first the most likely successors to the Germans were the Ukrainian nationalists, ultimately under the leadership of S. V. Petliura. The nationalist army, based on insurgent peasant forces, fought for a socialist and anti-Russian program. The nationalists' enemies were not only Bolsheviks, but also Russian counter-revolutionaries who dreamt of the recreation of a united empire.

The nationalists, however, were able to hold Kiev, the capital, only for a few weeks; they had to retreat in advance of the Bolshevik invasion. It was at this time, in January 1919, that the mass killing of Jews began. As long as the Petliurists had a foothold in the country, they continued to carry out pogroms. In the course of the following months they killed tens of thousands of people. The single bloodiest pogrom took place in February 1919, in Proskurov, in territory controlled by Petliura's troops. After an attempted Bolshevik rising, the local Petliurist commander, Semosenko, ordered his troops to massacre the Jews. In the course of three hours almost 2,000 unresisting people were cut down.[6]

Following Petliura's assassination by Samuel Schwartzbard in 1926 in Paris, and ever since, there has been a great deal of discussion concerning the Ukrainian leader's responsibility for the pogroms. The general picture, however, is clear.[7] On the one hand, legislation issued by Petliura's government emancipated the Jews, and the Ukrainian leader ultimately did repudiate pogroms and even named a Jewish Minister of "Jewish Affairs"; on the other, just like his unsophisticated followers, he believed that Jews were enemies of Ukrainian independence, and that they were pro-Bolshevik. He did much too little to impose discipline on his troops. Only in August 1919 did he issue a strongly phrased anti-pogrom manifesto, and there is reason to suspect that he did so largely because of his concern for European public opinion.[8] He realized that the survival of his movement depended on British and French good will. Petliura did little to prevent pogroms, because he benefited from them. Anti-semitism was a mobilization device for him. He believed that trying to curb the excesses carried out by his followers would needlessly alienate many of them.

Petliura's brand of nationalism did not find much of an echo among the Ukrainian peasants. From 1918 to 1921, the Ukraine, more than any part of the old Russian Empire, was plagued by anarchist peasant bands. Some fought against the Reds and against Petliura, but most of them considered the White Russians their greatest enemies. These well armed peasant groups differed from one another a great deal, and perhaps only in carrying out pogroms were they on common ground.

The most powerful and longest lasting of these bands was led by Nestor Makhno. He was a self-educated man, committed to the teachings of Bakunin and Kropotkin, and he could not fairly be described as an antisemite. Makhno had Jewish comrades and friends; and like Petliura, he issued a proclamation forbidding pogroms. In any case, his movement was based on the Eastern part of the Ukraine, where only relatively few Jews lived.[9] However, the anarchist leader could not or did not impose discipline on his soldiers. In the name of "class struggle" his troops with particular enthusiasm robbed Jews of whatever they had. He too, when he turned against Soviet power, did not hesitate to take advantage of the equation in the popular mind between Jews and Communists.[10] As a result, the troops of Makhno also devastated Jewish settlements and killed innocent people.[11]

The other anarchist leaders were far less scrupulous than Makhno. Not only did they not try to prevent pogroms, but themselves participated in them. Most of the leaders came from humble families and they directly and immediately expressed the mentality of the Ukrainian peasants. Their revolution was directed not only against landlords, but also against modernity and against city people whom they naively regarded as exploiters. To them the Jews stood for everything they disliked: Jews represented the outside world that suppressed and took advantage of the peasant.

The anarchist leaders, the so-called *atamans* or *batki*, felt no need to moderate their behavior because of a concern for foreign sensibilities: they expected and received no help from abroad. As a result, the anarchist pogroms were the most disorganized and bloody. Almost all pogroms included plunder; but taking Jewish property was a particularly important element in the attacks carried out by the anarchists.

The most bloodthirsty of the atamans was G. Grigorev, an unprincipled adventurer who at times supported Petliura, at times fought with the Red Army, and was finally prepared to join Denikin. He was prevented from doing so by Makhno, who captured and shot him. Grigorev turned against Jews with particular vehemence after he broke with the Soviet government. He denounced Lenin's regime as one dominated by Jews and vowed to free the country from "foreign elements." The ataman himself participated in the organization of the pogroms; during the spring of 1919, he was the greatest scourge of Ukrainian Jewry.

Fortunately for the Jewish population, the anarchists, including Grigorev, rarely controlled a great deal of territory and therefore the harm which they could do was limited. The situation quickly deteriorated when the most powerful anti-Bolshevik force, the Volunteer Army, entered the Ukraine.

II

The anti-Bolshevik movement, led by officers of the former Imperial Army, came into being almost immediately after the October Revolution. The Whites ultimately organized armies in the northwest and in Siberia, but the strongest and longest lasting, the one that presented the greatest threat to the existence of the young Soviet regime, was founded in the south, in Cossack districts. In the course of 1918 the Volunteer Army struggled to survive, first under the leadership of General L. G. Kornilov, and later under General A. I. Denikin.

The leadership of the Volunteer Army was in the hands of officers, and it was they who determined the character of the movement. Although the leaders never articulated it, the peasants correctly understood that the army fought for the re-establishment of old Russia. The great majority of the fighting men were Cossacks, who fought for their own purposes: protecting their privileges from the non-Cossack peasants, who had allied themselves with the Bolsheviks.

While the Volunteer Army fought in the northern Caucasus it had no need to confront the "Jewish question." Extremely few Jews lived in this region. Nevertheless, from the very beginning the antisemitism of the Cossacks and officers was evident. The Cossack leader and future General of the Volunteer Army, A. G. Shkuro, in the summer of 1918, herded the small Jewish community of Stavropol into the synagogue and threatened to burn the building on them unless they paid an exorbitant ransom.[12]

The liberal Kadet politician, N. E. Paramonov, who for a short time headed the propaganda agency of the Volunteer Army, hired a few Jews. He was soon dismissed. His successor, K. N. Sokolov, understood that the mood of the officers and Cossacks was such that no Jew could be tolerated working for the army even in a not particularly responsible position. His first act as head of the propaganda agency was to get rid of all the Jews. He reports in his memoirs that this move was necessary in order to win the confidence of the military men. His agency rapidly came to produce antisemitic propaganda.[13]

In the summer of 1919, the Volunteer Army was able to take advantage of strategic errors by the Red High Command. In June the Whites broke through enemy lines and within a short time occupied almost the entire Ukraine and even threatened Moscow. However, the Bolsheviks managed to mobilize new forces and defeat the armies of General Denikin. The White front was overextended and harassed by Makhno's troops; by December White forces were forced to evacuate the Ukraine once again.

The second half of 1919 was the most tragic period for Ukrainian Jewry. N. I. Shtif, on the basis of documents collected by a Jewish committee in 1922, distinguished three phases in the pogroms carried out by the Volunteer Army. He characterized the first weeks as a period of "quiet pogroms." In June and July 1919, in regions that had just come under White rule, the Cossacks attacked individual Jews, looted some villages and here and there raped women. In August, at a time when the Volunteer Army was advancing most rapidly, the pogroms turned into a mass phenomenon. Now looting occurred on a large scale. In this second period many Jews were murdered, but the attackers' main desire was to take Jewish property. It was still possible to buy off the murderers. The third period, November and December 1919, was contemporaneous with the decisive defeats of the Volunteer Army. This was a time for mass murder: the defeated took revenge on the defenseless.[14]

From the accounts of the survivors a typical pogrom can be reconstructed. Troops of the Volunteer Army, usually Cossacks, entered a little town. They immediately divided themselves into

Plate 10. Victims of a pogrom in an unnamed town in the Ukraine in 1920.

small groups of five or ten, often including officers. These groups attacked Jews on the streets, beat them and sometimes stripped them. Then they entered Jewish houses, demanding money and other valuables. The frightened victims handed over everything they owned without the slightest resistance. The pogromists then searched and destroyed the interior of the house. The destruction was frequently followed by rape. Sometimes the Cossacks forced the women to follow them, killing those who did not obey. The local population usually, but not always, joined the looting once the violence had begun. After several days of unrestrained murder and looting, the local commander would issue an order blaming the Jews for Russia's troubles, and therefore for their own misfortune, but promising that henceforth measures would be taken to preserve order. Since the soldiers knew the attitude of their commanders by experience, at this point the pogrom would either stop or turn into a "quiet pogrom," depending on the soldiers' perception of their superiors' attitude.[15] Methods of murder varied greatly. Generally the Cossacks shot or bayoneted their victims, but hanging, burning, drowning in wells, and live burials also occurred. There were recorded instances of people buried up to the necks in sand and then killed by horses driven over them.[16] Many victims were not killed outright but wounded and left to die. Thousands died of hunger, disease, and exposure after their houses were burned down and they had no one to turn to for help. There was nowhere to escape to, and in the very same town the appearance of fresh troops might start the wave of killing and looting once again.

Ironically, the Jews had awaited the coming of the Volunteer Army with high hopes. Although Jews were disproportionately represented in the Bolshevik leadership, the majority of the Ukrainian Jewry consisted of artisans and tradesmen, who had suffered as a result of Soviet economic policies, such as the restrictions on free trade. Moreover, the Jewish minority by and large had no interest in Ukrainian nationalism and therefore did not sympathize with Petliura. The Jews expected the return of law and order after a White victory, when they hoped to resume their normal lives.

Soviet agitators and publications, who held the Volunteer Army responsible for every sort of crime, real and imagined, did not play up the antisemitic outrages. Evidently Soviet propagandists understood that descriptions of pogroms carried out by the enemy was not good agitational material to win over the peasants.[17] Just as during the Second World War, every little Jewish settlement had to learn for itself by bitter experience.[18]

Friendly attitudes on the part of the unsuspecting victims toward their tormenters did not help them. Often the pogroms began by killing those Jews who participated in the good will delegation which greeted the entering army. In Korsun, for example, the town sent a mixed Christian and Jewish delegation, led by the rabbi, to meet the Volunteer Army. Next day the Bolsheviks retook the town and the rabbi went into hiding. The Bolsheviks captured and killed two Jewish members of the delegation. The following day the Volunteer Army chased out the Bolsheviks, and immediately started a violent pogrom, killing the rabbi as he came out of hiding.[19] It is abundantly clear from the evidence that the Whites had a preconception of Jews as enemies, and that there was nothing the Jews could do to convince them otherwise.

Self-defense against the Petliurists and anarchists was successful at times; against the Volunteer Army it was hopeless. Antisemitic propaganda often described Jews firing from windows on retreating White soldiers, or even imaginary Jewish detachments fighting against the Volunteer Army. These were pure fabrications. The behavior of the Jews of Kiev in particular became the subject of heated controversy. In October 1919, the Bolsheviks unexpectedly managed to occupy the city for a few days. After the Volunteer Army reestablished itself, antisemitic papers began an agitation blaming the Jews for the Bolshevik attack. *Vechernie ogni*, in its first edition after the recapture of the city, published detailed charges against individual Jews, giving names and addresses of those who had allegedly fired on the retreating soldiers of the Volunteer Army. The next day the liberal organ, *Kievskaia zhizn*, supported by politicians, including the mayor of Kiev, carried out an investigation showing that all the charges were entirely without foundation. In some instances there were no such house numbers as given in the original article. However, such attempts by moderate politicians to combat virulent antisemitism made no difference; at least partially as the consequence of the trumped up charges, the Jews of Kiev experienced their worst pogrom. V. V. Shulgin, editor of *Kievlianin*, and one of the most influential politicians in the White camp and an advisor to General Denikin, described the Kiev pogroms as politically harmful, because they created too much sympathy for the Jews.[20]

Ultimately the Jews realized that Soviet rule, in spite of its economic policies and in spite of the occasional pogroms carried out by ill-disciplined troops, offered the best chance of survival. White assumptions that the Jews were inveterate enemies of the anti-Bolshevik cause became self-fulfilling. After the Jews learned their lesson, sometimes entire settlements would follow the retreating soldiers of the Red Army. Indeed, many young Jews voluntarily enlisted in the Red Army.[21] White memoirists, including General Denikin and V. V. Shulgin, wrote gleefully that antisemitism was rife even under Soviet rule.[22] While this is partly true, it is equally clear that Soviet leaders were willing to fight against pogroms and punish the offenders. As a result, the victims of the Red Army numbered only a few hundred compared to the thousands slaughtered by the Whites.

Because of the very nature of the pogroms it is almost impossible to establish the exact number of incidents and victims. In the course of 1919 the number of pogroms was gradually rising until August, when they reached their peak. This was a moment when the Civil War was particularly bitter, and all the major participants in the civil struggle killed Jews. In the months that followed the main culprits were the soldiers of the Volunteer Army. In 1920, after the Whites were forced to evacuate the Ukraine, the number of incidents gradually decreased, and with the establishment of Soviet power they completely stopped in 1921.

Gusev-Orenburgskii, a Kiev researcher, collected evidence soon after the events and on the basis of his findings reported 35,000 deaths. Taking into account that his material came only from parts of the Ukraine, that entire families disappeared without trace, and that he believed that his statistics did not account for those who died of their wounds later, he estimated the total number of dead as approximately 200,000.[23] Even if we regard this figure as too high, it is likely that the dreadful slaughter carried out during the civil war killed about 10 percent of Ukrainian Jewry. This accounting, of course, does not include those who were raped, maimed, orphaned, or had their property and livelihood destroyed. According to Elias Heifetz, the Chairman of the Relief Committee for pogrom victims, one half of the murdered fell victims to the soldiers of the Volunteer Army.[24]

III

The Volunteer Army succeeded in murdering as many Jews as all other armies put together, because its pogroms were the most modern: they were the best organized, carried out like military operations, and the most ideologically motivated. Other attacks were carried out solely by peasants, whether belonging to armed bands or not, whereas the White army's pogroms were largely Cossack affairs, with non-Cossack officers and local inhabitants occasionally joining them. The antisemitism of these three participants were not the same; they had different methods, goals, and ideologies.

The antisemitism of the Ukrainian peasant has been frequently analyzed and it is the easiest to understand. However wretchedly poor the Jews might be, they were still seen as exploiters by the Ukrainians. The Jews, after all, formed a petty bourgeoisie, precisely that element of the exploiting class most familiar to the peasants who, in time of economic chaos, turned against those they considered responsible. The breakdown of order allowed the people to express their ancient hatreds. The peasant himself was a victim of occupying armies and requisitioning battalions, and his kinsmen had been dying on distant battlefronts. The Civil War, among other things, was a struggle of the village against the city, and for the backward, ignorant peasants the Jew epitomized the hated city. Petliurist and White propaganda identified the Soviet regime with the Jews to the detriment of both. Peasants exposed to brutal requisitioning policies often preferred to lay the blame on the Jews than on the Soviet regime.

It would be a mistake, however, to regard the peasantry as homogeneously antisemitic. There are numerous recorded incidents of peasants hiding Jews from persecution. Had the Ukrainians been uniformly hostile, the number of pogrom victims would have been much higher. Nevertheless, it is true that the peasants' antisemitism was a crucial pre-requisite for the pogroms: their attitude legitimized murders carried out by others. The murders were carried out by Cossacks, but these killers rarely encountered moral revulsion on the part of the peasants, or, more importantly, on the part of their officers. After destroying a Jewish settlement, the Cossacks would believe that they had simply contributed to the anti-Bolshevik cause. Had the murderers been regarded as such by their fellow men, it is unlikely that they would have long continued their behavior.

The majority of the Cossacks fighting in the Ukraine came from the Kuban. The Don Cossack army at this time was engaged in defense of their northern boundaries against the Bolsheviks. Above all, however, the Terek Cossacks had the most bloodthirsty reputation. Since the Kuban, but especially the Terek, had a tiny Jewish population, it cannot be said that the Cossacks learned to hate the Jewish "exploiters" from their childhood; their anti-semitism could not have been deep-rooted. It is therefore somewhat ironic that those who did most of the killings had been traditionally the least concerned with the "Jewish Question." The involvement of the Cossacks in the "Jewish Question" had been the same in the previous decades: Cossacks had looted peaceful citizens. Convinced that the Jews were vicious enemies, the Cossack murderers felt no compunction in taking their property. Many persuaded themselves of the Jewish danger to such an extent that it became natural to kill. It was, in any case, much easier to destroy the "enemy" in a Jewish settlement than on the battlefield.

Loot was the driving force and antisemitism, fanned by official propaganda, only justified the looting. The pogroms carried out by the Cossacks of the Volunteer Army differed from other pogroms in as much as these were better organized and removal of Jewish

property was more systematic. Goods were often taken by wheel-
barrows to the railroad station and shipped home. On occasion
women came from the distant Kuban and Terek in order to
participate in the distribution of stolen property.[25] The Volunteer
command, which could not organize the supply of the army properly
and could not pay the fighting men adequately, never took an
uncompromising stance against looting. The unruly behavior of the
Cossacks often turned the Russian and Ukrainian peasants against
the White cause. It is perhaps not surprising that with such a record
of protecting civilians, the Volunteer command did not come to the
aid of the Jews when they were looted.

The leaders and officers of the Volunteer Army were obsessed with
antisemitism. Secret reports, obviously not meant as propaganda,
make it clear that this antisemitism, full of paranoid delusions,
bordered on the pathological. In the thousands of documents in the
White army archives there is not a single denunciation of pogroms.
On the contrary, the intelligence agents simply assumed that Jews
were responsible for all miseries – whether Bolshevism, inflation, or
defeat in battle.[26]

The language and imagery of the reports is comparable to that of
Nazi tracts. For example, a White Secret Service agent reporting
from the Ukraine on the political situation, devoted as much space
to the discussion of the activities of the Jews as to all other subjects
put together. He wrote:

No administrative step would help; it is necessary to neutralize the microbe
– the Jews... As long as the Jews are allowed to do their harmful work, the
front will always be in danger... The Jew is not satisfied with corrupting the
soldier. Lately he has been paying even greater attention to officers. But he
is most interested in young people. Clever [Jewish] agents, under the cover
of patriotism and monarchism, mix with young soldiers, and with the help
of cards, women and wine they lure the debauched youth into their nets.

One must contemplate the picture of a Jewish conspiracy sending
out agents to lure the innocent young officers by card games and
women in order to appreciate fully the pathological mentality of the
White leaders. It must be emphasized that such thinking was not an
aberration among a few people, but an attitude that was taken for
granted in the White camp.

Jews were blamed especially for economic problems and inflation.
"We must not forget that the whole industry, and above all trade is

in the hands of the Jews; enormous supplies of all kinds of goods are hidden by them. They do not take these goods to the market, but on the contrary, spare no effort to buy more and hide them." The agent recommended that no humanity should be shown to these enemies, since they exploit mercy and such humane treatment alienates the populace.[27] The same theme appears in dozens of other reports.

Foreign observers reported with amazement on the extent of the antisemitic sentiment among the officers. An English journalist, John Hodgson, who stayed for some time at Denikin's headquarters, wrote:

The officers and the men of the army laid practically all the blame for their country's trouble on the Hebrew. Many held that the whole cataclysm had been engineered by some great and mysterious society of international Jews, who, in the pay and at the order of Germany, had seized the psychological moment and snatched the reins of government.[28]

He writes elsewhere: "When America showed herself decidedly against any kind of interference in Russia the idea soon gained wide credence that President Woodrow Wilson was a Jew, while Mr. Lloyd George was referred to as a Jew whenever a cable from England appeared to show him lukewarm in support of the anti-Bolsheviks."[29] Denikin and his closest advisors were no better. To a Jewish delegation which complained about the "excesses," Denikin replied:

Gentlemen, I will be honest with you. I do not like you Jews. But my attitude toward you is based on humanity. I, as Commander in Chief, will take steps to prevent pogroms and other acts of lawlessness and will punish severely those who are guilty. But I cannot guarantee that in the future there will be no excesses.[30]

Denikin, just like other antisemites, held Jewry as a whole responsible for the "crimes" of those who fought on the Bolshevik side. He believed and proclaimed that Bolshevism and Judaism were virtually identical. In that case how could the Russian people be asked to fight against one and not the other? The commander-in-chief privately deplored the pogroms, which seemed to him manifestations of barbarism. While he disapproved of "excesses," his belief in collective responsibility and his conviction that popular hatred against the Jews was justified, made those "excesses" possible.

Among the influential groups at the White headquarters there was none to defend the Jews. The record of the Orthodox Church was especially poor. In imperial Russia the Church had contributed to antisemitism among the peasantry by allowing priests to blame the Jews for the crucifixion of Christ. In fact traditionally the worst time for pogroms was Easter. During the Civil War many priests described Bolshevik Russia as a country ruled by anti-Christ and attempted to persuade their listeners that socialism was a Jewish creation.

Even among the reactionary and antisemitic priesthood Father Vostokov stood out by his agitation. He established a conspiratorial monarchist organization, "The Brotherhood of the Life-giving Cross," whose goal was to fight "Jewish Freemasonry." On one occasion he proposed to lead a crusade of priests armed with holy icons against "Jewish Bolsheviks."[31] Vostokov's pogrom agitation was so violent that in September 1920 General Wrangel had to restrain him. His demagoguery fired the crowds who, after listening to him, chanted hysterically: "Beat the Jews! Save Russia!" Vostokov undoubtedly was an extreme case, but there were hundreds of priests everywhere who denounced the Jews as enemies of Christ and blamed them for the misfortunes of the Church during the Civil War. The hierarchy of the Church repudiated neither Vostokov nor pogrom agitation in general. A Jewish delegation turned to Metropolitan Antony of Kiev for help. On 10 November 1919 *Kievskoe ekho* published an interview with the Metropolitan, who among other things, said: "In answer to a request [to denounce pogroms] by Jewish representatives I suggested to them that first they should turn to their coreligionists and ask them to leave the Bolshevik establishment forthwith."[32] The White Army had only a rudimentary propaganda network, and therefore it greatly depended on the Church for ideological support. In many villages, where priests had been persecuted by the Bolsheviks, the Church had acquired new prestige. That the Church used this power to inflame antisemitic feelings, rather than to combat them, caused the death of thousands of people.

Even the liberals, led by the Kadet party, failed to come to the aid of the Jews. This failure was all the more remarkable if we remember that in the past liberals had repeatedly condemned the tsarist authorities for organizing and allowing pogroms, and took a leading role in proposing legislation leading to the emancipation of the Jews. The last Kadet conference in Russia, held in November 1919 in

Kharkov, refused to condemn the Volunteer Army for the massacres. Just like Orthodox churchmen, the liberal politicians in their resolution called on the Jews to repudiate Bolshevism in order to save themselves, disingenuously blaming the Bolsheviks for organizing pogroms in the rear of the Volunteer Army in order to create confusion.[33] Nothing illustrated more clearly the bankruptcy of Russian liberalism than this resolution on the Jewish question. The liberal politicians were unwilling to alienate the generals even for the sake of their most cherished principles.

Given the mood prevailing in the White camp, it is not surprising that the Volunteer Army introduced anti-Jewish legislation. Denikin, for example, forbade Jews to buy land at the Black Sea coast in the name of preventing speculation.[34] The Volunteer Army leadership consciously attempted to exclude Jews completely from political life. The first, and perhaps most important step, was the removal of Jewish officers from the army. There were very few of these. In tsarist times Jews could not become officers. However, during the few months existence of the Provisional Government, a few Jews succeeded in receiving their commissions. A number of these joined the Volunteer Army at its inception, and participated in the first bloody campaigns. Denikin, under the pressure of antisemitic officers, dismissed them from active service. In July 1919, a Jewish delegation requested him to reinstate the officers, arguing that their very presence in the army would show the population that not all Jews sided with the Bolsheviks and so undermine pogrom agitation.[35] The commander-in-chief refused the request. If he would not protect even those who had fought with him at the most difficult times, how could other Jews expect help from him?

In territories occupied by the Volunteer Army, Jews were systematically excluded from positions of authority. Jewish judges, members of city councils and district assemblies had to leave their posts.[36]

Denikin's crimes were primarily crimes of omission. He allowed *Osvag*, the propaganda agency, to spread the most vicious antisemitic propaganda: its posters always portrayed Bolsheviks as Jews. It fabricated stories about Jews firing on retreating White Army soldiers and forming anti-Volunteer detachments. Denikin allowed his subordinates, such as General K. K. Mamontov, to issue proclamations such as: "Arm yourself and rise against the common enemy of our Russian land, against Jewish Bolshevik communists... The evil force which lives in the hearts of Jew-Communists will be eliminated."[37]

In July 1919, Denikin refused a Jewish request that he should condemn pogroms, saying that such a proclamation would only arouse the suspicion that he had sold out to the Jews. He told the delegation that the only solution was a general improvement in the moral climate and the repudiation of all forms of lawlessness. Finally, in October 1919, Denikin relented and did denounce pogroms. He addressed his troops in Kiev: "I have received reports on the use of force by the Army against Jews. I require you to take energetic measures to stop these and institute harsh measures against those found guilty."[38] This proclamation was immediately followed by the bloodiest pogroms in the history of Kiev. It is not surprising that no one took this denunciation of pogroms seriously. Soldiers and officers assumed that such statements were issued merely to appease foreign public opinion. Significantly, the high command did not punish the criminals. Official investigating commissions were farcical. Jews were coerced to testify that no pogroms had occurred at all. The government forbade newspaper reports of pogroms. The military governor of Kiev was General A. M. Dragomirov, who was a friend and ideological comrade of V. V. Shulgin, the ideologue of White antisemitism. The Metropolitan of Kiev interceded on behalf of those who had been convicted of mass murder. General Dragomirov, not surprisingly, pardoned every one of them. By contrast, when a delegation of trade unionists protested to Dragomirov the arrest of four of their Jewish colleagues, the general threatened them with court-martial for their impudence.[39]

On the basis of the available evidence it is fair to conclude that it was the high command and the officer corps of the Volunteer Army that were primarily responsible for the bloody pogroms. The Cossacks correctly understood that their superiors not only did not condemn their behavior, but also shared their prejudices.

IV

Antisemitism among the White officers was so wide-spread, so deeply felt and passionate that one must ask now this obsession can be explained. Of course, the imperial officer corps had traditionally been antisemitic. Jews could not be commissioned and even during the First World War, at a time when the army desperately needed officers, potential candidates were required to show that neither their parents nor their grandparents were Jewish.[40] The officers had looked down on Jewish soldiers and mistreated them. The great majority of them approved tsarist policy, which regarded Jews as a hostile and alien minority, whose very existence somehow threatened the Russian people. The High Command of the army carried out cruel anti-Jewish policies immediately from the outbreak of the war: Jews were stigmatized as potential enemies and spies, they were forbidden to enter Galicia, they were chased out of their little towns at twenty-four hours notice, and the army took hostages from them, "in order to assure the good behavior of others."[41]

Yet this conventional antisemitism was mild compared to the murderous obsession which the officers developed during the Civil War. Had they been asked to explain themselves, they no doubt would have pointed to the large number of Jews in leading positions in the Soviet regime. White propaganda constantly emphasized this point and there is no reason to doubt the sincerity of the propagandists. Obviously, however, this cannot be the full explanation. After all, most Jews were not communists and most communists were not Jewish.

The antisemites objected not only to Jews participating in the Communist Party, but to their participation in politics in general. In their words and actions they made it abundantly clear that they would not tolerate Jews in public life. Jews were not to have the rights of other citizens, however they behaved. The White officers passionately disapproved of the emancipation legislation of the Provisional Government. In their mind, in a distorted fashion, Jewish emancipation came to stand for all the modernizing and Westernizing ways of liberals and socialists. Jews became a symbol of modernity at a time when conservatives felt deeply threatened by change. Jews became a symbol of the other, the alien, what was not part of ancient Russia.

Baron Meller-Zakomelskii, a participant in the White movement and an associate of General Denikin, wrote a little pamphlet in 1923, entitled "The Dreadful Question. About Russia and about the Jews." This short work well summarizes the mentality of the conservative members of the White movement. In it the author explicitly coupled Jews and modernity, and argued that Russia must repudiate the modern world in order to save its soul. He described Jews as the Anti-Christ. In one of his concluding and rather confused paragraphs he wrote:[42] "The concepts of 'Europeanization' and 'progress' irreparably lost the appeal of the unfamiliar. And while

Europe will continue to follow on the road to 'progress,' following
the Red star of Jewish socialism, Russia, already knowing the end of
this road, with terror will look around in the desert and will recover
its sight."

The revolution was a painful challenge to conservatives. Liberals
by and large explained the collapse of the old regime by pointing to
its failures. But how were those who believed that imperial Russia
had been a just society to deal with the recent great events? The
army officers had always proudly regarded themselves as apolitical,
by which they meant that they uncritically accepted the existing
imperial regime as the best for Russia. Now that military men came
to play a major role in a civil war, they were forced to articulate a
program; they had to announce the goals of their movement. They
were intellectually and emotionally unprepared for such tasks.

The war was a dreadful period for the officers. The values which
they had unquestionably accepted turned out to be irrelevant. In a
modern war technology mattered more than courage; cavalry
charges rarely won the day. The officers saw a dreadful slaughter of
their comrades and men. It quickly became obvious that the bulk of
the Russian people, the peasants, did not share their idea of
patriotism and the Tsar and his ministers were indisputably
incompetent. Worse was to follow. The revolution not merely
threatened their way of life and privileges, but revealed the depth of
hatred of peasants against their masters, soldiers against their officers.
The imperial regime was no longer there to protect them.

It is perhaps understandable that the intellectually unsophisticated officers were full of bitterness and hatred. It is difficult for
anyone to look at the world anew; it is difficult to construct a new
world view that takes account of unpleasant realities. The officers,
instead of throwing overboard their long cherished ideas, reasserted
them with vigor. They always disliked Jews; now their antisemitism
reached pathological proportions.

This new and passionate antisemitism was born out of a need to
explain, not so much to others, as to themselves, why the revolution
had occurred. In the view of the reactionary officers it was the alien
Jews who were primarily responsible. They were the microbes that
destroyed the healthy body politic of old Russia. As the officers
became even more frustrated by the confusing world around them,
their antisemitism became increasingly pathological. They murdered
more and more Jews and it was necessary to justify themselves by

thinking up sinister Jewish conspiracies. Perhaps paradoxically, participating in pogroms increased antisemitism. Antisemitism was not simply an element in their *Weltanschauung*; it was the focal point. It alone enabled them to make sense of a world that to them seemed senseless. In this respect, at least, the White officers were precursors of the Nazis.

It has been a debated point whether antisemitism helped or harmed the White cause. Denikin and some of his fellow generals believed that participating in pogroms undermined the discipline in the army. Antisemites, such as Shulgin and Denikin, disapproved of pogroms primarily for that reason. On the other hand, antisemitism was a trump card in the hands of White propagandists. Associating Bolshevism with Judaism harmed not only the Jews, but also Soviet power. Many peasants, in particular among the Ukrainians, sided with the Whites at least partially because of their antisemitism.

There is, however, another way to look at the problem. Antisemitism was a delusion. It allowed the White leaders to avoid looking at the world as it was. Although such a palliative may have brought short-term psychological benefits, those who delude themselves are usually condemned to defeat.

NOTES

1 This article is a greatly revised and expanded version of a section in my book, *Civil War in South Russia, 1919–1920* (Berkeley, 1977), 166–77.

2 See the description of some spectacular brutalities at the beginning of the Civil War by I. Borisenko, *Sovetskie respubliki na Severnom Kavkase v 1918 goda* (Rostov on Don, 1930), i, 70.

3 The material on which this article is based comes largely from Jewish and Volunteer Army sources. How the pogroms were carried out is taken exclusively from Jewish sources. Following the Civil War Jewish organizations collected material concerning Jewish suffering. There is no question about the reliability of sources; however, given the conditions, it was difficult to collect evidence from all parts of the Ukraine. As a result, we can only estimate the number of victims and no modern day researcher can come up with precise figures. I base my statements on antisemitism among the Whites on Volunteer Army records and contemporary pamphlets. They are very revealing.

4 On Red Army pogroms see I. Cherikover, *Antisemitism i pogromy na Ukraine, 1917–1918 gg.* (Berlin, 1923), 144–5.

5 Ibid., 164–7.

6 Elias Heifetz, *The Slaughter of the Jews in the Ukraine in 1919* (New York, 1921), 41–2.

7 See the articles by Taras Hunczak, "A reappraisal of Symon Petliura and Ukrainian–Jewish relations, 1917–1921", and by Zosa Szajkowski, "A reappraisal of Symon Petliura and Ukrainian–Jewish relations, 1917–1921: a rebuttal," *Jewish Social Studies*, XXXI, 3: 163–83, 184–213.

8 This manifesto is reprinted in *Material Concerning Ukrainian–Jewish Relations during the Years of Revolution. [1917–1921.]* (Munich, 1956), 68–9.

9 Makhno's comrade, Voline, a Jew, passionately defended his chief against the charge of antisemitism. See Voline, *The Unknown Revolution* (New York, 1974), 697–700.

10 Elias Heifetz, *The Slaughter of the Jews*, 74.

11 See the description of a Makhnovite pogrom in S. I. Gusev-Orenburgskii, *Bagrovaia kniga. Pogromy 1919–1920 gg. na Ukraine* (Harbin, 1922).

12 General Tikhobrazov, *Vospominaniia*. MS. Columbia University, Russian Archives, chapter 26, 10. During the Second World War Shkuro fought on the German side. After the war he was captured and executed.

13 K. N. Sokolov, *Pravlenie generala Denikina* (Sofia, 1921), 103–5.

14 N. I. Shtif, *Pogromy na Ukraine. [Period Dobrovol'cheskoi armii]* (Berlin, 1922), 10–14.

15 Ibid., 17–23.

16 Zvi Gitelman, *Jewish Nationality and Soviet Politics. The Jewish Sections of the CPSU, 1917–1930* (Princeton, 1972), 161.

17 The Soviet authorities did publish anti-pogrom brochures. See for example *Evrei, klassovaia bor'ba i pogromy* (Petrograd, 1919). However, these brochures did not make a point of emphasizing the brutalities of the enemies.

18 Shtif, *Progromy na Ukraine*, 7.

19 Ibid., 16.

20 A. A. Goldenveizer, "Iz Kievskikh vospominaniakh", *Arkhiv Russkoi Revoliutsii* (Berlin, 1922), 6, 268–9. Shulgin, the rabid reactionary, chose to return to the Soviet Union after the Second World War. As far as the "Jewish Question" was concerned, one may assume, he found little to criticize in Soviet politics.

21 Heifetz, *The Slaughter of the Jews*, 97–8.

22 A. I. Denikin, *Ocherki russkoi smuty* (Paris and Berlin, 1921–25), 5, 151 and V. V. Shulgin, *Chto nam v nikh ne nravitsia* (Paris, 1930), 9.

23 Gusev-Orenburgskii, *Bagrovaia kniga*, 15.

24 Heifetz, *The Slaughter of the Jews*, 73.

25 Shtif, *Pogromy na Ukraine*, 19.

26 These reports can be found in Wrangel Military Archives, file 146, Hoover Institution (Stanford, CA).

27 Report of Olfer'ev, 14 November 1919, Taganrog, Wrangel file 166, 22–5.

28 J. E. Hodgson, *With Denikin's Armies* (London, 1932), 54–5.

29 Ibid., 55.

30 Tikhobrazov, *Vospominaniia*, 10.
31 I. M. Kalinin, *Pod znamenem Vrangelia* (Leningrad, 1925), 126–7.
32 Shtif, *Pogromy na Ukraine*, 71.
33 Resolution of the Conference of the Party of People's Freedom, Kharkov, 3–6 November 1919, Wrangel file, 129.
34 Denikin, *Ocherki russkoi smuty*, 5, 145.
35 Ibid., 150.
36 Shtif, *Pogromy na Ukraine*, 73–6.
37 Ibid., 65.
38 Ibid., 84.
39 Ibid., 15.
40 Peter Kenez, "A profile of the pre-revolutionary Officer Corps," *California Slavic Studies* (Berkeley, 1973), VII, 148.
41 "Dokumenty o presledovanii Evreev", *Arkhiv Russkoi Revoliutsii* (Berlin, 1928), XIX, 245–84. These documents, published by anti-Bolshevik *émigrées* show how widespread, passionate and constant antisemitism was among Russian officers, including the highest circles.
42 Baron Meller-Zakomel'skii, *Strashnyi vopros. O Rossii i evreistve* (Paris, 1923), 45.

Conclusion and overview

Hans Rogger

After Tsar and vodka, pogrom may well be the Russian word most widely understood and used by non-Russians. It is certain that the phenomenon it describes is invariably associated with the Empire of the Tsars and the mistreatment of its Jewish subjects. As recently as 1975, the *New Columbia Encyclopedia* wrote of Russia as "the birthplace of the pogroms," and of the term as one that "came to be applied to a series of violent attacks on Jews in Russia in the late nineteenth and early twentieth centuries." Although the events which gave it currency lie in the distant past, the word was thought sufficiently familiar to be employed by a mass-circulation American newspaper in 1988 without translation or explanation.[1]

Of equal durability and acceptance as the term itself is the belief that Russian pogroms were organized by the tsarist government, perpetrated with its connivance or, at the very least, tolerated by it as a welcome diversion from revolutionary assaults upon the old regime.[2] This standard view, which originated for the most part with Russian-Jewish observers who were contemporaries to the horrors they tried to understand, was restated in its purest and simplest form in an *émigré* scholar's article in 1941:

The aim of the Tsarist pogroms was clearly and explicitly political: to drown the Russian Revolution of 1905 in Jewish blood, to frighten the Jews away from taking part in the movement, to divert the anger of the discontented masses by setting them a suitable scapegoat. The decisive manner in which the government met the 1905 strikes by staging more than 500 pogroms constitutes an eloquent proof of this fact.[3]

An identical view was offered some thirty years later by an author who applied it to the pogroms of the 1880s:

These were not just sporadic outbreaks against Jews of a particular townlet, erupting spontaneously among an illiterate peasantry; they were surreptitiously organized by the authorities to occur simultaneously at hundreds

314

of Jewish settlements throughout the Pale. Pogroms were systematic, an integral part of deliberate tsarist policy. They were meant to...divert the attention of the masses from internal difficulties, worsening economic conditions, military defeats, and discontent over the repression of the numerous nationalities; to check revolutions and workers' strikes; to present an easy scapegoat for pent-up hostility; and to keep the Jews "amenable."[4]

The assumption of official authorship or complicity has been rejected or modified by recent historical research, some of it carried out by the authors of this volume and reflected in their contributions.[5] Yet it persists, even in the scholarly literature where, for example, the Russian government is said to have manifested its "black-hearted policy" by encouraging, arranging, or instigating pogroms in an effort to deflect discontent onto an unpopular minority and win public favor.[6]

To dispose decisively of the question (and degree) of governmental responsibility in all cases of anti-Jewish violence is impossible at this late date, even with better access to archives than has so far been granted. Still, it must be posed again; less to place or remove blame than for the sake of historical accuracy and, above all, for a better understanding of the sociopolitical order in which pogroms occurred and of the forces at work within it. It is equally important to ask, and to do so in a comparative historical and international perspective embracing Western Europe, Russia, and the United States, whether this form of ethno-religious violence was uniquely and peculiarly Russian; why it or something like it occurred at certain times and places, under different polities, and against others than Jews.

In spite of the necessarily narrow and sensible definition adopted for present purposes by John Klier, it is not self-evident, as he has pointed out, that pogrom, even in Russia, always connoted an anti-Jewish act. That connotation first arose in the wake of the 1881–2 riots; it entered into common consciousness and usage in those that followed in the twentieth century. But as late as the revolutionary year 1905 and beyond, a distinction was often made between "anti-Jewish" or "Jewish" pogroms and those inflicted by peasants upon the gentry, by rural or urban mobs upon students and intellectuals, by Azeris and Armenians upon each other.[7] Social turbulence and mass rage, the blind destructiveness which might strike out in any direction, were always implicit in the word and they shaped the initial reactions of officialdom to the excesses of 1881. It was the

events of that year also that led its critics to conclude that the state
which had in the century since the Pugachev rebellion successfully
and in short order contained all outbreaks of social and political
unrest could and should have done so in this case.

It seemed unthinkable that with all its awesome power, its
informers, policemen, and soldiers – who were thought to be more
numerous and ruthless than those of any other European country –
the Russian government was incapable of preventing or quickly
stopping the despoliation and killing of peaceful, law-abiding
subjects. Only the instigation or indulgence of the highest authorities,
it was held then and later, could account for the nearly simultaneous
eruption of anti-Jewish disorders in well over a hundred localities,
some of them major cities with sizable contingents of police and
troops, in eight southern provinces of the Empire. Failure to suppress
the depredations of the mobs in less than two or, more often, three
days was seen as added proof of the reluctance, the deliberate
sluggishness of the forces of order. When it came to the protection of
Jews, their conduct was in sharp contrast with that displayed in
peasant disturbances. Did not the mere appearance of a detachment
of Cossacks, at most a salvo of warning shots and a few arrests,
usually suffice to disperse a mutinous village crowd?

Jewish commentators and a governmental commission agreed
that whenever and wherever during 1881–2 local administrators had
shown determination and energy, they had been able to stifle or
altogether to prevent pogroms. Simon Dubnow, the Nestor of
Russian-Jewish historians, concluded that the northwestern provinces of the Pale of Jewish Settlement had not been touched by the
pogrom wave because Governor-General E. I. Totleben had left no
doubt in the minds of his subordinates and the populace that mob
violence would not be tolerated. The contradiction implicit in that
widely accepted conclusion was not explained or explored. If
atrocities against Jews were sponsored or permitted by the state and
its chief servants, why were their hints, orders, or wishes heeded in
some parts of the Pale but not in others? Why were there pogroms
in Ukraine but none in Belorussia and Lithuania and only one in
Russian Poland? And the Warsaw pogrom of December 1881,
Dubnow asserted, was staged, "on orders from above," to convince
Europe that pogroms were not exclusively a product of barbarian
Russia. Even the Bessarabian city of Kishinev, the scene in 1903 and
1905 of some of the most vicious outrages, was all but undisturbed.[8]

Since local officials did not respond in uniform fashion to such promptings as might have come from the capital, factors other than central planning or guidance must have come into play. Such an assumption is buttressed by a similar pattern of regional variations in the incidence and intensity of pogroms during 1905. Notwithstanding stronger evidence than exists for the earlier period of coordination and collusion by agencies or allies of the national government, their role was not decisive or, at a minimum, was less important than commonly thought.

The temptation to see a hidden hand in unexpected outbreaks of collective violence is great, and some of the very men who were held responsible succumbed to it. Alexander III could not believe that simple people, the narod, had turned upon the Jews of their own accord. The Tsar and his Minister of the Interior, N. P. Ignatiev, suspected revolutionary agitation before embracing the more comforting explanation of popular resentment at Jewish exploitation. For believers in the basic goodness of the common folk, in the spread of enlightenment and the artificiality of Judeophobia, it was almost a necessity to accuse some outside agency, whether governmental or not: the Holy League in 1881, the Union of Russian People in 1905. How could one otherwise make sense of the reappearance of long-dormant "medieval" passions and hatreds among the Russian masses "who are, religiously speaking, a tolerant people and whose relations to Jews have, on the whole, been marked with friendliness." To blame planning and organization for the pogroms, and the Emperor, his chief ministers, and a small clique of court dignitaries for the sufferings of the Jews brightened a gloomy picture and absolved the people of guilt for the injustices committed by their rulers.[9]

Inducements for seeing government as the chief culprit also came from the example of Europe. For much of its history, the state (or its sovereign) had been the foremost protector, indeed ally, of the Jews against their enemies; in the nineteenth century it had effected their emancipation. The states of Europe had neither eradicated antisemitism nor ended all forms of discrimination. But they were moving in that direction, unlike the eastern counterpart which after 1881 reversed such small advances as had been made in the preceding two decades and retreated from what appeared to be a universal movement towards equal rights. Most importantly, conservative and liberal governments in the West were at one in the principled, vigorous defense of Jewish lives and property.

Not just the enormity of what had taken place in Russia, but the

mere fact that it could happen at all in a presumably well-ordered
state, shocked and stunned contemporaries. It made them turn back
to the massacres of the Middle Ages for precedents and parallels and
caused them to focus on the Tsar's government as the agency that
had caused or made possible their repetition. In doing so, they and
historians after them failed to consider the record of modern Europe
and the possibility that however aberrant the acts committed or
omitted by the Russian state may have been, the behavior of the
masses was not. A brief look at the history of anti-Jewish violence in
the West may help to place in a clearer light what transpired in
Russia.

I

Most of that history has only been written in the recent past and that
– along with their favorable preconceptions concerning Western
society – may be the reason why students of the pogroms ignored the
first outbreak in modern times deserving of that designation: the so-
called Hep-Hep Riots which seized large parts of Germany in 1819.
Beginning on 2 August in Würzburg, they moved quickly to other
towns and rural districts of Bavaria, then to Baden, Hesse,
Württemberg, and beyond. At least forty cities were affected,
including Hamburg in the north, Leipzig and Dresden in the east,
as well as Copenhagen, Prague, Cracow, and Riga outside the
German lands.[10] The disorders differed in intensity and duration,
and there is much that we do not know about the specifics of their
course and character. But it has never been assumed or alleged, as
was done for 1881 or 1905, that the Hep-Hep movement began and
spread as a result of conspiracy or coordination. Its speedy crossing
of political and geographical boundaries was no doubt facilitated by
proximity and the ease with which news traveled; it fell on soil made
receptive by polemicists and agitators who fanned ancient dislikes
and articulated new resentments. Their critics complained of the
Jews demanding or being given civil rights; of their entry into
localities, trades, and professions from which they had been barred;
of their causing or worsening an economic downturn, unemployment, and crop failures at the end of the Napoleonic Wars.
There was bitterness against "upstart" Jewish financiers and
bankers – the house of Rothschild in the Frankfurt ghetto came
under physical and verbal attack – and in the country districts
against Jewish grain merchants, cattle dealers, and money lenders.

Nationalist feeling against conservative governments and Jewish outsiders, who were sometimes said to be in league, ran high and tensions were heightened by measures of control, the Carlsbad Decrees, taken against political subversives just as the troubles began.

The fears they aroused of a wider insurrection made governments decide to put an end to the turmoil. In Bavaria, the King ordered the military to suppress it and held local councils responsible for losses suffered by Jews. The Grand Duke of Baden did likewise: dispatched police patrols throughout the Duchy. He demonstratively visited the home of his banker, where he remained until the crowds besieging it had dispersed. Before the Frankfurt Senate was able, with difficulty, to restore order, Metternich offered troops on behalf of the federal Diet. Such resolution limited damage to homes and businesses and appears to have prevented the loss of life. It did not avert all outbreaks and their territorial expansion over a period of two months; nor did it assure their prompt repression everywhere nor their termination in less than three days. In Würzburg, the police, even after receiving support from the military, were unable to impose order before additional troops arrived. In Heidelberg, the police and civic guard looked on passively while Jewish properties were looted by crowds who were stopped only when students of the university intervened. In Hamburg, although the Senate imposed a curfew and police fired on violators, the troubles lasted longest. Only minor incidents occurred in Prussia and Austria.

The rigorous dedication to civic tranquility on the part of Germany's most conservative states was not the sole reason for their relative immunity from trouble. Since they were holding the line against an expansion of Jewish rights, the issue was not as contentious there as in the free cities and more liberal principalities. Especially in those states where Jewish emancipation had been introduced in 1806–8 under French pressure, it continued to be a subject of heated debates. The mere possibility of an improvement in the legal condition of Jews or of their increased presence, fueled the nationalist antisemitism of professors and journalists, while it deepened the hostility of their competitors in business, trades, and crafts. Although the riots contained a strong admixture of lower-class social protest, they were preceded, and in that sense prepared, by the resistance of men of education and property to Jewish emancipation, to the threat it posed or symbolized to their values and privileges. The voices advocating greater freedoms for Jews were drowned out by the clamor of street and press, and in its face governments thought it prudent to preserve Jewish disabilities.[11]

This was not the first time that the prospect of Jewish entitlement set off verbal protests, followed by demonstrations and governmental retreat, nor was it to be the last. On a very much smaller scale, the German pattern had been prefigured in eighteenth-century Britain. In 1753, a Whig ministry's introduction of a measure allowing for the naturalization of resident Jews stirred up the opposition of parliamentary Tories and London merchants, who were then joined by the city's Lord Mayor, aldermen, and council. When the bill became law, the campaign against it gathered strength. Alarmed by petitions, public meetings, and riotous crowds, the cabinet effected its repeal. Objections against the bill had in the first instance been economic and anti-Whig, but arguments that it would tend "to let in a swarm of foreigners, especially Jewish foreigners, to lord it over Englishmen and Christians" had the wider resonance.[12]

Revolutionary France, the birthplace of Jewish equality, was no more free of such troubles than were less enlightened regimes. The National Assembly's grant of full citizenship in 1790 to the "Bordelais," Sephardic Jews who had lived in France for generations, gave rise to angry outcries by clergy and nobles against doing the same for the more numerous Ashkenazim of Alsace and Lorraine. This enflamed the endemic antipathy of their neighbors whose more tangible protests forced the Assembly to take the Jews under its special protection. Neither this gesture, nor the Emancipation Law of November 1791, assured acceptance or safety for the Jews of Alsace. Complaints and attacks against them were a prime factor in Napoleon's ten-year suspension of Jewish rights, the "Infamous Decree" of 1808.

Although it was allowed to lapse after his fall and full emancipation was achieved under the July Monarchy, anti-Jewish outbreaks were a common occurrence in the Alsatian countryside throughout the first half of the nineteenth century. They usually followed political upheavals in the capital, becoming particularly violent in the spring of 1848, when the laxness of local authorities contributed to their spread and severity. Sixty communities were affected – one historian has described the disturbances in two of these as pogroms – and hundreds of Jews sought the safety of the cities or even of Switzerland.[13]

"Pogroms" was used with full justification for the cases of looting, assault, and ravaging of synagogues that during more than two decades followed the Crémieux decree of 1870 and the subsequent naturalization of Algeria's 35,000 Jews. They were a little-assimilated minority, most of them poor, whose supposed weight in local elections, in business and agrarian credit operations made them the object of an antisemitic campaign with leftist, anti-capitalist overtones. It did not achieve its aim of getting the home government to repeal Jewish enfranchisement. But it found a wide appeal among colonists from France, Spain, and Italy, and in the wake of the Dreyfuss Affair it scored significant, if temporary, electoral gains in Algeria's cities, where extraordinary measures were taken against Jews, from the denial of hospital admissions to the revocation of trading licenses.

In metropolitan France, the affair had also given a strong boost to anti-Jewish organizations and agitators who in January–February 1898 helped to bring about or exacerbate riots in fifty-five places. Half of these were sufficiently serious to terrorize the Jewish population and alarm the authorities into taking stern counter-measures. In spite of the fact that several of the riots lasted for three or more days and involved from 1,000 to 4,000 rioters – students, conscripts, and hooligans, as well as adult artisans, shopkeepers, even solid citizens – there were no deaths, few injuries and limited damage to Jewish shops and businesses, particularly department stores. The Jews of Algiers were not so fortunate during the pogrom of 22–4 January. Besides devastating entire streets of Jewish shops, the crowds assaulted individuals, in one or more cases with fatal results. The scale and duration of their rampage have been attributed to the encouragement of city officials, to the complaisance of the military, or the inaction of the police. Yet the casualty toll of nine rioters and forty-seven policemen seriously injured, with one of the former killed, suggests that the forces of order were not altogether passive and that they may, for a time, have been overwhelmed by the mob. In France, too, it has been charged, the police were either ineffective or in league with rioters. If this was so, they had ignored the wishes and warnings of their superiors.[14]

In the German and Austrian lands, as it had in French Alsace, the spring of the revolutionary year 1848 saw the recurrence of mass violence which has been compared with the persecutions of the Jews in the Middle Ages, with the Hep-Hep movement of 1819, and the

Russian pogroms of the 1880s. These outbreaks were largely the work of peasants who in a time of political and economic crisis – catastrophic harvest failures in 1845 and 1846, food shortages, and soaring prices – directed their anger against Jewish traders and creditors but also towards noble landlords, manorial rent offices, clergy and teachers who had lent them money. Incitement had no part in these rural disturbances, but did so in some cities, where economic antisemitism was accompanied and activated by propaganda against a revolution that threatened conservative interests and promised Jewish equality. As economic conditions improved and the liberal movement gained ground, the disturbances subsided. They left a legacy of fear among rural Jews, who abandoned the countryside in growing numbers, and of caution among the advocates of emancipation, which was not completed until another two decades had passed. In their revelation of the depths and virulence of popular Judaeophobia, the events of 1848 confirmed that it was under the protective shelter of the state that Jews were most likely to find tranquility and well-being. As a leader of German Jewry wrote in 1854:

All in all, we Jews recognize ... that among all elements of modern age it is the state, and above all and in particular the bureaucratic state, that has been and still is most open-minded towards us, since in every period of storm and stress the people rose up against us, and in every period of reaction it was nobility and the upper bourgeoisie who did the same.[15]

The coming of emancipation, favored by a long period of economic expansion and social stability, did not spell the demise of antisemitism, which became during the depression of the 1870s a catch-all ideology and mass movement in several countries. Nor did the remarkable degree of Jewish acculturation, assimilation, and integration bring a cessation of collective violence against them. But it did become less frequent and explosive and remained largely confined to parts of the continent where there was a persistence of nationality conflicts, of problems of underdevelopment, or both.

Thus, while the numerous manifestations of German antisemitism found their loudest expression and echo in Berlin, it was in two eastern provinces of the Reich that they provoked excesses against Jewish homes and shops. Beginning in West Prussia in April 1881, they reached their height during the summer in Pomerania, one of country's poorest regions, and did not end until September through the employment of troops and firearms. In the Dual Monarchy, troubles erupted the following year in several Hungarian towns, in connection with the Tisza-Eszlar ritual murder trial. The same charge was brought in Bohemia in 1893 and 1899, where anti-Jewish riots coincided with industrial unrest as well as Czech demonstrations for universal suffrage and language parity. Prague was the scene of attacks, led by Czech students, on German and Jewish estab-lishments, including synagogues, in 1897, and of still more serious anti-Jewish disorders, begun by new recruits, on 16 and 17 October 1899. Police and gendarmes managed to control these outbursts, sometimes with difficulty. Resistance was more severe than elsewhere in the Empire in the West Galician peasant pogroms of 1898. Although dozens of rioters were wounded and twelve killed on 16 June, the disturbances continued to grow for more than a week and culminated in a three-day pogrom. As in Russia, rumors that the emperor had given permission to despoil the Jews emboldened the crowds.[16]

Peasant poverty and anger were factors also in the Romanian rebellion of 1907 against the owners of large estates and their lease-holders. In Moldavia, where over 40 percent of the latter were Jews, they were the chief targets and victims. Few of them appear to have been killed, but the government, which put down the rising with a loss of 10,000 peasant lives, was fortified in its determination to allow only selective and individual naturalization of Jews. While legal equality and citizenship for most of them came in 1919 at the insistence of the Western powers, xenophobic antisemitism remained a feature of Romanian political and social life between the wars. Clashes, provoked for the most part by students, occurred throughout the 1920s. There was a major outbreak in Oradea Mare in 1927 against Jews and Magyars which spread to other cities in Transylvania and claimed two dead and many wounded.[17]

The nationality and class conflicts that the First World War had embittered and bequeathed to the newly independent states of Eastern Europe resulted in Jewish persecutions in Poland, Hungary, and Czechoslovakia which were more serious than any the affected communities had yet experienced. Within days of the proclamation of the Polish Republic on 3 November 1918, pogroms by soldiers, peasants, and townsmen erupted in Galicia and were repeated there and in other parts of the country for more than a year. They were most murderous in ethnically mixed regions where Jews were accused of disloyalty to the Polish cause and of collaborating with Ukrainians, Lithuanians, or Bolsheviks in the fighting over the new state's frontiers. Hundreds were killed and many more wounded, most of them by soldiers whose antisemitism was inflamed by agitation and indulged or stimulated by their commanders. Besides being identified with the nation's foreign enemies, the victims were also blamed for the economic dislocations and destitution that afflicted all segments of the population in the wake of the war. This happened again in the Great Depression. From 1935 to 1939, Polish Jewry became the object of administrative and economic discrimination and of physical attacks in towns and villages. Fatalities and injuries were at least equal in number to those of 1918–19.[18]

Hungary's "White Terror," following the overthrow in the summer of 1919 of a Communist government headed by Bela Kun, a Jew, brought pogroms to a nation in which Jews had been a favored and prosperous minority for over half a century. Made fearful and traumatized by their own loss of power and status, the old elites who had protected them were no longer able or willing to do so. Along with other Hungarians, many of these elites viewed the terror unleashed by the right as necessary for the defense of their interests and of the fatherland against leftists and Jews. Both were viewed as carriers of an alien ideology and agents of a foreign power, and little distinction was made between Marxists and Magyar patriots when undetermined numbers of Jews were killed in some fifty towns, usually by soldiers or armed bands.[19]

Czechoslovakia's emergence out of the tribulations of war and revolution was similarly marred by outbursts of popular antisemitism, notwithstanding the sympathies of its liberal founders for the Jewish minority. The "pogrom-like incidents" reported from all parts of the state were far less destructive, however, than those in Poland and Hungary and of shorter duration. Only in Slovakia, which the armies of Bela Kun had tried to recover for the short-lived Hungarian Soviet Republic, did long-standing complaints against Jewish estate-owners and innkeepers, now fused with denunciations of Jewish Bolsheviks and Magyarizers, turn into major violence.[20]

Not even the nearly total extermination of Poland's Jews in the Nazi death camps could save the remnant from what has been called "the most savage pogrom in Polish history." Forty-two men, women, and children were massacred in the city of Kielce on 4 July 1946, and many more – 1,500 according to one source – lost their lives between the end of the war and the summer of 1947. What, if anything; who, if anyone, provoked this last and, in view of the time and place, most vicious assault upon a defenseless and decimated minority, remains in doubt. The strength of traditional Jew-hatred, made worse by the example of the Germans and the ruinous effects of their occupation, may be a sufficient explanation. It would make unnecessary the hypothesis of Jews being killed because some of them served, or welcomed, the new communist government and its Soviet masters. Here as elsewhere, though more improbably, the detonation of deep-seated communal enmities has been ascribed to conspiratorial instigation. A British intelligence officer is said to have organized pogroms in order to destabilize the Communist regime and weaken its hold.[21]

Jewishness, with whatever negative connotations the larger society attached to it, was evidently the irreducible common denominator in all these attacks; it cannot account for their timing, severity, and origination. How they came to be started, just how large was the part played in each by spontaneous combustion, incitement, organization, and orchestration is as difficult to establish in this as in most forms of group violence. So is the measurement of how much of it was bound up with, was indeed the expression of, political and social grievances for which Jews became substitute or secondary objects. Finally, it is impossible to ascertain in most cases whether crowd or mob action followed a "natural" rhythm and subsided of its own accord or was subdued only by official force. The spotty historical record cannot furnish unequivocal or uniform answers. It does, however, allow for the making of distinctions and of some general observations.

The most obvious and least contentious of these is that tsarist Russia was neither the birthplace of pogroms nor the only country in which collective violence against Jews occurred and recurred during the nineteenth and twentieth centuries. Nor can the way Europe's governments dealt with their Jewish subjects – that is, their legal status – be considered decisive in determining whether they were set upon by groups of their neighbors over a larger or smaller territory for various periods of time. Pogroms or riots were experienced by Jews who were emancipated and by those who were not, by rich and poor, under monarchical and republican regimes of the most diverse political coloration, in cities as well as in country districts, in times of peace, war, and revolution.

The Hep-Hep movement in particular casts doubt on the proposition advanced by Dubnow that the careful preparation and engineering of the Russian pogrom "epidemic" of 1881 could be inferred from its breaking out in, or spreading to, many places almost at once. Other indications buttressed his conviction that all but sporadic or isolated pogroms were impossible if central and local authorities, and especially the former, were firmly set against them: the toleration of riots for the "customary" two or three days, until they threatened to get out of hand; their resumption in 1882; and their cessation, as if by magic, when at last St. Petersburg made clear that they must cease.[22]

Evidence from Germany in 1819, as well as from other times and places, indicates that large and small eruptions were rarely, if ever, the result of prior planning or coordination. Discrimination and propaganda, by pointing to Jews as the source of popular discontents and miseries, made them particularly susceptible to attacks which antisemitic agitators and organizations may have helped to spread. They did so in Germany (1881), France (1898), and Poland (1936). But none of these outbreaks was attributed to deliberate, much less careful, organization. Where such a charge was made, as in Poland after the Second World War, it has not been substantiated. Only in conditions of near anarchy, of ethnic and civil war, such as befell Poland and Hungary in 1919, can wholesale assaults upon Jews be said to have originated in the license consciously given to armed men to cleanse their country of its external and internal foes. Even then, it is an open question how much of the brutality can be laid to the brutalization and ill-discipline of the perpetrators and how much to the direction and permissiveness of their superiors and betters.

There was, in fact, no common pattern to the beginning of anti-Jewish violence. It might start with a tavern brawl, the drunken hooliganism of newly inducted recruits, the rumor that a Christian child had been abducted, the arrest of youthful troublemakers by gendarmes, a Jew's resistance to being insulted or robbed, or his mere presence in a public place. Riots could also be in the nature of an annual rite, taking place on Good Friday or Easter, during fairs or market days. They could be the accompaniments of revolutions or rebellions in which Jews were attacked along with other symbols of old and new oppression: tax collectors, manor houses, convents, machines, and railroads. They occurred during political crises and heated electoral contests, with partisans of one or another side decrying Jewish machinations, money, and numbers as a threat to themselves or the nation.[23]

Whether a given incident escalated into a full-fledged riot was influenced by a variety of factors and conditions, from the political to the meteorological. It could be, but rarely was, simply a function of the steps authority took or failed to take. No form or level of government viewed the excesses of turbulent crowds with equanimity; yet how quickly and efficiently they were or could be controlled depended on a number of variables. What guardians of the public peace felt about Jews might be one of these. In most places and in normal times – that is, when structures and lines of authority were intact – the prejudices harbored by policemen and soldiers, officers and officials, did not keep them from doing their duty. From 1819 to 1918, disciplined commitment to the maintenance of order was the rule. Suspicions that major deviations from it were inspired by anti-Jewish sentiments can neither be dismissed nor documented. It is probable that delay or an apparent lack of vigor in restraining a mob and protecting Jews usually had other causes. In all but the biggest cities, the regular police were too few to cope with civil disorders of any magnitude. By the time it was realized how large and unruly they had become and troops were summoned, valuable hours and days could be lost, which multiplied if a garrison was some distance away. Even when military units intervened forcefully, they did not always prevail until reinforced. On occasion, rioters were enraged rather than cowed by the resistance they met. The problem of control was complicated if disorders engulfed a larger territory in an unpredictable, wave-like fashion. Yet in all of them, property suffered more often than did persons; there were few injuries and fewer fatalities among the attacked.

This did not change until the First World War and its aftershocks introduced violence on a vast scale into the lives of millions, habituated them to its exercise, and weakened inner and outer restraints. One can only speculate whether it was the latter or the former that deserve most credit for the comparatively lower level of destructiveness and brutality that distinguished European pogroms from their Russian counterparts. The discipline and professionalism of army and police were surely important; so was the refusal of the state to countenance violence from below and a high regard for law and order in the relatively stable bourgeois societies of the West. The safeguards the middle and upper strata demanded for themselves, they were prepared to extend most readily to those Jews they recognized as members, if lesser members, of their class. In that respect, emancipation, or merely the expansion of residential and occupational rights, made Jews less conspicuously different in the urban setting. It allowed some to achieve a prosperity and prominence that carried a measure of influence, even of power. Larger numbers had been enabled to leave the backward, agrarian sectors where their economic role, their traditional way of life, their very appearance had facilitated their being singled out as alien exploiters. The rights the European states conferred were a contract which could not be breached without damaging the social and legal norms on which they rested. In Russia, where these norms – like the contract between state and society – were less fully developed and accepted, greater reliance was placed on control and command, and these were tested more severely than in the rest of Europe.

II

Measured by the calamities that befell Russian Jewry in 1905 and the Civil War, its sufferings in 1881–2 appear minor. The greatest hurt may have been psychic, leading many to abandon hope for a gradual but certain improvement of their condition. Compared with earlier manifestations of anti-Jewish hostility, however, the pogroms of the eighties were as painful in their material as in their emotional impact and could not be shrugged off as isolated incidents. Property damage, through the looting and destruction of homes and businesses, was estimated at 9 to 10 million roubles and the number of affected families at 60,000, of whom 20,000 were made homeless. The deepest and most lasting trauma was inflicted by reports, most likely exaggerated, of physical assaults on men, women, and children and of injuries, killings, and rapes. No reliable count of victims exists, and the number of dead, which has been placed at anywhere from fifty to "a few hundred," appears to have been comparatively small. But even if only property were lost, this betokened a greater malevolence and insecurity than Jews had theretofore experienced in the Russian Empire or in contemporary Europe.[24]

Given that fact, given the length and breadth of the troubles and the reactionary course upon which Alexander III and his ministers embarked, it is not surprising that they should have been blamed for this turn of events. But the oft-repeated charges that the government, or some conspiratorial group acting with or without its knowledge, was responsible, have been disproved by the investigations of I. M. Aronson and M. J. Ochs, exemplified by their contributions to this volume. Their careful reading of the documentary record, their interpretations of the conduct, capabilities, and calculations of the authorities and their presumed auxiliaries, demonstrate that it was not in the interest or power of either to unleash a storm of terror upon the Jews. Officialdom at all levels, no less than Jews, revolutionaries, and members of the Holy League, were surprised by the pogroms, unprepared for the scope and persistence of the riots which continued in spite of the authorities' efforts at pacification through orders and exhortations. All suspicions of official, semi-official, or unofficial preparation and orchestration having been shown to be unfounded, spontaneity must be listed above all others in the hierarchy of proximate causes.

The very first outbreak, which set off the rest, began in the most ordinary manner: with a quarrel between a Jewish taverner and one of his customers during Easter week in Elisavetgrad (Kherson Province), notwithstanding the precautionary measures taken by a conscientious and fair-minded chief of police. Although little was or perhaps could be done to prevent riots before their actual occurrence, once it was realized that they were not isolated or occasional, minor clashes, the Ministry of the Interior and its provincial agents issued the appropriate instructions and condemnations. This was as true of the anti-Jewish Ignatiev as it was of his more liberal predecessor Loris-Melikov. Both Totleben and his colleague at Ekaterinoslav, Governor I. N. Durnovo, issued stern, cautionary proclamations. The so-called Northwest Region commanded by the former (the provinces of Vilna, Kovno, and Grodno) remained at peace; Ekaterinoslav did not. In Kiev, the capital of the Southwest Region (the provinces of Kiev, Volynia, and Podolia), Governor-General A. R. Drenteln, a military man with a well-deserved reputation as a Jew-hater, placed police and troops on alert and ordered the suppression of any disorders which might begin. An incipient riot in Kiev was, in fact, stifled, but a few days later, on Sunday 26 April, a major and most destructive pogrom broke out. Neither Drenteln's personal appeals and intervention – he was at one point thrown to the ground by a rush of looters he interrupted at their work – nor the rifles of his soldiers, who killed one person and wounded two on 27 April, were able to restore calm before three days and nights had passed.[25]

In some places this was achieved more quickly, giving rise to the question whether the authorities on the spot might not have acted with greater swiftness, decisiveness, and rigor. Drenteln, for example, was faulted for not employing firearms until the second day. In Elisavetgrad, troops were withdrawn prematurely because all seemed quiet. When recalled they remained inactive for several hours and the crowd took this to be approbation. Warsaw was haphazardly patrolled during the December disorders, and not until the worst had passed was a systematic plan for its pacification implemented. In Odessa, foresight and firmness limited damage; nonetheless, rioting continued for four days. Both Count P. I. Kutaisov, the Tsar's special emissary to the pogrom region, and the Committee of Ministers deplored the widespread failure to muster the resoluteness required for the prompt repression of violence. In conscious or unconscious ways, lack of sympathy for the unpopular minority they were called upon to defend may have contributed to delay and restraint on the part of some administrators and officers. But more compelling and pragmatic considerations provide a better explanation for their conduct, especially of the senior ranks who would have to answer for any negligence to St. Petersburg.[26]

To begin with, there was a genuine reluctance to shoot into unarmed crowds, whatever the nature of the disturbance, until all other means of persuasion had been exhausted. The calling of troops by civilian authorities was itself a confession of failure and made more difficult by the resistance of military commanders to having their men do the work of the police, which was considered distasteful and demoralizing. Neither psychologically nor by training, experience, and numbers were the armed forces equipped for crowd control in such large-scale and wide-spread urban confrontations as the pogroms.[27]

When the Tsar, angered by the recurrence of pogroms in 1882, demanded that everything be done to prevent and stop them, his new Minister of the Interior, Dmitri Tolstoi, wrote to the Minister of War that there were too few troops in the south and southwest. He insisted not only on their augmentation and subordination to the police, but called for a redeployment of the army to meet internal security needs. The War Ministry rejected his proposal, on grounds stated, among others, by Drenteln: strategic considerations had to be paramount and the stationing of troops where disorders were not actually expected made impossible their training, as had already happened in the summer of 1881. They were, nonetheless, called upon ever more frequently, to the great annoyance of the generals who warned that using soldiers as policemen and having them fire on their countrymen would make them unreliable and unavailable to defend the nation's frontiers. To the end of the old regime, the regulations governing the use of troops in civil disturbances were in dispute between the military and their colleagues in the civil bureaucracy, with a resultant lack of clarity as to when, by whom, and how they were to be committed and commanded.[28]

Even where garrisons were of substantial size and led by resolute commanders, they were rarely handled with the requisite skill, being split up into too many small detachments or dispersed over too wide a territory. Nor could the lower ranks always be trusted to proceed vigorously against "their own people" on behalf of Jews. Alexander III declared himself saddened and disturbed by reports that some soldiers would have preferred to attack Jews rather than rioters. In several instances, they sympathized and drank with looters, accepted stolen goods from them and sometimes released those they had caught. When the apparently exceptional case of an officer who had taken part in a pogrom was brought to the Emperor's attention, he called it a disgrace. Such behavior and outright dereliction of duty, though rare, were most frequent among the lowest level of officialdom and the woefully undermanned, ill-paid, and poorly trained provincial police units. Their inadequacies and undependability had been cause for concern long before 1881, when some of the rank and file showed little inclination to risk life and limb fighting neighbors and coreligionists whose anti-Jewish feelings they shared. There were cases when, confronted and outnumbered by angry crowds whom verbal warnings or warning shots did not deter, they retreated until rallied by superiors or reinforced.[29]

Testimony to the obstinacy of crowds, which was experienced not only by lonely and lowly policemen, is abundant. In Borispol (Poltava province), rioters, most of them drunk, attacked the district police officer and a lieutenant of gendarmes who had called upon them to disperse; the latter was knocked off his feet (or horse) by a brick thrown at his back. Not until the shots of Cossack rifles had killed and wounded several of the crowd did the rest take to their heels. In Kiev, Cossacks withdrew before a hail of stones and one of their officers was beaten while a gendarme colonel was unable to stop a group of marauders. Mobs prevented the arrest of rioters or freed them in several places and even put small military units to

flight. The American Embassy reported from St. Petersburg that the
police had not dared to interfere in some of the worst outrages and
that railroad officials had refused to run trains for Jewish refugees
because they feared attacks from infuriated mobs "debauched with
liquor and plunder."[30]

Failure to have immediate recourse to firearms may have been
dictated also by the possibility of its enraging rather than pacifying
pogrom-makers. This was demonstrated in Smela (Kiev province) at
the time of the bi-weekly fair. A large mass of workers from local
factories and workshops, as well as peasants who had come from
nearby villages with their wives and carts, reacted to verbal
warnings and blank shots with cries of "don't shoot," advanced
upon the outnumbered soldiers, and threatened their officers when
gunfire killed two of the crowd. Additional troops were summoned,
but did not arrive until twenty-six hours later.[31] The presence of
women and children or curious bystanders was another deterrent to
the prompt and massive application of deadly force. It was ultimately
effective when brought into play, but there were many possible
reasons for withholding it besides the subtle or not-so-subtle workings
of prejudice: lack of foresight and experience, sheer incompetence,
irresolution, divided authority and confusion. To account for the
unruliness of townsmen and peasants is a more difficult and
speculative enterprise; it was not an altogether novel phenomenon,
but since the cholera riots of 1830–1 it had rarely become so
worrisome and explosive.

Refusing to accept as genuine the emancipation edict of 19
February 1861 because it did not give them all they thought their
due, peasants of Bezdna and neighboring villages in Kazan province
gathered by the thousands to demand true freedom (*volia*) in the
name of the Tsar. Their conviction, fed by rumors, that the ruler
sided with them in their quarrel with landlords and officials, made
them ignore repeated exhortations to return to their homes and
fields until several volleys of infantry fire killed at least fifty and
wounded hundreds. Ten years later Odessa became the scene of the
largest pogrom before 1881; it was also the longest and largest urban
disturbance in forty years and was not quelled completely until the
fourth day. During Easter week of 1872, the streets of the Ukrainian
city of Kharkov were virtually taken over for two days by unruly
holiday makers, many of them industrial workers, who had been
angered by efforts to restrain them. They routed the fire brigade and

the police, broke into precinct stations where they scattered or destroyed the files, and stoned the governor. Troops brought from Kursk and Poltava were unable to restore order until reinforced.[32]

A number of factors came together in 1881 that help to explain why stubbornness in the face of authority coincided with or was occasioned by the harassment of Jews. The resentments and discontents the lower classes of town and country harbored were aggravated for many during and after the Russo-Turkish War of 1877–8. Peasants expected at its end to receive new allotments of land from a gracious sovereign; poor harvests in several southwestern provinces deepened their yearning and increased their bitterness when hoped-for benefactions did not materialize. Their disappointments were shared in the towns where between one and two-thirds of the inhabitants were peasants who had temporarily or permanently left their villages in search of work and bread only to find a scarcity of both, low wages, and high prices. It was about these, the common people, the masses, that a perceptive minister of the Tsar wrote in 1879 that they were easily reached by rumors or promises of some new grants or favors: "Under the influence of these rumors and promises, they are capable of refusing to submit to the nearest governmental authorities and seek out enemies where the authorities do not perceive any."[33]

Jews had, however, already been singled out as ruthless exploiters and competitors of the simple people in the early years of the decade by the governors-general of New Russia and the southwest. Their analyses of conditions in the territories entrusted to them reflected and influenced a growing body of opinion which linked the evils attendant upon the spread of capitalist commerce and industry with the sudden influx of Jewish traders and entrepreneurs. For a larger public this identification was facilitated in the sluggish economy of the late 1870s by several newspapers which pilloried the profiteering of Jewish army contractors during the Turkish war in particular and the abuse of their excessive economic power by Jews in general. *Novoe vremia*, a St. Petersburg daily, led this campaign and in March 1880 sounded the alarm: "The Yid is Coming." The press had gained a genuinely popular audience during war, and even in the villages, where literacy was abysmally low, the arrival of the newspaper and its being read out were eagerly awaited and its contents discussed. What the press or its readers articulated created a broader awareness for what many had already observed for themselves: the presence of large numbers of Jews where there had once been few or none and the visibility of what Dubnow called a "new Jewish plutocracy."[34]

This development had its beginnings in the New Russian territories of which Odessa was the center and which had first been opened to Jewish settlement by Catherine the Great. In 1794, 246 of Odessa's 2,345 inhabitants were Jews. Between 1854 and 1892, their numbers grew from 17,080 (18·9 percent of the total) to 112,235 (33 percent). The numbers of Jews in Kiev grew thirty-six times in the half century between 1860 and 1910, whereas the general population increased 6·7 times, with most of the Jewish increase occurring in the first half of that period. What was happening in the thriving cosmopolitan city on the Black Sea and in the capital of the Ukraine replicated events and trends throughout the southern provinces. Only 2·5 percent of the country's Jews had lived there in 1847; fifty years later it was 13·8 percent. A selective easing of residential and occupational restrictions in the first decade of Alexander II's reign, a kind of mini- or pre-emancipation, and a benign business climate had greatly accelerated Jewish outmigration from Lithuania and Belorussia. New laws and new opportunities also favored the rise of a small but important group of wealthy manufacturers, entrepreneurs, and prominent professionals. Negative reactions to the increase in Jewish rights, numbers, and riches were magnified when economic misfortune struck individuals or the region as a whole.[35]

Nowhere was the Jewish "threat" to status, livelihood, and power reflected more clearly than in the interpretations contemporaries offered of the pogroms and the remedies they proposed. Charges of Jewish impertinence, insolence, and rapaciousness, the abuse of rights granted, the displacement of Christian doctors and grain brokers, railroad employees and common laborers, had already figured in official reports and the press as a cause of the Odessa troubles in 1871. Ten years later, that indictment was repeated almost in its entirety in Count Kutaisov's account of the pogroms. Just one generation, he reported, had seen humble Jewish middlemen turn into millionaires, factory owners, and landed proprietors and, what was worse, becoming ever more impudent. That is what seemed to rankle most and was objected to time and again – the demand, as Kutaisov put it, "that the native population honor and respect this moneyed aristocracy. The people became indignant at their behavior and could not get used to the idea of having to acknowledge the Jews as their 'masters.'" Their very character had changed, another official complained. Where they had once been a quiet element, timid and frightened, they no longer knew limits or modesty and even engaged in politics. Both Jewish effrontery and greed had to be reined in, Drenteln declared, a sentiment found all across the social spectrum. It was strongest where a significant, assertive Jewish presence was of recent date and therefore especially unsettling.[36]

Pereiaslav in Poltava province, where the Jewish population had almost tripled since 1847, provides a telling illustration. By putting and keeping Jews in their place, small traders and craftsmen (*meshchane*) thought to allay their own anxieties and prevent the recurrence of the pogrom that had raged in their city from 30 June to 2 July 1881, a pogrom in which some of them most likely took part. Before a local committee that had been formed at the governor's behest to find ways of "removing the abnormal relations between Christians and Jews," representatives of the *meshchanstvo* repeated earlier demands that Jewish newcomers be expelled and made additional ones that revealed the range and depth of their concerns. Prominent Jews were to resign from their positions in local government, on various public boards and committees, for which vanity and presumption had made them reach. Their women were urged to display in their dress and demeanor the modesty appropriate to their station and not to flaunt the silk, velvet, pearls, and gold that came from the "sweat, blood, and tears of the unfortunate Russian people." For the sake of their moral and physical well-being, Christian women should no longer serve in Jewish homes and Jews should cease to denigrate and belittle Christian townsmen. But humbling Jews, the latter realized, was not the best or only way to protect status and interests. As many proposals were made, in several towns, for inhibiting Jewish business activities (including calls for their expulsion and the destruction of machinery they had introduced) as for teaching them humility.[37]

At the lowest end of the social scale, resentments and opinions were expressed not by petitions or delegations, but by stones, sticks, and shouts. These were directed physically against the taverns and shops of Jews and verbally against their supposed eminence and power, symbolized for the Kiev rioters by a local family of brewers and sugar magnates. "Brodskii" or "To Brodskii's" was their cry, along with "Enough of the Jews lording it...they have grasped

everything...Everything costs dear and we suffer because of them."
Although targets and formulations may have been inspired rather
than homegrown, the repetition of such cries and actions in many
places shows that they were grounded in real experiences, values,
and feelings. Otherwise it is hard to understand why so many rioters
expressed disbelief when they, rather than Jews, were attacked or
punished. To do so seemed an inversion of the moral order, a sheer
perversity which was evidence that the Jews had bought the military
and the police.

Migrants from the inner-Russian provinces, from which most Jews
were barred, must have been especially affronted, their sense of the
fitness of things violated, when they met members of this despised
and alien group as rival job seekers, as employers, as buyers or sellers
of prime necessities. The "barefoot brigades," those homeless, roving
bands of laborers who were in several localities the main perpetrators
of pogroms, consisted for the most part of members of the peasant
estate who had, like most Jews with whom they clashed, fled from
poverty to the towns, ports, factories, and workshops of the south.
The other social category identified most often among arrested
rioters were *meshchane*, townsmen of the lower class. In Elisavetgrad,
for example, among 488 rioters whose status is known, the
meshchane formed the largest contingent with 181, closely followed
by 177 peasants; only 72 of these were locals, the rest coming from
three Ukrainian and five Great Russian provinces. In Kiev, where
202 peasants were the biggest group among those detained, more
than half came from outside the province, a third more from outside
the region. Of 379 individuals arrested in the city, 81 were
meshchane.[38] In Odessa, 453 peasants led the list (of 1,270 detainees
whose social category could be established; the total was 1,385),
followed by 376 meshchane and 313 ex-soldiers. They, or reservists,
also formed the third largest group in Kiev and some other cities.[39]

If the pogroms, as has been pointed out, were primarily and
originally an urban phenomenon and a projection of the fast-
growing southern cities' social and ethnic tensions, they also
reflected, as did the cities themselves – some of them no more than
overgrown villages – the problems of rural Russia and its people.
Not only did the disorders spread to the countryside or peasants
come from there with their carts to share in the pillage once they had
begun. Most of the railway and construction workers, the day
laborers, freight handlers, and vagrants among the pogromshchiki

were peasants who had left their villages recently or temporarily. "*Prishlyi liud*" (newcomers, drifters), the governor of Kherson called them, and "a restless element." The discontents which had made them walk or ride great distances for a better livelihood were worsened rather than assuaged in raw industrial settlements or urban slums and their awareness of being Russian or Ukrainian was heightened in a multi-ethnic environment. Often without regular employment, shelter, and the steadying influence of the families they had left behind, their disgruntlement and disorientation made them give credence to the tales of Jewish perfidy which circulated after the assassination of Alexander II on 1 March 1881 by members of the "People's Will."[40]

There can be no doubt that the killing of the "Tsar–Liberator" was part of the causal pattern of the pogroms, if for no other reason than that the accession of a new ruler, whatever the circumstances, always gave rise to expectations of the most varied kind, to fears and uncertainty. In 1881, after a period of mounting revolutionary terror, liberal calls for reform, and wavering at the heights of power, the First of March was followed by two months or more of panic, rumors, and alarms. Almost every report from the provinces spoke of the Jewish role in the conspiracy that had aimed at Russia's ruin by regicide. Disseminated by local rabble rousers and mischievous rumor mongers, such stories came to fix upon the Jews as solely or primarily responsible for the evil deed which, it was claimed, the martyred Tsar's son now permitted, or even ordered, avenged. The tale circulated in Elisavetgrad before the first pogrom and widely thereafter, leading a gendarme commander in Kiev to express doubt whether quiet would quickly return to that city. "The common people are too strongly aroused against the Jews whom they accuse of the murder of the Tsar and of economic oppression."[41]

In Kiev also, suspicious individuals were telling illiterate folk that the Tsar had commanded the beating of Jews and *pany* (Polish: landlords, masters) for killing his father. Whether they thought doing so was authorized or not, felt stirred up by the few revolutionary handbills they saw, or willfully misinterpreted what they heard, peasants in a number of instances believed and said that once the Jews were dealt with, it was the turn of the landlords whose estates they would divide. In rioters' minds, both were antagonists, most certainly outsiders if Polish, and treated as such when the opportunity arose, with little regard for their rights and none for their property. In the case of the Jews, the disparity between their legal and social inferiority on the one hand and their real or imagined economic power on the other was a constant irritant, as well as a virtual warrant or provocation to attack them in politically or economically troubled times. The people, Kutaisov wrote, were convinced that settling scores with Jews was not a crime since they did not enjoy the same rights as other citizens. Their rightlessness did, indeed, embolden and envenom their attackers.[42]

To see the events of 1881 as growing out of social distress and ethno-religious antagonism is the larger part of the story, but not the whole of it. Besides these deeper causes and favoring conditions of a temporary nature, accident played its part, as did ordinary greed, envy, and malice, which habit and culture easily turned against Jews. Accident and malice did their work on Christmas Day in Warsaw. During morning services in a Catholic church, a shout of "Fire" started a stampede in which some thirty worshippers were crushed to death. Another cry, that Jewish thieves had sounded the false alarm, was taken up, and the pogrom that would continue for three days began at two o'clock. Taunting or beating Jews could also be the Sunday or even May Day recreation of drunken rowdies and workers smashing and looting their homes and shops; peasants plundering them a form of opportunistic appropriation. Their raids on Jewish agricultural colonies can certainly be considered as such.[43]

During the final two decades of the century there were only sporadic pogroms. Few of these were of sufficient seriousness to have attracted the notice of historians, who did not lay them at the door of the government or its agents. Nonetheless, the very fitfulness of these disturbances, their failure to come together in a wave, were seen as proof that this could easily have been prevented in 1881 and strengthened suspicions that the will rather than the ability to do so had then been lacking. Measures of control and containment may, in fact, have been improved in subsequent years. A law of 1891 established criminal liability "for open attacks of one part of the population upon another" and the Galician pogroms led to increased watchfulness on the Russian side of the frontier. Yet neither in the manner in which they arose, nor in the way they were dealt with, did the isolated clashes of the 1880s and 1890s differ from their predecessors. Except for the killing of a Tsar, the same superficial and deeper causes, lesser frictions and larger grievances, were operative in the same areas of the Empire, with but two geographical exceptions: Nizhnii-Novgorod (1884) and Lodz (1892). That the greater vigilance of the authorities alone prevented a recurrence of the earlier epidemic is doubtful; more likely it was a lower level of distress and anxiety.[44]

Only in the metallurgical and mining center of Iuzovka is it possible to connect the serious workers' riot and pogrom of 1892 with a national catastrophe – the famine of 1891 which struck the central provinces and the cholera epidemic which followed in its wake. Neither directly affected Ekaterinoslav province and the Donets basin in which Iuzovka was located. But the "half-starved, ill-clothed workers [who] wandered wearily hundreds or even thousands of versts" from their homes in Tula, Kursk, and other stricken areas carried the disease with them to the crowded slums and hovels of the factory settlement whose population had doubled between 1889 and 1891. Medical and police initiatives to keep the plague from spreading to Iuzovka gave added nourishment to the workers' anger and to their distrust of bosses, officials, and foreigners.

Trouble began on a Sunday with the looting of food shops and taverns and the stoning of constables and Cossacks who were forced to withdraw and to surrender the prisoners they had taken. Not until Monday, with the central bazaar already in ruins, did a still larger crowd, having been turned away from a factory office building, attack the homes and shops of Jews. Although from the start there was invective against Jewish doctors for "poisoning our brothers" – as there had been against non-Jewish doctors elsewhere during the cholera – Jews were only the secondary target of the riot. In every other respect, it replicated a familiar sequence of popular exasperation, its violent expression, and relatively quick suppression.[45] In the much larger and longer convulsions and confusions of 1905, pogroms against Jews were both a product of revolution and a form of reaction against it, seen or welcomed as such by those defenders of the autocracy who had come to identify and denounce Jews as the spearhead of the radical opposition.[46]

III

Kishinev, which became a by-word for pogrom throughout much of the world, has often been viewed in the light of 1905 as one of the preliminary engagements fought by the counter-revolution. It did, in its bloodiness, presage what was to happen two years later. For all the signs of preparation by a reactionary local newspaper, agitators, and organizers; in spite of its negligent or criminal toleration by key officials on the spot, the violence still bore familiar features: its outbreak on Easter Sunday, the use of the ritual murder libel, the complaint that Jews were too powerful in the city's government and economy.

Since the Bessarabian capital (or province, for that matter) was not a center of revolutionary activity, of industrial or agrarian unrest, to stage a pogrom there – as Minister of the Interior Viacheslav Pleve was charged with doing – as a warning to disaffected elements, and Jews in particular, was bound to be an enterprise of dubious utility. Its very "success," which not even its fomenters could have foretold, embarrassed the putative sponsors in government and proved to be counterproductive. The provincial gendarme administration noted a closing of ranks on the part of all revolutionaries and an increase in their activities. Pleve, although he showed no sympathy for the victims, agreed: what had taken place was inadmissible; it discredited the local authorities, complicated matters at the center, and must not be allowed to happen again.[47]

The death and devastation wrought at Kishinev were due chiefly to the pusillanimous dithering of the governor, who made late and ineffective use of the troops at his disposal and did not, until a day and a half had passed, give the garrison commander the full authority he had requested to deploy his units as he saw fit. "The Kishinev pogrom serves as a sorry indictment of the state of civil-military relations...in Russia," their foremost student has written. If this was not new, neither was official antisemitism nor the circumstances and conditions which had created an audience for the preaching of Jew-hatred and facilitated its mobilization.[48]

Jews, who in 1847 accounted for 12 percent of the city's population, made up 46·3 percent in 1897; 80 to 90 percent of local industry – mainly small enterprises processing agricultural products – were in Jewish hands, as were the large commercial firms, warehouses, and printing presses. The bulk of Kishinev's Jews, however, were small traders, shopkeepers, artisans, and laborers who were no better off than their Christian counterparts and competitors; like them they suffered from the depression which set in at the end of the 1890s. The number of Jewish families in need of charity nearly doubled between 1895 and 1900 and a survey of the province's economy registered in 1902 a steady decline in the income of all trades, their growing competition and impoverishment. In a city of mixed ethnicity, which owed its growth mainly to in-migration (of Russians and Ukrainians, as well as Jews), local concerns and conflicts over status and livelihood were as important as local rabble rousers in providing men and motives for a pogrom, and more important than the possible machinations of distant bureaucrats.[49]

The latter cannot be taxed with arranging the violence at Gomel (Mogilev province) in September 1903 or the more than forty incidents that occurred over a wide area in 1904, about half of them staged by reservists mobilized for the war with Japan. Men called to the colors had been known to riot and attack Jews in peacetime; their behavior in 1904 foreshadowed the frustrations that unruly peasant-soldiers discharged against them and other civilians a year later.[50]

Events in Gomel were equally ominous. Beginning with an altercation between a Jewish tradeswoman and her customer, they led to a free-for-all in which a peasant was killed and which, with the help of rumors and calls for revenge, escalated into a full-scale pogrom, in spite of the orders Pleve had issued after Kishinev and the best efforts of the city's chief of police. The troops he summoned put a stop to the rampage, which was led by workers of the railway shops and joined by peasants from nearby villages, but in the process army units killed and wounded several Jews as well as rioters.

This was a first: the victimization of the intended victims by those charged with their protection. Here, in a stronghold of Jewish proletarian radicalism, a lesson might usefully be taught, and it was administered, apparently without premeditation but also without regrets or apologies, to members of the Bund's armed fighting squads. These had been formed earlier in the year in various cities of the Pale for the defense of the party's demonstrations and Jewish communities. At Gomel, 200 squad members (some 30 of them Christians) had succeeded in limiting damage and casualties; they had also inflicted them. Confused and conflicting accounts make it impossible to reconstruct precisely what took place, whether the officers in command of army units deliberately shielded pogromists or moved as vigorously against them as against the Bundist defenders. That the latter did engage the military was, however, admitted by the Bund itself. It did not, as charged by the authorities, plan and prepare a "Russian pogrom" to avenge Kishinev. But the Bund's members were proud to have demonstrated their courage to themselves and the world with arms and determination. They did so again in 1905.[51]

It was their greatest crime, the principal point of the indictment made against the Bund in 1903 and final proof of the leading part Jews were said and believed to be playing in the revolutionary movement. The official fixation on Jewish subversion as the prime source of Russia's troubles was certainly misguided. It could reach pathological dimensions, as in Foreign Minister V. N. Lamzdorf's "analysis" of the 1905 Revolution, an event which should, in its depth and breadth, have demonstrated the insubstantiality of the charge. Yet that the Jewish contribution, in word and deed, to the offensive against autocracy was substantial, and disproportionately so, had been true (and understandable) since the 1880s and was demonstrated again at the turn of the century, when the Bund became the first and largest Marxist party in the Empire.[52]

Such facts and fears created or strengthened a disposition on the part of hard-pressed conservatives inside and outside of government to look upon pogroms as a comprehensible, even legitimate form of self-defense by loyal Russians, and by some as a way of rallying support and intimidating opponents. No pogrom policy or system, as it has been called, was adopted by the government, approved by its responsible ministers or the Tsar. But the extremity of their situation made them, and therefore their subordinates, less willing and able, in psychological as well as practical terms, to oppose, to speak out against, and to punish outrages against Jews committed by men who claimed to be acting in the name of Tsar and fatherland. Failure to do so gave rise to a belief in the "indulgent wink" of the authorities. The restraints and rationality that were operative in and after 1881 had been weakened by 1905, when not merely property and public order were at stake but the very survival of the regime. In that process, Gomel marked a turning point, less in what was done there to Jews by pogromists and soldiers than in subsequent interpretations of what transpired.[53]

The very first of these, offered by Governor Klingenberg of Mogilev, set the tone. He told a delegation of Gomel Jews that they bore the moral responsibility for the hostility that brought death and suffering to their people. It was not caused, as were the troubles twenty years before, by Jews exploiting Christians, but by their leadership and initiation of every anti-governmental movement, of the Bund and all Social Democracy. Jews had become insolent and insubordinate; they no longer respected the established authorities. "Always and everywhere they manifest their contempt and intolerance for Christians," the governor declared, and to illustrate the extreme impudence of which Jews were guilty, he mentioned the bicyclist who had run into his wife and the gymnasium student who had failed to apologize for accidentally brushing up against the person of Her Excellency.

You no longer bring up your children as you should, you cover up for them... You spread the ideas of disobedience and rebellion among the uneducated classes; but the Russian people do not want this and turn against you... Jews arming themselves and firing upon troops who are there to protect them – has there ever been anything like it? Under such circumstances it is not for us to defend you; we must defend ourselves against you.[54]

Jews who were tried, along with their attackers, for the disturbances at Gomel, were similarly accused: not merely of acts they had supposedly committed, but of conduct and attitudes which the state prosecutor found as offensive and provocative as the governor. Since the proceedings, unlike those of Kishinev, were held in open court, there was seemingly no fear that official sins of omission or commission would be revealed. On the other hand, the indictment and trial could serve as a warning against the formation of self-defense units and a declaration that in this, as in other respects, Jews had transgressed the limits of the permissible. That alone can explain the inclusion in a judicial document of ill-tempered criticism of their misbehavior.

The Jews of the city of Gomel... have in the recent past not only borne themselves arrogantly but even defiantly. Insults by Jews to peasants and workers have occurred ever more frequently; even towards members of the educated Russian public they have been openly scornful; for example, forcing even army officers to make way for them on a sidewalk and being rude to Christian customers in stores.[55]

To equate and arraign, in virtually the same breath, as both Klingenberg and the prosecution had done, armed resistance and bad manners, shows how profoundly they were shaken by the Jews' refusal to remain in the inferior position to which law and custom consigned them. Challenges to state authority, to the dominance and superiority of Russians, did not of course, come exclusively from Jews. Nor were these challenges resisted and resented only by holders of high office and status. Many ordinary Russians were also upset and frightened by the prospect of radical changes in accustomed patterns of hierarchy and preferment; and it was they – soldiers, policemen, Cossacks, peasants, priests, civil servants, and townsmen of the lower classes – who without and sometimes with the indulgence of their betters and bosses were most active in the pogroms of 1905. The assistant station master at Golta, a small town in Kherson province, spoke for them when he burst out, on learning of the October Manifesto's promises of political and civil rights for all, that now it was time to beat the Jews, "or we'll have to clean their boots."[56]

Just ten days after he had reluctantly put his signature to the October Manifesto, Nicholas II wrote a letter to his mother which is worth quoting at length. Besides displaying his moral insensitivity and dislike of Jews, it describes how substantial numbers of Russians received the news of 17 October, how they responded to the strikes and demonstrations that preceded and followed it.

In the first days after the Manifesto, the bad elements boldly raised their heads, but then a strong reaction set in and the whole mass of loyal people took heart. The result, as is natural and usual with us, was that the people (*narod*) became enraged by the insolence and audacity of the revolutionaries and socialists; and because nine-tenths of them are Yids (*zhidy*), the people's whole wrath has turned against them. That is how the pogroms happened. It is amazing with what unanimity and suddenness they took place in all the towns of Russia and Siberia. In England, of course, they write that these disorders were organized by the police; as always – the old, familiar tale! But not only Yids suffered; so did Russian agitators, engineers, lawyers and such-like vile people. Events in Tomsk, Simferopol, Tver and Odessa showed clearly how far an infuriated crowd can go. They surrounded houses in which revolutionaries had barricaded themselves, set fire to them and killed everyone who came out.[57]

Nicholas' gratification at what loyal Russians were doing was as genuine as his surprise at their doing it simultaneously over widely scattered parts of his Empire. Neither he nor his chief advisers could or did foresee how the concessions which they had expected to tranquilize the country would be received by it. There was confusion and disarray, a loss of confidence and command, at all levels of authority, especially in the provinces. The Manifesto took even governors unawares and they were left to their own devices in coping with the explosive celebrations of victory over autocracy and with counter-demonstrations and attacks upon them by patriots and monarchists. Some governors, higher local officials, and military commanders opposed pogroms determinedly and successfully, against Jews as well as other enemies of Tsar and fatherland; others welcomed or tolerated such violence as part of the battle against revolution; a few abetted it.[58]

In view of such differing reactions, one cannot speak of the pogroms of 1905 as government-sponsored or arranged; not if by government are meant the ruler, the appointed head (Sergei Witte) and members of his cabinet. Nor were the sinister forces and shadowy figures at court, in the bureaucracy, their auxiliaries in the political arena, all those who were indubitably present and willing to move in extra-legal ways against *kramola* (sedition), yet ready to do so in a coordinated fashion. Thus, the pogrom proclamations which a certain Captain Kommisarov arranged to have printed on a secret press in the Police Department, with the knowledge of at least some superiors, did not appear until the worst of the October pogrom wave had spent itself.[59]

The "Black Hundreds," the rightist groups and parties that allegedly distributed and acted upon these appeals, were still in an embryonic state. The largest and most rabid, the Union of Russian People, began to organize on 22 October, was not formally launched until 8 November, and held its first public meeting on 21 November. No provincial branches existed before January (Saratov), February (Odessa), or summer 1906 (Kishinev, Kiev, Pochaev). Moreover, the majority of pogroms erupted almost immediately upon publication of the Manifesto and occurred in provinces that had suffered most heavily in 1881–2. They are best viewed as the combined result of local instigation, tensions, and conservative protest, the outgrowth of the political crisis that had held the country in its grip for a year, rather than the product of central directives. Dubnow's picture of their origin must be discounted: "in hundreds of cities the carefully concealed army of counter-revolutionaries, evidently obeying a prearranged signal, crawled out from beneath the ground to indulge in an orgy of blood."[60] The signal, if there was one, was the October Manifesto itself, and the conflicting ways in which it was interpreted and received. As Professor A. Ascher concluded in his masterly study of 1905:

One cannot agree... that the pogroms began in response to a signal from St. Petersburg or that they would not have taken place at all without official inspiration or approval. The random character of the pogromshchiki's acts of violence, the failure of local officials to follow one clearly defined policy, and the absence of evidence incriminating Witte's government, argue against this interpretation. Most of the officials found wanting were charged not with instigating the disorders but rather with neglecting to take prompt action to end them.[61]

There was more to it, however, than mere neglect; above all, loss of control and self-control, an angry and often blind lashing out against those who had long been known as troublemakers and who were now blamed for the breakdown of order, for the disruptions of daily life and work caused by strikes, demonstrations, and armed clashes. That these did not end on 17 October, but mounted to become virtually a civil war, shocked the holders of power, property, and privilege into a hardened determination to resist further encroachments. It also mobilized elements of the lower strata of town and country. They felt threatened by a revolution that brought no tangible benefits, offended their religious, national, and dynastic sentiments, and was led by men and, *horribile dictu*, women who were perceived as alien: not only Jews and Poles, but also Russians from the other side of the class barrier – professionals, intellectuals, students. It was the confluence of the conservative reaction among the elites and the traditionalist ones among the masses that made for the broad sweep of the pogroms. The foot soldiers of counter-revolution were most numerous where socioeconomic and ethnic tensions were of long standing; they also appeared where months of political conflict and contention had created great confusion and vexation in the popular mind.

Peasants in Chernigov province declared that with the October Manifesto the Tsar had given them permission "to beat the Jews and pany until January." In other provinces, sometimes aroused by the clergy, they threatened teachers, veterinarians, physicians. In one Moscow district they thought the Manifesto a gentry ruse and feared that intelligenty and strikers would come from the capital to despoil their villages. The masses in uniform offer the best illustration of how disorienting the pressures of revolutionary turmoil could be. Some mutinied against the indignities and rigors of their service, as on the cruiser "Potemkin," acted as the unwitting or obedient instruments of repression (in Lodz, Revel, and Moscow, for example) and started or took part in pogroms (Rostov-on-Don, Ekaterinoslav). Workers, too, on occasion "combined revolutionary barricades with the pogrom politics of the Union of Russian People."[62]

Although the overwhelming majority of pogroms was triggered by the Manifesto, fuel for the rightist reaction it provoked had been accumulating for some time. To that process, the antisemitic and reactionary part of the press, clergy, and bureaucracy made an essential contribution, as did the Imperial Manifesto of 18 February 1905 which called on loyal Russians to unite against their foreign and domestic foes. It could be taken as a summons to organize and to act but before October organization remained weak and scattered, while action against Jews and others remained until then largely the work of policemen and soldiers. Exasperated and demoralized, outnumbered and under almost constant stress, taunts, and attacks, they went on rampages against their presumed tormentors, sometimes quite aimlessly, especially in the non-Russian borderlands. But reports of violence by (and against) police and Cossack charges against innocent civilians, demonstrators, and strikers came from all over the country beginning in early 1905.

The police of Kursk brutally beat and dispersed student demonstrators with the help of peasants. The marshal of the Tambov nobility mobilized "Black Hundred" ruffians to prevent political action by the zemstvo. In a townlet of Mogilev province, the police issued arms to peasants in advance of a May Day demonstration by Jewish workers. A medical journal related that in a village of Saratov province, drunken peasants, "influenced by the preaching of the local clergy about 'sedition' and 'internal enemies', had assaulted the school... A pogrom began." Policemen, some of them in mufti, started or took part in pogroms in Zhitomir and elsewhere. Together with Cossacks they assailed ordinary citizens in Rostov-on-Don; in Brest-Litovsk it was drunken reservists. Units on their way to Manchuria staged anti-Jewish riots in five cities in May and June; at a Kiev railway station they beat to death two Jews distributing revolutionary leaflets. By October, even the police in St. Petersburg, the City Council declared on the 24th, had "ceased to be an organ guaranteeing the personal safety or property of the population." Armed soldiers and sailors mutinied in nearby Kronstadt, raiding and wrecking businesses and homes. In the Georgian capital of Tbilisi, soldiers defying the orders of their officers rioted and looted for two days.[63]

The high number of Jewish casualties in October is attributable to the general breakdown of discipline and authority revealed in the examples cited. They manifest the impossibility of relying on men and methods of control which had already proved deficient in 1881 and were stretched to the breaking point by revolution. Inadequacies in the size, morale, and training of the forces of repression were multiplied many times over in 1905. From Bloody Sunday in January – which an English diplomat was convinced the London police could have handled with 300–400 men without resorting to extreme measures – until the bloody suppression of the Moscow rising by the Semenevskii Guards in December, troops and police showed themselves unequal to the task of preserving order. When this required protecting Jews, inability was compounded or caused by an unwillingness which was not necessarily concerted or sanctioned from above. Even when it was and a governor or city prefect allowed a pogrom to proceed, police or soldiers at times intervened to prevent or end it. So did troop commanders or their civilian counterparts in a number of cities; in others, their orders were ignored.[64]

Insubordination and the shortcomings of soldiers and police, along with the negligent incompetence of their superiors, still provide only a partial explanation of the heavy toll exacted by the pogromists. The latter were goaded on not merely by the example and appeals of rightist rabble rousers in or out of uniform. They also knew that their ugly work was viewed with favor or indifference by men of authority. Without clear guidance from St. Petersburg, where divided counsels and confusion reigned; fearful of being overwhelmed by a still-rising tide of revolution; sympathetic to those who resisted it; and themselves counting on the sympathy of like-minded officials in the central government, its representatives in the provinces must bear a heavy responsibility for what they did as well as for what they neglected to do.

Men such as Neidhardt and Kaulbars in Odessa, Generals Bezsonov and Drake in Kiev, Governors Kharusin in Kishinev, Khvostov in Chernigov, Kurlov in Minsk, Sleptosov in Tver, and Azancheev-Azanchevskii in Tomsk, did not merely fail to move quickly and unequivocally against outbursts of "patriotic" wrath. They also condoned or stimulated them by word and deed. Sleptsov's benign passivity in the midst of a group of rioters could only be taken by them as a sign of approval and encouragement. Bezsonov's inaction was considered deliberate by an investigating Senator while his remark to pogromists that it was all right to riot (*gromit'*) but not to plunder was an invitation to do both. When asked to stop a pogrom, Khvostov reportedly replied that he could not prohibit a patriotic manifestation. His Tomsk colleague was accused by a Duma deputy and others of instructing the police and fire brigades not to hinder the excesses of the mob. His observation that the mood of the troops was entirely on the side of the crowd, while correct, may have served also as a rationalization for not ordering them until the third day of disorders to use armed force. They obeyed and quiet was restored. The pogrom wave receded even before the government recovered full control over the length and breadth of the country. In that recovery, and especially in the defeat of the urban revolution, a substantial minority of the population, for reasons which did not always coincide with those of the authorities, acted wittingly or unwittingly as their allies.[65]

Not until the height of the Civil War that followed the Bolsheviks' coming to power in October 1917 was there a renewal of large-scale violence against Jews that was more massive and murderous than any the Empire had yet experienced. It was preceded by scattered Cossack raids on Jewish communities near the front lines in the world war, raids which must have been stimulated by the High Command's denunciations of Jews as spies, shirkers, and war profiteers. It seemed obvious even to the Council of Ministers that the generals were determined to blame the Jews for their failures, and as the military situation deteriorated, the voices raised against them grew in volume and number. When the old regime collapsed, with the country's administration, armed forces, and economy disintegrating, the need and wish to see the Jews as authors of the nation's misfortunes grew even stronger in many segments of society, in spite of the lifting of all Jewish disabilities (20 March 1917) and in part because of it.[66]

Less so than at any previous time in Russian history, during the eight months of the Provisional Government's fragile rule, were there men and movements who disposed of the means to instigate or order pogroms. And more so than ever before did such central authority as existed – the government, the All-Russian Congress of Soviets and its Executive Committee – inveigh forcefully and repeatedly against all forms of persecution. In the midst of rising anarchy, their appeals and commands availed little against the physical and verbal abuse of Jews, whether as speculators and hoarders in time of desperate shortages; as members of the socialist parties who had treacherously encompassed the fall of the Tsar and

Russia's ruin; as freshly empowered citizens or functionaries of the new order. Soldiers of the Second Siberian Corps refused to have Jewish officers; so did a Moscow regiment which also would not allow speakers from the Soviet, "which was in Jewish hands," to address it. The municipal Duma of Soroki in Bessarabia was dispersed, and its members assaulted, for having elected a Jew as its head. During local elections in August, the villagers of Ocrianovo (Voronezh province) shouted "Down with commissars, teachers, and Jews," as they burned ballot boxes. "Outsiders, foreigners, stay away from our villages!"[67]

The crumbling of state power left Jews more vulnerable than they had been before the February Revolution, and as early as May pogroms broke out in Nizhnii-Novgorod and Bessarabia, soon to be followed in Elisavetgrad and other Ukrainian towns. Mounting antisemitism and pogroms caused the Procuracy in Petrograd to ask for a special law against incitement to murder and looting. By the end of June, these forms of violence had assumed such worrisome proportions that the Soviet sent a commission of inquiry to the Ukraine, Bessarabia, and Odessa. In September and October, some sixty pogroms in the Ukraine were reported to the Soviet's Executive Committee, and in the name of their 500,000 comrades, Jewish soldiers appealed to it for relief.[68]

All this was but a prelude to the unspeakable horrors inflicted upon the Jews of the Ukraine during the Civil War years of 1919–20. They were savaged by White Armies and, to a lesser degree, by Red forces, by Ukrainian, Cossack, and Anarchist forces and by the large and small bands of peasants, marauders, and deserters who followed in their wake or operated on their own. A fratricidal conflict of ever-changing fronts, in which every armed hand was raised against almost every other, left only the narrowest loyalties intact and made Jews the universal outsiders. There were few islands of safety, not even the remotest village or the most heavily Jewish town. Numbers or self-defense units rarely offered protection, for it was not urban mobs, as had been generally true in 1881 and 1905, but sizable detachments of armed men who descended upon Jewish communities and decimated them. Pogrom, with its connotation of ethno-religious discord and socioeconomic tensions, was hardly an adequate description for these military actions.

Nor did it require a spark, an incident, a provocation to bring about a massacre. Men and officers, including the higher White commanders, considered Jews fair game for loot, for "contributions," revenge, or bloody sport. Three years of brutalizing warfare, two revolutions, and civil strife had removed the moral, legal, and prudential inhibitions that had been operative in earlier years. For the White Armies, lacking a strong bond of belief, the war against the Jews became a virtual necessity and program, as demonstrated by Peter Kenez in the present volume. White Armies carried these beliefs beyond the south into Central Russia, Siberia, and Belorussia.

The fewest pogroms and deaths – 8·6 percent of the former and 2·3 percent of the latter, according to one count – were caused by the Red Armies, mostly in the early part of 1918. On occasion, they had found the equation Jew–bourgeois a useful one, but a determined campaign of penalties and propaganda among the soldiers convinced the latter that hunting Jews was not acceptable behavior. "It is herewith ordered," the Council of People's Commissars decreed in July 1918, "that pogromists and persons inciting to pogroms be outlawed." The Soviet regime vigorously enforced its sanctions against the violent expression of antisemitism during and after the Civil War, and thereby assured the physical security of Jews under its control. It required the reimposition of a strong state power, ruthless consistency in its application, as well as compelling practical and ideological reasons to end Jewish victimization. The weakening of one or more of these factors had made possible the pogroms; their total disappearance and abandonment during the Civil War was the primary cause of the slaughter of Jews in the Ukraine.[69]

IV

Under the heading, "An American Kishinev," the New York *Outlook* of 29 September 1906, commented on the outrages that had been perpetrated against the Negroes of Atlanta, Georgia, on the preceding weekend. "Temporarily, civilization has been suspended," the journal's editorialist wrote, and the city... "disgraced... For brutality, wanton cruelty, fiendish rage and indiscriminate savagery one would have to turn to accounts of massacres in Russia or Turkey for a parallel." Although in his view the riot differed from the Russian variety in that it was not instigated and abetted by the government and the military, headline and text made clear that he thought not just a city but the country as a whole had been shamed by deeds which had heretofore blemished only despotic regimes and benighted nations. Yet six months earlier, in Springfield, Ohio, a mob, prevented by the sheriff from lynching two blacks suspected of murdering a white, vented their frustration by attacking the town's Negro section, its bars, slums, and homes, setting fire to them and driving out the inhabitants. Until the militia, called out by the governor, thwarted them at the end of the second day, the rioters, as described by a reporter, were "simply a band of savages who had left civilization behind them."[70]

If the Atlanta disturbances – because of the mayor's indecisiveness, the greater number of casualties, their longer duration – reduced the significance of Springfield, there was, nonetheless, a long history of communal violence in American cities that could as easily have served for a parallel as Kishinev. The pattern and targets, though racial rather than religious outsiders, bore a striking resemblance to Russian and some European pogroms. An 1829 attack, lasting three days, on the Negro quarter of Cincinnati, which made half of that city's black population flee to Canada, was the first of many major racial clashes in the Age of Jackson. The historian of that "turbulent era" has recorded a constant stream of anti-immigrant, anti-Catholic, anti-black, and anti-abolitionist riots, of electoral, labor, and vigilante violence, of bitter battles fought by working-class nativists against state militias equipped with rifles and cannons. The most furious and frequent were directed against northern blacks, in this as well as in later periods.[71]

Long-standing biases and cultural animosities were embodied and given near-universal sanction in state and federal laws until the end of the Civil War. They in effect declared the United States to be a white man's country and denied even free blacks full civil and political rights. The chimerical fear of being inundated and corrupted by a "separate and degraded people," as Jackson's Attorney General Roger Taney called members of the "African race," lay at the root of northern resistance to equal citizenship for blacks. Yet since they were free men, exclusion could not be total, and in growing numbers they made use of such opportunities as were open to them for free movement, education, economic improvement, organization, protest, and petition. In the latter they had vocal white allies, who helped to expose the disparity between northern profession and practice, between the advances some Negroes were making and the supposed depravity of the race. Although most were and remained poor, a small black middle class had emerged in northern cities. Its relative well-being stirred as much resentment as did the majority's competing with native whites and Irish immigrants for employment or the demands for justice made by abolitionists.[72]

Indeed, it was tolerant Philadelphia, the "Capital of Conscience," of Quakers and abolitionists, that experienced the greatest number of large and small-scale attacks upon blacks in the two decades after 1829. They closely followed the example of Cincinnati and were repeated elsewhere. Hundreds or thousands of whites invading black neighborhoods; their tearing and burning down houses, beating and sometimes killing the inhabitants; attacks on the sheriff's posse or police; fire fighters showing little enthusiasm for their task – such accounts closely resemble those emanating from the Pale of Settlement, and first of all from hospitable, broad-minded Odessa. The similarities extend to the flurry of feathers from pillows and comforters that became the hallmark of Russian pogroms, the hated or envied symbols of the well-being that some Jews, like some blacks, had attained. Of the 1834 Philadelphia riot, where prosperous blacks were singled out, M. Feldberg, citing contemporary sources, has written:

For three nights the rioting remained uncontrolled by public officials…Crowds looted the property of blacks, pocketing silverware and cash, burning or breaking what they could not carry. "The furniture of the houses was broken into the smallest fragments; nothing escaped; the bedding was carried into the streets, ripped with knives, and the contents scattered far and wide. The bedsteads, chairs, and tables were hacked to chips." People as well as property suffered at the mob's hands. One black was killed, many were badly hurt, and the constabulary suffered several injuries as well. A reporter for the *Philadelphia Gazette* noted that "The mob exhibited more than fiendish brutality, beating and mutilating some of the old, confiding and unoffending blacks, with a savageness surpassing anything that we could have believed men capable of."[73]

Predominantly, but not exclusively, it was the young and disadvantaged who took out their hostilities and sometimes their excess energies, in what has been called recreational violence, against blacks. More than one mob contained, besides native workmen and Irish laborers, established members of the community, artisans, doctors, lawyers, and dentists, as well as some constables and elected officials. Economic difficulties and hard times were the stronger element in lower-class Negrophobia, as in the attempted burning of a Philadelphia warehouse into which Irish dockers had driven black stevedores. Both groups, however, saw Negroes challenging more than their livelihood: their very place in the social and moral order was at stake. For both, race became a "substitute form of hierarchy" and to maintain or restore their status they, like their Russian counterparts, employed legal and extra-legal discrimination, high flown arguments and inarticulate violence.[74]

To preserve public order and white dominance, to inhibit the rising influx of blacks, which was all the more threatening since it coincided with the arrival of native and immigrant job seekers in the cities, northern state legislatures, voters, and city councils adopted a variety of measures between 1820 and 1850 that reduced the rights of blacks: political disenfranchisement in Pennsylvania, an end to Negro admission in Illinois, and attempted expulsion in Ohio. Special taxes and passes, residential and educational restrictions were imposed; bonds to insure good behavior were required; and laws passed that voided contracts made with blacks and barred their testimony in cases to which a white was party.[75]

Status anxieties were a powerful motive in these enactments, and even more so in the customary denials of equal access to theaters, schools, restaurants, and public transport. When a New York Federalist opposed giving the franchise to the "whole host of Africans that now deluge our city," he feared as much as the political consequences the equality of condition the vote would tacitly confer upon a group "already too impertinent to be borne." Blacks who rose above their station, who expressed in their dress or deportment claims to respect and consideration to which they were not thought to be entitled, invited ridicule in the press and rough treatment in the streets. Even those who wished them well deplored their finery and ostentation as provocative and, like the meshchane of Pereiaslav and the governor of Mogilev (though with better grace and motive) advised modesty and deference. A Philadelphia citizens' committee, citing depression, white unemployment, and the hiring of Negroes as causes of the 1834 riot, asked that leading blacks, to forestall future violence, impress upon their people "the necessity, as well as the propriety, of behaving themselves inoffensively and with civility... taking care, as they pass along the streets or assemble together, not to be obtrusive."[76]

Nothing before or after equalled the furious looting, arson, beating, and killing carried out by thousands of men, women, and children – mostly working-class Irish – during the New York City draft riots of July 1863. Only on the fifth day, with the help of large numbers of troops, were the authorities able to end the state of near-anarchy into which America's largest city had been plunged. The "black pogrom" of New York was, like the Jewish one of Iuzovka, the smaller part of a larger social protest, galvanized in this instance by the Enrollment Act. It exempted from call-up men who could pay 300 dollars for a substitute to serve in "the rich man's war the poor were being forced to fight" and for which Negroes were widely blamed. In the wake of the July days, white mobs attacked black communities in a dozen other cities. Changes in the draft law helped to restore peace. But the war that ended slavery and led at last to the constitutional recognition of black citizenship, also exacerbated racial hatreds by the economic and human sacrifices it had exacted and by the prospect of "two or three million semi-savages" escaping bondage and flooding the northern states.[77]

As profound and unsettling in its impact and consequences as the Russian Revolution of 1905, the American Civil War was, however, the only national calamity or crisis that acted as a magnifier and trigger of collective violence. It was both more episodic and endemic in the United States than in Russia and it was typically set off by economic, social, and demographic shifts, by regional or even local tensions, rather than by singular events and actions of a national scope.

The Chinese Exclusion Acts, for example, by which Congress suspended (1882, 1884) and then banned (1902) the entry of Chinese laborers, were responses to a campaign conducted by western labor unions. They followed the anti-Chinese riots of Los Angeles (1871) and San Francisco (1877) and the more than fifty that occurred throughout the West in the 1880s. "From Seattle to southern California, from the Pacific to the Rocky Mountains, Chinese ghettos were mobbed or burned out, their residents dispersed or murdered." As was true elsewhere, the anger of working-men at having their wages depressed and their jobs taken by outsiders did not remain without rationalizations that their spokesmen and political allies based almost exclusively on racial grounds.[78]

From its very foundations, the American Federation of Labor not only advocated keeping Chinese and all other Orientals out of the country; it did so in crudely and viciously racist language. Its 1893 convention charged that the Chinese brought "nothing but filth, vice and disease"; declared that "all efforts to elevate them to a higher standard had proven futile"; and held them responsible for "degrading a part of our people on the Pacific Coast to such a degree that could it be published in detail the American people would in their just and righteous anger sweep them from the face of the earth." The Federation's president, Samuel Gompers, a Jewish immigrant, told its members in 1901 that "every incoming coolie... means so much more vice and immorality injected into our social life." Three years later he referred to black strike breakers as "hordes of... huge strapping fellows, ignorant and vicious, whose predominant trait was animalism."[79]

The articulation of such primitive prejudices by the leader of a movement that had once refused affiliation to locals whose constitutions contained discriminatory clauses is directly traceable to the migration of blacks into northern industrial cities. Beginning in the 1880s, it reached massive proportions between 1910 and 1920, a time of business expansion and labor scarcity intensified by the world war and the curtailment of European immigration. The black exodus from the South placed enormous strains on housing, public transit, and recreational facilities, aggravated job competition when servicemen returned from the war, and led to a deterioration of race relations that had in the two decades before 1900 improved in northern states.[80]

Structural changes that war helped to accelerate heightened racial tensions both before the European conflict began and after it ended. If in Atlanta and Springfield, Illinois (1908), tales of sexual assault, assiduously trumpeted by local papers, inflamed passions, just as the ritual murder fiction had done in Kishinev, the still greater riots at East St. Louis, Illinois (1917), and Chicago (1919), as well as several lesser ones, began without such preparation. In the "Pittsburgh of the West," where some 40 blacks and 9 whites were killed, as in Chicago, where about two-thirds of the 38 dead and 537 injured were Negroes, the immediate cause was not the violation of sexual taboos but punitive or admonitory attacks designed to keep the "invaders" in their place, away from white work places, neighborhoods, parks, and ballot boxes. The rancor of the mobs grew when blacks defended themselves or went on the offensive; the police then turned upon them with vigor they had previously failed to muster. There were instances of policemen participating in the rioting, poor coordination of their efforts, as well as deliberate neglect of duty and an insufficiency of manpower. Events followed much the same course in Detroit in 1943.

Persistent racial frictions and minor clashes were exacerbated by an influx of black labor, the resulting housing shortage, and the federal government's imposition of equal employment standards in defense industries. White workers, many of them also recent arrivals from the South, resented these, staged walkouts, and were supported in their feelings and incited to their actions by white supremacists like Gerald L. K. Smith. Police misconduct and ineptness helped greatly to turn a Sunday night incident in an amusement park into a full-fledged race riot. Here, as in East St. Louis and Chicago, national guard or federal troops had to be called in, though there were delays in summoning them, in their dispatch, or confusion over who was authorized to order it. In Detroit, delay was due to bureaucratic bungling; in East St. Louis, the number of guardsmen was inadequate; they and their commanding officer were inexperienced and biased. In Chicago, the police chief and mayor waited three days before they either admitted or recognized the need for outside help.[81]

The year 1943 also saw a major racial disturbance in Los Angeles, the so-called Zoot-Suit Riots, in which large mobs of "Anglos," mainly soldiers and sailors, hunted and brutalized young Mexican–Americans whom press and police had for more than a year vilified and harried as hoodlums and gang members. One police official described Mexicans as being "biologically" predisposed to criminal behavior and the conduct of his men was in keeping with that characterization. "In no reported cases did the police intervene, except to help beat Mexicans."[82]

Detroit and Los Angeles were not the last outbreaks of racial violence in American cities, but they were the last in which minority communities were the objects of massive aggression by the majority. The assertiveness Negroes had begun to display in Detroit and on some earlier occasions, fundamentally changed the nature of racial conflict in America's inner cities. Like the Harlem riots of 1935 and 1943, those that seized the nation's black ghettos in the 1960s, even when they were triggered by an act of white aggression, were vehement and destructive protests against a system of segregation and deprivation that persisted though it had lost all legal sanction and much of its approval in the larger community. The vocal and firm commitment of the federal government and most of the nation's political elite to formal equality ended neither discrimination nor poverty. Instead, it revealed in all its sharpness the gap between law and reality, promise and fulfillment, from which sprang the frustrations and despair that made Watts, Harlem, Newark, Detroit, and thirty other black ghettos rise up in virtual rebellion between 1964 and 1967. Changes in law and majority attitudes, plus the physical, moral and political power of which the minority had shown itself capable did, nonetheless, make the pogrom-like violence that had been all too common in northern cities for over a century a thing of the past. These changes also put an end to the lynchings that had been the southern way of controlling blacks who rebelled against their subordinate condition and violated the taboos of race.

v

More clearly still than does the history of West European Jewry, the melancholy record of race relations in America confirms that popular antagonism toward a feared or despised out-group could turn violent as easily in a liberal polity professing egalitarian values as under a centralized, reactionary regime that rested on a hierarchy of status and ethnos. To be sure, codes and customs hemmed in Russian Jews almost as tightly as American Negroes, and there is much in the treatment and perception of the former, who were, with few exceptions, a distinct and peculiar presence in the Russian setting, that can only be called racist. Yet in neither country, and least of all in Western Europe, can the state's laws or actions be seen as the root cause of collective acts of persecution. If anything, official discrimination, the legal definition and strict maintenance of inferiority – although taken or invoked by their perpetrators as justifying such acts – more often than not served to prevent them. For it was usually when long-standing relations of sub- and superordination were in dispute, when the existing barriers of exclusion were breached or relaxed, when the state was no longer felt to be their enforcer, that its aggrieved subjects took matters into their own hands. It was after they had done so that the governments were persuaded to impose or tighten legal disabilities. Such was the case in the France of Napoleon, in the Russia of Alexander III, and in the northern states during the three decades before the Civil War.

It is equally clear that the state's forceful and active intervention was needed not merely to stop the ill-treatment of Jews or blacks once it had begun. Also required, if its termination was to be more than temporary, were unmistakable condemnations from the highest levels of authority, as well as the passage of laws that removed the stigma of second-class citizenship, affirmed equal rights, and provided fit punishment for their violation. Principle, pragmatism, or a combination of the two led the governments of Europe in the nineteenth century, revolutionary Russia between 1917 and 1923, and the United States in the 1960s, to brand as impermissible the terrorizing of minorities and to prosecute it.

Success was not total, and especially in the social and private spheres, racism and prejudice survived to invade the public realm and policy, most banefully in Nazi Germany and Stalin's Russia. The most perfect and possibly unique example of a state organized and coordinated outburst of "popular wrath" occurred in the Third Reich on "Kristallnacht," the misnamed pogrom of November 1938. In the USSR, the anti-cosmopolitan campaign and the Doctors' Plot of Stalin's last years once again made antisemitism a poisonous ingredient of domestic and foreign policy. In neither dictatorship, however, was there a recurrence of the paradigmatic or classic pogrom, for the state jealously and successfully reserved to itself the monopoly of violence and repression.

Not until the loosening of Stalinist rigidities under Mikhail Gorbachev was there a pogrom – of Muslim Azeris against Christian Armenians in the new industrial city of Sumgait in February 1988 – in which 31 (by official count) or anywhere from 350 to 600 Armenians were killed in the course of three days. It elicited familiar charges of culpability and neglect against the regime and its local agencies. While these charges cannot be dismissed, there is reason to ask whether the Communist Party and the Soviet state can have wanted or welcomed a calamity that necessitated a costly and colossal military presence, infinitely complicated the task of government, and was certain to endanger the reforms on which the leadership had embarked and, possibly, the leadership itself. Most credible is the accusation levelled against the Sumgait police, most of them presumably Azeris, that they stood by without interfering. The statement of the Soviet Deputy Minister of the Interior, that they "proved to be not up to the job in these extreme conditions," may be taken in more than a technical sense and is a likely, if partial, explanation of the significant number of casualties.[83]

In all popular disturbances, and particularly in those of a racial, ethnic, or religious kind, the attitudes and performance of the police

are factors of the utmost importance. For some students of Russian
pogroms and American race riots no others are of equal weight.
"When disorder starts," Justice Thrugood Marshall, then a director
and counsel of the NAACP, wrote in 1943 about the Detroit riot of
that year, "it is either stopped quickly or permitted to spread into
serious proportions, depending upon the actions of the local police."
In Detroit they "enforced the law with an unequal hand." Yet it is
far from certain that an energetic and impartial use of force by the
police, or military, can carry the day quickly at all times, and in all
circumstances, against crowds that form, melt away, and reform in
unpredictable patterns. The history of urban violence suggests
otherwise both before and after the days of specially trained riot
squads, of water cannons, tear gas, dogs, and helicopters, especially
in the United States where that history has been better studied and
documented than anywhere else.[84]

During New York's draft riots, mobs repeatedly compelled a
sizable police force to retreat. Neither courage nor discipline kept
over a hundred of its men from being wounded, thirty-two of them
seriously. Of the soldiers who came to their aid, thirty-five suffered
serious and thirty-eight lesser injuries before their numbers and fire
power took effect. At least ten of the military and police were shot
or beaten to death. In 1919, failure of the Washington police to
check an incipient riot may indeed have set the stage for the larger
one that followed. But the concerted efforts of the police, cavalry,
infantry, marines, and citizens on its second day were "powerless to
quell the mobs that surged through the principal business streets and
the Black districts." Dubnow half admitted the possibility that in the
Starodub pogrom of 1891, the police proved powerless against huge
hordes of plunderers and incendiaries. The conclusion is inescapable
that bias, mixed signals from above, or lack of determination are not
the only explanations for what many have seen as the willful
derelictions of duty by the guardians of the public peace.[85]

On those occasions – and they have been most fully attested in the
United States – when policemen did precipitate or prolong a riot,
they expressed the pervasive prejudices of their communities.
However deep-rooted and widely shared these may have been,
however essential in preparing the ground for attacking a minority
and branding it as a menace to majority dominance and well-being,
prejudices do not of themselves produce pogroms or riots. They can
be activated in a multitude and multiplicity of ways: by minor

frictions and clashes of a traditional kind; by inflated or fabricated tales of vile deeds; by the advent of crises or catastrophes; by wars and revolutions. In the majority of cases we have surveyed, it was the stress of changes in the urban environment that created the most fertile soil for the intensification of latent antagonisms, for their mobilization and eruption.

American race riots and Russian pogroms (before the Civil War) were predominantly urban phenomena. They took place in cities and regions to which blacks and Jews were relative newcomers and where their presence in unprecedented numbers was perceived as a threat. The sense of being swamped and displaced by waves of immigrants of alien stock and race stemmed not alone from the fact of geographical mobility. It was also fed and enlarged by fears of the still greater hordes supposedly waiting to break out of the areas to which they had been confined – the American South and the northwestern parts of Russia. Demographic dread appears to have been a major contributor to urban tensions where the minority's numbers grew quickly, especially in countries where its overall numbers were large. To quantify what might at different times and places have been the critical mass that exhausted toleration and envenomed attitudes is impossible. There is, nonetheless, a positive correlation between a minority's size in a community or country and the frequency and severity of attacks upon it. Going from west to east, from the smallest to the largest of Europe's Jewish communities, the incidence of pogroms increased. In America it did so with the rising waves of black migration from south to north; in Russia with the movement of Jews from northwest to southwest and south.

For both groups, such movement was a form of emancipation from below, a partial escape from old constraints, a grasping of economic opportunities that were also sought by others or considered the preserve of older inhabitants and elites. In the best of times tolerance was strained in the burgeoning, undergoverned cities of an untamed capitalism, the raw commercial or industrial centers that acted as magnets for all manner of folk, most of them poor and not too discriminating in their search for a livelihood. When economic difficulties and/or political discord heightened insecurities, frustrations, and disappointments, these were apt to be discharged against the most visible, most alien, and most recently arrived outgroup. That is why the cities of the Russian South and the American North were the primary locus of race riots and pogroms, rather than the more stable, if less benign, environments that so many Russian Jews and African–Americans had left behind them. As Belostok and Atlanta showed in 1906, no region of either country was immune from outbreaks of massive violence. But it was much less frequent and widespread where older forms of social control and separation were maintained, where rates of development were lower and slower, where change was more likely, therefore, to be experienced as an outrage against norms the dominant community, the "superior" race or nationality, considered just and proper.[86]

Given the temporal and geographical limits of our survey, and the unsatisfactory base of evidence for its European and Russian parts, no claim is made for the universal applicability of its conclusions – not even to all the examples we have considered and certainly not to the vast number we did not, whether in India, Pakistan, or Sri Lanka; Northern Ireland, Yugoslavia, or Cyprus; Nigeria, South Africa, Turkey, or Iraq. It may be that no amount of comparing, analyzing, or theorizing will ever make fully comprehensible why so many so often mistreated their fellow humans as if they were a lesser species. The temptation is great to say, as did Freud in a letter to Arnold Zweig: "With regard to Antisemitism, I don't really want to search for explanations; I feel a strong inclination to surrender to my affects in this matter...and my wholly unscientific belief that mankind on the average are a wretched lot. Naturally, I am not reproaching you with having managed not to surrender to this irrational affect." Historians and social scientists, too, must resist the inclination to surrender and keep searching for facts and explanations.[87]

NOTES

1 *Los Angeles Times* 10 January 1988, 12. Since then, the word has become even more familiar as a result of the ethnic clashes in various parts of the Soviet Union.

2 See, e.g., the editors' introductions to S. M. Dubnow and G. Ia. Krasnyi-Admoni, *Materialy dlia istorii antievreiskikh pogromov v Rossii*, 1 (Petrograd, 1919), where Dubnow describes 1881 as the "era of systematic pogroms"; 1903 as initiating pogroms as a "permanent governmental institution" (ix, xi); and Krasnyi-Admoni speaks of the "pogrom ideology" of the central government (xxxi). The latter did, however, absolve the government of direct responsibility for the outbreaks of the eighties and charged it mainly with failure to take immediate and stern measures for their suppression. Volume II

(Petrograd 1923) of this valuable collection of documents was edited by Krasny-Admoni alone. Subsequently cited as *Materialy* I or II.

3 Jacob Lestschinsky, "The anti-Jewish program: tsarist Russia, the Third Reich and independent Poland," *Jewish Social Studies*, III (1931), 143.

4 Joseph Nedava, *Trotsky and the Jews* (Philadelphia, 1972), 22.

5 Most often this has been done for 1881–82. See S. M. Berk, *Year of Crisis, Year of Hope* (Westbrook, CN and London, 1985), 39–44.

6 R. F. Leslie, ed., *The History of Poland Since 1863* (Cambridge, 1980), 48.

7 A definition which extends to "national, racial, economic or other hostility" is given in *Bol'shaia Sovetskaia Entsiklopediia*, XLV (1940), cols. 763–4. An older and broader use of the word occurs in a Russian translation of Heinrich Heine's poem "Es reiten die blauen Husaren" in which *Kriegsvolk und Landesplag* were rendered as *voenshchina, zemskii pogrom* by the poet A. A. Fet in 1890. See his *Stikhotvoreniia i poemy* (Leningrad, 1986), 583. I am grateful to Professor Emily Klenin for providing this reference.

8 S. M. Dubnow, *History of the Jews in Russia and Poland*, trans. I. Friedlander (Philadelphia, 1916), II, 276, 283; *Evreiskaia Entsiklopediia* (St. Petersburg, 1906–13), XII, col. 616; *Materialy*, II, 531; *Die Judenpogrome in Russland* (Cologne and Leipzig, 1910), I, 187–8, 378.

9 R. Kantor, "Aleksandr III o evreiskikh pogromakh, 1881–83 gg.," *Evreiskaia Letopis'*, I (1923), 151; P. A. Zaionchkovskii, *Krizis samoderzhaviia na rubezhe 1870–1880-kh godov* (Moscow, 1964), 385; Samuel Joseph, *Jewish Immigration to the United States* (New York, 1914), 63; Lestschinsky, "The anti-Jewish program," 142; Louis Greenberg, *The Jews in Russia*, 2 volumes in one (New Haven, 1965), II, 47.

10 There is, surprisingly, no monographic study of the Hep-Hep riots. I have relied on the following: *Encyclopaedia Judaica* (Jerusalem, 1971–72), VIII, cols. 330–31; Utz Jeggle, *Judendörfer in Württemberg* (Tübingen, 1969), 90–97; Jacob Katz, *From Prejudice to Destruction* (Cambridge, MS, 1980), 92–104; E. O. Sterling, "Anti-Jewish riots in Germany in 1819; a displacement of social protest," *Historia Judaica*, XII (1950), pt. 1, 105–52; Simon Dubnow, *Weltgeschichte des jüdischen Volkes* (Berlin, 1925–30), IX, 22–4. It is noteworthy that the unknown author of a memorandum prepared for the Pahlen Commission in 1882 and published by Dubnow in 1909 argued for the non-spontaneous eruption of the pogroms by analogy with Germany where, he wrote, there had been no "systematic attacks [on Jews] in the press or by the masses" until the appearance of the Anti-Semitic League in 1879. See "Antievreiskoe dvizhenie v Rossii v 1881 i 1882 g.," *Evreiskaia Starina*, I (1909), 91.

11 In 1819, for example, the Senate of Hamburg suspended the emancipation of the city's Jews, confirmed their exclusion from guilds, and demanded that they conduct themselves with discretion and

reserve. Hans-Gerhard Husung, *Protest und Repression im Vormärz* (Göttingen, 1983), 106–7.

12 T. W. Perry, *Public Opinion, Propaganda, and Politics in Eighteenth-Century England. A Study of the Jewish Naturalization Act of 1753* (Cambridge, MS, 1962), 85; George Rudé, *Paris and London in the Eighteenth Century* (New York, 1971), 322–3.

13 Patrick Girard, *Les Juifs de France de 1789 à 1860* (Paris, 1976), 54, 123.

14 On Algeria and the French riots of 1898, see *Encyclopaedia Judaica*, II, col. 616; Richard Avoun and Bernard Cohen, *Les Juifs d'Algérie* (Paris, 1982), 127–39; Michael Marrus, *The Politics of Assimilation* (Oxford, 1971), 208, 235; Stephen Wilson, "The anti-Semitic riots in 1898 in France," *Historical Journal*, XVI (1973), 789–806; Zeev Sternhell, "Roots of popular anti-Semitism in the Third Republic," in Frances Malino and Bernard Wasserstein, eds., *The Jews in Modern France* (Hanover, NH and London, 1985), 117–18.

15 Quote from W. E. Mosse, Arnold Paucker, and Reinhold Rürup, eds., *Revolution and Evolution. 1848 in German-Jewish History* (Tübingen, 1981), 41. Cf. ibid., 32–41, 100–3; Istvan Deak, *The Lawful Revolution* (New York, 1979), 85; W. O. McCagg, Jr., *A History of Habsburg Jews, 1670–1918* (Bloomington, IN, 1989), 78, 85, 136.

16 H. Schultheiss, ed., *Europäischer Geschichtskalender 1881* (Noerdlingen, 1882), 155, 223, 230, 234, 240; Hans-Ulrich Wehler, *Bismarck und der Imperialismus* (Cologne–Berlin, 1969), 471, and the frequent reports from West Prussia and Pomerania of the *Frankfurter Zeitung*, 6 August through 10 September 1881. On Hungary: Jörg Hönsch, *A History of Modern Hungary*, tr. K. Traynor (London and New York, 1988), 32–3; *Encyclopaedia Judaica*, VIII, 1090–1; XV, 1155–6. On Bohemia: H. J. Kieval, *The Making of Czech Jewry* (New York, 1988), 64–74; M. A. Riff, "Czech antisemitism and the Jewish response before 1914," *Wiener Library Bulletin*, XXIX (1976), 8–19; McCagg, *A History of Habsburg Jews*, 178–9. On Galicia: Frank Golczewski, *Polnisch–Jüdische Beziehungen 1881–1922* (Wiesbaden, 1981), 74–84.

17 Daniel Chirot and Charles Ragin, "The market, tradition, and peasant rebellion: the case of Romania in 1907," *American Sociological Review*, XL (1975), 431–2; R. W. Seton-Watson, *History of the Roumanians* (Cambridge, 1934), 386–7.

18 Golczewski, *Polnisch–Jüdische Beziehungen*, 181–264; Lestschinsky, "The anti-Jewish program," 157–8; McCagg, *A History of Habsburg Jews*, 203; Israel Cohen, *A Report on the Pogroms in Poland* (London, 1919); Jerzy Tomaszewski, "Pinsk, Saturday 5 April 1919," *Polin*, I (1986), 227–51; Josef Lewandowski, "History and myth: Pinsk, April 1919," *Polin*, II (1987), 50–72; Ezra Mendelsohn, *The Jews of East Central Europe Between the World Wars* (Bloomington, 1983), 40–2.

19 Mendelsohn, *Jews of East Central Europe*, 97; Ervin Pamlény, ed., *A History of Hungary*, trans. L. Boros, et al. (London, 1975), 456; Hoensch, *History of Modern Hungary*, 98; McCagg, *History of Habsburg Jews*, 203.

20 Mendelsohn, *The Jews of East Central Europe*, 150–1; Kieval, *The Making of Czech Jewry*, 185–6; *The Jews of Czechoslovakia. Historical Studies and Surveys* (Philadelphia and New York, 1968), I, 86, 151, 167–8, 226–7.

21 Michael Checinski, "The Kielce pogrom: some unanswered questions," *Soviet Jewish Affairs*, V (1975), 57–72; *Los Angeles Times*, 24 August 1987, 12; Stewart Steven, *The Splinter Factor* (London, 1974), 37.

22 Dubnow, *History*, II, 248–50, 256, 267, 282.

23 On the "calendar of violence" and its "ritual" character, see Eugen Weber, "Reflections on the Jews in France," in Malino and Wasserstein, *The Jews in Modern France*, 14; Michael Feldberg, *The Turbulent Era: Riot and Disorder in Jacksonian America* (New York, 1980), 81; R. C. Cobb, *The Police and the People: French Popular Protest, 1789–1820* (Oxford, 1970), 20. Mosse, et al., *Revolution and Evolution*, 36–7. For the connection between anti-Jewish and other forms of violent protest, see ibid., 35–6; R. J. Goldstein, *Political Repression in Nineteenth-Century Europe* (Totowa, NJ, 1983), 154; Husung, *Protest und Repression*, 22; Charles Tilly, *The Rebellious Century* (Cambridge, MS, 1975), 302.

24 S. W. Baron, *The Russian Jew Under Tsars and Soviets* (New York and London, 1964), 53. Berk, *Year of Crisis*, 35, citing a Russian–Jewish weekly, writes that "hundreds of Jews were killed, wounded, mutilated and raped." An Austrian diplomat estimated the number of Jewish fatalities at fifty, with "at least an equal number of demonstrators killed by the military." From E. R. Rutkowski, "Die revolutionäre Bewegung und die inneren Verhaeltnisse des Zarenreiches von 1877 bis 1884 im Urteil österreichisch-ungarischer Diplomaten," *Mitteilungen des Oesterreichischen Staatsarchivs*, IX (1956), 348–483.

25 *Materialy*, II, 38, 57, 116–30; I. M. Aronson, *Troubled Waters: The Origins of the 1881 Anti-Jewish Pogroms in Russia* (Pittsburgh, 1990); *Evreiskaia Entsiklopediia*, V, col. 612; Mina Goldberg, *Die Jahre 1881–1882 in der Geschichte der russischen Juden* (Berlin, 1934), 27–30; I. V. Galant, "Drentel'n i anti-evreiskie pogromy 1881 g.," *Evreiskii Vestnik* (Leningrad, 1928), 180–2; V. D. Novitskii, *Iz vospominanii zhandarma* (Leningrad, 1929), 186.

26 Novitskii, *Iz vospominanii*; *Materialy*, II, 243–4, 386–9; *Die Judenpogrome*, I, 143–4; Hans Rogger, *Jewish Policies and Right-Wing Politics in Imperial Russia* (Berkeley and London, 1986), 135, 143–4.

27 John Bushnell, *Mutiny Amid Repression. Russian Soldiers in the Revolution of 1905–1906* (Bloomington, IN, 1985), 32–3; *Materialy*, II, 288. Even in the hour of their extremity, in February 1917, the military authorities of Petrograd exercised restraint for three days before deciding on full-scale repression and ordering troops to fire on strikers and demonstrators.

28 Bushnell, *Mutiny*, 27; W. C. Fuller, Jr., *Civil-Military Conflict in Imperial Russia, 1881–1914* (Princeton, 1985), 106–8; *Kievskii i Odesskii pogromy v otchetakh senatorov Turau i Kuzminskogo* (St. Petersburg, 1907), 77–8;

Λ. N. Kuropatkin, "Dnevnik," *Krasnyi Arkhiv*, II (1922), 11, 13, 27, 40; "Iz zapisok A. F. Redigera," ibid., LX (1933), 95.

29 Doubts on whether soldiers could be trusted to put down civil disturbances were voiced as early as the 1820s and were repeated throughout the century and beyond. See E. K. Wirtschafter, *From Serf to Russian Soldier* (Princeton, 1990), 73; Daniel Field, *Rebels in the Name of the Tsar* (Boston, 1976), 75; P. A. Zaionchkovskii, *Samoderzhavie i russkaia armiia na rubezhe XIX–XX stoletii, 1881–1903* (Moscow, 1973), 34; Λ. K. Wildman, *The End of the Russian Imperial Army* (Princeton, 1980), 31. The inadequacies of the police are described by Patricia Herlihy, *Odessa: A History, 1794–1914* (Cambridge, MS, 1986), 163; D. T. Orlovsky, *The Limits of Reform* (Cambridge, MS, 1981), 96, 142, 150; Neil Weissman, "Regular police in tsarist Russia, 1900–1914," *Russian Review*, XL (1985), 47–8. Alexander III's comments from Kantor, "Aleksandr III," 150, 152, 154, 156.

30 Kantor, "Aleksandr III," 151, 157, 158; *Materialy*, II, 249–50; *Die Judenpogrome*, I, 53; Germany, Auswärtiges Amt, *Akten* (microfilm reel 306); Kiev Consul Reitz to Bismarck, 2 August 1881 (NS); *Frankfurter Zeitung*, 13 August 1881, 2; "Anti-evreiskoe dvizhenie," 93; Cyrus Adler and A. M. Margalith, *With Firmness in the Right: American Diplomatic Action Affecting Jews, 1840–1945* (New York, 1946), 204.

31 Goldberg, *Die Jahre 1881–1882*, 30–1.

32 Field, *Rebels*; Herlihy, *Odessa*, 301. The events in Khar'kov were reported in dispatch no. 182 of 8 May 1872 (NS) by the US chargé d'affaires in St. Petersburg, Eugene Schuyler. National Archives of the United States, Dispatches of US Ministers to Russia, 1808–1906. Microcopy M-35, Roll 24.

33 P. A. Valuev quoted in Zaionchkovskii, *Krizis*, 100; Goldberg, *Die Jahre 1881–1882*, 19–24; I. M. Aronson, "Geographical and socio-economic factors in the 1881 anti-Jewish pogroms in Russia," *Russian Review*, XXXIX (1980), 18–31; A. G. Rashin, *Naselenie Rossii za sto let, 1811–1913* (Moscow, 1956), 120–9.

34 Rogger, *Jewish Policies*, 127–9; John Klier, "The Russian press and the anti-Jewish pogroms of 1881–2," *Canadian–American Slavic Studies*, VII (1983), 199–221; Dubnow, *History*, II, 186, 193–4, 202; *Materialy*, II, 241; I. D. Sosis, "K istorii anti-evreiskogo dvizheniia v tsarskoi Rossii," *Trudy Belorusskogo Gosudarstvennogo Universiteta*, no. 6–7 (1925), 177. Continuation in no. 12 (1926), 82–94.

35 Herlihy, *Odessa*, 251; M. F. Hamm, "Continuity and change in late imperial Kiev," in Hamm, ed., *The City in Late Imperial Russia* (Bloomington, IN, 1986), 92–3; *The Universal Jewish Encyclopedia* (New York, 1939–43), VI, col. 382; *Evreiskaia Entsiklopediia*, IX, cols. 522, 526; *Encyclopaedia Judaica*, XIV, col. 443; A. J. Rieber, *Merchants and Entrepreneurs in Imperial Russia* (Chapel Hill, NC, 1982), 57, 60–1.

36 Kutaisov quoted by Sosis, "K istorii," no. 6–7, 180, Drentel'n by Novitskii, *Vospominaniia*, 180, 182. As an example of how the suddenness

of the Jewish influx was perceived by a man of the left, the Populist V. V. Bervi-Flerovskii, see his "Vospominaniia," in *Golos Minuvshogo*, no. 5–6 (1916), 265–8.

37 Goldberg, *Die Jahre 1881–1882*, 36–7; *Materialy*, II, 325–48; *Frankfurter Zeitung*, 8 August 1881, 2; D. Rivin, "Istoricheskie itogi pogromnoi epokhi," *Evreiskaia Starina*, IV (1911), 422, Sosis, "K istorii," no. 6–7, 186.

38 Sosis, "K istorii," 182–3; *Die Judenpogrome*, I, 53. On antisemitism among Kiev workers and radicals' efforts to combat it, see B. A. Engel and C. N. Rosenthal, trans. and eds., *Five Sisters: Women Against the Tsar* (New York, 1975), 230–1.

39 *Materialy*, II, 537, 532–3, 539–40; Goldberg, *Die Jahre 1881–1882*, 38; on permanent and seasonal migration to cities and their rapid growth, see Joseph Bradley, *Muzhik and Muscovite. Urbanization in Late Imperial Russia* (Berkeley, 1985), 31–2 and D. R. Brower, "Labor violence in Russia in the late nineteenth century," *Slavic Review*, XLI (1982), 418.

40 On peasant participation in pogroms and villages affected by them: *Materialy*, I, 125–7, 132, 138, 165, 234, 296, 298, 305, 342 and II, 529–30; Kantor, "Aleksandr III," 156. Information on religion, ethnicity, and family status of workers in one city is provided by Herlihy, *Odessa*, 241–51. On the migrant or "prishlyi" element also see Sosis, "K istorii," no. 6–7, 183.

41 *Materialy*, II, 8, 75, 83, 90, 102, 116, 243, 277, 395–6; Novitskii, *Vospominaniia*, 184. Popular disorientation, caused by uncertainty and feelings of political as well as socioeconomic insecurity, is also seen as a factor in the French riots of 1898 by Wilson, "The antisemitic riots," 801.

42 *Materialy*, II, 10–13; Sosis, "K istorii," *Trudy*, no. 12 (1926), 87.

43 *Trudy*, no. 6–7, 186; S. D. Corrsin, "Warsaw," in Hamm, *The City*, 140, 143–4; Rutkowsky, "Die revolutionäre Bewegung," 457. Goldberg, *Die Jahre 1881–1882*, 35; *Materialy*, II, 529. There was "opportunistic rioting and looting" during the New York City draft riots of 1865. See Adrian Cook, *The Armies of the Streets* (Lexington, KY, 1974), 199.

44 The 1891 law in *Ministerstvo iustitsii za sto let* (St. Petersburg 1902), 213–14. See Michael Ochs, "St. Petersburg and the Jews of Russian Poland, 1862–1905" (Ph.D. dissertation, Harvard University, 1986), 220–1, for precautions taken in Poland after the Galician pogroms.

45 T. H. Friedgut, "Labor violence and regime brutality in tsarist Russia: the Iuzovka cholera riots of 1892," *Slavic Review*, XL (1987), 245–65; Brower, "Labor violence," 417–18, 427.

46 Heinz-Dietrich Löwe, *Antisemitismus und reaktionäre Utopie. Russischer Konservatismus im Kampf gegen den Wandel von Staat und Gesellschaft* (Hamburg, 1978), 57–65; *Materialy*, I, 130–295; *Die Judenpogrome*, II, 5–37.

47 I. G. Budak, ed., *Istoriia Kishineva* (Kishinev, 1966), 145; P. P. Zavarzin, *Zhandarmy i revoliutsionery* (Paris, 1930), 65. On the role of Pleve, whom he finds to be guilty of at least negligent homicide, see E. H. Judge, *Plehve. Repression and Reform in Imperial Russia* (Syracuse, NY, 1983), 93–101.

48 Fuller, *Civil-Military Conflict*, 109–10. In spite of his judgment on the incompetence and irresponsibility of civil and military authorities, Fuller is convinced that the pogrom was planned in advance and was well organized, that the governor had prior knowledge of it and did nothing to forestall it.

49 Budak, *Istoriia*, 83, 90, 94, 138; *Jewish Encyclopedia*, VII, col. 512; *Encyclopaedia Judaica*, X, col. 1064; *Evreiskaia Entsiklopediia*, IX, col. 504; *Universal Jewish Encyclopedia*, VI, col. 403; *Sovetskaia Istoricheskaia Entsiklopediia*, VII, col. 391.

50 Bushnell, *Mutiny*, 42; V. I. Gurko, *Features and Figures of the Past: Government and Opinion in the Reign of Nicholas II*, trans. Laura Matveev (Stanford, 1939), 249; Ochs, "St. Petersburg," 227.

51 Löwe, *Antisemitismus*, 65–8; M. L. Mandel'shtam, *1905 god v politicheskikh protsessakh; zapiski zashchitnika* (Moscow, 1931), 19–40; Dubnow, *History*, III, 87–90; *Die Judenpogrome*, II, 37–44; H. J. Tobias, *The Jewish Bund in Russia* (Stanford, 1972), 227–8.

52 Lamzdorf's "Zapiska ob anarkhistakh," dated 3 January 1906, in no. 6 of *Sbornik sekretnykh dokumentov iz arkhiva byvshogo Ministerstva Inostrannykh Del*, published by the People's Commissariat of Foreign Affairs (Petrograd, 1918), 264–72. His view that Jews took the leading role in the revolutionary movement was shared not only by Nicholas II, Pleve, Witte, and lesser officials, but also by Austrian and German diplomats. See Hans Heilbronner, "Count Aehrenthal and Russian Jewry, 1903–1907," *Journal of Modern History*, XXXVIII (1966), 394–406. For other assessments, see Novitskii, *Vospominaniia*, 180; *Die Judenpogrome*, I, 245–6; N. M. Naimark, *Terrorists and Social Democrats. The Russian Revolutionary Movement Under Alexander III* (Cambridge, MS, 1983), 92, 202–11; Leonard Schapiro, "The role of the Jews in the Russian revolutionary movement," *Slavonic and East European Review*, XL (1961–2), 148–67.

53 "Indulgent wink" from Bernard Wasserstein, "Patterns of communal conflict in Palestine," in Ada Rapoport and Steven Zipperstein, eds., *Jewish History. Essays in Honour of Chimen Abramsky* (London, 1988), 620. Gomel is described as a turning point by Löwe, *Antisemitismus*, 67–8.

54 Löwe, *Antisemitismus*, 66; *Bulletin de l'Alliance Israélite Universelle*, 2ième série, no. 28, année 1903 (Paris, 1905), 57–8.

55 B. A. Krever, comp., *Gomel'skii protsess; podrobnyi otchet* (St. Petersburg, 1907), 6.

56 *Die Judenpogrome*, I, 234. Wasserstein "Patterns of communal conflict," 619, remarks on the frequent presence of "low-level authority figures," such as policemen and soldiers, among anti-Jewish rioters in Palestine.

This applies to Russia as well, where the category included postal employees and railwaymen. The latter were for the most part ethnic Russians and, to a lesser extent, Ukrainians, even on lines serving the non-Russian areas of the Empire. See Henry Reichman, *Railwaymen and Revolution; Russia, 1905* (Berkeley, 1987), 43–4.

57 "Perepiska Nikolaia II i Marii Fedorovny (1905–1906 gg.)," *Krasnyi Arkhiv*, XXII (1927), 169.

58 Evidence on the wide diversity of reactions to the Manifesto and to its public reception on the part of civilian, military, police, and Church authorities is voluminous and can only be sampled. See, i.e., E. K. Beliaeva, "Chernosotennye organizatsii i bor'ba s revoliutsionnym dvisheniem v 1905 g.," *Vestnik Moskovskogo Universiteta, Seriia Istoriia*, no. 2 (1978), 42–3; "Dekabr'skie dni v Donbasse," *Krasnyi Arkhiv*, LXXIII (1935), 107; Abraham Ascher, *The Revolution of 1905. Russia in Disarray* (Stanford, 1988), 316; Bushnell, *Mutiny*, 133; *Die Judenpogrome*, I, 192, 209, 252, 279; Mikhail Agursky, "Caught in a crossfire: the Russian Church between Holy Sinod and radical right (1905–1908)," *Orientalia Christiana Periodica*, L (1984), 168.

59 The notion of prior, or nationwide, organization was rejected by Senator Turau (*Kievskii i Odesskii pogromy*, 74–6). Cf. *Die Judenpogrome*, I, 273, 314–15; Löwe, *Antisemitismus*, 97; Bernard Pares, "The Russian government and the massacres," *Quarterly Review*, CCV (1906), 586–615; E. R. Zimmerman, "The right radical movement in Russia, 1905–1917" (Ph.D. Dissertation, University of London, 1968), 278.

60 Dubnow, *History*, III, 127. On the Union of Russian People, Don C. Rawson, "Voices from the Right, Russian monarchists and the revolution of 1905," unpublished book ms (1989). For the geographical dimensions of the pogroms, see *Die Judenpogrome*, I, 187–91; *Evreiskaia Entsiklopediia*, v, col. 618 and Dubnow's preface to Iliia Cherikover, *Antisemitizm i pogromy na Ukraine, 1917–1918 gg.* (Berlin, 1923), 10–12.

61 Ascher, *The Revolution of 1905*, 260–61.

62 "Agrarnoe dvizhenie v 1905 g. po otchetam Dubasova," *Krasnyi Arkhiv*, XI–XII (1925), 183; Scott Seregny, *Russian Teachers and Peasant Revolution* (Bloomington, IN, 1989), 176–7; Bushnell, *Mutiny*, 64, 69–70, 131–5; V. E. Bonnell, *Roots of Rebellion* (Berkeley, 1983), 327; Laura Engelstein *Moscow, 1905* (Stanford, 1982), 139–40; Löwe, *Antisemitismus*, 90.

63 Rex Rexheuser, *Dumawahlen und lokale Gesellschaft* (Cologne–Vienna, 1980), 170; R. T. Manning, *The Crisis of the Old Order in Russia* (Princeton, 1982), 426, n. 73; N. A. Bukhbinder, "Evreiskoe rabochee dvizhenie v 1905 godu; Pervoe maia," *Krasnaia Letopis'*, no. 7 (1923), 7; N. M. Frieden, *Russian Physicians in an Era of Reform and Revolution, 1856–1905* (Princeton, 1981), 296; Seregny, *Russian Teachers*, 148–9; Tobias, *The Jewish Bund*, 315–16; Bushnell, *Mutiny*, 56, 78–80; Ascher, *The Revolution of 1905*, 257, 266, 269, 324. Examples of police engaging

in excesses against students and in pogroms are given in *Kievskii i Odesskii pogromy*, 126, 131, 192.

64 For instances of unwillingness or inability to proceed against pogromists and revolutionaries, see *Kievskii i Odesskii pogromy*, 49–53, 56–7, 64, 74–6, 145, 158–61, 165; Pares, "Russian massacres," 596; F. W. Skinner, "Odessa," in Hamm, *The City*, 304; W. D. Santoni, "P. N. Durnovo as Minister of Interior in the Witte Cabinet" (Ph.D. dissertation, University of Kansas, 1968), 164; "Zapiski Λ. F. Redigera," 91; Löwe, *Antisemitismus*, 92–3. For examples of action taken against pogroms and pogromists, see ibid., 93–4; *Die Judenpogrome*, 1, 293; Bushnell, *Mutiny*, 186; Henry Reichman, "The 1905 Revolution on the Siberian Railroad," *Russian Review*, XLVII (1988), 39; *Kievskii i Odesskii pogromy*, 176.

65 *Kievskii i Odesskii pogromy*, 22, 59–63, 182, 184, 190; Ascher, *The Revolution of 1905*, 258, 260; Gary Hanson, "The Tomsk pogrom: gromili, Jews, intelligentsia and workers alike," unpublished paper, 1988; V. K. Korostovets, *Neue Väter–Neue Söhne. Drei russische Generationen* (Berlin, 1926), 228; Pares, "Russian massacres," 597; I. I. Petrunkevich, "Iz zapisok obshchestvennogo deiatelia," *Arkhiv russkoi revoliutsii*, XXI (Berlin, 1934), 405–7; Löwe, *Antisemitismus*, 94.

66 Löwe, *Antisemitismus*, 146–50, 167–70; Rogger, *Jewish Policies*, 100–1. R. P. Browder and A. F. Kerensky, eds., *The Russian Provisional Government, 1917* (Stanford, 1961), 1, 211–12, contains the law of 20 March 1917, which did not specifically refer to Jews: "All restrictions established by existing legislation on the rights of citizens of Russia by reason of their adherence to a particular religious denomination or sect or by reason of nationality are abolished."

67 For condemnations of pogroms by the Provisional Government, the First All-Russian Congress of Soviets and its Central Executive Committee, see Cherikover, *Antisemitizm*, 205–10. Examples of popular resistance to Jewish rights in: Browder and Kerensky, *The Russian Provisional Government*, II, 863, 1644, 1648 and W. G. Rosenberg, "The zemstvo in 1917 and its fate under Bolshevik rule," in Terence Emmons and W. S. Vucinich, eds., *The Zemstvo in Russia* (Cambridge, 1982), 398.

68 Marc Ferro, *The Russian Revolution of February 1917*, trans. J. L. Richards (London, 1972), 301–2; Marc Ferro, *October 1917*, trans. Norman Stone (London, 1980), 225, 321 (n. 4).

69 Cherikover, *Antisemitizm*, 13–14, 20, 24–35; *Encyclopaedia Judaica*, XIII cols. 698–701; *Jüdisches Lexikon* (Berlin, 1927–30), IV, pt. 1, cols. 983–7; Benjamin Pinkus, *The Jews of the Soviet Union* (Cambridge, 1988), 85; Zvi Gitelman, *Jewish Nationality and Soviet Politics* (Princeton, 1972), 158–68.

70 Joseph Boskin, ed., *Urban Racial Violence in the Twentieth Century* (Beverly Hills and London, 1969), 4–8; Allen Weinstein and F. O. Gatell, *The Segregation Era, 1863–1954* (New York, 1970), 112–28.

71 Feldberg, *Turbulent Era*, 38 (for Cincinnati) and passim.

72 L. F. Litwack, *North of Slavery. The Negro in the Free States, 1790–1860* (Chicago, 1961), 52–3, 178–85; G. B. Nash, *Forging Freedom. The Formation of Philadelphia's Black Community* (Cambridge, MS, 1988), 148–58.

73 Nash, *Forging Freedom*, 274; Feldberg, *Turbulent Era*, 41–2.

74 Feldberg, *Turbulent Era*, 26, 40, 76; Feldberg, *The Philadelphia Riots of 1844. A Study in Ethnic Conflict* (Westport, CT, 1975); Nash, *Forging Freedom*, 213.

75 Litwack, *North of Slavery*, 64–112, 159–68.

76 Ibid., 75, 101–2; Nash, *Forging Freedom*, 213.

77 Cook, *Armies of the Streets*; P. A. Gilje, *The Road to Mobocracy. Popular Disorder in New York City, 1763–1834* (Chapel Hill, NC, 1987), 285; Jules Archer, *Riot! A History of Mob Action in the United States* (New York, 1974), 65–70; Larry Kincaid, "Two steps forward, one step back," in G. B. Nash and Richard Weiss, eds., *The Great Fear. Race in the Mind of America* (New York, 1970), 45–6, 51.

78 Alexander Saxton, *The Indispensable Enemy: Labor and the Anti-Chinese Movement in California* (Berkeley, 1971), 113–16, 201–12; Shi-Shan Henry Tsai, *The Chinese Experience in America* (Bloomington, IN, 1986), 56–72.

79 Alexander Saxton, "Race and the house of labor," in Nash and Weiss, *Great Fear*, 105, 114–15; Eric Foner, ed., *America's Black Past* (New York, 1970), 299–300.

80 Foner, *America's Black Past*, 324–6; A. H. Spear, *Black Chicago. The Making of a Negro Ghetto, 1890–1920* (Chicago, 1967), 129–46; E. M. Rudwick, *Race Riot at East St. Louis, July 2, 1917* (Carbondale, IL, 1964), 217–18.

81 Rudwick, *Race Riot*, 218–20, 223, 227–30; Spear, *Black Chicago*, 201–22; Boskin, *Urban Racial Violence*, 2, 23, 25, 32, 35, 41; D. H. Bennett, *Demagogues in the Depression* (New Brunswick, NJ, 1969), 282–6. On the part rumor and symbols play in provoking crowds, see N. J. Smelser, *Theory of Collective Behavior* (New York, 1962), 116.

82 Boskin, *Urban Racial Violence*, 46–9; Carey McWilliams, *North from Mexico* (Philadelphia, 1949), chs. 12–13; Stanley Coben, "The failure of the melting pot," in Nash and Weiss, *Great Fear*, 153.

83 *New York Times*, 29 March 1988, A2; Sergei Grigoryants, "Tragedy in the Caucasus," *Glasnost Information Bulletin*, nos. 16–18 (January 1989), 6; George Soros, "The Gorbachev prospect," *New York Review*, 1 June 1989, 18, believes that the Sumgait pogrom was "instigated by the notorious local mafia, which is controlled by KGB official G. A. Alieev, in order to create a situation in which Gorbachev would lose, no matter what he did." Although that possibility cannot be ruled out, hard evidence is still lacking. Cf. R. G. Suny, "Nationalism and democracy in Gorbachev's Soviet Union: the case of Karabagh," *Michigan Quarterly*

Review, XXVIII (1989), 481–506. Comment on the Sumgait police from *Los Angeles Times*, 19 April 1988, 2.

84 Marshall in Boskin, *Urban Racial Violence*, 41.

85 Gilje, *Road to Mobocracy*, 285; Cook, *Armies of the Streets*, 213–32, lists dead and wounded policemen and soldiers. On Washington: Boskin, *Urban Racial Violence*, 28–9; Dubnow, *History*, II, 412.

86 A. Q. Lodhi and Charles Tilly, in their study of "Urbanization, crime and collective violence in nineteenth-century France," *American Journal of Sociology*, LXXXIX (1973), 296–318, call into question the linking of crime, collective violence, and disorder to urban growth and conclude that "the gross correlation over time is negative: rapid urban growth, little collective violence. Collective violence fluctuated much more directly as a function of the quickening and slowing of struggles for power at the national level." Although in some cases of ethnic violence described here such fluctuations did occur in connection with larger political conflicts, the discharge of social and economic tensions caused or exacerbated by migration to urban and industrial centers, appears to have been more important and more frequent. This holds true of recent ethnic clashes in the Soviet Union. According to a poll reported in *Sotsialisticheskaia Industriia* (16 August 1988), the movement of workers from one area to another was considered a major factor in stirring up nationality discontent. Political changes at the national level did, of course, facilitate the expression of discontent but cannot be said to have caused it.

87 Freud's letter, dated 2 December 1927, in E. L. Freud, ed., *Letters of Sigmund Freud and Arnold Zweig*, trans. Elaine and William Robson-Scott (New York, 1970), 3.

Bibliographical essay

Avraham Greenbaum

A bibliographic essay on pogroms in Russia should first define what a pogrom is, since anti-Jewish disturbances are not necessarily included in that category. We define a pogrom as a serious anti-Jewish riot, usually lasting for more than a day and often abetted by the authorities actively or passively. It was in the nature of the Russian pogroms from about 1881 on to spread over entire areas and to come in cycles which took about three years to subside. We find it convenient to use the following period division:

A   Pre-1881
B   1881–1884
C   1903–1906
D   1917–1921

General Works. A partial bibliography of the subject is the relevant part of Gershon C. Bacon and Gershon D. Hundert's bibliographic essay on Russian Jewry.[1] Bacon covers the pogrom literature of the post-1881 period selectively in his surveys of Russian antisemitism and of the Russian Jews in revolution and civil war. His work includes source materials and studies in Russian and Western languages as well as Yiddish and Hebrew, and is quite up to date though unfortunately not indexed.

Useful articles on the pogroms in encyclopedias can be found in two works, far apart in time: *Evreiskaia entsiklopediia*[2], undated but published around 1910, i.e. after the tsarist censorship had lapsed. The entry "Pogromy v Rossii" ("Pogroms in Russia") is extensive and detailed, consisting of twelve closely printed columns. Its first part, up to 1900, was written by the well-known historian of Russian Jewry, Iulii Gessen; the pogroms of the first decade of the new century were described by Daniel Pasmanik, a publicist with Zionist leanings. More concise, and more interested in causes and effects than in the details of the pogroms, is the Israeli historian Yehuda Slutzky's article "Pogroms" in the *Encyclopedia Judaica* (1971).[3] Here the bibliography is weighted in favor of the 1917–21 period. Slutsky does not take a stand on the controversial question of Simon Petliura's responsibility for the Civil War pogroms in the Ukraine (see section D). On the other hand, the statement that Odessa was saved during this period by the Jewish "self-defense" is too categorical. Odessa, the most pogrom-prone city in Russia (see Section A), was more probably saved by what amounted to foreign occupation.

After looking at the general histories we agree with Bacon that the most detail is provided by Simon Dubnov [Dubnow], *History of the Jews in Russia and Poland* (henceforth *HRP*).[4] Dubnov wrote the old-fashioned kind of narrative history; the modern reader may be irritated by his "black and white" approach to the Jewish problem in Russia, and his polemical style when taking on such an emotionally charged phenomenon as the pogrom waves. All this having been said, it remains true that Dubnov describes many of these outrages in detail – detail which varies with the importance he attaches to a particular pogrom – while later historians give little detail and concentrate on the politics and the results.

HRP, which does not reach the Civil War period, is excerpted from the general history the author was completing at the time. The final manuscript was apparently cut somewhat by the author or publisher, so that *HRP*, which appeared only in English, is slightly more extensive – especially in quotations from reports and documents – than the general history which appeared in translation after the First World War.[5] We note that the Russian original of the general history, termed definitive by the author, appeared in Riga in the last years before the Holocaust and is hard to find.[6] We also note with regret that its English translation, which finally appeared long after Dubnov's death, is awkward at best, erroneous in a number of places, and cannot be recommended.[7] Valuable observations on the pogroms – especially those at the beginning of this century – and the Jewish reaction can also be found in Dubnov's memoirs, at the end of which he appended his "auto-biography."[8]

In the post-Holocaust period the only general and complete Jewish history of academic value, much used by students nowadays, is the composite work published in Jerusalem in Hebrew at the end of the sixties and now available also in English.[9] Shmuel Ettinger, who wrote on the modern period, is more interested in interpretation than in description. In the pogrom context he emphasized the factor of economic competition. Ettinger, like many others, does not believe the 1881 pogroms were instigated from above, but the government's hesitation in suppressing them encouraged the wave. In his interpretation, the Balta pogrom of 1882 was more than the government could tolerate and led to the dismissal of the Minister of the Interior, Ignatiev, after which the outbreaks became sporadic.[10]

As for histories of Jews in Russia, those have been appearing with increasing frequency in the last fifty years. First was the two-volume work by Louis Greenberg around the time of the Second World War.[11] Greenberg does give the pogroms a fair amount of attention, though referring to Dubnov for more detail. He is interested in proving that the pogroms were a result of hostile policies and an inimical social climate fostered by the reactionary regimes of the last two Tsars. Much less interest in the subject is shown by Salo W. Baron, the great modern Jewish historian, who wrote a heavily criticized monograph on Russian and Soviet Jewry in the sixties and revised it in the seventies.[12] Baron may have been influenced by his well-known opposition to the "lachrymose school" of Jewish historiography. Here is the place to warn the reader against overly relying on indexes: Baron happens to call the Odessa pogrom of 1871 a "disturbance," and as a result one does not find it in his index under "pogroms."

The most recent history of the Jews in Russia, published in 1986 and directed mainly at the Israeli college student, is that of Benjamin Pinkus.[13] Very concentrated, it devotes only one-third of the space to the tsarist period; for the pogroms Pinkus is content with a statistical summary and the most important bibliographical references. His book may not be a good example, but the impression is inescapable that historians give less attention to the pogroms as they recede in time. Two recent studies of Russian Jewry by John Klier and Michael Stanislawski, taken together, provide a detailed study of the pre-pogrom period.[14]

Documentary material. There were two successful attempts to publish primary material: the first by a commission to investigate the pogroms established by the World Zionist Organization soon after 1905, and the second by Russia's Jewish Historical-Ethnographic Society soon after the 1917 revolutions. The Zionist Organization, being an unofficial body, had to content itself with press excerpts, eyewitness reports, and the like, but tried to give systematic attention to all places visited by a pogrom in the 1903–6 period, and also produced an introductory volume on the earlier pogroms.[15] Leo

Motzkin, who edited the volumes under the pseudonym A. Linden, even gave some attention to the rarely discussed pre-1881 period (see Section A). The post-1917 collection, edited by Dubnov and Krasnyi-Admoni, utilized the recently opened archives of the former Ministries of the Interior, Justice, and the Department of Police. The work, carried out in Petrograd under the very difficult conditions of the time, ended when the Soviet authorities withdrew their support. Of the two published volumes, which for technical reasons could not be in chronological order, the first deals with the Dubossary and Kishinev pogroms of 1903, the second with the pogroms of the 1880s.[16]

Much documentary material on the various pogroms was collected in Hebrew translation by the Israeli historian Israel Halpern in his wide-ranging anthology of Jewish heroism.[17]

A PRE-1881

It is widely assumed that Russia, as distinct from pre-partition Poland, did not know pogroms until 1881. There were, however, some earlier anti-Jewish riots which some writers call pogroms. All but one took place in Odessa, in the years 1821, 1859, and 1871. The Odessa pogroms are noted, but minimized as chance occurrences, in Gessen's old encyclopedia essay.[18] Other writers make do with the outbreak of 1871, which lasted for four days and was definitively a pogrom by our definition. It presaged the much more destructive pogrom of ten years later, and served as a warning to assimilating personalities such as the historian and jurist Ilia Orshanskii, who lived through the pogrom and has left us a graphic description.[19]

To date there is no complete history of the Jews of Odessa, but Steven J. Zipperstein's recent book helps to fill the gap and is currently the best source for the early Odessa pogroms.[20] Their basic cause was economic competition between Greeks and Jews, though religious prejudice brought about the earliest outbreak in 1821. A little-known book by a visiting German missionary reports that rumors in the area of religion nearly caused another Odessa pogrom in 1873.[21] The religious factor is not always given its due weight by twentieth-century historians.

Motzkin casually refers to a pogrom in the Bessarabian town of Akkerman in 1865.[22] This is evidently the least known of all the pogroms; Gessen omits it in his pogrom article in the Russian-language Jewish encyclopedia but mentions it without detail in the same work's article on Akkerman, which he wrote as well.[23] After the First World War even the literature on Akkerman no longer mentions this outbreak, an example of the Talmudic saying that "the later troubles cause the earlier ones to be forgotten." Like thousands of others the Akkerman community was destroyed in the Holocaust; it had previously suffered a serious pogrom in 1905.[24]

B 1881–1884

The pogrom wave of 1881–4 – in the opinion of many writers, 1881–2 with sporadic follow-ups – has received a good deal of attention because it was a historical turning point in a direction which no one would have predicted. The general histories abound with descriptions of Jews, especially young Jews, losing their faith in Russia and its culture and becoming Zionists, revolutionaries, Diaspora nationalists, or simply emigrants. Scholarly writing on the more narrow topic, the pogroms and their causes, began in tsarist Russia when the lifting of censorship in 1905 made open discussion possible with Dubnov beginning the process in the historical journal he edited.[25] This period enjoys unusually good bibliographic coverage due to the fact that the only extensive bibliography of Russian-language literature about the Jews, unfortunately never continued, was published in 1892 and lists nearly 150 items relating to the "besporiadki" (disorders) some ten years earlier.[26] Tsarist documents on them can be found in the collection edited after the revolution by Dubnov and Krasnyi-Admoni.[27] When Dubnov left Russia he had some police records of the time in his possession, and these were used in an interesting article by E. Tcherikower, which argued that the pogroms were organized by the "Sviashchennaia druzhina" (Holy Brotherhood) formed secretly by some aristocrats to protect the Tsar from harm.[28] Links between the Holy Brotherhood and antisemitism in the *émigré* Russian press are explored in the work of Shmuel Galai.[29] Foreign links to the Russian pogroms, and the treatment of the pogroms in the Russian press, are examined in two articles by John Klier.[30] It should be noted that these pogroms are not blamed by historians on the government directly though to Dubnov, who saw the entire 1881–1917 period as one long war by the authorities against the Jews, the point hardly mattered. One exception to the general consensus acquitting the authorities from direct responsibility for the pogroms is a recent article by Omeljan Pritsak which argues, on the basis of memoir evidence in Russian and Ukrainian, that the pogroms – or at least the first pogrom of 1881 in Elisavetgrad – were carefully organized, allegedly by officials from the capital.[31]

The first book on the pogroms of the eighties is a German dissertation printed in part in 1933.[32] Some fifty years later another book on the main pogrom year, by Stephen M. Berk, proves to be a disappointing pastiche of related topics such as antisemitism, emigration to the US, and even the rise of some unimportant Judeo-Christian sects.[33] Berk's book does include a useful bibliographical essay and is at least up to date. I. Michael Aronson's doctoral dissertation deals not with the pogroms but with their "bureaucratic" aftermath, i.e. the various government commissions founded in their wake, and especially the high-level Palen Commission.[34]

One item which might be considered as source material relating to the commissions' activity is the memorandum by the Odessa "crown rabbi" Simeon Schwabacher, the original German text of which has been preserved in the Jewish National and University Library in Israel.[35] Aronson also published an article directly concerned with the pogroms in their geographic aspect, as did Yehuda Slutzky in Hebrew.[36] Of course we cannot indicate in this essay all the articles on the topic; there is a concentration of them in the journal *Heavar*, nos. 9 and 10 (1962–3).[37]

An interesting sidelight to the pogroms of the eighties is the Polish issue. The Poles tended to pride themselves – at least until their own pogroms upon regaining independence in 1918 made the argument no longer tenable – on being free of the pogrom plague, of being too civilized to treat their Jews, dislike them though they did, in this manner.[38] The Warsaw pogrom of December 1881 threatened to refute this theory. But even Jewish historians who had little love for the Poles, such as Dubnov and Yitshak Grünbaum, credited the Warsaw pogrom to Russian instigators and pointed out that Polish society universally condemned it.[39] Poland under Russian rule – with some minor exceptions discussed in Grünbaum's essay – remained free of pogroms.

C 1903–1906

The work of Heinz-Dietrich Löwe provides essential background for the rise of a new wave of pogroms after the turn of the century.[40] Of these pogroms, the one which took place in the Bessarabian city of

Kishinev in April 1903 had the biggest effect. This is true even though the pogrom wave of October 1905 left many more victims in Odessa alone than Kishinev's forty-five dead. The very name of Kishinev became a byword for a new government-sponsored barbarism, and a whole literature arose around this pogrom. The world was taken by surprise by the reopening of what seemed a closed chapter, and by the increase in brutality: what had previously been mainly rampages of pillage and destruction were now routinely accompanied by murder and rape. Book-length works of protest appeared in the US[41] and in Germany,[42] which also provide considerable detail on the pogrom itself. A Hebrew memorial volume on the sixtieth anniversary brings no new material but keeps the memory alive.[43] The memoirs of the former governor of Bessarabia, which appeared in several languages including English a few years after the pogrom, give an unusual slant by opposing the pogrom phenomenon but absolving the government, at a time when almost everyone else was pointing an accusing finger at the Minister of the Interior V. K. Pleve as the organizer.[44] The reappraisal of Pleve's role has been carried further in the work of Edward Judge and Shlomo Lambroza.[45] Another source consists of fragments of an investigative report by the famous Hebrew poet Hayim Nahman Bialik. His full report, together with some related material, was finally published in 1991, more than half a century after the poet's death.[46]

Bialik's name brings us to a controversial aspect of Kishinev. On the basis of existing descriptions it is normally assumed that the Jews of Kishinev did *not* defend themselves, and that the more or less organized Jewish "self-defense" which played an increasingly important part in subsequent pogroms came about as a result of the Kishinev disgrace. Bialik's well-known poem "The City of Slaughter" contributed to this impression.[47] An Israeli born in Kishinev has tried to absolve his parent's generation from this charge of cowardice and helplessness, though it is doubtful that he can make an impression on the textbook writers who shape the historical consciousness of the next generation.[48]

The Kishinev pogrom was only the first of a wave. We have already had occasion to mention the one in nearby Dubossary.[49] Much more severe and extensive were the riots which broke out through much of Russia in the week after the Tsar's manifesto of 17 October 1905, in an attempt by the reactionaries to avenge their defeat upon the Jews. The near anarchy in Russia at the time, and the attention given to the revolution itself, made these riots difficult to document, but in Odessa alone the number of victims ran into the hundreds. The most extensive documentation of this period, on a province by province basis, is the second volume of the work edited and partly written by Motzkin in 1909.[50] Those interested in a specific town should not forget the hundreds of memorial volumes published since the Holocaust by former residents of the destroyed communities. These volumes, usually not particularly scholarly, are often the only source of what happened in the town. The most recent bibliography of these volumes appeared in 1983.[51]

The pogroms of this period interest scholars dealing with the regime of the last Tsar. One of them, Hans Rogger, questions the premise that the government instigated or organized these pogroms. He finds it "fairly certain that the pogroms were not approved as a matter of high policy at or near the level of central government."[52]

For recent research which places the pogroms of this period into a wider context, and which challenges many prior assumptions about the motives and identity of the pogromshchiki, see the unpublished doctoral dissertation of Charters Wynn, "Russian labor in revolution and reaction: the Donbass, 1870–1905" (Stanford, 1987).

D 1917–1921

For the general background of the Russian Civil War, see the work of Peter Kenez.[53] The pogroms of the Civil War period far surpassed in brutality and number of victims anything that had gone before. In some ways – especially since killings were sometimes carried out as a kind of "national duty" without the usual robbery – they bear comparison with the Holocaust some twenty years later; the great interest in the Holocaust may in turn have reduced attention to the Civil War pogroms. The years are 1917–21, but before 1918 and after 1920 there were few. Most of the pogroms were concentrated on Ukrainian territory in 1919 and perpetrated by the Ukrainian nationalists, but almost all warring armies, not to speak of armed bands, engaged in pogroms at some time or another. The pogroms by Denikin's Volunteer Army were numerous and have become the subject of some special studies (see below). Less known are depredations carried out against the Jews in Belorussia by the soldiers of Stanislav Bulak-Balakhovich.[54] Relatively free of the pogrom scourge were the Anarchists of Makhno and the Soviet troops. In the early twenties some Jewish reports emphasized Soviet pogroms,[55] possibly to counter the right-wing propaganda which equated Jews and communists; but more recent histories pointed out that the pogroms by Soviet troops were sporadic and – unlike those of other armies – were severely punished by the commanders.[56] The fact that the Ukrainian nationalist leader Simon Petliura was unable and apparently unwilling to stop the pogroms by his troops made him one of the most hated figures for the Jews of the time, and led to his assassination in Paris in 1926. This deed, and the trial following, which became a trial of the pogrom organizers and led to the acquittal of the assassin Shmuel Schwartzbard, became the subject of a popular book some twelve years ago.[57]

In 1919 one of the first big pogroms, that in Proskurov in February, left over 1,700 dead in its wake. The total number of pogrom dead is in the tens of thousands; the number, 100,000, often found in popular histories and articles, apparently confuses the dead with the total number of victims, which include many wounded.[58] Two small works on the pogroms came out before the Civil War had ended;[59] Leo Motzkin – again anonymously – edited a work on the subject written by Joseph Schechtman and sponsored by the Committee of the Jewish Delegations in 1927, at a time of strong interest after the Petliura assassination.[60]

After the twenties interest in the Civil War pogroms ebbed. Elias Tscherikower's major work on the subject of the pogroms in the Ukraine in 1919 was not published until after his death and then only in part and in Yiddish.[61] An earlier work by him, on the relatively mild pogroms of 1917–18, came out in Yiddish and Russian in the early twenties when interest was at its height.[62]

The question of Ukrainian responsibility has led to some apologetic literature by the Ukrainian nationalists now in exile; these tend to blame the Bolsheviks for the strained relations between Ukrainians and Jews.[63] The specific question of Petliura's responsibility caused a polemical exchange on the subject between a Jewish and a Ukrainian scholar some years ago in the New York journal *Jewish Social Studies*.[64]

Some additional sources are Tcherikower's unpublished archive and the memoirs of A. Revutsky.[65] Tcherikower had a life-long and almost obsessive interest in the Ukrainian pogroms and compiled as complete a list as possible of the victims. His archive is at the YIVO Institute for Jewish Research in New York. Revutsky was one of the Ministers for Jewish Affairs in the Ukrainian government, who came and went during the period of Ukrainian independence, finding it impossible to serve in a government which granted national autonomy to its Jewish citizens but could not protect them from its own armies.

As noted before, the Ukrainian nationalists were not the only pogromists. The pogroms staged by the Volunteer Army of General Denikin also killed thousands, and have been studied by two writers: the Yiddish scholar and publicist Nahum Shtif[66] and the later historian of the Zionist revisionist movement Joseph B. Schechtman.[67]

The terrible events of this period were taken up in some depth in fiftieth-anniversary articles devoted to the topic by the Israeli journal *Heavar*.[68] The most important article is by Slutzky. He discusses the problem of responsibility for the pogrom by all sides; and comes – albeit with caution – to the conclusion that the Soviet camp was worse than generally assumed, and that, contrary to earlier reports, the Anarchist peasant bands of Makhno were not pogromists.[69] A number of articles in the issue deal with various "self-defense" organizations which had been set up by the Russian Jews after Kishinev and were now active for the last time. There are also memoirs by those who themselves experienced the pogroms in their youth.

NOTES

1 Gershon D. Hundert and Gershon C. Bacon, *The Jews in Poland and Russia: Bibliographic Essays* (Bloomington, 1984).

2 *Evreiskaia entsiklopediia*, XII (1971), cols. 611–22.

3 *Encyclopedia Judaica*, XIII (1971), cols. 694–701.

4 S. M. Dubnow [Dubnov], *History of the Jews in Russia and Poland from the Earliest Times until the Present Day*, trans. by Israel Friedlander, 3 vols. (Philadelphia, 1916–20) reprinted in 2 vols. with some additions (New York, 1975).

5 S. Dubnov, *Weltgeschichte des jüdischen Volkes*, trans. A. Steinberg, 10 vols. (Berlin, 1925–9); *Divre yeme 'am 'olam*, trans. B. Krupnik (Karu), 10 vols. (Tel Aviv, 1923–4); reprinted frequently with minor additions and changes.

6 Dubnov, *Vsemirnaia istoriia evreiskogo naroda*, 10 vols. (Riga, 1936–8). The last three volumes, called *Noveishaia istoriia evreiskogo naroda*, were also published in an earlier and more accessible edition (Berlin, 1923).

7 S. Dubnow, *History of the Jews*. trans. M. Spiegel, 5 vols. (South Brunswick, NJ, 1967–73).

8 S. Dubnov, *Kniga zhizni*, 3 vols. (Riga and New York, 1934–57); in Yiddish: *Dos bukh fun mayn lebn*, 3 vols. (Buenos Aires, 1962–3). The

Hebrew and German versions published in the thirties are incomplete. An English translation is a great desideratum.

9 *Toldot 'am Yisrael*, ed. H. H. Ben-Sasson, 3 vols. (Tel Aviv, 1969); in English: *A History of the Jewish People* (Cambridge, MA, 1976). Unfortunately the entry "pogroms" in the index has no further breakdown.

10 Ben-Sasson, *A History of the Jewish People* (see previous note), 881–3.

11 Louis Greenberg, *The Jews in Russia*, 2 vols. (New Haven, CN, 1944–51); reprinted in a one-volume edition (New York, 1976).

12 Salo W. Baron, *The Russian Jew under Tsars and Soviets* (New York, 1964) 2nd revised and enlarged edition, 1976; reprinted in paperback, 1987.

13 Benjamin Pinkus, *Yehudim be-Rusiya uve-Berit ha-Mo'atsot* (Sde Boker, 1986).

14 John D. Klier, *Russia Gathers Her Jews: The Origins of the Jewish Question in Russia, 1772–1825* (DeKalb, IL, 1986); Michael Stanislawski, *Tsar Nicholas I and the Jews: The Transformation of Jewish Society in Russia, 1825–1855* (Philadelphia, 1983).

15 *Die Judenpogrome in Russland*, ed. Leo Motzkin, 2 vols. (Cologne, 1909).

16 *Materialy dlia istorii antievreiskikh pogromov v Rossii*, ed. S. M. Dubnov and G. Ia. Krasnyi-Admoni [vol. 2 edited by Krasnyi-Admoni alone] (Petrograd, 1919–23).

17 *Sefer ha-gevura*, ed. I. Halpern, 4 vols. (Tel Aviv, 1950–80). See especially vol. 3.

18 *Evreiskaia entsiklopediia*, XII, col. 611.

19 Il'ia Orshanskii, "K kharakteristike odesskogo pogroma," in his: *Evrei v Rossii* (St. Petersburg, 1877), 156–74.

20 Steven J. Zipperstein, *The Jews of Odessa: A Cultural History, 1794–1881* (Stanford, 1985).

21 Ferdinand Weber, *Reiseerinnerungen aus Russland* (Leipzig, 1873) 22.

22 Motzkin (see above, n. 14), I: 14; cf. M. Fischer, ibid., II: 91 ("ein geringfugiges Pogrom").

23 *Evreiskaia entsiklopediia*, I, cols. 636–7.

24 An Israeli memorial volume on the Akkerman community describes the 1905 pogrom but does not mention the one in 1865; *Akerman ve-'ayarot ha-mehoz* (Tel Aviv, 1983), 38.

25 Dubnov. "Antievreiskoe dvizhenie v Rossii v 1881 i 1882 gg.," *Evreiskaia starina*, I (1909), 88–109, 265–76; Dubnov, "Iz istorii vos'midesiatykh godov," ibid., 8 (1915), 266–95.

26 *Sistematicheskii ukazatel' literatury o Evreiakh na russkom iazyke* (St. Petersburg, 1892); reprinted Cambridge, MS, 1973; items 356–599.

27 *Materialy* (see above, n. 15), II.

28 Elias Tcherikower, "Naye materialn vegn di pogromen in Rusland onyeb di 8oer yorn," *Historishe shriftn*, II (1937), 444–65. Dubnov's archive was then in the Yiddish Scientific Institute (YIVO) in Vilna,

and is today in the successor institution, YIVO Institute for Jewish Research, in New York.

29 Shmuel Galai, "Early Russian constitutionalism, 'Vol'noe Slovo' and the 'Zemstvo Union'. A study in deception", *Jahrbücher für Geschichte Osteuropas*, N.F., xx, 1 (1974), 35–55.

30 John D. Klier, "Russian Judeophobes and German antisemites: strangers and brothers." *Jahrbücher für Geschichte Osteuropas*, xxxvii, 4 (1989), 524–40; "The Russian Press and the anti-Jewish pogroms of 1881," *Canadian–American Slavic Studies*, xvii, 1 (1983), 199–221. See also the same author's "*The Times* of London, the Russian press, and the pogroms of 1881–2," *The Carl Beck Papers*, no. 308 (1984), 1–26.

31 Omeljan Pritsak, "The pogroms of 1881," *Harvard Ukrainian Studies*, i–ii (1987), 8–43.

32 Mina Goldberg, *Die Jahre 1881–1882 in der Geschichte der russischen Juden* (dissertation, University of Berlin, 1934). Only sixty pages of the dissertation were printed.

33 Stephen M. Berk, *Year of Crisis, Year of Hope: Russian Jewry and the Pogroms of 1881–1882* (Westport, CT, 1985).

34 I. Michael Aronson, "Russian Bureaucratic Attitudes towards the Jews, *1881–1894*" (dissertation, Northwestern University, 1973).

35 Simeon Leon V. Schwabacher, *Denkschrift über die in den südlichen Provinzen Russlands vorgefallenen Unruhen* (Stuttgart, 1882).

36 I. M. Aronson, "Geographical and socioeconomic factors in the 1881 anti-Jewish pogroms in Russia," *The Russian Review*, xxxix (1980), 18–31; Yehuda Slutzky, "Ha-geografia shel pera'ot TaRMA," *Heavar*, ix (1962), 16–25.

37 Unfortunately the Israeli journal *Heavar* (22 issues, 1952–76), which dealt with Jewish history in Russia, is no longer being published.

38 A good example is the statement made by the openly antisemitic Polish National Democrat Roman Dmowski to the American Jewish leader Louis Marshall in 1918: "There never was a pogrom in Poland," *Louis Marshall, Champion of Liberty: Selected Papers and Addresses* (Philadelphia, 1957), ii: 586.

39 Dubnov, *HRP*, ii: 280–3; I. Grünbaum, "Die Pogrome in Polen," in *Die Judenpogrome in Russland*, i: 146–51.

40 Heinz-Dietrich Löwe, *Antisemitismus und reaktionäre Utopie* (Hamburg, 1987).

41 Cyrus Adler, *The Voice of America on Kishineff* (Philadelphia, 1904); Isadore Singer, *Russia at the Bar of the American People: A Memorial to Kishineff* (New York, 1904).

42 Told [Berthold Feiwel], *Die Judenmassacresin Kischinew* (Berlin [1903], a Palestine-oriented book.

43 *Ha-Pogrom be-kishinev bi-mlot shishim shana*, ed. H. Shurer et al. (Tel Aviv, 1963).

44 Serge P. Urussov, *Memoirs of A Russian Governor* (London and New York, 1908); reprinted New York, 1970.

45 Edward H. Judge, *Plehve: Repression and Reform in Imperial Russia, 1902–1904* (Syracuse, 1983); Shlomo Lambroza, "Pleve, Kishinev and the Jewish question: a reappraisal", *Nationalities Papers*, XII, 1 (1984), 117–27. See also Lambroza's "Jewish responses to pogroms in late imperial Russia," in Jehuda Reinharz, ed., *Living With Antisemitism: Modern Jewish Responses* (Hanover and London, 1987), 253–74.

46 H. N. Bialik, "Geviyat 'edut mi-pi nifge'e prea'ot Kishinov bi-shenat 1903," *Heavar*, I (1952), 18–30; ibid., X (1963), 150–4; *'Eduyot nifgee Kishinov 1903*, ed. Yaakov Goren (Afel, 1991).

47 Bialik, *Selected Poems*, ed. I. Efros (New York, 1965), 114–28.

48 David Doron, *Geto Kishinev veha-pogrom ha-softi* (Jerusalem, 1976), 27–33. Urussov, *Memoirs*, 52–3, mentions a Jewish self-defense organization of doubtful effectiveness in Kishinev. See also Shlomo Lambroza, "Jewish self-defense during the Russian pogroms of 1903–06," *Jewish Journal of Sociology*, XXIII (1981), 123–34.

49 *Materialy*, I.

50 Motzkin, *Die Judenpogrome in Russland*, II.

51 Zachary M. Baker, "Bibliography of Eastern European memorial Books," in *From a Ruined Garden: The Memorial Books of Polish Jewry*, ed. and trans. J. Kugelmass and J. Boyarin (New York, 1983), 223–64.

52 Hans Rogger, "The Jewish policy of late tsarism: a reappraisal," *Wiener Library Bulletin*, XXV, 1/2 (1971), 42–51; reprinted in Rogger, *Jewish Policies and Right-Wing Politics in Imperial Russia* (London and Oxford, 1986), 25–39.

53 Peter Kenez, *Civil War in South Russia, 1919–1920* (Berkeley, 1977).

54 See the entry on Bulak-Balakhovich in *The Modern Encyclopedia of Russian and Soviet History*. On the anti-Jewish depredations of his troops in the Pinsk area see Azriel Shochat in *Pinsk, sefer 'edut ve-zikaron*, I, pt. 2 (Haifa, 1977), 198–202 and the literature cited there. I thank Professor Shochat for calling this item to my attention.

55 E. G. Elias Heifetz, *The Slaughter of the Jews in the Ukraine in 1919* (New York, 1921), 201–2, 328.

56 Baron, *The Russian Jew*, 1976 edn, 184; Pinkus, *Yehudim be-Rusiya*, 190.

57 Saul S. Friedman, *Pogromchik: The Assassination of Simon Petlura* (New York, 1976); in Hebrew see M. Kotik, *Mishpat Shvartsbard* (Tel Aviv, 1972).

58 Tcherikower knew of c. 20,000 dead, and there were obviously more; see his *Di Ukrayner pogromen in yor 1919* (New York, 1965), 11. Baron, *The Russian Jew*, 1976 edn, 184, thinks the number "easily" exceeded 50,000, but has no evidence for this claim.

59 Heifetz, *The Slaughter of the Jews*; American Jewish Congress, *The Massacres and Other Atrocities Committed against the Jews in Southern Russia* (New York, 1920); S. I. Gusev-Orenburgskii, *Kniga o evreiskikh pogromakh na Ukraine v 1919 g.* (Petrograd, 1921).

60 *The Pogroms in the Ukraine under the Ukrainian Governments, 1917–1920* (London, 1927); published also in French. The Committee of the Jewish Delegations, formed in Paris in 1919 at the Peace Conference, stayed in existence to protect worldwide Jewish interests until the task was assumed by the World Jewish Congress.

61 Motzkin, *Die Judenpogrome in Russland*, II.

62 Cherikover (Tcherikower), *Antisemitizm i pogromy na Ukraine, 1917–1918* (Berlin, 1923); also in Yiddish: *Antisemitizm un pogromen in Ukrayne 1917–1918* (Berlin, 1923).

63 See e.g. *Material concerning Ukrainian-Jewish Relations during the years of the Revolution, 1917–1921*, ed. F. Pigido (Munich, 1956).

64 *Jewish Social Studies*, XXXI (1969), 163–213.

65 A. Revutzky, *In di shvere teg oyf Ukrayne* (Berlin, 1924).

66 Nahum Shtif, *Pogromen in Ukrayne: Di tsayt fun der frayviliger armey* (Berlin, 1923), published also in Russian.

67 Joseph B. Schechtman (Shekhtman), *Pogromy dobrovol'cheskoi armii na Ukraine* (Berlin, 1932).

68 *Heavar*, XVII (1970).

69 Slutzky, "Be'ayat ha-ahrayut li-pera'ot Ukraina," *Heavar*, XVII: 27–43.

Index

African–Americans: riots and lynchings of, 351–5, 356–8
Akkerman, 376–7
Aksakov, Ivan, 30
Akselrod, Pavel, 63, 65, 66, 73–4; and response to pogroms of 1881–4, 81, 82, 102, 117–21
Albedynskii, P. P., 167, 168, 169–71, 173–4
Alexander, II, 6, 8, 9, 20, 48, 165; assassination, 39, 40, 45, 46, 47, 50, 51, 64, 77, 100, 101, 103, 104–5, 191, 337
Alexander III, 3, 11, 39, 45, 51, 56, 64; and the pogroms of 1881–4, 67, 68, 72, 169, 182, 317, 328, 331
Alexeev, E. I., 212
Algiers: pogrom of 1898, 321
Alliance Israélite Universelle, 233
Alsace: pogrom of 1848, 320
American Jewish Yearbook, 222–3
anarchists: and pogroms of 1919–21, 294, 296–7, 300, 350, 382
Armenians, 359
artels, 75
Austro-Hungarian Empire, 145
autoemancipation, 144
Azeris, 359

Baku, 40
Bakunin, M. A., 72, 296
Bakuninists, 103
Balta, 120; pogrom of 1882, 41, 375
Baron, Salo W., 375
Bekman, V. A., 199
Belorussia, 3–4, 14, 111, 334, 381
Belostok (Bialystok): pogrom of 1906, 227, 231, 237–8
Bender, 170, pogrom of 1904, 213–14
Bessarabets (Bessarabian), 196–7, 201, 204, 206, 214, 215, 224

Bessarabia, 191; mobilization pogroms (1904), 215; pogrom of 1904, 216; pogrom of 1905, 228, 231
Black Americans, *see* African–Americans
Black Hundreds, 14, 224–6, 231, 233, 237, 240, 259, 262, 278–80, 345, 347
Black Repartition (*see* Chernyi Peredel)
Bloody Sunday, 195, 219, 347
Bogdanovich, I. P., 45
Bohemia: pogroms of 1893 and 1899, 323
Bolsheviks/Bolshevism, 256, 292, 300, 307, 311
Borispol, 331
bosiaki (barefoot brigade), 47, 336
Brafman, Iakov, 20–1, 29, 31
Bulak-Balakhovich, S., 381
Bulanov, A. P., 63, 80, 81, 82
Bulatsel, P. F., 224
Bulygin, Alexander, 223
Bund (General Jewish Workers' Part in Russia and Poland), 151–2, 192, 220, 223; and Jewish self-defense, 208, 217–18, 221, 223–4, 226, 256, 258, 259, 341–3
buntarstvo, 101, 103

Cahan, Abraham, 111, 112, 121
Cassini, Arthur, 207
Catherine II, 3–4, 5, 250, 334
Census of 1897, 138, 156, 159, 208, 253; and Jewish population, 138–9; and Jewish occupational patterns, 140
Chatskin, I., 27
Cheka, 293
Chernigov, 228, 346
Chernyi Peredel (Black Repartition): and pogroms of 1881–4, 62–97, 98, 106–10, 109, 113–14, 118
Chernyi Peredel, 63, 65, 66, 79, 81–3, 109, 113
Chertkov, M. I., 173

Chezmenkov, I. D., 198, 201, 202–3, 207, 210
Chinese Exclusion Acts, 355–6
Chmielnicki, Bogdan, 14
Chudnovskii, Solomon, 124–5
Civil War (United States), 352, 355
Civil War (Russian), 292–311, 349, 350, 374, 380, 381
Clergy, 55, 170–1, 179, 215, 346, 347; and pogroms of 1919–21, 306–7
Committee of the Jewish Delegations, 381
Congress Poland (*see* Poland, Kingdom of)
Cossacks, 14, 17, 18, 27, 75, 176, 213, 256, 266, 331, 339, 347; and the pogroms of 1919–21, 297, 298, 299, 302–4, 349, 350
Council of Ministers, 40, 41
Crémieux decree (1870), 321
Czas (Time), 181, 183
Czechoslovakia, 324
Czestochowa, 178, 179, 192

Davidovitch, M., 206
Deich, Lev, 63, 82, 114, 117–21, 123, 124
Delo (The Cause), 22
Den (The Day), 16, 21, 31–2
Denikcn, A. I., 294, 298, 301, 305, 307–9, 311, 380, 381
Di arbeiter shtimme (The Workers' Voice), 150–1
Doctors' Plot, 359
Dondukov-Korsakov, A. M., 32
Dragomirov, A. M., 308
Drenteln, A. R., 329, 330, 334
Dreyfuss Affair, 321
Dubnow (Dubnov), S. M., 41, 86n, 181–2, 203, 224, 239, 316, 325, 326, 332, 345, 360, 362n, 363n, 376, 377, 378; on Jewish national identity, 154–5
Dubossary, 197, 202, 210, 376, 379
Dubrovin, A. I., 224, 225, 235
Duma (1906), 155, 235, 237, 238; (1916), 291
Durnovo, I. N., 203, 329

Easter Week, 326; and pre-1881 pogroms, 18, 19, 21, 23; and pogroms of 1881–4, 40, 41, 45, 46, 50, 167, 171, 176, 329; and pogroms of 1903–6, 196, 198, 205, 214, 251, 255–6, 339; and pogroms of 1919–21, 306
Ekaterinoslav: pogrom of 1883, 41, 329; mobilization pogroms (1904), 215; pogrom of 1905, 228
Elisavetgrad, 53; pogrom of 1881, 40, 45, 54, 67, 100, 105, 329, 336, 337, 378

Emigré, 83
Eruv, 171–2

France: Jewish emancipation 319–20; pogroms of 1898, 321

Gabin, 176–7, 179
Galicia, 181, 309, pogroms of 1918, 323
Gapon, Georgii, 219
Gelfman, Gesia, 39–40
Gessen, Iu. I., 373, 376, 377
Getsov, I., 63, 76–7, 113–14
Gintsburg (Guensburg), Horace, Baron, 68, 69, 98
Golczewski, F., 182–3
Golos (The Voice), 16, 28–9, 30
Gomel: pogrom of 1903, 192, 207–11, 212, 218, 340–1, 342, 343; and legal proceedings, 211, 218, 343; and police and military, 208–9
Gorbachev, Mikhail, 359
Gostyn, 172
government policies toward Jews, 3–11, 40–1, 51, 141–2, 159, 211, 314–15; and the pogroms of 1881–4, 164–85, 316–17; and the pogroms of 1903–6, 196, 206, 207, 210–11, 211, 212, 218, 221, 237–41, 250, 257, 260
Greenberg, Louis, 99, 203, 224, 239, 375
Grigorev, G., 297
Grinefest, S., 63, 113, 116
Gringmut, G., 235
Grodno: mobilization pogroms (1904), 215; pogroms of 1904, 216; pogrom of 1906, 227
Gruenbaum, I., 181–2
Grujec, 173, 174, 175
Gurevich, G., 117–19, 122, 123, 124
Gurko, Io. V., 171
Gurko, V. I., 226
Gurvich, I., 111, 113

halakha, 156–7, 171–2
Hebrew language, 152–6
heder, 9, 10
Hep-Hep Riots, 318–21, 325
Herzl, Theodor, 148, 221–2
Hibbat Zion (Lovers of Zion), 146–8
High Commission for the Review of Existing Legislation on the Jews (Palen Commission), 24, 363
Holy League, 317, 329
Holy Week, *see* Easter
Hungary, 324

Ignatiev commissions, 40
Ignatiev, Nikolai Pavlovich, Count, 7,
    40-1, 54, 68-9, 70, 168, 203, 211,
    244n, 317, 329, 375
Illiustratsiia (Illustration), 18
Imeretynskii, A. K., 175
Iskra (The Spark), 222
Iuzovka: pogrom of 1892, 338-9
Ivan IV, 13

Jewish Chernoperedeltsy (*see also* Jewish
    Populist and Jewish socialists), 99, 113,
    115, 117
Jewish community (Russian), 137; Census
    of 1897, 138-40, 253; culture, 152-6;
    economic condition, 141-2, 148-9;
    education, 156-9; emancipation
    during Russian Revolution of 1917,
    292; and emigration, 139-40, 144-8;
    internal migration, 140; labor
    movement, 148-52; and nationalism,
    152-6; occupational patterns, 140; in
    Odessa, 252-4; political leadership,
    143-8; population 138-40, 334;
    religion, 156-9; urban population, 139
Jewish Daily News, 204
Jewish emancipation, 322, in France,
    319-20; during Russian Revolution of
    1917, 292
Jewish emigration, 46, 51, 139-40; as a
    result of pogroms of 1881-4, 143-8; to
    Palestine, 143-4, 145-7
Jewish Historical-Ethnographic Society, 375
Jewish labor movement (*see also* Bund),
    148-52
Jewish narodniki, *see* Jewish populists
Jewish Narodovoltsy (*see also* Jewish
    Populists and Jewish socialists), 99,
    112-13, 115, 117
Jewish nationalism, 152-6
Jewish New Year, *see* Rosh Ha Shannah
Jewish Populists/Populism, 98, 99, 110,
    112, 113
Jewish press, 152-6
Jewish Question, 7, 11, 18, 28, 29, 30, 51,
    82, 83, 119-21, 138, 151, 303; and
    education, 156-9; and the religious
    community, 156-9
Jewish socialists, 221; and pogroms of
    1881-4, 99-100, 102, 110, 111-12,
    116, 117, 119-25, 126n, 148-9, 150; in
    Vilna, 150-1

Kadet Party, 306-7
kahal, 8, 20

Kalisz, 175, 178
Katkov, M. N., 26
Kattowitz, 146
Kaulbars, A. V.: and Odessa pogrom of
    1905, 225, 233, 262-7, 269-72, 348
Kherson, 40, 53; mobilization pogroms
    (1904), 215; pogrom of 1904, 216;
    pogrom of 1905, 228
Kielce: pogrom of 1946, 324-5
Kiev, 66, 334; disorders of 1113, 13;
    pogrom of 1881, 40, 54, 100, 105,
    112-13, 329, 331, 335, 336, 337;
    mobilization pogroms (1904), 215;
    pogrom of 1904, 216; pogrom of 1905,
    228, 231; pogroms of 1919-21, 300-1,
    308
Kievlianin (The Kievan), 29-30, 301
Kishinev: pogrom of 1903, 160, 166, 172,
    174, 192, 195-207, 208, 210, 212, 238,
    255, 316, 339-40, 341, 356, 376, 379;
    legal proceedings, 210-11, 218, 219;
    and police and troops, 199, 201-3, 204,
    205, 209, 238; police report on, 206;
    property damage, 200; deaths and
    injuries, 200; participants, 204
Klingenberg, Governor of Mogilev, 342,
    343
Kolivshchyzna, 14
Kommisarov, M. S., 237, 345
Kongresowka (*see* Poland, Kingdom of)
Kornilov, L. G., 297
Kotsebu, P. E., 21-4, 26, 28, 32
Kovalskaia, E., 65
Kovno: pogrom of 1904, 216
Kraevskii, A. A., 28
Krakow, 181
Krasnyi-Admoni, g., 164, 166, 184, 376,
    377
Kremenchug, 53
Kremer, Arkadi, 149-50
Kristallnacht, 359
Krushevan, P. A., 196, 201, 204, 210,
    224
Kun, Bela, 324
Kuropatkin, A. N., 215-16
Kursk, 347
Kutaisov, P. I., Count, 44, 51, 56, 86n,
    330, 334, 337
Kutno, 178
Kuzminskii, A.: and Odessa pogrom of
    1905, 265-9, 271-2

Lamzdorf, V. N., Count, 222, 342
Land and Liberty (*see* Zemlia i Volia)
Lavrov, P. L., 72, 107, 108-9, 117

League for the Attainment of Full Rights for the Jews of Russia, 155
Leo XIII, 172
Levkov, S., 63
Lieberman, A. S., 72
Lilienblum, M. L., 143–8
Lipkin, I. B. Z., 158
Listok Narodnoi Voli (Narodnaia Volia Sheet), 70
Lithuania, 14, 63, 141, 334
Lodz, 223
Lomza, 170; mobilization pogroms (1904), 215
Lopukhin, A. A., 206, 234–7, 238
Loris-Melikov, M. T., 40, 52, 54, 68, 167, 329
Lovers of Zion (*see* Hibbat Zion)
Lowicz, 176
Lublin, 177

Makhno, Nester, 296–7, 298, 382
Mamontov, K. K., 307
Martov, Iulii, 150
maskilim, 98, 102
May Laws, 41, 139, 191, 221, 226, 241
Medem, N. N., Governor of Warsaw, 167, 168, 171, 173–5, 180, 183
Menshevism, 63, 256, 280
Mexican–Americans, 357
military, 33; and Odessa pogrom of 1871, 27; and pogroms of 1881–4, 45, 53–5, 176–7, 181, 183, 330–3; and pogroms of 1903–6, 199, 202–3, 204, 205, 208–9, 212, 213, 217–18, 235–6, 237
Miliukov, Pavel, 195
Ministry of the Interior, 21–2, 40–1, 237, 240, 259, 329
Minsk, 63, 111, 113, 116; pogrom of 1905, 192, 231
mobilization pogroms (1904), 213–16
Mogilev, 113, 347; mobilization pogroms (1904), 215
Moldavia (Romania), pogroms of 1907, 1920, and 1921, 323
Monarchist League, 238
Moscow, 47, 63, 66, 139
Moskovskie vedomosti (Moscow Gazette), 26–8
Motzkin, Leo, 103, 110, 227, 239, 376, 380, 381
musar talks, 157–8

Narodnaia Volia (The People's Will), 62, 337; and pogroms of 1881–4, 64–5, 70–1, 73, 82, 91, 98, 101, 103, 106–9, 111, 118, 121, 123–5

Narodnaia Volia, 64–5, 70–1, 73, 82, 91, 98, 101, 110
narodniki (*see also* Populists), 22, 62, 81, 101
National Committee of Jewish Self-Defense, 255
Nazi Germany, 359
Neidhart, Dmitri: and Odessa pogrom of 1905, 233, 237, 248, 262–72, 348
New York draft riots (1863), 354, 360
New York Relief Committee, 205
Nicholas I, 8, 9, 138
Nicholas II: and pogroms of 1903–6, 196, 207, 210, 212, 219, 222, 224, 234, 238, 239, 240, 248, 261, 344; deposition of, 292
Nizhnii Novgorod: pogrom of 1884, 42
Novoe vremia [The New Times], 10, 39, 45, 192, 224, 333
Novo-Minsk, 176
Novorossiiskii telegraf (New Russian Telegraph), 45, 46, 80

October Manifesto (1905), 225–7, 231, 232–3, 234, 248, 249, 259, 260–1, 267, 278, 344, 345, 346, 380
Odessa, 116, 334; pre-1881 pogroms, 15–33, 40, 376; pogrom of 1821, 17, 251; pogrom of 1849, 17–18, 251; pogrom of 1859, 18–20, 251; pogrom of 1871, 20–33, 124–5, 251–2; pogrom of 1881, 40, 251, 330, 332; pogrom of 1905, 231–3, 237, 248–81, 379, 380; economic conditions, 277; Jewish community of, 252–4; Greek residents and pogroms, 15–17, 22, 25, 27, 30–1, 251–2, 376; pogromists during 1905, 272–81; population of, 249, 250, 252, 253
Odessa Aid Committee, 233
Odesskie dni (Odessa Days), 256–7
Odesskii novosti (Odessa News), 268
Odesskii vestnik (Odessa Herald), 18, 19, 24–6, 27, 28
Okhrana (Political Police), 24, 236, 237, 240, 267
Ornshtein, S. S., 31
Orshanskii, I. G., 31, 32
Ostrovets: pogrom of 1904, 217

Pale of Settlement, 5–6, 26, 40, 51, 56, 72, 73, 111, 143, 146, 164, 165, 166, 168, 192, 248, 316; abolition of, 292; geographic area, 138–9; Jewish population of, 138–9, 156, 192; and labor movement, 149–52

Palen Commission, *see* High Commission for the Review of Existing Jewish Legislation on the Jews
Palestine, 111, 119; Jewish emigration to, 143, 145-7
Paramonov, N. E., 298
Parchev: pogrom of 1904, 217
Passover, 197, 198
Passover, A., 68
People's Will, The (*see* Narodnaia Volia)
Periaslav, pogrom of 1881, 335
Perovskaia, Sofia, 39
Petliura, S. V., 294, 295-7, 300, 374, 381
Pinsker, Leo, 144-5, 146
Piotrkow, 177, 179
Plekhanov, Gregorgii, 63, 65, 82, 91, 107-9
Plekhanova, Rozaliia, 116
Pleve (Plehve), V. I., 203-4, 206, 207, 221, 224, 340, 341, 379
Plock, 170, 172
Pobedonostsev, K. P., 39, 55
Podolia, 228
Pogroms, 6, 11, 164; common usage of term, 35n, 314, 315, 373; etymology, 34n; features of pogroms, 14, 33-4
Pogroms, pre-Modern, 13-14; Kiev (1113), 13; Polotsk (1563), 13; Ukraine, 13-14
Pogroms, pre-1881 in Odessa, 15-33, 124-5, 251-2, 376; government responses, 21-4, 32-3; the press, 16-22, 24-32
Pogroms of 1881-4, 3, 11, 34, 39-57, 328-9; in Balta, 41, 375; in Ekaterinoslav, 41, 329; in Elisavetgrad, 40, 45, 67, 100, 105, 329, 336, 337, 378; in Gabin, 173-4; in Kiev, 40, 100, 105, 329, 331, 335, 336, 337; in Nizhnii Novgorod, 42; in Odessa, 40, 251, 330, 332; in Periaslav, 335; in Smela, 105, 332; in Warsaw, 40, 177, 330, 338; Alexander III on, 67, 68, 72, 169, 182, 317, 328, 331; and the central government, 44, 46, 51-5, 68-70, 141-2, 159, 164-85, 316-17; and Chernyi Peredel, 62-97; and emigration, 143-8; as a result of modernization and industrialization, 46-8, 51, 137; and Narodnaia Volia, 64-5, 70-1, 73, 82, 91; physical damage, 143; in Poland, 164-85; police and the military, 45, 53-5, 176-7, 178, 180, 183, 330-3; and Populism/Populists, 97-134; and the press, 39, 45-6, 49, 70-95; statistics, 143, 328

Pogroms of 1903-6, 44; in Belostok, 227, 231, 237; in Bender, 213-14; in Bessarabia, 215, 216, 228, 231; in Chernigov, 228, 346; in Ekaterinoslav, 215, 228; in Gomel, 192, 196, 207-11, 218, 340-1, 342, 343; in Grodno, 215, 216, 227; Iuzovka (1892), 338-9; in Kherson, 215, 216, 228; in Kiev, 215, 216, 223, 228, 231; in Kishinev (1903), 160, 166, 172, 174, 192, 195-207, 208, 209, 210-11, 212, 218, 219, 238, 255, 316, 339-40, 341, 343, 356, 376, 379; in Kovno, 216; in Lomza, 215; in Minsk, 192, 231; in Mogilev, 215, 347; in Odessa, 231-3, 237, 248-81, 379, 380; in Ostrovets, 217; in Parchev, 217; in Podolia, 228; in Poltava, 228; in Rovno, 218; in Samara, 216; in Saratov, 347; in Sedlits, 227, 238; in Simferopol, 231; in Smela, 217-18; in Smolensk, 216; in Sosnovitsy, 217, 218; in Vitebsk, 215, 216, 218, 231; in Volynia, 216; in Warsaw, 223, 378; in Zhitomir, 223-4, 347; and the central government, 196, 205, 210-12, 218, 250, 257; and Jewish self-defense, 192, 198, 202, 208, 209-10, 217-18, 223-4, 228, 255-6, 279, 341-3, 379; mobilization pogroms (1904), 213-16, 341; police and the military, 199, 202-3, 204, 205, 208-9, 212, 213, 217-18, 235-6, 237, 239, 240, 260-2, 264-74; and the press, 196-7, 201, 204, 206, 214, 215, 222, 224, 225; statistics on, 228, 229, 231
Pogroms of 1919-21, 293-311; in Kiev, 300-1, 308; in Proskurov, 295, 381; and antisemitic propaganda, 307-8; role of S. V. Petliura, 294, 295-7, 374; statistics, 302; and officers in Volunteer army, 304-6, 308-11
Pogroms outside Russia: in Algiers (1898), 321; in Alsace (1848), 320; in Bohemia (1893 and 1899), 323; in France (1898), 321; Hep-Hep Riots (1819), 318-21, 325; in Kielce (1946), 324-5; in Moldavia (Romania), pogroms of 1907, 1920 and 1921, 323; in Pomerania (1881), 322-3; in Prague (1897), 323; in West Galicia (1898), 323; in West Prussia (1881), 322
Poland, Kingdom of (Russian), 5, 20; and pogroms of 1881-1903, 164-85; and pogroms of 1903-6, 216

Poale-Zion (Workers of Zion), 220
police, 17, 21, 23–4, 33, 52–3, 366n; and
    Odessa pogrom of 1871, 23–4, 27, 54,
    55; and pogroms of 1881–4, 178, 183,
    330–3; and pogroms of 1903–6, 199,
    201–3, 204, 205, 208–9, 212, 213,
    217–18, 235–6, 237, 239, 240, 260–2
Polish Republic, 323
Polish Social Democrats, 223
Polish Socialist Party (PPS), 223
Pollan, A., 197
Polotsk: pogrom of (1563), 13
Poltava, 53, 228
Pomerania, pogrom of 1881, 322–3
Populism, 62, and pogroms of 1881–4, 82,
    97–134
Populists, 22; and pogroms of 1881–4, 82,
    97–134 (*see also* narodniki)
Poslednie izvestiia (The Latest News), 222
Potemkin, 256, 346
Prague, pogrom of 1897, 323
Pravitelstvennyi vestnik (Government Herald),
    24
Pravo (Law), 211
Press coverage: and pre-1881 pogroms,
    16–22, 24–32; and pogroms of 1881–4,
    39, 45–6, 49, 70–95, 98, 101, 107, 109,
    110, 113–14, 181, 333; Jewish press,
    152–6; Polish press, 179, 181, 183; and
    pogroms of 1903–6, 196–7, 201, 204,
    206, 211, 212, 214, 215, 222, 224,
    225
Pribyleva, A. N., 115
Proskurov: pogrom of 1919, 295, 381
Protocols of the Elders of Zion, 192, 292
Provisional Government, 292, 307, 309, 349
Pugachev rebellion, 316
Purishkevich, V. M., 224

Raaben, R. S., 197–9, 201, 202–3, 207, 210
Rachkovskii, P. I., 235
Rafalovich, David, 27
Raffalovitch, Arthur, 215
Rasputin, Grigory, 291
Rassvet (The Dawn), 21, 143
Ratner, M. B., 112–13
Reclus, Elisee, 119
Red Army, 293, 294, 297, 301
revolution, Russian (1905), 192, 195,
    219–39, 241, 248, 314, 355; October
    general strike, 226–7; October
    Manifesto, 225–7, 231, 232, 234, 248,
    249, 259, 260–1, 267, 278, 344, 345,
    346, 380; and Odessa pogrom, 248–81
revolution, Russian (1917), 291–2, 297, 350

ritual murder, 16, 42, 164, 196, 197, 202,
    204–6, 214, 242n, 339, 356
Romanenko, G. G., 101, 103, 105–9, 114,
    115, 124, 128n, 129n
Rosh Ha Shannah, 216, 217
Rothschild, Edmund de, Baron: financing
    of Palestine settlement, 147
Rovno: pogrom of 1904, 218
rumors: as justification for pogroms, 33,
    164, 292, 323; and Odessa pogrom of
    1859, 19; and Odessa pogrom of 1871,
    22, 30; and pogroms of 1881–4, 40, 42,
    45, 47, 49, 50, 55, 67–8, 86n, 170,
    172–3, 176, 181, 182, 337; and
    pogroms of 1903–6, 197, 204–6, 214,
    217, 223, 251, 256
Russian Assembly, 224
Russkii vestnik (Russian Herald), 19
Russo–Japanese War, 194, 212–16, 218,
    219, 254–5, 341; Jews in, 215
Russo–Turkish War, 333
Rybachenko, M., 197

St Petersburg, 47, 63, 66, 67, 72, 113–14,
    115, 139, 165, 166, 175, 180, 183, 207,
    219
St Petersburg Aid Committee, 227
Samara: pogrom of 1904, 216
Sanktpeterburgskie vedomosti (St Petersburg
    Gazette), 25, 30–1
Saratov, 347
Schchedrin, Nikolai, 65
Schechtman, J., 381
Schiff, Jacob, 214
Schwabacher, S., 378
Schwartzbard, Samuel, 295, 381
Sedlits, 227; pogrom of 1906, 238
self-defense (Jewish), 192; during pogroms
    of 1903–6, 199, 202, 208, 209–10,
    217–18, 223–4, 228, 243n, 341–3,
    255–6, 278, 379; during pogroms of
    1919–21, 300, 374, 382
Sheftel, M. I., 63, 82
Sheremetev, S. D., 238
Shkuro, A. G., 297–8
Shulgin, V. V., 301, 308
Simferopol, 231
Sion (Zion), 21
Smela: pogroms of 1881–4, 105; pogrom of
    1904, 217–18, 332
Smolensk: pogrom of 1904, 216
social cosmopolitanism, 98, 99–100, 117,
    122, 123
Social Democrats, 220, 226, 257, 260, 278,
    280, 342

socialist revolutionaries (*see also Narodniki*), 45, 52
Socialist Revolutionaries, 112, 219, 223, 226, 257
Society for the Promotion of Culture among Jews, 98
Sokolov, K. N., 298
Solskii, D. M., 104
Sosnovitsy: pogrom of 1904, 217, 218
Southern Russian Workers Union of Kiev, 65, 66, 67, 106
Stavropol, 298
Stefanovich, Ia. A., 63, 82, 108
Stolypin, Peter, 248
Stroganov, A. G., Count, 19
Sumgait, 359
Suvorin, A. A., 224

Talmud, 157
Tikhomirov, Lev, 105, 108, 110
The Times (London), 28
Tisza–Eszlar trial, 42, 242n, 323
Tolstoi, D. A., 10, 41, 330
"To the Ukrainian People", 101, 105
Totleben, E. I., 316
Trepov, D. F., 234, 236, 239
Tscherikower (Cherikover), Elias, 102, 110, 124, 125n, 126n, 377, 381–2

Ukraine, 45, 47, 49, 66, 77, 191; premodern pogroms, 13–14; Chmielnicki revolt, 14; pogroms of 1881–4, 105, 169–70, 174, 183; pogroms of 1919–21, 293–311
Union of Russian People (URP), 224–5, 232–3, 235, 317, 345, 346
Urusov, S. D., 207, 215, 235
Ustrogov, A. I., 196, 205, 207

Vestnik narodnoi voli (Herald of Narodnaia Volia), 108
Vilenskii vestnik (Vilna Herald), 39, 45
Vilna, 72, 73, 111, 113, 115, 116; establishment of rabbinical seminaries, 9–10; Jewish socialists, 150–1
Vitebsk, 111; mobilization pogroms (1904), 215; pogrom of 1904, 216, 218, 231

Vladimir Aleksandrovich, Grand Duke, 69
Voitinskii, V. S., 102
Volunteer Army: and pogroms of 1919–21, 293–311; officers and pogroms, 304–6, 308–11, 380, 381, 382
Volynia: pogrom of 1904, 216
Voskhod (The Dawn), 153–4, 222, 248

Warsaw, 169, 171, 173, 174, 175, 180; pogrom of 1881, 177, 182, 183, 330, 378; pogrom of 1905, 378
West Galicia, pogroms of 1898, 323
West Prussia, pogrom of 1881, 322
White Armies, 14; and pogroms of 1919–21, 293–311, 350
White Russia, 63, 141
Witte (Vitte), S. Iu., 207, 226–7, 234, 236, 345
Wolf, Lucien, 221–2
Wolfe, Bertram, 225
World War I, 291–2, 308, 323, 327, 374
World War II, 326
World Zionist Organization, 148, 375

yeshiva/yeshivot, 9, 156–7, 159
Yiddish language, 152–6
Yom Kippur, 216

Zack, A. I., 68
Zagorskii, K. Ia., 63, 76–7, 114, 115
Zasulich, Vera, 63, 82
Zemlia i Volia (Land and Liberty), 62, 63, 65; and pogroms of 1881–4, 66–7, 70–7, 93–5
Zerno (The Seed), 63, 65, 66, 74–7, 81–3, 93–4, 96, 107, 113–14
Zheliabov, Andrei, 39, 125
Zhitomir: establishment of rabbinical seminaries, 9–10; pogrom of 1905, 223–4, 347
Zionism, 3, 32, 98, 99, 103, 377
Zlatopolskii, Savelii, 114–15, 116
Zoot–Suit Riots, 357
Zundelevich, Aron, 124
Zyrardow, 168